TO MATT,

THANKS FOR ALL YOUR SUPPORT AND COMMITMENT
TO BRITISH BASEBALL. YOU'RE NOT BAD
FOR A BOLTON FAN!

BEST WISHES,

CONFLICT

The Yankees, the Red Sox and the War for My Heart

Ryan Ferguson

CONFLICT

ALSO BY RYAN FERGUSON

Planet Prentonia: The Real Story of Tranmere Rovers

DEDICATIONS

For my fiancée, Patrycja, who told me not to delete this
manuscript.

For my mum, Cheryl, who set her alarm for 01:00 am just to
record baseball games on VHS tapes.

For my dad, Mike, who kept baseball newspaper clippings
whenever he found them.

For my brother, Nathan, who has listened to my baseball
ramblings since we were kids.

For my grandad, Neville, may he rest in peace.

For Henry Chadwick, the world's first great baseball writer, born
in Exeter, Devon.

For Jonny Gould, Josh Chetwynd and everyone at *Baseball on
Five*, without whom I would not have discovered this grand old
game.

CONTENTS

PROLOGUE

PART FOUR: London Calling

EPILOGUE

"I was walking near the London Eye and I ran into a couple people wearing Yankee hats. They had no idea who I was." – Aaron Judge

PROLOGUE

Field of Dreams

Attending your first ballgame is a rite of passage. It typically happens when you are five or six years old, maybe earlier in particularly passionate families. You travel in the car with your dad, pay for box seats on the first base side, and ascend a ramp into the verdant nirvana of America's national pastime. You enjoy a hot dog, smear mustard all over your shirsey, and maybe even catch a foul ball in your oversized mitt. The routine is commonplace.

By contrast, my first ballgame came when I was 24. On a warm Saturday afternoon in June 2019, I boarded a London Underground train with my brother, Nathan, and my girlfriend, Patrycja, bound for Stratford, home to England's Olympic Stadium. That is where the Yankees played the Red Sox in a most unusual series, making fantasies come true, and that is where I found salvation from years of internal conflict.

After a hair-raising journey, we emerged from the dingy labyrinth of tunnels and concourses into a buzzing maelstrom of baseball jerseys, caps and chatter. It was special to eavesdrop on a dozen conversations, hearing fragmented tales of Bill Buckner and Babe Ruth. I could not believe this was happening. Years of delirious devotion found an exclamation point, and a British celebration of this befuddling game meant more than words can convey.

Brimming with anticipation, we slalomed through the festive streets of London, bathed in excitement and sunshine. We passed through a shopping centre then caught a glimpse of the monolithic stadium, the first major league ballpark I had ever seen. It was a beautiful yard unlike any other.

Pacing towards the metallic hub of aspiration, my life flashed by in cinematic slow motion. Conceived in childhood and incubated in adolescence, the distant goal of one day attending a major league ballgame was birthed in adult disbelief. I gawped at the stadium with a satisfied smile. A lump formed in my throat. Despite campaigning for eons, I never contemplated what victory would actually feel like. Rarely are such impossible objectives realised, and the sheer ingenuity of it all caught my breath.

Our tickets were scanned, our bags were searched, and then we progressed into the rampant hive of activity that resembled my ultimate dream come true. Walking through the gates, we became eternal characters in the most fabled sports rivalry of all, joining untold millions in a timeless crusade of war and peace, hate and love, Boston and New York.

Floating through the fluorescent concourse, I inhaled the sweet aroma of *baseball*, that fine panoply of charred beef, sickly sugar, stale beer and hallowed grass. Stalls offered a wide range of food and drink from the soul of Americana. Peanuts and Cracker Jack. Burgers and candy floss. Hot dogs of interminable length. They had it all. Vendors carried beer. Stores displayed popcorn in replica batting helmets. There was a live band and large screens showing pre-game coverage from Fox. It felt like we had stepped into another world. A *fantasy* world. The world of my childhood hopes.

One of six kids born to parents on the British breadline, I never had a chance to visit the United States of America, yet from an early age, I found the place bewitching. There was something so commanding about its size and something so thrilling about a land that discovers new parts of itself every day. I could not get enough.

To me, the USA was rather like Narnia – close enough to inspire bold ambitions, but so unattainable as to straddle fiction. My efforts to visit America were routinely scuppered for various reasons – financial, psychological, logistical – and I'm still yet to set foot in what feels like my spiritual heartland. In the end, America came to me before I went to it. Such is the spellbinding power of the place, and such is the unappreciated genius of its people.

Arranging big league ballgames on another continent is incredibly challenging, but the way things came together in London was spellbinding. In a huge stadium seating 60,000 spectators, our tickets were on the back row, deep in left field, way out in foul territory. We could barely have been further from home plate, but I could barely have been happier.

With temperatures soaring over 30°C, the air was heavy, humid and unbreathable. Expectation sizzled through the stifling clouds, and the slightest movement resulted in perspiration. In such evocative conditions, we climbed the transparent steps leading to the seating bowl. Music thumped and neon flashed in every direction, boisterous accoutrements of an event without equal. My heart pounded with resounding urgency.

We turned the final corner, ascended the final steps and captured a final vignette of the clear blue sky. Then we found solid ground. Then we were washed in luscious green. Then it all unfurled before us, like oh so many movies. The field, majestic and meticulous. The infield dirt, beautiful and beguiling. The foul poles, innocuous yet inspiring. It was my very own field of dreams.

Then there was the crowd. Oh boy, was there a crowd. Sprinkled around the field like candy on a cake, believers of all ages joined in a summer collage of red, white and blue. Pensioners wore old school Yankee hats and millennials embraced full replica Red Sox jerseys. Fans of other teams donned their colours, too, creating a rainbow of baseball awakening.

I envied the decisiveness of those around me. While others rolled out of bed that morning and easily picked their outfit for the sacred day, I stuffed a cap for each team in my backpack, hedging my bets against a faulty heart. In a sea of dedicated diehards, I was an undecided voter. I longed to experience such blissful states of nonchalance.

Before taking our seats, way up in the gods, we managed to find a great vantage point overlooking the left field bullpen. Never in the field of human history has anybody been more excited than I to see Larry Rothschild, the Yankees' pensionable pitching coach. It was all so surreal.

Masahiro Tanaka, the Bombers' ace, walked slowly across the field to complete his warmups. He played catch with batterymate Gary Sánchez then progressed to throwing from the bullpen mound beneath us. I studied the finer details of his delivery, gaining a newfound appreciation for the devilish movement of big league pitches. It seemed impossible to hit such wicked projectiles, and my respect for major league batters was duly fortified.

When he was finished, Tanaka threw a ball to a gaggle of Japanese fans on the front row, tipping his cap. I was impressed by the mutual respect between this superstar and his fans. The romantic poetry of baseball sprang to life before my eyes, and its compassionate difference to every other sport was illustrated profoundly.

The lineups were announced amid cacophonous fanfare. There was Aaron Judge and Didi Gregorius, Mookie Betts and Xander Bogaerts. There was Gleyber Torres and Brett Gardner, Andrew Benintendi and Rafael Devers. There was a galaxy of distant heroes suddenly brought to life. You could almost reach out and touch them. You could barely believe it was true.

Both sets of players stood along the baselines, their elegant uniforms contrasting beautifully with the turf. Those hallowed Yankee pinstripes and that proud Boston red. That is when it hit me: I was about to watch the greatest rivalry in sports. I was actually in the building for a competitive contest between the Boston Red Sox and the New York Yankees, two teams with a grip of my heart. The life of an ostracised baseball fan came full circle as the far-off focus of my splintered adoration played ball in my backyard.

To some, staging Major League Baseball games in London was nonsensical. It was a gimmick, a money-making stunt, an event shrouded in pointless vainglory. I understood those mainstream concerns, but to me, and to many like me who harbour a tangible love for baseball despite living in Britain, there has never been a happier moment. Many could die in peace, their keenest wishes granted, and the enormity of that achievement rendered me speechless.

The lump in my throat swelled as the national anthems of two proud allies shattered the scene before us. A star-spangled banner smothered left field with a union jack splayed across right. Goosebumps trembled across my whole body. Tears formed in my eyes. The hairs on the back of my neck stood on end. We did it. We actually pulled it off. Major League Baseball came to London, and nobody can ever take that away.

The crowd numbered 59,659 when all was said and done. The last big league game to draw a larger attendance occurred 16 years earlier. Since then, MLB has taken its product around the world, from America and Canada to Japan, Australia and beyond. But nowhere were the masses so engaged, and so thoroughly *giddy*, as in the United Kingdom. Nowhere did baseball create such a ripple of excitement as that enjoyed by London. Nowhere did this seductive game feel more at home than in its estranged ancestral hotspot.

An island of calm in that river of fanfare, DJ LeMahieu, the Yankees' leadoff hitter, strode to the plate at 6:10 pm GMT, signalling the start of something great and heralding the end of an ancient wait. Rick Porcello, workhorse for the world champion Red Sox, toed the rubber in opposition. Rolling waves of noise rained down on the field. Our moment finally arrived.

For years, my pre-game routine was to sit back, turn up the volume and squint at a modern device beaming baseball around the world. Now, things were different. Now, I cheered loudly, finding my hidden voice. Now, I stood up, clapped my hands and peered out at the diamond. I was *part* of this game, no longer an idle bystander. That felt great, and I hollered my dizzy approval.

Porcello got the sign from Christian Vázquez, his catcher. He came set then drove towards home plate with the first major league pitch ever thrown on European soil: a two-seam fastball at 88 mph, down and in.

Strike one.

The two-game series for my heart was underway.

RYAN FERGUSON

"Good evening, fellow baseball nuts, and welcome to *Baseball on Five*." – Jonny Gould

PART ONE

Where It Began

CHAPTER ONE

The Essence of Fandom

I was born 3,115 miles from Fenway Park. To the east, that is, not even to the west. A great body of water separates my homeland from America's most beloved ballpark. That body of water is the Atlantic Ocean.

I'm British, a fact that has typically precluded any professional or even casual involvement with Major League Baseball for the vast majority of its existence. Despite having a profound influence on the very *creation* of baseball, and indeed staking a claim to original authorship of the sport, the United Kingdom has only a miniscule community of fans, followers and influencers dedicated to the game. For the longest time, baseball barely registered on the radar in mainstream Britain, and only marginal gains have been made in modernity.

Football, as in soccer, is king on these shores. In fact, it is king, queen, prince and princess. We live and die with the highs and lows of so many football clubs, allegiances to which are passed through generations like treasured family heirlooms.

England does not have just one football league, nor a system of interconnected divisions. It has a wide-ranging, all-encompassing *pyramid* containing more than 480 leagues, home to over 5,000 clubs of varying expertise.

Even in the fourth tier of professional football here, far removed from Premier League opulence, more than 8,000 people regularly attend matches, a testament to the adoration that we have for this sport. The college football obsession of Bible Belt America is a useful comparison, except our *entire nation* is aglow with Bissinger-like preoccupation.

Football is the opiate of Britain, providing shelter from the mundane progression of everyday life. Football binds families together, filling silences and starting conversations. It infiltrates every aspect of society, serving as the foremost vehicle of civic pride in cities and towns, villages and hamlets. We get awfully emotional about football, quite unlike anything else on the global sporting sonar. Football matters to us. It matters like little else.

I was born on 4th October 1994 in Wirral, a leafy peninsula of 330,000 souls nestled betwixt the rivers Mersey and Dee near Liverpool, the revered city of John, Paul, Ringo and George. I grew up in Bromborough, a large village in Wirral's southern quarter. Our borough is a quiet place, leafy and natural, possessing great views and fine beaches. I love the serenity that makes it tick.

Newspaper archives suggest the most common use of a baseball bat in Wirral is to bludgeon another human amid various shades of criminality. Fanatical boosters of the Boston Red Sox do not typically hail from such alien turf. This is true England, not New England. Nobody seems to care.

Fittingly, the only sporting loyalty I inherited was that to Tranmere Rovers, a humble football club at the heart of Wirral that has fluctuated between the second and fifth divisions for its entire 136-year existence, never reaching the Premier League and rarely encountering joy.

Until winning the fifth tier playoffs at Wembley Stadium in 2018, Tranmere waited longer between promotions or trophies than any other professional club in the country. They are experts in salvaging heartbreak from the cusp of euphoria, finding ever more creative ways to shatter hopes and fuel despair. They are masters of near-miss trauma, often threatening to win but typically losing when it matters most.

Unlike the polished titans obsessed with public image, Tranmere reflects the flawed nature of our existence. Life is a struggle, with many bumps in the road. It is not all about success and happiness, and Tranmere teaches you that. The club has driven me to tears more often than it has catapulted me to joy, but that is okay. That is *real*. It educates you about dealing with adversity and maintaining dreams. It gives you a grounding in life and tells you that nothing comes easy.

For decades, perhaps *forever*, this star-crossed football club from this rough and rugged town has fought bravely to deliver results befitting its imposing stature. In that quest, pain - unbearable pain - has greeted us habitually, but thousands have fallen in love with this club, this story and this feeling. It is inside us, and little can be done to quell the tide.

To support Tranmere Rovers is to believe in unseen dreams. To invest in this peninsula jewel is to fight against prejudice and stereotype. To adore such a beautifully flawed concept is to feel true love, requited or not. It is about much more than mere sport.

Once touched by the Shakespearian reality of Tranmere Rovers, you are a character for life. It courses through your veins and pours through your heart. You are subjected to the same feelings of raw anguish and occasional ecstasy as the chosen few who believe. You are special, different from the norm, and that should be celebrated in dramatic hues.

From the cradle, I was raised on a steady diet of Tranmere mythology. My dad shared stories of bygone matches at Prenton Park, the team's home stadium. He told of famous nights beneath the floodlights when Wirral's otherwise anonymous footballers slayed some of the largest giants the game can muster.

Rovers *have* enjoyed occasional triumph, but their story is overwhelmingly one of teary endings and misbegotten promises. Tranmere *have* beaten huge clubs like Arsenal, Manchester City, Chelsea, Leeds and Newcastle, but they fit more logically as underdogs than as alpha males. Our hometown heroes *have* reached a League Cup final and played in European competition, but the agents of history view them more as footnotes than as leading protagonists.

We were never meant to lead from the front, and historians have guarded that maxim with austere sincerity. Still, there are chronic misconceptions about this football club, and those who see things differently have a duty to correct the record.

Suitably indoctrinated, I attended my first Tranmere match in 2001, instantly falling in love with the boisterous crowd and the verdant grass, the susurrus of expectation and the scent of burgers cooking on a distant grill. I was hooked, and there was no turning back. Tranmere Rovers became the most important thing in my life.

Every Christmas as a kid, I received the latest replica kit, to be washed daily after hours spent in the garden pretending to score goals for the hometown eleven. I collected autographs and read match programmes incessantly, absorbing the club's history. I attended matches all over the country, bonding with my dad and brother in a shared passion. I became possessed by the football demon, spinning into tantrums whenever Rovers lost, which was more often than they won. There was no greater force in my life than that snakebitten club from Birkenhead.

I once embarked on a 600-mile continuous round trip to watch Tranmere draw 0-0 with Dover Athletic. I was out of my house for 25 hours in total, and the match took place closer to Paris, France than to Wirral, England. Football inspires such nonsensical devotion from British fans, to a point where extreme passion is normalised. We are *expected* to provide such support, even when faced with logistical and emotional challenges. If we do not turn up on the terraces each Saturday, friends and family know that something is badly wrong.

In this regard, life is hard for Tranmere fans, who live in the shadow cast by heavyweight neighbours across the river. From Prenton Park, you can reach two Premier League stadiums by driving less than ten miles through the Mersey tunnel. Anfield is home to Liverpool, among the most successful football clubs in the world, while Goodison Park hosts Everton, a bygone powerhouse yearning for glory.

On Merseyside, the vast majority of people support Liverpool or Everton, preferring easy lives of mild success to arduous battles for dignity. As a Rovers rooter, I was heavily outnumbered at school. Encountering a fellow Tranmere fan was a rare occurrence. We lived in restrained anonymity, strangers in our own hometown.

As a means of starting conversation, local people often ask if you are a red or a blue, referring to the iconic colours of Liverpool and Everton, respectively. They promptly grow confused when you answer as a white, dumbfounded at the mere existence of a club called Tranmere Rovers.

"Who do you really support?" I'm frequently asked.

"What is your *Premier League* team?"

"Surely you cannot just follow Tranmere?"

Well actually I can, and I do. There is no other way of being true to my values.

Gleeful Liverpool fans celebrating success was the soundtrack to my childhood. Finding anybody on my council estate who actually attended their matches proved impossible, but the instinct of mere casual observers was to associate with Liverpool whenever the topic of football arose. Even fervour for Everton paled in comparison to love for Liverpool, leaving my beloved Rovers nowhere to be seen, lost in the sea of replica red shirts that flooded our peninsula.

For years, then, I have been teased and ridiculed for supporting Tranmere by hypocritical people who live 15 minutes from the team's stadium. Throughout my life, I have been at once furious and fascinated by that concept. The brazen fraudulence of such defection contravenes prevailing logic, yet it has gone largely unreported for most of our existence. To this day, I'm dumbfounded by the stunning duplicity of local football fans, and I'm proud to stand up for my subjugated brethren.

In a nation of partisan underpinning, less than 2% of Wirral's population typically attends Tranmere matches at Prenton Park, a grave anomaly that morphs into resentment on my part. Clubs in similarly sized conurbations like Leicester, Coventry and Portsmouth attract support from upwards of 8% of their immediate population, stretching above 10% in places. However, the sacred traditions of supporting your local team are corrupted on Merseyside, where generations have neglected Tranmere in pursuit of instant satisfaction across the river. I could never forgive those addled souls. I could never let it go.

Bigger clubs look down on Tranmere as irrelevant, but as diehard fans, we have a football club that represents our town and its people, rather than its sponsors and their corporate shareholders. After all, that is the true meaning of a football club: to represent its area and its values around the country and perhaps overseas. Identifying as a fan of said club is therefore a bold expression of one's metaphysical infrastructure. The line between business and passion is suitably blurred.

We want our team to represent our town in a positive manner. We want Tranmere to beat other clubs and stake a claim to superiority. That is the tribal, rudimentary essence of football fandom. We remain invested because we long for that satisfaction, rather like a drug. Even through regular defeat and frequent relegations, we continue to attend matches because Tranmere is like a family member you can never reject. The club needs us as much as we need it, and that is the definition of true *support*.

In this regard, smaller football clubs like Tranmere are more human and personable than the constructs of commerce that flood the Premier League. Elite football is akin to window-shopping, with glass separating you from the action, whereas lower league football is a humble farmers' market, all blood and guts and emotional bidding.

Supporting a third division football club is not an accessory of coolness; it is an intrinsic part of our makeup. It is an unconscious tic and a thoughtless habit. There is an untouchable force, buried deep in the soul, that just compels us to believe. No amount of money can replicate that feeling.

Associating with Tranmere gives me a sense of belonging. It provides an identity and extends a template of moral reasoning. Without that alluring focal point, that prepacked concise *worldview*, my existence would lack direction. There would be no cause for exasperation, an understated catalyst of action, and there would be no outlet for internalised frustration.

No single nation is more passionate about a particular sport than Britain is about football. Sure, hockey is huge in Canada. Yes, table tennis is omnipresent in China. And of course, cricket enjoys a phenomenal spread of participation around the world. But the English infatuation with football defies all comparison. We invented this game and gifted it to the world. Our love for it is therefore similar to that of a mother for her new-born child.

There are even subtle differences between British sporting fandom and American sporting fandom. There is a permanence to US sports that somehow muffles the intensity of its emotion. The franchise model offers teams a baseline coolness that differs sharply from the unhinged desperation of England's wild hierarchy. The *certainty* of Americana makes it easier to take for granted.

The major North American sports leagues offer recurring jousts of the privileged few. The same teams compete every year, and there is little stigma attached to failure. In fact, the worst team in any given baseball, basketball, hockey or gridiron season is afforded a dubious prize: picking first in the subsequent amateur draft, getting a premium opportunity to replenish its roster.

By contrast, English football is a primal fight for survival, a high-wire act devoid of plush safety nets. By embracing a meritocracy of promotion and relegation, of classified success and public humiliation, British football fandom takes on an altogether deeper meaning. The bond between teams and fans becomes intermingled as a result, encouraging a broad dichotomy of driving cultures and definitive socioeconomic profiles.

Essentially, football clubs are hubs through which the frustrated and forgotten express their love for a particular area or for a specific ideal. The players represent us, and that is a sacred honour. Rivalry, occasionally spilling into genuine hatred, is a core constituent of this British footballing passion. It stimulates interest around an otherwise simplistic game, adding communal purpose to a humble pursuit.

Of course, there are storied rivalries throughout North American sports, but they thrive almost superficially, without elaborate networks of causation. They are simpler than the sporting feuds of Europe, stitched together by expansive hyperbole as opposed to deep-seated political and financial differences.

The sterilised, serialised environment of North American sports encourages a unity of outlook and a homogeneity of approach. The system is eminently replicable and essentially predictable. Americans view sports as entertainment, and consumption is the mode of accessibility. Soccer, on the other hand, is bathed in bespoke individuality, and *participation* is the engine of its appeal.

In short, baseball is a product *to be* loved, whereas football is a product fashioned *by* love. Both sports orbit an empowering force of feeling, but the *strain* and *gradation* of that emotion is malleable. Baseball is an accessory, whereas football is a necessity. One is a pastime, but the other is religion.

Few artistic ventures captured this polarisation better than *Green Street*, a 2005 film about extreme football fandom in which Pete Dunham, the movie's main character, is tasked with entertaining Matt Buckner, his American brother-in-law who is attempting to restart his life after being expelled from Harvard.

Pete introduces Matt to the seedy underworld of West Ham United, a proud London football club of working class rigour. When Pete attempts to explain the team's rivalry with Millwall, a local enemy, immortal dialogue springs from the screen:

Matt: "What about Millwall?"

Pete: "Ah, where to even fucking begin with Millwall? Millwall and West Ham fans hate each other, more than any other fans by far."

Matt: "Sort of like the Yankees and the Red Sox?"

Pete: "More like the Israelis and the Palestinians."

Although much derided for its woeful imitation of British accents and its tenuous grasp of reality, *Green Street* remains memorable for this legendary exchange. It captures the difference between football and baseball fandom better than any prose I have encountered. As a longstanding fan of both sports, I'm in a strong position from which to pontificate, and I echo the sentiments of Pete Dunham. Baseball is a matter of life and death, but football is much more important than that.

Our planet is aglow with such football enmity. In Scotland, the war between Celtic and Rangers treads religious and sectarian minefields. In Turkey, the battle between Fenerbahçe and Galatasaray penetrates every tenet of society. In Serbia, the conflict between FK Partizan and Red Star Belgrade has spilled into murder. There is no such thing as friendship in the timeless war of football. Every club must fight for itself.

The catalysts of football rivalry are multifarious, but the depth of feeling is communicable. A match that does not matter to one person will be a pivotal modifier of mood for somebody else. One man's disinterest is another man's obsession. Here in England, local derbies from Hartlepool to Plymouth are the most important dates in any season for a disparate range of people, and abhorrence is the crux of competition.

In this chamber of enflamed emotion, I learned to hate Liverpool FC from an early age. Just as kids born into Red Sox families are taught about Yankee arrogance, I was fed yarns about Tranmere being threatened by those bullies across the river. Such lessons are hard to unlearn, and my moral compass was hardwired accordingly.

I quarrelled with neighbourhood kids when Liverpool won. I celebrated with exuberant vigour when Liverpool lost. When my sisters brought boys home, I vetted them with probing questions about football, grilling their sentiments. I could not tolerate the laissez-faire instincts of local people who abandoned their own heritage just to taste triumph.

Through my prism of defensive antagonism, allegiance to Liverpool has ended friendships and started fights. I have perplexed loved ones with my hostility and angered strangers by questioning their morals. There are few boundaries to my loathing. Like an oppressed servant seeking autonomy, I never back down in the face of hostility, and I never stop living my complicated crusade for equality.

In bygone debates, I have expressed a willingness to use ten, twenty or thirty years of my life as currency to obtain a Tranmere Rovers victory over Liverpool at Anfield. Maturity has smoothed such prickly fantasies, granting me the gift of perspective, yet that baseline wisdom is impossible to unstitch.

It may be quieter now than in days of yore, but that background hum of fear and detest accompanies my baseball story. It lays a foundation for the web of confusion to come, and it permeates every facet of my being.

ᴓᴓᴓ

CHAPTER TWO

Triumph and Tragedy in the Depths of British Night

While Tranmere Rovers are my specialist subject, football in general holds an intriguing appeal to me. From an early age, I consumed *anything* related to the sport in any format. I read books. I collected stickers. I watched videos and wrote stories. There was no end to my inquisitiveness and no filter on my enthusiasm. Football was everything.

We did not have much money when I was young. With six children, my parents had to improvise to make ends meet. The meagre budget never allowed a Sky Sports subscription, while paying the internet bill could also be a transient obligation. Sport, particularly football, on terrestrial television was therefore a vital lifeline. Fortunately, I enjoyed a golden era in that regard, leading directly to my discovery of baseball.

Possessed of a voracious desire for football and the inimitable drama it creates, I began expanding my net in search of contentment. ITV held exclusive rights to broadcast live UEFA Champions League games in the 2000s, and I spent many wonderful evenings listening to Clive Tyldesley - the network's lyrical bard of football commentary - reporting from colossal European stadiums. I came to adore the stimulation of sports broadcasting, and scratching that itch led me to Channel Five, a ridiculed station buried deep in the terrestrial quagmire.

I was 9 years old for most of 2004, still a primary school pupil, still agog at the ever-expanding world. At that time, Five's sports offering - totally free from a paywall - was a veritable cornucopia of joy for such a young sports nut. To this day, I'm still astounded by what the organisation achieved.

Firstly, I became infatuated with Dutch football. Five replayed an entire match from the Eredivisie - Holland's top division - each week, with Ajax, PSV and Feyenoord taking centre stage. Those broadcasts typically began around midnight or shortly thereafter, usually in midweek, essentially to fill time between lurid quiz shows and turgid breakfast news broadcasts. I did not care. It was the highlight of my week, quite literally.

I developed a major sleeping problem, keeping myself awake to watch matches on a tiny bedroom television. Sometimes, I had to hang the aerial from my window to get a good signal, watching football through the flickering snow of incessant static. It was all worthwhile, however, because Ajax had Wesley Sneijder, PSV had Arjen Robben and Feyenoord had Robin van Persie. It was a brilliant time to fall in love with the Eredivisie.

Like a young sporting junkie, Dutch football led me to Argentinian football like cannabis leads to cocaine. Somewhat implausibly, Five also had rights to broadcast the Argentine Primera División, one of the top domestic leagues in South America. Boca Juniors and River Plate, those mysterious titans of world football, were suddenly alive in my council estate bedroom. I got even more excited. I got even less sleep. Surely this was too good to be true.

With minimal resources, Five became an understated hero-making machine. On any given night, viewers may have been treated to the genius of Juan Román Riquelme at La Bombonera or the goalscoring opportunism of Mateja Kežman in Eindhoven. Five even had Ashes cricket, heavyweight boxing, PGA Tour golf, NASCAR motor racing and world triathlon coverage at various points. The channel presented a veritable smorgasbord of sporting delight, and legions of fans enjoyed every minute.

In 2020, it would cost around £900 per year to access all of the sport that was free to view on my childhood television. I'm particularly grateful that Five made such a visionary commitment to sports, especially of the North American variety, and we should always remember the motivational force of *Sunset & Vine* – the channel's chosen production arm – in that endeavour.

Without such dissident groups, bound by a belief in the power of sports, millions of British fans never would have honed their athletic taste buds. Thousands more never would have found an outlet for pre-existing interests in the razzmatazz of stateside competition. A slew of networks *tried* to package that wonder, presenting late-night sport to sleepy audiences, but Five mastered the art. Nobody came close to its array of free content, and those who consumed it before money became king are among the luckiest rooters of our time.

The contemporary British love affair with North American sports began in 1982, when Channel 4 introduced a generation to Dan Marino, Joe Montana and the colourful world of NFL. Weekly highlight shows were devoured in unprecedented numbers, while more than 4 million Brits tuned in to live coverage of Super Bowl XX between the Chicago Bears and New England Patriots.

Throughout the 1980s, Britain endured great turmoil at the confluence of economic change, conflicting politics and a rebellious attitude towards modernisation. Such apathy and discontent spilled into the sporting arena, where football fans became increasingly violent. In turn, the middle class grew tired of football, criticising its turbocharged machoism. Among other pursuits, *American* football became an inclusive alternative, and families enjoyed the way it was readymade for television.

Gaining momentum, Channel 4 began showing live NFL games each week, and thousands identified with successful teams like the Miami Dolphins and San Francisco 49ers. My dad even stayed awake to watch the Super Bowl each year, starting a tradition I uphold to this day. It was a metamorphic age for the British sporting palate.

Seeking to capitalise on an expanding market, the NFL brought pre-season exhibition games to London in 1986, with the Bears and Dallas Cowboys kickstarting the annual America Bowl. NFL Europe, an offshoot development league, began play in 1991, scattering seeds that later bloomed into yearly International Series games in London and beyond.

Launched in 1997 under a credo of modernisation, Channel Five planned to build around that groundswell of interest in Americana. While many stations carried football in the UK, Five realised the untapped potential of *North American* sports coverage on these shores. Pivoting from traditional programming precedents, Five hoovered up broadcasting rights and created a transformative brand around bats, balls, hoops, pucks and helmets. No free-to-air broadcaster had ever attempted such an aspirational project in Britain.

With audacious chutzpah and primitive production, a biblical array of sport became the channel's lifeblood, late-night drama making amends for daytime dross. At various times, Five held the rights to NFL, NBA and NHL broadcasts, but coverage of Major League Baseball, presented by the immortal Jonny Gould, became the channel's longest-running show. It was the jewel in their sporting crown.

I first encountered Five's baseball coverage in the winter of 2004, a gift of pure serendipity. I was up late on a nondescript school night awaiting the Dutch Football Game of the Week, due to begin around 03:00 am. The Eredivisie replay never materialised, however, thanks to an overrunning baseball documentary. That documentary changed my life.

I was frustrated at first, impatiently awaiting the football. Bleary-eyed and sleep deprived, I watched the seconds tick by in numb agitation. Then I began to actually take notice of the programme before my eyes. Soon, I became *involved*, engrossed and absorbed. There was a magnetism to the film that I could not resist.

The story it told, that of the 2004 Boston Red Sox emerging from a three-game deficit to beat the New York Yankees to the American League pennant, was truly beguiling. I knew nothing about the protagonists, little about the context and zero about the sport in question, but the drama was otherworldly. The romantic miasma of history, that definitive essence of baseball, was overpowering. I was enthralled.

After beating the Yankees, Boston swept St Louis in the 2004 World Series, claiming its first baseball championship since 1918. The documentary reached a dazzling climax at Busch Stadium, where the coveted final out was recorded after 86 years of yearning. The golden crescendo brought a smile to my face. I felt a strange affinity with this victorious if unfamiliar team. They seemed like my kind of champions.

Duly inspired, I became a devout admirer of *Baseball on Five*, which carried live coverage from ESPN every Wednesday and Sunday evening - or, more accurately, every Thursday and

Monday morning - usually after stupendous reruns of *World's Wildest Police Videos* with Sheriff John Bunnell. The dulcet tones of Jon Miller and Joe Morgan illuminated the wee hours of British summer, and though ridiculed in America, those announcers became accidental heroes in the UK.

Aside from stupendous displays of baseball, the show also offered camaraderie, fellowship and sense of belonging to its viewers. The infectious enthusiasm and personable nature of its presenters transcended usual television productions. *Baseball on Five* had so many quirks and was far more natural, organic and human than any other sports programme. I feel lucky to have experienced its pomp.

The purpose of *Baseball on Five* was not to sell advertising, flog merchandise or make money. Accordingly, the people involved were not mercenary, distant or robotic. The show's sole aim was to educate people in, and entertain them with, baseball. Above all else, a love of the game pervaded.

Conveyed with such conviction and devotion, that message inspired those watching. A whole generation of British baseball fans cite the humble show as the genesis of their fandom, displaying gratitude to Jonny Gould, Josh Chetwynd, Erik Jansen, David Lengel, Todd Macklin and everybody else involved in its production.

Baseball on Five spurned a cult and moved a generation. If you watched it for any length of time, you will understand the indescribable, intangible burning of pleasure it evoked. That feeling will never be rekindled because times have changed, but we should not be sad that the glory years are over. We should be happy they happened at all.

⚾⚾⚾

The British baseball fan is a strange creature, and putting an age to the species is difficult. Organised baseball has been played in the United Kingdom since the 1880s, and it has enjoyed impermanent success during various eras. However, deciphering the genesis of authentic *passion* for the sport here, beyond regional indulgence, has befuddled investigators for years.

English newspapers made infrequent mention of baseball in the 1900s, while many football clubs adopted the game as a means of summer recreation in the 1910s. In this mode, though, British baseball is always an adjunct of something else. It is never a self-sustaining product of organic interest.

Conversely, in the 1930s, several attempts were made to establish a professional British baseball league, but the dream typically died amid issues with funding and connectivity between competing teams. Nevertheless, the BBC broadcasted its first live baseball game in 1936, a local contest between the Oldham Greyhounds and the Rochdale Greys. Slow but steady advances were made therefrom.

During World War II, the US Army borrowed equipment from the BBC to resuscitate its Armed Forces Network (AFN), a radio station dedicated to service members around the world. Its first transmission to US troops came in 1943, and the network subsequently spread throughout Europe, with outposts in France, Germany and elsewhere. Pancontinental expansion was subsequently inevitable.

While sports news broadcasts were a staple of the network's original output, live coverage of baseball and gridiron games came later. Indeed, interest in AFN transmissions from the 1960s onwards influenced Channel 4 as it took a visionary leap into NFL coverage. Adrian Metcalfe, the sports editor who brought American football to Channel 4, listened to AFN broadcasts when searching for new content. Without that original inspiration, decades of progress may never have happened.

The dominant medium of its time, radio was a significant propeller of worldwide sporting integration. In Asia, people learned to speak English by listening to AFN broadcasts. Behind the Iron Curtain, the AFN became a taboo portal to the outside world. The network was a bulwark of early globalisation, soothing tensions while pushing American diplomacy. Its seminal role in the globalisation of technology is terribly understated.

By the late-1970s and early 1980s, thousands of Brits listened to North American sports through these means, falling in love with the crackly narration of excitement and drama. AFN carried live play-by-play of the World Series each year, and esteemed announcer Gary Thorne was among the broadcasters during the 1990s.

However, if radio was insurrectionary in the fight for baseball coverage across Britain, the subsequent rise in personal computing and internet browsing was a grand accelerator of that crusade. As international newspapers reproduced stories online, and as sports teams saw the commercial opportunities inherent therein, baseball became available on the information superhighway, accessible to anyone with a modem.

MLB launched its own website in 1995, replete with news, digital boxscores and entertainment features. On 5th September 1995, a game between the Yankees and Seattle Mariners became the first live baseball broadcast in internet history. ESPN devised the concept after extensive testing, opening new avenues for consumers around the world.

"The game was played in New York and carried on local radio in Seattle," reported the *Los Angeles Times*. "But internet users from Los Angeles to Lagos were able to hear the play-by-play using freely available software called RealAudio."

Buoyed by these early successes, tech gurus built platforms for online video streaming, paving the way for mlb.tv, the ultimate gamechanger for overseas devotees. That package was launched in 2003, giving international fans the option to watch every major league game for the first time.

Accordingly, when considering the availability of such content, the British fan of *major league* baseball is an even younger specimen than the British fan of *domestic* baseball. The oldest active British fan of an MLB team - following news, enjoying games and generally *rooting* in the conventional sense - is probably around 75 years old. More realistically, members of the old guard are likely to be in their fifties or sixties. Junkies of the golden age, by contrast, are even younger.

Inspiring that new generation, *Baseball on Five* was first broadcast on Opening Day in 1997, beaming into British homes another contest between the Yankees and Mariners. Ken Griffey Jr. hit the first home run ever shown live on British television, and Seattle won 4-2 before a crowd of 57,586 at the Kingdome.

MLB found a new home in the after-dark void of UK broadcasting.

Raw and rudimentary, the show was initially carried sporadically as part of Five's late-night *Live & Dangerous* sports strand, with analysis from the lovable Todd Macklin and little else besides. A cheery Canadian, Macklin developed terrific pedigree working for The Fan 590, Fox Sports and the BBC before taking Five's baseball gig. He also moonlighted as an ice hockey analyst for the station, earning his corn with immense dedication and enviable stamina.

In its first season, despite sponsorship from the Coors beer company, *Baseball on Five* was notoriously bad. Tommy Boyd, a journeyman presenter with no expressed interest in baseball, was the first host, and a pretty lousy one at that. Aside from the splendid insight provided by Macklin, who had the patience of a saint, there was very little baseball knowledge on display.

All too often, those involved saw it as a show inconveniently *about* baseball, rather than as a *baseball show*. A presenter would introduce a replay of a key strikeout, only for the broadcasted clip to show an inconsequential groundball. Macklin would expound on the beauty of a long home run, yet the tape would be rewound as he spoke, debunking any stylistic subterfuge.

However, from amid the unrefined, disinterested wreckage, one man came forth to revolutionise the show, set Britain on a path to serious baseball fandom, and rewrite the laws of televisual production. One man. *Another* Canadian. Mr Erik Janssen.

A keen Montreal Expos fan, Janssen earned a film school degree in London before traversing the murky world of part-time projects and freelance gigs in the capital throughout the 1990s. Erik watched *Baseball on Five* during its first season and was appalled at its thorough lack of baseball acumen. Such was his infuriation, Janssen was moved to do something entirely out of character: he called Five to complain.

After reeling off the show's weaknesses from a handwritten list, Erik was invited to stop by and provide some advice on the finer points of baseball and production. After all, he appeared to know the game far better than anybody Five employed at the time, with the exception of Macklin, and the station was open to change. Janssen accepted the invitation, figuring it would provide a new hobby if nothing else. Ultimately, Erik found his calling in the gloom of a London studio.

Initially an unpaid voluntary mentor, Janssen wound up staying at Five for a decade, producing the baseball show and later working on NHL and NFL broadcasts. With self-effacing skill and understated enthusiasm, Erik revolutionised late-night sports programming in Britain. There has never been anyone like him, before or since, and there will never be anyone like him again.

Without his nocturnal imagination, the schedule would never have worked. Without his relaxed approach, the lovable culture would never have bloomed. And without his overlooked *ability*, a glorious epoch would never have materialised. Janssen was a true one-off, and we must remain abundantly grateful that he chose Britain as the beneficiary of his life's work.

In remoulding Five's baseball output, Erik's first task was to hire a new presenter. Never accused of open-mindedness, Boyd mysteriously disappeared one day in May 1997, citing a sworn hatred for baseball, which he branded 'glorified rounders.' In his stead, Jonny Gould - a bubbly, borderline hyperactive figure - was granted a three-show trial that, under Janssen's edict, blossomed into 11 colourful years and over 600 sensational episodes.

Born in Kenya but the archetypal Brit, Gould studied politics at Durham University before embarking on a varied acting career out of drama school. In 1994, Jonny transitioned to the broadcasting realm, eventually taking a sports analyst role alongside famed newsreaders Alastair Stewart and Mary Nightingale on ITV's *London Tonight*. A jack of all trades, Gould also maintained sidelines in charity auctions, quiz shows, conventional journalism and television voiceovers. His charisma could never be pigeonholed.

Known for his brash love of Chelsea Football Club, Jonny's career was characterised by a free-spirited determination. He rarely stopped to weigh up the pros and cons of a particular project; he preferred to wade in with heart and hustle, giving it his all while living in the moment. In this regard, his arrival at Five was a perfect marriage of time and texture. Gould threw his weight behind the baseball experiment, shooting from the hip and picking up the pieces afterwards. Such cavalier bravery illuminated the darkness.

With a new dream team at the helm, spearheaded by Erik and anchored by Jonny and Todd following a complete overhaul, the show exploded in performance and popularity. During the late-1990s, many of the core foundations and unmistakable mannerisms that made *Baseball on Five* so popular were put in place.

Every year, for instance, the presenters wore suave tuxedos for Game 1 of the World Series, a tradition of respect. They also developed humorous topical asides, rating national anthem renditions on makeshift scorecards and creating a wonderful sense of occasion.

Jonny learned along with everybody else, identifying with the Atlanta Braves and professing love for their third baseman Chipper Jones. People began to tune in not only to watch the baseball games, but also to enjoy the irreverent studio hijinks and personable analysis between innings. With Gould and Macklin, Five stumbled upon a winning formula, and Janssen knew better than to strangle the dynamic synergy that developed between the show's presenters and its viewers.

ESPN eventually made gestures towards the UK market, launching the North American Sports Network in 2002, but true baseball fans preferred the avuncular charm of *Baseball on Five* to the premium satellite options that sprang up periodically. Likewise, watching games on mlb.tv became a convenient stopgap for some, but the unpretentious geniality of Five reminded most of bygone simplicities.

The leisurely rhythm of baseball allowed Gould and friends to flourish. They could not have replicated the magnetism with any other sport. Football offers two 45-minute halves and a 15-minute break in between, packed with partisan sneering. By contrast, baseball has no clock, and it refuses to adhere to arbitrary constraints of time. The routine breaks between innings and during pitching changes encouraged personality and experimentation from the *Baseball on Five* crew, and each individual team member took that gift in a unique direction.

Creating a dedicated baseball community from scratch, Gould encouraged fans to write in with questions and comments. That function later expanded to email. Macklin answered the technical queries but also injected humanity into the conversation, making the show eminently relatable. Meanwhile, Gould offered satirical commentary on the travails of daily life, adding a reality to the show that greatly amused viewers. Three people even wrote in asking Jonny to propose on their behalf live on air. Such was the crazy camaraderie that held *Baseball on Five* together from supper until breakfast.

Gould was a law unto himself, pushing the boundaries of sporting context and political correctness. He did it all in the most charming manner possible, though, winning legions of fans across the country. In 1998, Oscar-winning director Francis Ford Coppola even emailed the show, thanking Gould and Macklin for their fantastic coverage of the World Series. *The Godfather* it was not, but *Baseball on Five* produced a similarly steadfast fanbase.

By the dawning millennium, the show regularly averaged six-figure audiences. It peaked at over 1 million viewers during the epochal Yankees-Mets Subway Series of 2000, a halcyon moment in Five's evolution. This was also a tremendous achievement in the wider arc of British broadcasting history: a low-budget show that chased darkened nights through to early mornings with *baseball* commanding the attention of so many people. It was truly unprecedented.

In a logical sense, the show's niche focus and comparative poverty should have doomed it from the outset. Nevertheless, *Baseball on Five* became a success through lovable improvisation. From a small studio at ITN in London, the programme had no delusions of grandeur. No smoke and mirrors were deployed in its making, and what viewers saw was a realistic show made by honest professionals. It was baseball for the everyman, all unbuttoned shirts and misplaced scripts. It was slapstick genius held together by sticky tape, and the magnanimity of it all was immense.

During the aforementioned Subway Series, viewers witnessed the show's sheer *normality* firsthand. At 06:00 am each morning, *Five News* broadcasted live from the same studio as the baseball programme, causing frequent clashes. When a marathon Game 5 pitching duel between Andy Pettitte and Al

Leiter stretched until sunrise, a classic dilemma brewed backstage.

Typically unruffled, Janssen learned from a previous embarrassment, when a 1998 Stanley Cup Finals game was cut prematurely by Five due to a similar scheduling conflict. Accordingly, as Mariano Rivera recorded the final outs of the World Series game, Erik ushered his presenters into a small box room off a nondescript ITN corridor, from where the show commenced.

Gould and Macklin finished their broadcast from a tiny cupboard, signing off for the season as Joe Torre's team won its third consecutive world championship. Imagine Buster Olney or Joe Buck working in such conditions. Our guys were a different breed.

In this regard, it is hard to conjure an exemplary equivalent in American television because *Baseball on Five* was so damn uncommon. Even for its time and its jurisdiction, the show was unique, the sole baseball *programme* in our entire country. The show's intimacy cannot be reconstructed, while its blend of pure expertise and workmanlike credibility is unimitated in the pantheon of sports broadcasting.

Harvesting such momentum and public affection, *Baseball on Five* teetered on the brink of mainstream appeal. Among celebrity viewers were high-profile comedians and Premier League footballers, elite actors and ambitious politicians. Gould played to the crowd while staying true to his core audience of students, insomniacs, breastfeeding mothers and sleep-deprived gambling addicts. The equipoise of viewer demographics was beautiful. *Baseball on Five* was community in action, togetherness symbolised by coffee at midnight.

Ex-Kansas City Royals pitcher Brett Barash was a studio guest during the 2001 World Series, won by the Arizona Diamondbacks from a Yankees team attempting to galvanise its city in the wake of terrorist-wrought devastation. Macklin bowed out after that Fall Classic, leaving the show and returning to Canada with his wife. A gaping void emerged, eventually filled by a boisterous man with a boyish love for the game.

"I had actually never seen the show before I tried out for a position prior to the 2002 season," recalled Josh Chetwynd when I interviewed him for a feature article in 2015. "I had been working at Major League Baseball as a communications executive when it became clear neither Brett Barash nor Pat Garrigan [another short-lived Macklin replacement] were coming back.

"I had TV experience when I worked as a reporter covering the entertainment industry for *USA Today*, so I was comfortable in front of a camera. I also had a baseball background, from NCAA Division 1 at Northwestern University, to a brief stint as an independent ball professional in the Frontier League, and for a number of years catcher for Great Britain.

"So the MLB folks asked me if I wanted to try out. I sat next to Jonny Gould in a room with a camera and we riffed quite well. I was thrilled to get the job. So much so, I pushed off plans to return to the States to go to law school."

Born in London to British-American parents, Chetwynd grew up in Los Angeles. With two degrees in journalism from his prestigious alma mater, Josh cut his teeth reporting for *USA Today* and *The Wall Street Journal*, mainly focusing on Hollywood. Josh also wrote for *The Times* and *Chicago Tribune* before becoming involved with MLB International and, by extension, *Baseball on Five*. He seemed predestined for the role.

A thoughtful Red Sox fan, Chetwynd gave the show an injection of energy, his youthful spontaneity, unbridled passion and exhaustive attention to detail aiding its professionalism and affirming its educative properties. While in the hot seat, Josh introduced instructional features about baseball history and the ballparks of MLB. His *60-Second Rant* segment was an instant hit, and Chetwynd brought an intellectual focus to the show, which was occasionally chaotic.

First and foremost, Josh saw his mission as to arm viewers with a sound level of understanding so they could enjoy the baseball and frolics on offer. He succeeded in the most remarkable way, without coming across in the slightest arrogant, pretentious or condescending. British baseball needed Josh Chetwynd, and our understanding of the sport was greatly enriched by his commitment.

"I can easily say that Five was the most enjoyable job I've ever had," said Chetwynd. "I'm a late-night person by design, and I just loved the people and the work. It was very different to reporting, and certainly different to doing a live game, which I did at the World Series for the BBC. But the laidback nature and the pure fun we had is something I will always cherish.

"I was always aware that I was serving two different audiences: those who knew the game really well and those who might be tuning in for the first time. My goal was to never talk down to the audience, whether I was explaining the grip of a two-seam fastball or going over what exactly a balk was. I wanted to be clear but not patronising."

To that end, Chetwynd taught me more about baseball than anybody else. British readers are likely of a similar viewpoint. Josh explained the fundamental minutiae for beginners and for experts without making it tedious or overwhelming for either. He hit an elusive sweet spot that few have managed to find, looming as one of the most informative baseball experts on either side of the Atlantic.

With Josh, much like with baseball itself, there was always another layer of fact, history and trivia. For instance, he taught me not only the myriad of different pitches, but how, why and when a pitcher may elect to hurl them. Ultimately, then, *Baseball on Five* furnished me not only with casual enjoyment, but also with an encyclopaedic knowledge of the game.

In this respect, I regard the people behind the show, chiefly Chetwynd, as epic crusaders in the battle to expand and enrich America's game on British shores. Their continuous commitment to baseball facilitated my appreciation thereof, and that is true for many seamheads across the country. We should always remember the selflessness that made *Baseball on Five* tick, for without it, many of us would still be untouched by the greatest game of all.

Midway through the 2003 season, Josh returned to Arizona to study law. Five scoured the market for a stopgap replacement before hiring another lively, intelligent and downright hilarious expert by the name of David Lengel. It soon became obvious that the family had a new, eternal member.

The quintessential Mets fan, all relentless energy and gaudy New York enthusiasm, Lengel was a graduate of history and political science with future aspirations to work in those fields. A man of boundless vitality and tremendous wit, Davey poured fuel on the open fire of entertainment, trading tongue-in-cheek barbs with Jonny and forming a mesmeric bond with his audience.

Mellower than his predecessor, Lengel made the role his own with stunning rapidity, forming new traditions, developing new mannerisms and concocting new ways for the show to expand. He was the perfect foil for Gould, sharing the same sense of humour and tiptoeing close to the same fault lines of acceptability. Their partnership was raucous, and it propelled *Baseball on Five* into new territory.

Often considered so laidback as to be horizontal, Davey took his work very seriously, deep down. After all, who else would commute from Brooklyn to London on a regular basis merely to work through the night on a niche sports programme? Davey did that for a 10-week stretch at one point, crisscrossing the pond while also working on documentaries at ESPN. We should never forget such enormous sacrifices.

I will always have a special place in my heart for Lengel because he was the co-host when I first discovered this addictive show and this therapeutic sport. Chetwynd returned later, coinciding with my hardball zenith, but Lengel sparked the fire. Along with Gould, Davey brought baseball to life in my childhood bedroom, for which I'm eternally grateful. Nobody can ever take that away.

Among the humorous segments created by Gould and Lengel, *Weaver Watch* was perhaps the most beloved. When Jeff Weaver endured an erratic spell with the Yankees in 2003, *Baseball on Five* found its major league doppelganger. Famously wild, Weaver posted a 5.99 ERA one year. He also frequently led the league in hit batsmen. Jonny and Davey presented highlights of every Weaver start, complete with side-splitting soundtracks and playful mockery. Viewers loved the satire.

When Weaver won a World Series ring with St Louis in 2006, the segment was retired. However, it returned sporadically when *Jered* Weaver, Jeff's younger brother, made his big league debut with the Angels. Chetwynd even got to interview Jered on the show years later, a nostalgic treat for old school viewers. The segment came full circle, and it was weirdly emotional to watch.

If each television personality has a signature moment, Lengel's came during Game 3 of the 2005 World Series between the Astros and White Sox. First pitch was scheduled for shortly after 01:00 am GMT, and a 14-inning war ensued at Minute Maid Park. In the studio, Davey began to wilt, consumed by the searing heat of production lights, stricken by the attendant numbness of sitting still for five hours straight, and haunted by the steady, inexorable encroachment of morning.

The game went on, and on, and on. Twelfth inning, tied. Thirteenth, tied. Pitching change after life-threatening pitching change. At-bat after interminable at-bat. The guys simply ran out of words, and Lengel was left in a crumbled heap of exhaustion between innings, warmly derided by Gould as - of all things - *soft*core.

Mercifully, the game ground to a cherished conclusion when the White Sox scored two runs in the fourteenth and somehow closed out the longest contest - in terms of innings played and time taken - in Fall Classic history. Jonny and David signed off just before 07:00 am, closing the most monumental broadcast in *Baseball on Five* lore.

When mlb.com later pinched Lengel to front its video output, Chetwynd returned in 2006 for another three-season stretch as colour analyst. My passion was stoked anew as Josh brought gravity to proceedings. I soaked up the baseball ephemera and committed it all to memory. A kid could barely wish for a better learning tool, and I used it to great effect.

Spurred by the show's popularity, Five even sanctioned live, on-site broadcasts of MLB All-Star Games, adding another unique chapter to the fairytale. When Gould and Chetwynd fronted the show from Pittsburgh's PNC Park for the Midsummer Classic in 2006, another apex was reached. They repeated the trick a year later, broadcasting live from AT&T Park in San Francisco.

Around this time, when trying to find a sequel for *Weaver Watch*, the show managed to persuade Curtis Granderson, a genuine star with the Detroit Tigers, to become a stateside ambassador. *Granderson Watch* featured a weekly conversation with Curtis, broadcast every Sunday night, in which he answered a viewer question sent in by email. Granderson always was one of baseball's good guys, and we have a special place in our hearts for him to this day.

Another short-lived feature was *The Baseball Library*, filmed with Phill Jupitus, a successful British comedian of mainstream renown. Jupitus fell in love with the Red Sox while travelling in Boston during the mid-1990s, and he often spoke of feeling more comfortable at Fenway Park than at *Upton* Park, the home of his beloved West Ham United.

In his *Baseball on Five* segments, Jupitus sat in a large baseball glove chair and read from a different book each week. Mixing in his trademark humour, Phill introduced viewers to *The Natural*, *Boys of Summer* and *Veeck as in Wreck*. In one episode, he even revealed a Red Sox tattoo on his arm. Such is the unpublicised passion for baseball in the hushed backwaters of Britain, and such is the extent of love we harbour for our distant major league teams.

These professional synergies of *Baseball on Five* eventually morphed into close personal comradeship. A sense of brotherhood meshed the crew together, and the guys embarked on annual summer road-trips across America, watching ballgames at different stadiums. The resultant footage, stitched together like a home movie by Erik, was frequently uproarious. I doubt those films would be transmittable today.

"We were like brothers on those road-trips," Chetwynd recalled. "It was inevitable that we would be scrapping off camera and exhausted by each other's idiosyncrasies come the end.

"The best trip, in my opinion, was the last one, in which we went to the Astros' Triple-A affiliate, the Round Rock Express. The people were so nice, and Jonny threw out a pretty nice first pitch!

"We ultimately had a dizzy bat race, in which I beat Jonny and knocked him down in the process. Jonny is so crazy competitive and, if you asked him, to this day he would say I deliberately dropped him. Alas, we just ran into each other and it was an accident. Still, he couldn't handle losing."

Perhaps if the presenters were not so friendly, caring and passionate, so thoroughly adept at selling the game to swathes of undecided observers, baseball would have passed me by.

Perhaps I would never have been sucked in. You see, *Baseball on Five* was not so much a community as a family, with everybody bringing something to the table. It was a quirky metaphor for life, and such a triumph could never be replicated today.

"I really loved every member of the group," said Chetwynd a little mawkishly. "It was like family. Of course, Jonny was centre of the universe. It is impossible not to love the man, even though he is amazingly self-absorbed and forgetful. Still, he is charming beyond belief and, at his core, a very warm-hearted man.

"Erik has a fantastic, wry sense of humour. He would be in the control room trying to make us laugh. He is also very talented at what he does, but in an understated way, which always meant a laidback environment.

"David is truly one of the funniest people. When he took over for me for the year-and-half I went back to the States, people would tell me 'you guys are so different!' When I saw him on air for the first time, I totally understood. He puts it all out there and his demeanour and attitude is so funny. Off camera, he is incredibly giving and generous. He is the type of guy who would really go to bat for his friends at the first word of a request.

"I also got to work with Mike Carlson, better known for his NFL work, and Mark Webster. Both are great guys, albeit very different personalities. Regardless of who I sat across from, I always thought there was a good chemistry. Primarily, because we were almost always having fun."

That communal spirit is missing from modern television, which is a pawn of unfettered capitalism. From literal seventh inning stretches and the haphazard celebration of British baseball highlights through to the endless saga of in-game trivia, *Baseball on Five* was the last great programming experiment before everything became too serious.

I will always be indebted to these guys, and I will always adore their contributions to my life. Without their guts, guile and unimaginable creativity, I never would have found baseball, and the years of happiness therefrom never would have happened. That is an enormous gift to be savoured. That is the luckiest quirk of my life.

If I close my eyes and drift away, they still broadcast baseball in my dreams. There is Jonny, caught eating chocolate as the camera cuts back from an unexpected pitching change. There is Davey, exasperated by another Yankees montage. And there is the family, unseen but definitely heard, that welcomed me into a secluded pastime all of its own.

Baseball on Five was a show for the times and a movement of the people. It was a tale of bouffant hair, Hawaiian shirts, fantasy baseball meltdowns and demonic ballpark food. It was iconic – hugely and truly *iconic*. More than anything, though, *Baseball on Five* was a monument to human decency, commitment and belief. They built it, and we came. There is no finer miracle in the history of British sports.

CHAPTER THREE

Bromborough Library

With unreliable access to the internet at home as kid, learning more about a topic and broadening one's horizons required a visit to the local library, housed in a rather ugly building at the edge of Bromborough's centrepiece village. That is where I first began consuming baseball content, muddling my way through vague rulebooks and dissecting boxscores three days after games had finished. That is where I found myself.

The library was my happy place. I can still picture its utilitarian design, with a marble foyer and ginger carpet tiles. My mum took me to the library three or four times per week, enjoying some peace while I embarked on wild expeditions of the mind. It always seemed to be cold and dark outside, an endless winter of discontent, but the library's warm embrace was unprejudiced.

Most people visited Bromborough library to use the photocopier or to return vague autobiographies of middle-class suburban banality. I, on the other hand, was there to learn about baseball. Nobody has ever shared such a random objective.

At the time, Bromborough library had two or three baseball books, but – naturally – they were broad in focus. I recall an old coffee-stained manual by Ian Smyth, in which he explained baseball using stick men and line drawings. There was also an educational pamphlet issued by *BaseballSoftballUK*, the game's appointed development agency in Great Britain. I made light work of those titles, poring over them briskly. I was then ready for heavier substances, and incredulous librarians arranged for seemingly nonsensical books to be delivered from other libraries in Wirral.

Bebington had a copy of *The Bill James Historical Baseball Abstract*, and it was ferried to Bromborough especially for me. I read all 1,024 pages. Next, I pushed enough buttons that Bromborough purchased a copy of *Idiot* by Johnny Damon, spiritual leader of the Red Sox team I admired. That was consumed rapidly, as well. My demand for hardball literature outstripped the local supply, however, and I was forced to get creative in pursuit of satisfaction.

I kept a folder of baseball notes and scribbles, doodles and drawings. I slowly pieced things together, understanding the complex rules and appreciating the game's undulating history. If something confused me, or if I became inquisitive about a certain aspect of baseball, I tried everything to solve the quandary or find the answer. I was usually successful.

Bromborough library also had a bank of computers, allowing members to surf the internet. The first 30 minutes were free, then you had to pay for each subsequent half-hour. We did not always have enough cash to extend the browsing time, but the kind old women who ran the library occasionally boosted my credit anyway. They knew I was working on something important.

When using the library computers, people my age played games or printed pictures to colour. I trawled mlb.com and the *Boston Globe* Extra Notes column, which was then free to read online. Baseball captured my soul intravenously, creating the closest thing to a natural lifelong baseball fan as Britain could possibly muster.

In terms of bespoke rooting optics, I associated with the Red Sox simply because of that thrilling documentary screened by Five. A spectre of romance engulfed the team, and it was exciting to be involved with such a monumental movement. There and then, I did not know the consequences of that fairly innocent blooming of allegiance, but it haunted me for years when adult issues came to the fore. Oh, to be young and free.

It was difficult to follow baseball in such splintered, distant fashion, with half-hour bursts of internet and the sporadic availability of books. Such was my tenuous grasp of baseball current affairs as a 10-year-old Brit, I discovered that Pedro Martínez, the great Red Sox ace, had signed with the Mets four months after the ink had dried on his contract. I mistook Pedro for Manny Ramírez - my favourite player - in the brief clip Five showed of him holding aloft a Mets jersey. Only after Gould broached the topic in Opening Day discussions did I realise it was actually Martínez, not Ramírez. Such were the vagaries of falling in love with baseball as a poor British kid.

The first ballgame I ever watched live - purposely, at least - was Opening Night in 2005. Old Yankee Stadium provided the backdrop as David Wells made his Red Sox debut against the Bronx Bombers. All I remember from the game is Wells wearing a sand-coloured glove. A quick search of Baseball-Reference.com reveals that the potbellied southpaw lasted just 4.1 innings and surrendered four runs on 10 hits as the Yankees won 9-2. A crowd of 54,818 crammed into the famous old yard, consuming the competing talents of Ramírez and David Ortiz, Derek Jeter and Alex Rodriguez. Randy Johnson got the win for New York. It was a very strange season.

Midway through that campaign, *Baseball on Five* showcased the latest work of Craig W Thomas, a British author who fell in love with the Red Sox. Published in April 2005, *Roads to Redemption*, his ode to the sport from an English perspective, was a triumph of passion and perseverance. It was the ultimate guide to Major League Baseball for Brits of typical footballing persuasion, a labour of love that greatly enriched the niche community to which it was dedicated.

Sourcing *new* baseball books in Bromborough was akin to seeking Budweiser in the desert. Librarians grew tired of my requests to ship obscure tomes from far-off locales at great expense. Accordingly, with a fresh title to chase, I eschewed the library and pestered my mum for a trip to Birkenhead, the main commercial thoroughfare of Wirral. We did not have a car, so the train had to suffice. I hoped for the best but expected the worst. I knew the odds of locating such an obscure grail were crushingly miniscule.

When we eventually arrived at Waterstones bookstore, I dug through the sports section, paying close attention to the new releases. After a prolonged search, I somehow found what I was looking for: Thomas' opus. Quite why or how such a book wound up in Birkenhead, of all places, is still largely ineffable, but it did, and I was the gleeful beneficiary.

It took me four months to read *Roads to Redemption* for the first time because I tried to commit every word to eternal memory. In one section, which provided a potted history of baseball, I remember being simultaneously perplexed and amused by some of the names, with actual people named Three Finger Brown and Nap Lajoie playing this great game.

Thomas funded the book himself, setting up a publishing house – *Inside Corner Books* – to force completion. Years later, I came to befriend Craig, at least in the distant guise of modern social media interaction. He loathes any mention of the book and deems it a failure, despite the cult following it sparked. Craig has since fallen out of love with baseball, a sad realisation for hardcore traditionalists.

Thomas' self-ridicule be damned, *Roads to Redemption* was an ideal tool for the British baseball learner. The book contained a guide to each of the 30 major league franchises, with a brief synopsis of team histories, ballparks, players and achievements. It was my first in-depth and prolonged exposure to the glorious history of America's national pastime. It was also a gateway to heavier substances.

Soon, I read *Faithful*, which chronicled the historic 2004 Red Sox season. To me, Stephen King was - and will always remain - just a baseball writer. I do not think I have ever enjoyed a book more than his diary collaboration with Stewart O'Nan. For the first time in my life, I could not put a book down. I caught the baseball bug, and it was impossible to shake free.

Around this time, my sister Kim lived with her boyfriend and they had the luxury of an Amazon account. That always seemed somehow *mystical* to me. It was like a secret club that I would never likely join. Whenever I got some money - from birthday gifts or for completing chores around the house - I would peruse Amazon and supply a handwritten list of baseball books for Kim to purchase on my behalf. She probably got tired of my incessant orders, but she processed them, nevertheless. Without that crucial lifeline, my baseball library would have been imaginary.

I also have fond memories of mum buying me a plastic sleeve to protect whichever baseball book I was reading at any given time. That was her unspoken way of encouraging me to read and of pushing me towards a better life built on solid education. I took that sleeve everywhere, including school, sneaking off to find a quiet space in which to float away and connect with my idyllic American fantasies. Those daydreams lifted me from squalor.

I naturally progressed to read extensively about Boston baseball history, with works by Dan Shaughnessy, Peter Gammons and Tony Massarotti warming up many a winter evening. I can barely remember doing anything *other* than devouring baseball books between 2005 and 2008. My knowledge and understanding improved by osmosis, as did my vocabulary.

When reading the incisive, achingly beautiful prose of such accomplished writers, it is difficult to be unmoved. Soon, I began imitating these literary heroes in my own writing, using words and phrases and tempo discovered in their books and columns. My schoolteachers could never decipher the genesis of such an eloquent approach, but I kept experimenting with bold language. That soon became my trademark style, an eye for sharpened generalisation bathed in hyperbole.

From an early age, I wanted to be like Roger Kahn, Jerome Holtzman or Grantland Rice. I wanted to write about baseball with regularity and panache. I wanted to cover sunny weekend games at Fenway Park, smoking a Cuban and punching thunderously at a typewriter. I wanted to make a name for myself in the bronze-hued heritage of America's national pastime. There was no other ambition in my heart.

However, after reading *Moneyball* early in my literary baseball adventure, another passion began to emerge along parallel lines. Michael Lewis, the book's accomplished author, took the reader inside the clubhouse, the draft war room and the magic computer of general manager Billy Beane, posing as a fly on the wall as the Oakland A's transformed baseball with their use of advanced analytics. We had rarely seen anything like it.

At the time, seamheads everywhere became fascinated by sabermetrics and fantasy baseball. We longed to be in control, overlooking baseball organisations like suave general managers. I entered innumerable fantasy leagues, competing with grown men anonymously. There was something so mysterious about baseball operations, and I wanted to contribute my ideas.

Fantasyland, an elaborate diary by Sam Walker, spoke to that dream. A talented journalist, Walker entered Tout Wars, the most gruelling fantasy baseball league in America, chronicling the experience for all to explore. With real money at stake, Walker used objective data to draft and manage his team. He even hired Nando Di Fino, a fully-fledged data scientist, to create a genuine baseball operations department for a fictional ballclub. It was just about the coolest thing I had ever heard.

When high school teachers asked about my future career aspirations, running the Boston Red Sox was not considered a realistic aim judging by their stifled laughs of indignation. But that is what I wanted to do, more than anything else. I wanted to be Theo Epstein, the Yale graduate who cracked the code and delivered a world championship to Boston for the first time in 86 years. I even signed off fan mail to Jonny Gould as *Ryan Ferguson, Future General Manager of the Boston Red Sox*. There was a clear plan in my head.

In this regard, I was deeply introverted as a child. Losing myself in books, creating parallel universes away from the pressures of social conformity, was a blissful passion. To the extent that it systemised my thoughts, baseball saved me from outright loneliness. It gave structure to my relentless contemplation and mixed excitement with my modest disaffection. It *differentiated* me, and that is a powerful concept.

When there was nothing else to do, or nobody else to converse with, there was baseball and its endless cast of heroes, legends and near-mythic warriors. There was always Babe Ruth and Joe DiMaggio, Ted Williams and Ty Cobb. There was Gould and Chetwynd, Janssen and Lengel. There was baseball, and what more can a kid want?

In retrospect, the seeds of anxiety and obsessive-compulsive disorder – conditions that later derailed me – were scattered in this baseball-obsessed childhood. As a kid, I was defined by an inescapable *otherness*. My parents showed more love than the norm. I played baseball in the street, often alone, stopping only at the encroachment of dusk. When it rained, I read on the stairs wearing my ubiquitous navy Red Sox cap. In short, I was abnormal. I did not fit in.

The books I enjoyed were almost exclusively about baseball and almost certainly aimed at people triple my age. As a pre-teen, I tackled Jim Bouton's nuanced satire, Seth Mnookin's sharp analysis and Peter Gammons' investigative power. It all seeped into the mind and into the blood. Baseball gave me my appreciation of words, the greatest gift I have ever received. It opened a world of private opportunity, and I never looked back.

I remember reading *The Ultimate Baseball Road Trip* by Josh Pahigian and Kevin O'Connell then planning my own excursion through the United States. I usually woke up before reaching my intended destination, but harbouring such dreams is the entire point of life. There is no meaning here except that which we create, so sketching an impossible baseball pilgrimage of the mind was perfectly acceptable.

You see, it did not take much to make me happy back then. After the 2005 World Series, for instance, my dad returned from the village one day with clippings from the *Daily Mirror* newspaper of Oliver Holt reporting on the White Sox winning their first world championship in 88 years. I did not root for Ozzie Guillén's team, but I treasured those scraps of paper for years. I still have them in a drawer to this day. They represented rare baseball reporting from a British outlet, and they intensified my ambition for a major league career, far removed from the council estates of Wirral. They showed me what was possible, and I never looked back.

Such exposure to America's pastime on these shores was rare and short-lived. When opportunities arose, they had to be taken. I remember spending my pocket money on baseball films, finding battered VHS tapes and DVDs in charity shops. I also remember watching *Fever Pitch* at the local cinema, although the rom-com entwined in Red Sox mania was renamed *The Perfect Catch* here to avoid confusion with Nick Hornby's famous football memoir.

Telling the story of Ben Wrightman, a teacher whose obsession with the Red Sox stunts his romantic potential, that movie had a profound impact on me. Though often criticised, *Fever Pitch* burnished my love for the Red Sox. It offered a harmless insight, embellished or otherwise, into Boston baseball mania, and I lapped it up. For the first time, I explored the extent of my own hardball infatuation, which continued to grow as a result. I wanted to become the British equivalent of Wrightman, even if such a lousy objective jarred with my immediate culture.

Resembling a Red Sox memorabilia store, Ben's apartment fascinated me, and I began transforming my bedroom into a similar baseball shrine. Framed photos of bygone legends and modern heroes filled every available space. I crafted a replica Green Monster and Citgo sign from wood, recreating Fenway

Park in the most unlikely location. I even made a name plaque for my door, complete with the team's iconic logo.

I had figurines and banners, cards and pennants, trinkets and flags. I stencilled my own Red Sox hall of fame on the ceiling, inscribing sacred names like Tris Speaker and Smoky Joe Wood for posterity. I was obsessed. Deeply and madly obsessed. The Red Sox were my life.

While sacred allegiance to Tranmere Rovers was forever ringfenced as my ultimate overarching priority, baseball surged ahead of football as my favourite sport. There was a subtle beauty to baseball that defied succinct explanation, a lyrical continuity that marked the progression of life. To me, baseball represented humanity's best attempt at creating something perfect. And the Red Sox? Well, they were the ballclub most worthy of devotion.

So deep was my affection, I wore a Curt Schilling shirsey that was a size too small. So strong was my passion, I bought battered baseball cards on eBay. So huge was my intrigue, I read tirelessly about every aspect of the team's soul. There was no end to the yearning.

Millions of people rise and fall with the travails of Boston baseball, but the mechanics of *my* love affair with the team were unique. I did not have access to newspapers in stores or daily sports radio in cars. I could not find baseball video games anywhere, nor could I watch games every night on television. Unlike most *Brits*, I never once went on holiday as a kid, so summer trips to Florida were not even possible. For me, following the Red Sox required stamina and ingenuity, faith and perseverance. The challenges were real, but I managed to overcome them.

By borrowing books, scanning the internet, watching *Baseball on Five* and exploring the limits of my own imagination, I created a homespun ecosystem of baseball. I kept the passion alive, even when it was easier to simply give up, and the rewards were phenomenal.

By printing pictures at Bromborough library, collecting scraps of baseball news, playing catch with a backyard wall and watching films whenever they became available, I conjured a personal *association* of baseball. My instincts were not always correct, and I made plenty of rookie mistakes, but nothing deterred me from accessing the game and understanding its glory. I was determined to debunk stereotypes and have my diverse opinions heard. I wanted to prove that *anybody* can love baseball, regardless of their nationality or background, and that mission drove me forward.

Baseball is a complicated sport, not only to play but also to understand as a spectator. The rulebook is a tome, and rare permutations continue to spring up hundreds of years after the game was created. The strike zone - baseball's most important piece of real estate - is literally *invisible*, while balls and strikes - baseball's omnipotent currency - are figments of faulty human interpretation. The game is an organism, changing before our eyes, and explaining it to a newcomer is a thankless task.

Indeed, new British fans often struggle to grasp the full gamut of baseball minutiae. It can be difficult to purposely *learn* the infield fly rule from a textbook, for instance, just as the theory of balks can be monolithic when starved of exemplary context. Likewise, the suicide squeeze play can baffle premeditated newbies, especially those who discover baseball at a later stage. Consciously *choosing* to take an interest in this game often leads to confused irritation. It takes years to master the detail, and immersion is the most efficient method of doing so.

I'm fortunate that, despite living in England, I discovered baseball as an absorbent kid rather than as a grouchy adult. Early exposure injected the game into my bloodstream, and natural repetition helped my passion develop organically rather than arbitrarily. You could say I was an American kid in an English body. My baseball dogma was innate, and that trait distinguished me from many compatriots.

In the space of two, maybe three years, I surged from my first encounter with baseball to becoming the most intense and knowledgeable Red Sox fan in the UK. I went from never hearing of Boston to never shutting up about it. There was no official British fan group or booster chapter at that point, but if there was, I would have been the president. Even if I was only 12 years old.

⚾⚾⚾

CHAPTER FOUR

World Series Champions

The illustrious Boston teams of my halcyon age were held together by manager Terry Francona, one of the most infectious personalities in baseball history. Entering the dragon's den of Boston, with its merciless media and relentless fanbase, Francona had to convince a lot of people about his abilities. He succeeded in the most emphatic way possible and is now considered among the greatest managers who ever lived.

A previous stint as skipper of the Philadelphia Phillies yielded little success, but Francona found his calling with the Red Sox. Massaging some of the largest egos baseball has ever known, 'Tito' was a skilled conduit between the front office intelligentsia and the clubhouse plebeians. Scarcely has baseball seen a more altruistic manager, and rarely has Francona been afforded the necessary respect for his Bostonian toil.

In his debut season at Fenway, Francona won the World Series. Before him, the last Red Sox manager to hoist a world championship flag was Ed Barrow, a snazzy dresser born in 1868. Tito had a magic touch, and it was brilliant to watch him rewrite baseball history by the Charles.

While his khaki-wearing bosses and his hairy-chested players received greater acclaim, Francona stitched the two factions together, conducting a beautiful symphony with homespun pragmatism. Terry was the ordinary author of the *extra*ordinary 2004 miracle. People went to war for Francona, whose deceptive casualness defined an era.

Tito tried to keep his team honest amid a landslide of global affection, but his efforts were routinely undone by ownership, which sold the Red Sox' soul for celebrity razzmatazz. Boston underperformed in 2005 and 2006, failing to meet rigorous standards as pressure mounted. A civil war brewed inside the team's baseball operations enclave, and the resultant disconnect between player recruitment, in-game philosophy and overarching business strategy derailed plans for a dynasty.

In 2007, however, Francona delivered Boston's first division title since 1995, putting the Red Sox back in October contention.

I followed the team closely throughout the season, growing more excited about its prospects with each passing month. Gameday, a new product from MLB, allowed me to watch digitised recreations of games in real-time, even if video footage was eons in my future. I often stayed awake until sunrise watching static animations of exultant wins and stinging defeats. Kids today do not know they are born.

The 2007 campaign was punctuated with moments of immense satisfaction as a sense of expectation congealed in New England. Every night, there was a new hero, and that procession of big hits and bigger hearts made baseball experts sit up and take note. Something different was happening in Beantown.

In April, for instance, the Red Sox tied a major league record by hitting four consecutive home runs in a Sunday night contest with the Yankees, turning a 3-0 deficit into a 4-3 lead in the space of 13 pitches. Five carried that game live here in Britain, and I watched in spellbound fascination, just like thousands of Brits who caught the Red Sox bug during their exponential rise.

Sparking the immortal third inning rally, Manny Ramírez took a plump fastball from Yankees lefty Chase Wright and drilled a solo shot over the Green Monster in left field. It was a signature Manny moon blast, all relaxed authority and swaggering confidence. I was relieved to see my favourite player bust out of a lengthy slump. There was nothing more exhilarating than watching Ramírez on a tear.

Much maligned, JD Drew strode to the plate after Manny, keen to kickstart his spluttering Red Sox career. Wright hung a 79-mph breaking ball over the plate, and Drew whipped his bat through the zone with the zeal of a trained opportunist. Connecting like a rapier, Drew skied the baseball to deep centre field, where it landed in the distant bleachers. Fenway came alive.

Amid a hive of excited chatter, Mike Lowell stepped in and promptly golfed a laser over the left field wall. The attendant horde shrieked in disbelief, emitting the kind of euphoric soundtrack that is impossible to fake. In the *Sunday Night Baseball* broadcast booth, Jon Miller delivered a timeless call: "Now Lowell! And this game is going to be tied up! That one's headed for New Hampshire!"

The rolling waves of exasperation had barely subsided when Jason Varitek teed off on another lifeless fastball, chest-high and hittable. The go-ahead run soared through the dank night sky, ushered on a majestic parabola by the *oh my god* pleas of a sellout crowd. Fenway could not contain such a missile, and the Red Sox bludgeoned their way in front.

Wily Mo Pena tried to hit a fifth straight home run, eyeing the major league record, but Wright recovered with a strikeout. Lowell parked another homer in the seventh, however, and the Red Sox eventually won the game, 7-6, verifying one of my greatest highs watching baseball.

That night, the Red Sox did not hit four *wall-scraping* home runs in a row. They launched four consecutive *bombs* off the same pitcher. Lansdowne Street took a beating, and that lyrical little bandbox had never seen anything like it.

Indeed, Fenway rocked to its ancient foundations, a spine-tingling buzz greeting four straight dingers for the first time in the park's history. With four swings of the bat, the Red Sox surged ahead, stunning everybody. This was my first live exposure to true Boston *greatness* against New York, and it spoke to a monumental powershift in the historic grudge. Another enchanted season was about to unfurl, and I felt lucky to experience the ride.

On Mother's Day, 13th May 2007, Red Sox fans were treated to another of the team's periodic miracles. Down 5-0 to Baltimore entering the bottom of the ninth inning, Boston fought all the way back to win in walk-off fashion. Julio Lugo beat out an infield hit to drive home the winning, and I was left shaking my head in disbelief.

The fairytale continued when young pitcher Jon Lester returned to major league action following successful treatment for non-Hodgkin's lymphoma. Diagnosed in the summer of 2006, Lester underwent chemotherapy during the offseason and gradually rehabbed in the minor leagues. Jon made his 2007 debut against the Indians at Jacobs Field on 23rd July. He allowed just two runs on five hits through six innings, pitching Boston to victory. Lester's story reinvigorated the Red Sox, whose multifaceted attack received a new dimension.

As if to bookend the historic campaign, 23-yeard-old Clay Buchholz threw a no-hitter in just his second career start early in September, blanking the Baltimore Orioles 10-0. Fresh-faced and brimming with confidence, the livewire Texan mixed and matched his pitches beautifully, navigating one of the most epic games of Red Sox modernity.

Every morning, I woke and rushed to the family computer - which eventually had a wired internet connection - to check the boxscores online. On that particular occasion, I remember the surging excitement when my homepage, redsox.com, twinkled with a banner headline of Buchholz celebrating his masterpiece. It was a harbinger of glory to come.

That 2007 Red Sox team will always occupy a special place in my heart. It resembled the fruit of Theo Epstein's labour, as homegrown talent developed in the Boston farm system coalesced around a veteran core to create an unstoppable force. The long-term plan delivered a dynamic juggernaut, and the Red Sox became a Swiss Army Knife of baseball domination.

Kevin Youkilis was solid at first base. Dustin Pedroia, all guts and snot, was American League Rookie of the Year at second. In the outfield, Jacoby Ellsbury made a great first impression, bringing raw energy and blinding speed to the table. Meanwhile, Lester was set to emerge as the next great Red Sox ace.

Of course, the veteran nucleus played a crucial role in allowing those younger guys to flourish. David Ortiz hit .332 with 35 homers and 117 RBI. Lowell had a banner year, driving in 120 runs and delivering regularly in the clutch. Ramírez showed less power than usual but was still a formidable presence at the plate, while Drew made an understated contribution in his first Boston season.

The pitching staff was rather bipolar, but it somehow managed to hang around in games long enough for the offence to exact damage in metronomic fashion. Josh Beckett was a reliable bulldog, winning 20 games and sporting a 3.27 ERA, while Daisuke Matsuzaka, Curt Schilling and Julián Tavárez got enough outs to help Boston win 96 games.

The Red Sox swept Anaheim in the American League Division Series but fell behind Cleveland, three games to one, in a subsequent joust for the pennant. However, as they always seemed to do under Terry's command, Boston rallied with sinister intent when facing elimination, blowing the Indians away with three successive victories by a combined score of 30-5. I could scarcely believe my eyes.

In Game 6 of that 2007 ALCS, Drew once again answered his critics by delivering a huge clutch hit. With the Red Sox teetering on the brink of death, Drew came to the plate in the first inning amid screeching desperation. The game was scoreless and the bases were loaded. Two outs had been recorded, forming a subtle microcosm of Drew's career. However, for once, JD morphed into the storybook superstar everyone said he would be rather than shrinking into the overrated bust everyone seems to remember.

As he pounced on a pitch from Fausto Carmona and drove it 415 feet into the centre field bleachers at Fenway, Drew was on top of the world. After years of battling to reach the summit of expectation, he finally conquered his own demons. The Red Sox surged ahead, 4-0, and never looked back. They won Game 7, too, securing the American League title.

The Colorado Rockies awaited in the World Series amid a historic run of their own. Entering play on 16th September with a mundane 76-72 record, the Rockies proceeded to win 14 of their final 15 regular season games, necessitating a one-game playoff with San Diego to determine the National League wildcard spot. A 13-inning marathon ensued, but the Rockies emerged victorious. They then swept back-to-back playoff series - against Philadelphia and Arizona - to claim the first pennant in team history.

Entering the Fall Classic, then, Colorado had won 21 of its previous 22 games, a monumental achievement in the capricious world of baseball. Unperturbed, and in a true mark of their historic potency, the Red Sox plotted a route of calm assurance to another world championship, sweeping the Rockies in brutal fashion. Colorado seemed invincible, but Boston's hardnosed pragmatism won out.

Indeed, no team had ever entered the World Series with more momentum than the 2007 Rockies. That the Red Sox destroyed their hopes so clinically, setting a record for the most runs ever scored in Game 1 of a World Series, speaks to the sheer talent of

Francona's club. Nothing fazed those guys, and they were relentless in pursuit of victory.

I watched every pitch of the 2007 World Series live on Five, shivering in the early morning frost. I kept notes, rather than filling out a scoresheet, and those thoughts became my first unpublished articles about baseball, a seminal moment. As the Red Sox soared ahead with inimitable ease, I rejoiced at the wonder of it all. There was no end to the capabilities of that team.

I remember Pedroia greeting Jeff Francis with a lead-off home run in Game 1, cool and commanding. I remember Lowell, himself a cancer survivor, hitting a go-ahead double in Game 2, concise and confident. I remember Matsuzaka spanking a two-run single through the infield in Game 3, crazy and comical. I remember it all.

I remember the historic emergence of Ellsbury and the dominant pitching from *everyone*. I remember the huge contributions by bit-part players like Coco Crisp, Bobby Kielty and Lugo. I remember Schilling emptying the tank. I remember the sense of mounting exhilaration.

Most of all, though, I remember Jonathan Papelbon gazing through the mile-high mist of Coors Field in Game 4, peering in at the fingers of Varitek from the mound. I was unhinged with excitement. My body trembled uncontrollably. Seth Smith, a helpless rookie, embodied Colorado's final strike and its final opportunity, trailing by three games to none. The end was near.

Papelbon got the sign: *fastball, pump it in strong*. He pouted and paused, allowing the rolling waves of October adrenaline to wash over his body and pour over his shoulders. He came set then exploded with arrogant ease, blowing a high fastball beyond Smith's desperate swing. Varitek held on for dear life, clasping in his mitt an object of instant history. For the second time in four seasons, the Boston Red Sox were champions of the baseball world. Jon Lester got the win.

Over 4,500 miles away, I collapsed in a heap at 05:10 am, quivering with joy. Watched by the eyes of so many immortals living in photographs around my bedroom, I celebrated the first sporting success of my life. Tranmere had never won anything for as long as I had followed them. They never came close. However, the Red Sox gave me a tangible shot at glory. They delivered when it mattered most, an oxymoron of their own history. They ruthlessly swept the surging Rockies, adding another title to Boston's growing pantheon. They encouraged me to dream, and then they backed up their bluster with glittering results.

Such moments rest at the very extremes of human emotion, occurring but once or twice in a lifetime. They are typically accompanied by an emphatic outpouring of jubilation, untrammelled and vociferous. For me, in 2007, that was not the case. I was 13 years old and watching in secret. My parents were asleep in the next room, separated by paper-thin walls. I screamed into a pillow, muffling any clue of my early morning baseball escapades. School was due to start in around three hours, so certain economies of truth were required to maintain an easy life.

Ultimately, then, rooting for a Major League Baseball team from Britain was a somewhat sordid passion. It was a lonely journey to salvation. But for the first time in my life, I was a champion. The Red Sox authored one of the greatest moments of my existence, and that can never be airbrushed from history.

I did not pop champagne corks or party into the morning. I was a high school pup, remember. I could not even *buy* alcohol at that point. I did purchase one of the replica Red Sox World Series rings when they eventually hit the market, though, and I figured to pass it down through future generations.

That never happened, for reasons that will soon become clear, but the 2007 Fall Classic will always remain special to me. It was the culmination of my baseball *enlightenment*, even if it was not a fulcrum of my baseball *maturation*. Great beginnings do not guarantee happy endings, and my lifelong baseball addiction set out to prove that hypothesis.

⚾⚾⚾

"Don't worry, these guys have been trying to beat us for eighty years." – Yogi Berra

PART TWO

The Greatest Rivalry in Sports

CHAPTER FIVE

The Genesis of Hatred

Boston is an intense crucible of sporting passion. As the most beloved squad from that metropolis, the Red Sox are held aloft as a defining vehicle of immense civic pride. The Olde Towne Team has a more personal connection to its fanbase than any other franchise in Major League Baseball, and the attendant demands placed upon each representative are rigorous bordering on absurd.

More than any other city, Boston refers to its baseball heroes in mononymous fashion. Nomar, Manny, Papi, Xander, Mookie. Red Sox players are but an extension of New England families, welcomed into living rooms each night from Vermont to Maine, a loyal companion to summer conveyed through television, radio and any other means of articulating addiction.

There is a fine line between partisan obsession and defensive hostility. In Boston, quite literally The Hub of baseball, that line is often blurred, because few things define the Red Sox fan more than his or her hatred of the New York Yankees, that ultimate nemesis 200 miles to the south.

An old adage holds that people in Boston hate the Yankees more than they love the Red Sox. Such is the enmity between two of the most illustrious teams in baseball history. Such is the abhorrence of failure and the fear of defeat that washes along the eastern seaboard. Such is life amid the greatest sporting rivalry that ever came to pass.

Why do Red Sox fans hate the Yankees? Well, because the Yankees win. It is that simple. In fact, the Yankees win with greater regularity than any team from any sport anywhere else in the world. They are *synonymous* with winning, and that eats at Red Sox fans, who perceive their city, their culture and their baseball intelligence as supreme.

The Yankees have won 27 World Series titles. St Louis, the next-best team, has only managed to win 11. The Red Sox and Athletics have lifted 9 titles, ranking second in American League history, but New York has more than doubled their total output.

In the NFL, Green Bay has won 13 championships. In the NBA, Boston has won 17 titles. And in the NHL, Montreal has lifted 24 Stanley Cups. On a global stage, no team surpasses the New York Yankees in terms of silverware, success and dynastic power. The Bronx Bombers almost *define* glory at this point.

Such a reality jars with the notion, perpetrated by Red Sox Nation, that Boston baseball is of a superior style, heritage and meaning to that conjured by any other city. In this regard, Red Sox baseball is tinged with dizzy melodrama, each moment devoid of pragmatic proportion due to the sheer force of avidity. Nothing can be *normal* in Boston sports. Every event rests at the extremes of human emotion. Often, that leads to vitriol and invective. There is no filter on Beantown's consciousness.

The Red Sox and Yankees have shared a league, and subsequently a division, for their entire existence. Familiarity breeds contempt, and for the longest time, Red Sox fans saw all their hopes, dreams and ambitions run into a pinstriped buzzsaw.

If not for the Yankees, Boston would be the conclusive powerhouse of Major League Baseball. If not for the Yankees, Boston would have many more division titles, pennants and world championships than is presently the case. If not for the Yankees, Boston would be the bully, not the *bullied*.

If not for the Yankees.

Even in the modern age, where the Red Sox have won four titles in 15 years, this rivalry rests on Boston's unquenchable quest to eradicate the smug, relentless and arrogant omnipotence of New York. Sure, Yankees fans loathe the Red Sox, too, especially in light of those recent powershifts, but the Bombers always have the upper hand from a historical perspective. They always have 27 rings to fall back on. Such is the cosmic reality of baseball.

This is a rivalry founded on indignation, fuelled by paranoia and defined by David's seemingly noble insurrection against Goliath. This is a feud rooted in betrayal, animated by suspicion and heightened by the underdog attempting to destabilise the king. This is a convergence of fate, destiny and the biased interpretations of the same that has rarely been replicated in sports. It is Red Sox-Yankees and Yankees-Red Sox. Baseball barely comes into it.

If Yankee success is the elixir of toxicity between these storied teams, the *manner* in which that success is attained is the very foundation. The Yankees traditionally spend more money than everybody else, purchasing the best players and building uber teams that blow away the competition. Though that has changed under the aegis of Hal Steinbrenner, the Yankees are still considered staid, corporate and overly serious. With deep pockets and deeper resources, they take the fun out of baseball. At least according to the mainstream narrative.

Eyeing the robotic, almost *inevitable* parade of Yankee titles, baseball fans around the world have come to associate the game's most successful team with bourgeois arrogance. In a world that wants the underdog to succeed, the favourite is shunned as ruinous or outright evil. That role was tailormade for the New York Yankees, and they embrace it with irritating zest.

America casts its most famous sports team as a dictator to be toppled. People can relate to good versus bad. We like blue collar hustle outperforming bigwig complacency. There is something so damn *personable* about Average Joe beating the CEO. There is inspiration to be found in workaday spirit triumphing over inherited wealth, and there is poetry in the Red Sox beating the Yankees.

In the 2000s, that concept was amplified across the United States by a media machine erring on the side of symbolism. The social dichotomy embodied by two warring baseball teams captivated a populace and spread around the world. A narrative was born, and it never really went away. Baseball became a kaleidoscope of cultural difference, and identifying with one side or the other allowed people to express their pent-up rage.

With their shaggy beards and their ragtag culture, the Red Sox were good guys. With their policy banning facial hair and their expressionless pursuit of victory, the Yankees were inherently bad. With their iconic personalities and their cosy ballpark, the Red Sox were lovable. With their exorbitant payroll and their monolithic stadium, the Yankees were to be loathed.

A whole generation discovered baseball amid such an environment of contrasting values and splintered morality. I was part of that group. As a Red Sox fan, I disliked the Yankees because, well, that is what Red Sox fans do. That is just the way it has always been, from one generation to the next, and that is just the way it will remain, for many decades to come.

In the cauldron of competition, one can become so embroiled in a movement that all perception is impaired. We lose sight of alternative viewpoints and latch onto anything that confirms our deeply inaccurate biases. For a Red Sox fan, questioning *why* they dislike the Yankees is preposterous, akin to asking why Thursday follows Wednesday. It just does, and they just do, okay? Life would not be the same otherwise.

Well, a deeper analysis is needed, actually, to extract the true causes and sustaining features of the Red Sox-Yankees feud. We must dig further, right back to the genesis of this ancient grudge. We must journey back more than 300 years, to pre-Revolution America, where a downtrodden city outgrew its traditional foe.

⚾⚾⚾

Under colonial British rule, lasting into the 1700s, Boston was the hub of educational, cultural, artistic and economic power in continental America. Its location as the closest port to Europe was of great strategic importance, forming a gateway to trade, commerce and philosophical expansion. Meanwhile, the 1636 founding of Harvard, the country's first college, gave Massachusetts a veneer of lofty intellect.

By contrast, New York was deemed inferior, cast in the shadows as an overpopulated town of parochial outlook. It was the working class cousin of elitist Boston, the overlooked sibling of aristocratic Beantown. Originally dubbed *New Amsterdam* by rugged Dutch settlers, the city did not even get its evocative name until 1665. New York was a late bloomer, beholden to imperial intransigence.

With guts and guile, Boston became the engine of American independence, striving to overthrow colonial hegemony in all facets of life. The Boston Massacre of 1770 foreshadowed the American Revolution, while the Boston Tea Party was symbolic of the mounting fearlessness that culminated in revolt and led directly to the formation of the United States.

Quite ironically, Boston's influential role in driving American autonomy had the self-defeating effect of allowing New York to flourish. Free to create, trade and expand, New York mushroomed into a thriving metropolis. By the 19th century, its economy was transformed into a global colossus, outstripping that of Boston for the first time as resentment brewed.

Amid rampant industrialisation, New York's possession of the Erie Canal terminus spurred huge growth in manufacturing, shipping and financial services throughout the city. From a population of just 5,000 in 1700, New York swelled to welcome 123,000 inhabitants by 1820, the most of any city in the US. By 1860, that number soared to 813,000, a startling increase that defies description.

As the 1900s dawned, power in every sphere of consequence had pivoted to New York, stunning Boston into a frustrated state of paralysis. In the coming century, New York secured its position as the most prominent seat of western capitalism. Wall Street became the fulcrum of modern commerce. Broadway became the epicentre of contemporary entertainment. Times Square became the nexus of big dreams and grand articulation. While Boston prized regional domination, the Big Apple sought global recognition. The march of New York was irrepressible.

Those sentiments naturally translated to sporting competition, just as they did to politics, culture and finance. Baseball was the dominant game of America's gilded age, and it became one of the most accessible conduits to civic friction between the two great cities of that epoch.

In its formative years, baseball was a game of capricious rules, precedents and characteristics. Depending on where a game was played, and when, the sport could change subtly or considerably. There was no uniform code of conduct. Each conurbation played its own style of baseball, making it up as they went along. Naturally, Massachusetts and New York adhered to different brands of baseball, closely tethered to the disparate cultural textures of each region. Rarely did the codes intermingle, as deep-rooted traditions were fiercely upheld.

The Massachusetts game had four bases with home in the middle. Played on the amateur fields of New England, this version of the game drew inspiration from Philadelphia Town Ball, an influential strain. Fielders could record an out by throwing the ball at a runner, a practice known as 'soaking' or 'plugging.' Foul territory did not exist, and runs were plentiful. The first team to score 100 times won each game.

In contrast, the New York iteration, bound by the vaunted Knickerbocker rules, was far more civilised, refined and disciplined. The ball had to be pitched, not thrown violently. Foul lines were introduced, focusing the game's action. Three strikes constituted an out, and three outs comprised a half-inning. The team that had scored the most runs after nine innings was victorious.

A devout rival to the Massachusetts game, this new style of baseball was formalised by William Wheaton and William Tucker of the New York Knickerbocker Base Ball Club in 1845. Founded by sports enthusiast Alexander Cartwright, the Knickerbockers were the first real baseball team of serious renown. They are frequently credited with developing modern baseball as we know it, introducing uniforms and demanding commitment from their club members. Indeed, the Knickerbockers blazed a trail through America's early sporting dalliance, and their Elysian Fields diamond in Hoboken, New Jersey spoke to baseball's enduring mythological intrigue.

It was there in June 1846 that the Knickerbockers played the New York Nine, a rival team, in what was long considered the first 'officially recorded' baseball game of all-time. Driven by New York's evolving power, size and authority, this version of baseball surpassed all regional alternatives, morphing into the nationally recognised pastime enjoyed to this day.

In 1862, the Excelsior Club of Brooklyn barnstormed through New England, seeking to establish the Knickerbocker rules as a universal code of baseball. The Excelsiors defeated a Boston team known as the Bowdoins, 41-15, and then thrashed a merger of two other local clubs, 39-13. Somewhat begrudgingly, Boston teams began adopting the New York brand of baseball as a result. The Big Apple won out, and baseball fans became accustomed to such a concept in the decades ahead.

By 1869, the first professional baseball team, known as the Cincinnati Red Stockings, was established in acknowledgement of the Knickerbocker rules. By 1876, likeminded clubs had formed in enough cities to spawn the National League of

Professional Base Ball Clubs, which eventually became the National League of Major League Baseball that survives to this day.

Early in its expansion, the National League faced challenges from several upstart competitors, most notably the American Association, formed in 1882, which offered games on Sundays and sold alcoholic beverages to fans in its ballparks.

A rudimentary series between the winners of each league was attempted on several occasions, but the NL eventually undercut the AA by encouraging teams such as the Pittsburgh Pirates to defect. The AA disbanded in 1891, creating a void alongside the National League at the top of professional baseball. Ban Johnson, an ambitious entrepreneur, set out to bridge that chasm by developing the Western League, a comparatively minor circuit, into a sustainable alternative to the cutthroat NL.

With support from Charles Comiskey, powerful owner of the WL franchise that moved from Sioux City to St Paul, Johnson capitalised on the National League's contraction of teams in Baltimore, Cleveland, Louisville and Washington, D.C., to build an enticing product.

Johnson moved the Western League's Grand Rapids team to Cleveland, where they became the Indians. He also positioned Comiskey's Saints in Chicago, where they became the White Sox, in addition to scattering expansion teams in Baltimore, Boston, Philadelphia and beyond.

When the National League limited salaries to $2,400 in 1901, Johnson, Comiskey and the other owners grasped their chance to establish their offering - freshly rebranded as the American League - as equal to the NL in quality, potential and resources. The AL offered a greater rate of pay, and more than 100 players jumped to the new circuit, which staked a claim to major league status. The baseball ecosystem was altered forever.

In 1901 and 1902, the National League and American League fought a bloody war. Players were raided on either side, crossing the divide. Attendances rose and fell, fluctuating with kneejerk capriciousness. The egotistical presidents of each association, Johnson and Nicholas Young, pulled no punches while clinging to vacuous claims of superiority. Baseball welcomed the twentieth century with vehemence and vitriol. No quarter was asked nor given.

Finally, in 1903, a truce was declared and a definitive annual contest between the champions of each league was arranged to quantify the impassioned posturing. The World Series was born as contemporary baseball bloomed to fruition. There was a new holy grail for teams to chase, and that transformed the game in perpetuity.

❧❧❧

In baseball's awakening century, as the World Series became a jewel of serious gravity, Boston was the dominant force. The Red Sox, initially known as the Boston Americans, won the inaugural World Series from Pittsburgh in 1903. They added further titles in 1912, 1915 and 1916, building the first dynasty in major league history.

Tris Speaker, a regal outfielder, was one of the first baseball superstars of mass appreciation. A veritable hitting machine, Speaker swaggered through the outfield in Boston, where he was complemented by Harry Hooper, a reliable professional, and a cast of hardworking sticklers.

The early Red Sox were defined by dominant pitching, however, and their supremacy was illustrated by the immortal Cy Young winning 192 games in eight Boston seasons. Eventually a metonym for pitching excellence, Young birthed a tradition of great pitching that inspired later Red Sox hurlers like Smoky Joe Wood, Dutch Leonard and Carl Mays, all of whom won multiple championships in Beantown.

There was no greater team as professional baseball found its feet. In essence, the Red Sox were the Yankees before the Yankees even existed. They were baseball royalty, backed by a rambunctious fanbase and characterised by relentless momentum. Boston just *got* baseball, and other cities struggled to keep up.

For instance, New York did not have an American League team until 1903. The National League Giants, playing out of Manhattan and managed by the authoritative John McGraw, forbade such encroachment on their territory. However, amid the peace talks that created the World Series, Johnson requested a team in New York to compete with the Giants, adding intrigue and drama. McGraw eventually relented, and Johnson transplanted the Baltimore Orioles from Maryland to Manhattan.

Playing out of Hilltop Park, a ramshackle yard near Broadway, the New York American League team became known as the Highlanders. They faced their Boston rivals for the first time on 7th May 1903. Americans pitcher George Winter was knocked down in the first of many beanball wars. It was a portent of future controversy.

The first great Boston-New York pennant race unfurled in 1904, when the Americans and Highlanders fought until the final weekend of a brutal season to hoist the cherished flag. Naturally, the two teams met for a conclusive doubleheader on said occasion, creating a tense showdown to decide the American League championship. The Highlanders needed to win both games to claim their first AL crown. Boston needed just one victory to defend its pennant.

In the opener, Jack Chesbro, a firebrand ace, went to the hill for New York after winning 41 games. He was opposed by a strong Americans lineup and over 200 Royal Rooters, the rowdy Boston fan club led by local tavern owner Michael 'Nuf Ced' McGreevy that famously played instruments and waved banners at games.

Early in the fateful contest, unruly Boston fans danced on the dugouts at Hilltop Park, attempting to get under the skin of opposing players. McGreevy's tactics seemed ineffective through six innings, however, as New York nursed a 2-0 lead. Regardless, Boston fought back to tie the game in the seventh, eliciting raucous cheers from the barnstorming horde.

In the top of the ninth, perhaps perturbed by the vociferous fans who travelled to New York by train, Chesbro unleashed a wild pitch over the head of batter Freddy Parent and all the way to the backstop. Standing at third base, Lou Criger trotted home with the winning run, clinching the pennant for Boston in dramatic circumstances. Highlanders manager Clark Griffith fell to his knees in agony; the Royal Rooters played *Tessie*, their trademark ballad; and the Americans toasted their latest success, celebrating long into the night.

Due to a longstanding personal feud with Johnson, McGraw refused to allow his Giants to participate in a subsequent World Series, but Boston portrayed the confidence of champions, nevertheless. It would take the city 100 years to beat New York in another title-deciding baseball game.

◌◌◌

The World Series resumed in 1905 and the Giants won their first championship, beating Philadelphia in five games. McGraw enjoyed the Series after all, pitting his wits against the legendary Connie Mack. In subsequent years, however, other cities across the country made bids for baseball ascendancy, and the hardball vanguard faced stiff competition from ambitious upstarts.

Chicago became a particular rival to New York and Boston as the White Sox beat the crosstown Cubs to claim the championship in 1906. The Cubs responded by winning two straight titles of their own, while competitive teams in the industrial heartlands of Pittsburgh and Philly added depth to the evolving cosmology of big league baseball.

Following the 1907 season, Boston Americans owner John I Taylor rebranded his team, formally adopting the *Red Sox* nickname in tribute to their distinctive uniforms. A new logo was drawn up, and the team's trademark identity began to take shape.

Keen to keep up and distinguish themselves, the Highlanders added pinstripes to their home uniform in time for the 1912 season. The design was refined, debated and dropped altogether at various points in the ensuing years before becoming a hallowed symbol of baseball aspiration. Naturally, Boston was the first team to face New York as it christened the iconic outfit. A crowd of 12,000 witnessed the wardrobe change on Opening Day at Hilltop Park, and the Red Sox won, 5-3, kickstarting another season that ended in a championship.

Nine days later, the Highlanders were party to another *first* in the evolving rivalry, losing 7-6 to the Red Sox in the first official game ever played at Fenway Park. Despite a crowd of 24,000, Boston's new ballpark was pushed off the front pages by coverage of the *Titanic* sinking en route from Southampton to

New York. Decades later, some said it was an omen, because the concept of *coincidence* never really played well in New England. Indeed, all seemed fine on the surface in 1912, but the Red Sox ploughed towards unseen icebergs with reckless zeal.

A year later, while Boston reigned supreme as champions of the baseball world, their counterparts in New York were still defining their identity. The Highlanders moniker proved cumbersome when attempting to write newspaper headlines and media releases, vital cogs in baseball's march towards mainstream adoration. Accordingly, Jim Rice, sports editor of the *New York Press*, took to calling the team 'Yanks' or 'Yankees' in his paper, finding it sharper and more succinct.

The nickname gained popularity and the ballclub adopted it officially in 1913. The first ever Red Sox-Yankees game, in name as well as spirit, occurred shortly thereafter, adding another dimension to the gathering feud.

Around the world, *Yankee* or *Yank* is a colloquial nickname for any person of American nationality. In the southern United States, however, the term refers to northerners, specifically those from New England, in a derisive manner.

The phrase has roots in British colonial dialect, used in reference to Boston's fierce revolutionary soldiers. Indeed, the *Oxford English Dictionary* defines *Yankee* as a "nickname for a native or inhabitant of New England or, more widely, of the northern States generally."

Alas, lest we never forget that that the New York American League Baseball Club, so successful and prestigious, actually bears a nickname descriptive of the very region it despises. From an etymological perspective, perhaps the Boston Yankees makes more sense than the *New York* Yankees. Now how do you like *those* apples?

Regardless of nicknames and uniforms, slogans and marketing techniques, the Red Sox rumbled through the 1910s in clinical fashion, sweeping all before them. George Mogridge of the Yankees no-hit them at Fenway Park in 1917, twirling the first such game in the ballpark's history, but otherwise Boston dominated.

A young southpaw named George Herman Ruth was masterful for the Red Sox, pitching 29.2 consecutive scoreless innings in World Series play. That record stood for 43 years, and the prized phenom had three championship rings before he turned 24. There had never been a more exciting prospect in baseball history.

Boston bought Ruth from the minor league Baltimore Orioles midway through the 1914 season. At first, the crude kid was reluctant to move away from home, and his initiation with the Red Sox was often rocky. Nevertheless, Ruth barrelled his way to approval with dense determination, and the Red Sox reared a legend.

Brash and untamed, Ruth rivalled Walter Johnson, the Senators' famed fireballer, in a number of masterful outings. Possessed of a natural affection for the game, George Herman wanted to see and do everything all at once, and his simultaneous emergence as a hitter gave Boston a two-pronged weapon in its quest for eminence.

In 1918, Ruth went 13-7 as a pitcher, massaging a 2.22 ERA through 20 starts. He also played 95 games in the field for Boston, hitting .300 while leading the league with 11 home runs. There was an absurdity to Ruth's act that simmered as the Red Sox won another world championship that year. Some began to question whether Boston could contain The Babe and his carnival act.

"There was no doubt about his place in baseball now," writes Leigh Montville in *The Big Bam*, his seminal Ruth biography. "He was the number one attraction in the game. If there was a Most Valuable Player award in 1918, and there wasn't, he would have won it in a breeze. He was the best player on the best team, and if you listened, you would hear good young players compared now to Babe Ruth, not Ty Cobb, not anyone else. The best player deserved the best money, Ty Cobb money. The Babe had made $7,500 in 1918. Now he wanted $15,000 a year."

❧❧❧

As a franchise, the Red Sox had five World Series titles by 1918. They had won 33% of all Fall Classics *that had ever been played*, and Philadelphia was the only other team to claim more than two championships. The Red Sox also had the game's best player and its most colourful character. In short, Boston was the crucible of baseball. No city could compare.

All was not serene, however. When the Red Sox finished sixth in 1919, mustering a meagre defence of their world championship, owner Harry Frazee found himself in a bind. A noted theatre empresario, Frazee was losing money by the day. His Broadway empire required immense funding, and when a series of mediocre productions flopped at the box office, baseball's swashbuckling executive ran into trouble.

Born in Peoria, Illinois, Frazee carved a handsome reputation with theatrical successes such as *Fine Feathers* and *Adele*. A keen baseball fan, he then teamed with Hugh Ward, a friend, to buy the Red Sox from Joseph Lannin in November 1916.

Despite musical triumphs, Frazee did not really have much free-flowing capital, and $262,000 of the ballclub sale price was tethered to a three-year credit. When that credit came due, in November 1919, a perfect storm engulfed Frazee, who struggled to make ends meet.

Slumping attendances amid World War I hurt the beleaguered owner, who favoured his theatre investments over the Red Sox as a serious avenue to financial security. Accordingly, Frazee came to view baseball player sales as a tool for stimulating capital in his theatre business. The Red Sox were a pawn in Harry's game of high-stakes racketeering.

Boston drew criticism by trading frontline pitcher Carl Mays to the Yankees, but that was merely the start of Frazee's fire sale. Wally Schang, Herb Pennock, Everett Scott, Waite Hoyt, Joe Bush and Sam Jones were all sold to the Yankees. Ed Barrow, the man who allowed Ruth to play some outfield in Boston, also moved to New York, where he built a Hall of Fame resume as the Yankees' general manager. The Red Sox were gutted so Frazee, a New York resident, could continue putting plays on the stage in the Big Apple. An inferiority complex roared to prominence.

Unbeknownst to many contemporary fans, however, even Frazee's ability to trade players was impinged by grim extraneous circumstances. Johnson never really liked Frazee, and the AL president launched a scurrilous smear campaign that turned many team owners against Boston. As a result, most

Johnson allies refused to deal with Frazee, precluding the potential for trades. The Red Sox owner was essentially restricted to two potential transaction partners: the White Sox or the Yankees.

Working amid such draconian restraints, Frazee knew that Ruth, his star pitcher-hitter, was a highly valuable asset. The rambunctious Ruth broke the single-season home run record in 1919, thrashing 29 long balls in 130 games. Ruth hit more home runs that year than 10 major league *teams*, including both pennant winners. He also drove in 113 runs and got on base at a .456 clip. Few players had ever produced such a potent season.

Branded 'incorrigible' as a kid, Ruth grew up in the tough Baltimore neighbourhood of Pigtown, a place of minimal hope and bleak lawlessness. Suitably reckless as a youngster, Ruth was sent to St Mary's Industrial School for Boys, a correctional institute that kerbed his rowdiness. Still, George Herman was a crude and uncultured colt early in his baseball career, and the game's cognoscenti was not always receptive of his bluster.

Frazee grew impatient with Ruth's antics, believing the star wanted too much at a young age. Ruth repeatedly threatened to hold out for a bigger salary, and his thorough iconoclasm was difficult to comprehend for traditional baseball men who had always seen the game played in a sedate mode of hushed dignity. Ruth's flair singled him out, and the crusty nostalgists were not amused.

Meanwhile, Frazee struggled to find the money to repay his credit used to purchase the Red Sox. November seeped into December, intensifying the panic. Something had to give, and on the fifth day of January 1920, Ruth was sold to the Yankees for $125,000 and a personal loan to Frazee of $300,000, secured against Fenway Park. Chicago offered Shoeless Joe Jackson and $60,000 for Ruth, but Frazee opted for the larger financial windfall.

The sale of Ruth allowed Frazee to appease his creditors and consolidate his Broadway efforts. Future plays such as *My Lady Friends* and *No, No, Nanette* were particularly successful, but such glory became increasingly rare for the baseball team that once kept its predominant director solvent.

Frazee relied on the Red Sox to underpin his lifestyle, taking loans and making the club pay his non-baseball expenses. He frequently overdrew his salary, by as much as $21,659 in 1920, and his general insouciance for the future of baseball in Boston was flagrantly selfish.

"The Ruth deal was the only way I could retain the Red Sox," Frazee once told baseball historian Fred Lieb. Indeed, he only remained Red Sox owner until 1923, presiding over four more losing seasons before selling the team to Bob Quinn, a Johnson ally. Baseball was never the same again.

⚾⚾⚾

When Ruth swapped Boston for New York, the Red Sox had five World Series titles, the most in baseball history. The Yankees had none. New York won 26 world championships before Boston next managed the feat. They also clinched 39 pennants, confirming their status as the preeminent powerhouse of North American sports. The Yankees redefined winning while the Red Sox capitulated with stunning regularity. Rarely have we seen such a profound transformation.

Endowed with pinstripes, Ruth became the greatest player who ever lived, converting to the outfield full-time and mashing more home runs than anybody thought possible. The Yankees built a cavernous stadium to maximise his left-handed power stroke, and the resultant surge in attendances and marketing cache grew their resources beyond the kin of any competitor ballclub.

In the Bronx, George Herman morphed into *The Babe*, a storybook character who transcended the sport and personified the era. Ruth was known alternatively as the Great Bambino, the Sultan of Swat, the Colossus of Clout, the Behemoth of Bust, the Wazir of Wham, and the Maharajah of Mash. He was Santa Claus with a baseball bat, and everybody loved him.

Launching 714 career home runs, Ruth reinvented baseball, fuelled the Yankees' empire and catalysed the Red Sox' mutilation. His sale from Boston to New York became the single most infamous player transaction in sporting history. It altered the fate of two teams and two cities for almost a century henceforth. Harry Frazee had a lot to answer for.

Between 1920 and 2003, when the so-called Curse of the Bambino was in full effect, the Yankees finished ahead of the Red Sox on 66 occasions, or in 78% of all seasons. In 10 of the first 12 seasons after he swapped Boston for New York, Babe Ruth out-homered the entire Red Sox *team* on his own. In turn, it took the Red Sox 14 years just to reach the .500 mark again after losing their talisman, while a first-place finish came a further 12 seasons thereafter.

The Yankees soared from one dynasty to the next, winning two, three, four and five consecutive titles at various points. Boston, in contrast, became the ultimate baseball bridesmaid, winning the pennant but losing the World Series in 1946, 1967, 1975 and 1986.

Their rivalry was like that between a nail and hammer. One team existed merely to be thumped by the other. No amount of dreaming could alter that fate, and no blend of suspicious desperation rewrote the familiar script. The Yankees drove home their power with one clinical blow after another. Boston cowered in the corner, battered and bruised by the sinister sibling it once taught to fight.

⚾⚾⚾

CHAPTER SIX

Pride, Power, Pinstripes

A monumental crowd of 74,200 gathered in the Bronx on 18th April 1923 as Yankee Stadium, the first triple-decked sporting arena in America, enjoyed its grand Opening Day. Naturally, the Red Sox were in town, and just as naturally, the Yankees won, 4-1, sending the masses home happy.

Ruth hit the Stadium's first home run, setting the tone for a fine Yankees team that rolled to its first world championship six months later. Eleven of the 24 players used by New York that season previously played for the Red Sox. Boston sold its future to the Yankees, and loyal fans watched on in disbelief.

The Yankees added further titles in 1927 and 1928, aided by a strapping first baseman named Lou Gehrig, who teamed with Ruth to form the most powerful three-four punch in baseball history. Second baseman Tony Lazzeri and outfielder Bob Meusel added depth to a terrifying lineup that became known as Murderers' Row.

At the behest of ambitious owner Colonel Jacob Ruppert, the Yankees spared no expense in pursuit of victory. If a new player was needed to fill an area of weakness, New York typically made the move. Such a relentless commitment to success congealed into a demanding philosophy on River Avenue, which became the epicentre of global baseball domination.

In 1930, the Yankees raided Boston once again, trading Cedric Durst and $50,000 for Red Ruffing, an inconsistent hurler who was underappreciated by the Fenway faithful. Yankees manager Bob Shawkey tweaked Ruffing's delivery, and Red duly spent 15 years at the front of New York's rotation. Ruffing won 231 games for the Yankees and took six World Series rings to the Hall of Fame. As for Durst? Well, Cedric had just 330 plate appearances for the Red Sox. He hit .245 with 1 home run. Such was the lopsided nature of the Red Sox-Yankees crusade.

Powered by Ruth, the Yankees morphed into the richest, most powerful team on earth. Yearly attendance soared over 1 million as the Yankees became the first team ever to reach seven digits in fan support. Ticket prices were raised, feeding a supply chain of fame and success, while a stream of excellent players beat a path to the Bronx.

The explosion of tabloid media, radio and newsreel film beamed Ruth's image around the country and throughout the world. The Bambino's arrival in New York was the big bang moment for Yankee mystique, and America was never the same again.

"Of this, there can be no doubt," writes Marty Appell of Ruth's eminence in *Pinstripe Empire*. "He became the face of the Yankees as they emerged as the best-known team in sports. All discussions of Yankee greatness, dynasties and success begin with the Babe. Obtaining him proved to be the greatest transaction a team ever pulled off, and keeping his name and image front and centre proved to have enduring qualities for the franchise."

The first player to hit 200, 300, 400, 500, 600 and 700 career home runs, Ruth powered the Yankees to seven pennants and four World Series titles between 1920 and 1934. During a 22-year career, the Bambino played in 10 World Series, winning seven. He recorded a 0.87 ERA in Fall Classic play, complementing a 1.214 OPS and 15 home runs, including a possible called shot against the Cubs in 1932. Upon his retirement, no player in baseball history had won more world championships than Ruth. In short, he made the Yankees great, and future generations strained to honour his legacy.

Ruth passed the flame to Gehrig, who hauled the Yankees to three consecutive titles between 1936 and 1938 amid a consecutive games played streak that reached 2,130 contests. The team's reliable captain, Gehrig won seven World Series titles as an active Yankee. Though unrecognised in some almanacs, he also played eight games for the 1939 Bombers, who later won the world championship, too. That title was dedicated to the mountainous first baseman as he struggled with failing health. New York had never seen a winner like Gehrig.

Larrupin' Lou was forced into early retirement after doctors diagnosed him with amyotrophic lateral sclerosis, a disease that effectively kills the neurons that control voluntary muscles, gradually diminishing the sufferer into a state of paralysis.

Upon retiring, Gehrig - baseball's Iron Man - gave an iconic speech at a tearful Yankee Stadium, proclaiming himself the 'luckiest man on the face of the earth.' The legendary gamer passed away in June 1941, but New York won another championship in his memory, the ninth in club history.

That same summer, Joe DiMaggio, the next great Yankee, hit safely in 56 consecutive games, beating the club record of 29, the modern record of 40, and the all-time MLB mark of 44. When that stretch ended, the elegant centre fielder unleashed another 17-gamer, hitting safely in 73 of 74 ballgames.

It was, quite simply, the most outstanding achievement in baseball history to that point, and the whole nation was captivated. The daily buzz to see if Joe collected a hit provided a salve for people petrified of Nazi aggression amid World War II. Indeed, the great DiMaggio even knocked Hitler off the front pages. Nobody had ever done what he did, and the celebrations were epochal. There was new star in the pinstriped galaxy.

Joltin' Joe won the hearts of a nation with exquisite hitting, superlative defence and noble elegance. His rivalry with Ted Williams, Boston's definitive slugger, divided a populace and brought fresh invective to the ancient rivalry. Kids of the age grew up adoring Ted or Joe, imitating The Splendid Splinter or the Yankee Clipper. Passions were duly stoked.

As DiMaggio tore a hole in the failure-time continuum with his extraordinary streak, Williams authored a 1941 season of equal brilliance, finishing with a .406 batting average. Newspapers were full of commentary as to the comparative virtues of each accomplishment, while taverns from the Bronx to the Back Bay hummed with inexorable debate.

DiMaggio added 30 home runs and 125 RBI to his headline performance, while Williams clouted 37 dingers and knocked in 120 runs. The Yankees won the World Series, however, defeating Brooklyn, and DiMaggio won the Most Valuable Player award, to the chagrin of Sox boosters everywhere.

The DiMaggio-Williams dichotomy consolidated that between the Yankees and Red Sox as the ultimate power duel in sports. Dominic, Joe's younger brother, played for Boston, adding a further layer of intrigue.

The franchise figureheads were almost traded for one another, too, at least according to folklore. Allegedly, one drunken eve amid the duo's startling pomp, exuberant Red Sox owner Tom Yawkey met with Yankees officials over dinner. As the beer flowed, discussions turned naturally to Joe and Ted, just as they did in sequestered enclaves throughout the nation. Before long, the Red Sox and Yankees struck a verbal agreement to swap superstars, quite remarkably. Sober minds prevailed in the morning, though, and the trade was never consummated.

Nevertheless, future generations developed statistical models to project the likely impact of DiMaggio and Williams swapping ballparks. A righthanded hitter, Joe's natural swing plane carried balls towards Death Valley at Yankee Stadium, where the left-centre field fence lay 457 feet from home plate. A lefty swinger, Ted never struggled to reach the bleachers at Fenway, but the concept of him regularly aiming for that fabled right field porch in the Bronx, just 295 feet from home plate, made historians salivate.

Indeed, hardball mathematician Bill James once calculated that, by hitting balls into the gargantuan abyss of Yankee Stadium, DiMaggio lost more homers due to his home stadium than anybody in baseball history. Likewise, statistician Bill Jenkinson argues that, if he had played in a fairer stadium of modern construction, DiMaggio would have belted "about 225 homers during his home field career," as opposed to 148.

Accordingly, it is not unreasonable to suggest that, if Joe played his home games at Fenway for a considerable stretch of time, launching pop flies over the seductive left field wall, he would have topped 500 career home runs. Ultimately, the Clipper finished with 361 bombs, although he also missed three prime-age seasons due to military service between 1943 and 1945.

Williams also missed those seasons while serving in the Navy and Marine Corps. Ted later participated in the Korean War, as well, etching his name further into national folklore. Still, he finished his career with 521 home runs, and some analysts hold that, if the bizarre Yankees trade *did* materialise, Williams may have launched an assault on Ruth's sacred career record.

Alas, the progression of war diminished the zenith of both players and interrupted the intriguing subplot as both DiMaggio and Williams made huge sacrifices for their country. Joe briefly became a sergeant before settling into a largely ambassadorial role as a physical education instructor at a camp in Atlantic City, New Jersey. Meanwhile, Ted earned his naval aviator wings and became a fighter pilot, flying missions and training young enlisters.

To much relief, World War II finally ended in September 1945, and in 1946, for the first time since selling Ruth, Boston finished ahead of New York in the American League standings. St Louis awaited in the subsequent World Series, which the Red Sox lost in seven games, extending their championship drought to 28 years. Boston shortstop Johnny Pesky paused while handling a crucial relay throw late in Game 7, allowing Enos Slaughter to dash from first to home with the decisive run.

Regardless of such heartache, with Williams hauling Boston into contention, the Red Sox and Yankees were more evenly aligned than at any point since the demise of Harry Frazee. Pesky figured to get multiple shots at exorcising his demons.

To that end, a pulsating three-way AL pennant race captivated America in 1948. Entering the season's final weekend, Boston and New York both lay one-and-a-half games behind Cleveland, a surprise package led by fine shortstop Lou Boudreau. The Indians finished the season with a three-game series against Detroit, while the Red Sox and Yankees faced each other in two final games at Fenway Park.

Cleveland lost the first game to Detroit, cutting its lead to one meagre game. The nation was agog with chatter about a three-way tie for the pennant. However, the Red Sox trumped the Yankees, 5-1, in their series opener, while Cleveland also won. New York was duly eliminated as the Indians secured at least a tie atop the standings.

On the season's final day, Joe DiMaggio went 4-for-5 with three RBI, but Boston thwarted New York en route to a 10-5 victory. *Dom* DiMaggio went 3-for-4 with a home run as the younger sibling enjoyed his moment of adulation. Meanwhile in Cleveland, the Indians lost 7-1 to finish with a 96-58 record, identical to that of the Red Sox.

A one-game playoff was arranged for Monday 4th October at Fenway. The winner would face the Boston Braves, The Hub's decrepit National League entry, in a subsequent World Series. Such a crosstown classic seemed poetically irresistible. However, those plans were swiftly upended when Red Sox manager Joe McCarthy - of course a fabled Yankee - picked the inexperienced Denny Galehouse to start the do-or-die showdown rather than ace Mel Parnell. Cleveland won, 8-3, stunning the Red Sox en route to a world championship.

"McCarthy made his choice, and it didn't work out," Parnell told author Peter Golenbock years later for a book entitled *Red Sox Nation*. "After the ballgame, he said to me, 'I made a mistake, and I'll just have to live with it.'"

In this regard, Boston became the very *cradle* of mistakes, finding ever more outlandish ways to spark false hope and dash baseball dreams. Red Sox players resented momentary lapses in managerial decision-making. Local writers mourned the loss of immense opportunity. Executives scratched their heads while contributing to the problem. And as for the loyal fans? Well, they just had to live with it, too. There was no other choice. They were all hooked for life.

⚾⚾⚾

The following year, 1949, another topsy-turvy pennant race unfurled in the American League. Cleveland faded somewhat as the season reached a crescendo, but the Yankees and Red Sox were right in contention, as they always seemed to be, separated by one game atop the standings entering the final series.

Fittingly, the teams met for a two-game series at Yankee Stadium to conclude the regular season. Boston needed to win just one game to clinch the pennant. Managed by the loquacious Casey Stengel, New York required a sweep to reach the World Series. The equipoise was delectable as a new chapter was added to the storied rivalry.

Boston raced to a 4-0 lead in the opening game, watched by 69,551 in the Bronx. According to Baseball-Reference.com, the Red Sox had a 90% probability of winning the game, and thus the pennant, through two-and-a-half innings. But the Yankees were not done. More importantly, *Joe DiMaggio* was not done. New York came soaring back.

DiMaggio had been out of the lineup for two weeks, bed-ridden with bone spurs in his right heel and a mild case of pneumonia. Impatient and antsy, The Yankee Clipper regularly tried to speed up his recovery, attempting to put weight on his foot before falling back into bed, disconsolate and pained.

Few expected him to play in the season-ending series, but Joe awoke on the morning of the first game and discovered - rather miraculously - that he could stand and move without agony. Like a scene from a bad Hollywood baseball film, DiMaggio smiled wickedly and made his way to the ballpark. Then he broke Boston hearts. Again.

His team down by four in that first game, Joe led off the fourth inning by poking a ground-rule double into the Yankee Stadium abyss. Hank Bauer knocked DiMaggio in with a single and subsequently came around to score himself after a further base hit from Johnny Lindell and a sacrifice fly by Jerry Coleman.

Three straight singles to open the home fifth cut the Red Sox' lead to 4-3. DiMaggio scratched out an infield single, loading the bases and applying intense pressure. Billy Johnson grounded into a double play for the Yanks, but Tommy Heinrich scored to knot the game at 4. It stayed that way until the eighth inning, when Lindell, an unheralded outfielder, crushed a home run to deep left field, giving the Yankees a lead they never relinquished.

It was just Lindell's sixth long ball of the season, complementing a batting average below .250. He manged to hit just 72 dingers in a 12-year career spanning 854 games. So inadequate was his skill in the box, Lindell eventually gave up on hitting and became an effective pitcher. The keen practical joker from Greeley, Colorado became the first of many ordinary heroes to gain pinstriped immortality for extraordinary achievements against Boston. He was Bucky Dent before Bucky Dent was even born.

Still, Lindell's shot merely tied the American League standings. There was still one more game to be played, with a place in the World Series awaiting the victor. The winner of 21 games in 1949, co-ace Vic Raschi got the ball for New York while Ellis Kinder, a 23-game winner, toed the rubber for Boston. The old enemies traded blows once again.

Phil Rizzuto, the Yankees' pesky shortstop, led off the home first with a triple. Heinrich grounded out to the right side, driving him in to stake New York to an early lead. A tense game unfurled from there, with Raschi and Kinder exchanging zeros in a fast-paced war for supremacy.

Finally, in the bottom of the eighth, New York busted the game open. Heinrich blasted a solo home run, Jerry Coleman cranked a three-run double, and the Yankees built a 5-0 lead. They were three outs away from returning to the World Series, but Boston mustered a rally as Bobby Doerr tripled in two runs and Billy Goodman singled in another.

Ever dignified, the hobbled DiMaggio took himself out of the game to aid the Yankees' chances on defence. Raschi gritted his teeth to record the final out, a measly popup off the bat of Birdie Tebbetts. Heinrich squeezed the ball in foul territory, and the Yankees had their 16th pennant in franchise history. The Red Sox had blown it again.

Facing Brooklyn in the Fall Classic, Stengel's Yankees breezed to victory in five games, winning their 12th world championship of all-time. This triumph presaged the next great Yankee dynasty, as the Bombers became the only team in baseball history to win five consecutive World Series titles. New York also won 14 pennants in 16 years between 1949 and 1964, capturing nine championships in that span, an unprecedented run of sustained greatness.

Boston faded into the second division, meanwhile, finishing 23 games out of first place *on average* between 1951 and 1966. The stunning turnaround of 1949 consolidated the roles of master and underdog in this rumbling saga. The Red Sox were always chasing a pinstriped shadow.

⚾⚾⚾

Just as Gehrig succeeded Ruth, DiMaggio reluctantly passed the torch of Yankee greatness to Mickey Mantle, a precocious slugger from the mining towns of Oklahoma. With blonde hair, blue eyes and comic book muscles, Mantle debuted with New York in 1951, a big city culture shock personified. Through trial and error, Mantle learned to refine his rambunctious skill, and New York soon fell in love with its next great hero.

A natural centre fielder, Mickey was initially shoehorned beside DiMaggio in the outfield, and there was always ice between the staid legend and the cavalier colt tabbed to replace him. Joe resented Mickey's easy, unearned fame. Mickey sought Joe's respect, largely without success. They were inextricably linked in the pantheon of Yankee greatness, but Mantle never felt comfortable around DiMaggio. They were icons of very different times.

In the 1951 World Series against the Giants, Mantle suffered a torn anterior cruciate ligament after twisting his knee on a drainage hole in right-centre field at Yankee Stadium when DiMaggio called him off a ball late. The injury affected Mickey throughout his legendary career, and he never played another game without reams of bandages supporting legs that ached unbearably.

There is no telling what Mantle may have achieved if that injury never happened. He may have smashed every record in the book. He may have surpassed every name in the annals. He may have fulfilled his potential. Still, deep down, Mickey never felt worthy of playing centre field in pinstripes, filling the shoes of a living god. The pressure was immense, and he did not always deal with it in a healthy manner.

Despite battling chronic self-doubt and a relentless stream of injuries, Mantle authored one of the greatest careers in baseball history. A switch-hitter with superhuman power, Mickey slugged 536 home runs in 18 seasons, third all-time at the point of his retirement. He won three MVP awards, played in 20 All-Star Games and claimed the historic Triple Crown in 1956. Never before had baseball encountered a five-tool player of such stunning genius. Never before had the Yankees harnessed a clutch gamer of such titillating talent.

More than the numbers and accolades, though, Mickey Mantle humanised the maturation of American power. A country kid who spoke with a twang, Mantle oozed charisma and embodied hedonism. He was everything to every*one*, a handsome charmer who drank to excess and used vulgar language redolent of the Bambino himself. A notoriously prolific womaniser, Mantle somehow got away with it all, and he somehow kept his own persona in check. Mothers *and* fathers loved The Mick.

Grandparents, too. To dislike Mickey Mantle was to disparage the United States. There was no denying his oxymoronic purity.

Likewise, in the 1950s and 1960s, New York consolidated *its* position as the global epicentre of baseball. Playing in the Polo Grounds of Manhattan, the Giants had Willie Mays, a prodigious player with infectious enthusiasm. Fighting out of cosy Ebbets Field in Brooklyn, the Dodgers had Duke Snider, an underrated star with a gentlemanly manner. And then looming in the Bronx were the Yankees, led by Mantle, whose impish passion and pearly white smile defined an American epoch.

Between 1936 and 1957, when the Giants and Dodgers moved west, 17 of the 22 World Series played involved at least one team from New York. On 10 occasions in that span, Gotham hosted a crosstown series to determine baseball's world champion. The Yankees' Don Larsen even threw a perfect game against Brooklyn in the 1956 Fall Classic, underscoring the city's baseball prowess. The Big Apple was the crucible of modern hardball, and people were shocked when the Yankees did *not* win it all.

In 1960, that unthinkable notion of pinstriped defeat was taken to its artistic extreme by the Pittsburgh Pirates, who slayed the Yankees in seven iconic games. Light-hitting second baseman Bill Mazeroski hit the only Game 7 walk-off home run in World Series history, devastating the Yankees and thrilling 36,683 revellers at quaint Forbes Field. Mantle famously cried at his locker after the game, offering a glimpse inside the traumatic world of stress occupied by Yankee heroes. When *greatness* was expected, mere *excellence* did not tick the box.

Indeed, Mantle won 12 pennants as a Yankee, meaning that 66% of his career seasons finished with an appearance in the World Series. Mickey led the Bombers to seven world championships, two less than DiMaggio, but he still felt the dense weight of expectation. Upon Mantle's retirement in 1968, the Yankees had 20 titles in franchise history. The Mick thought it should have been more, however, and the demands of Yankeedom lent a certain paranoia to his pursuit of perfection.

Still, the sight of Mantle in those hallowed pinstripes, bulging out of a tight jersey and powdering baseballs into the upper deck, was synonymous with America's modernisation. The

Commerce Comet gave the populace somebody and *something* to believe in, as the country merged from old to new. An imperfect man, Mickey was the perfect star for his team, his town and his time. He stood forth as the ultimate symbol of contemporary aspiration.

"Who else - besides maybe Elvis - is lodged so firmly in pop iconography?" asks Jane Leavy in *The Last Boy*, her meticulous appraisal of Mantle's fame. "The transformation of The Mick over the course of eighteen years in the majors and forty-four years in the public eye parallels the transformation of American culture from wilful innocence to knowing cynicism. To tell his story is to tell ours."

He was the transformative icon of a complicated age. He was the blank canvas of post-war aspiration. He was a king among men, built from the fabled hankering thrust upon him. Even his name just sounded like baseball, people said. The Mick. Mickey. *Mickey Mantle*. America's childhood was over, and its ultimate boy was a Yankee god.

❧❧❧

As the Yankees cemented layer after dynastic layer to their classy heritage, Boston played the role of begrudging accomplice. New York needed a foil in its quest for mass appeal, and the Red Sox could not help themselves.

In 1951, for instance, hometown ace Allie Reynolds no-hit the Red Sox at Yankee Stadium. A decade later, divisive Yankees slugger Roger Maris launched a long home run off Boston pitcher Tracy Stallard, his 61st of the year, breaking Ruth's ancient record for most bombs in a single season.

Between 1946 and 1963, cuddly catcher Yogi Berra won 10 World Series rings with the Yankees, one for every finger. To this day, that is more than *the entire Red Sox franchise* has managed *forever*. Indeed, among non-Yankee ballclubs, only St Louis has won more titles than Berra, a quite remarkable illustration of pinstriped dominance.

"You can observe a lot just by watching," Berra once famously said. Indeed, just by watching baseball at Fenway, one could observe the Calvinist determinism of New England. The Yankees were predestined to be champions, according to local lore, while the Red Sox were doomed to eternal mediocrity. Baseball fortunes were decided by the smog of external fate, and that never smiled down on the guys in crimson stockings. There was little point resisting the inevitable anguish.

In 1966, Boston lost 90 games to finish ninth in the American League. Attendance at Fenway slumped to an average of 10,095 per game as the Red Sox endured an eighth straight losing season. Yawkey even threatened to relocate his team due to declining fan interest and the city's refusal to build a new ballpark. Hopes of success were suitably slim entering the 1967 campaign, but Boston embarked on an Impossible Dream that reawakened the franchise as a capable force.

Managed by Dick Williams, a first-year skipper, the 1967 Red Sox were young, brash and carefree. Led by Carl Yastrzemski, a great outfielder with a savant's batting eye, Boston started the season well and never looked back, gaining momentum with each improbable win. Before long, the crowds came back, and they brought newfound belief with them, fuelling the surge with naïve fairy dust.

Yastrzemski slugged 44 homers and drove in 121 runs that year. Rico Petrocelli, a great young shortstop, added a further 17 big flies, while Tony Conigliaro showed immense promise before suffering a freak injury when hit by a pitch. On the mound, Jim Lonborg put together the season of his life, winning 22 games with a 3.16 ERA. Boston suddenly had it all, and diehards pondered a miracle.

The Red Sox' resurgence coincided with a sharp downturn for the Yankees. Mantle was a 35-year-old first baseman in 1967, a shadow of his former self hitting .245. Whitey Ford embarked on his final tour of duty at 38 as New York endured its worst season since 1913, losing 90 games. The Yankees finished ninth, buried in the standings, as Boston surged ahead. Many New Yorkers had never known anything like it.

Still, a vein of dignity ran through the rivalry, and there was a mutual respect between the teams, whose hatred was born of frustrated admiration. On the whole, Yankee fans were philosophical about their legendary run stretching back decades, and they appreciated the cycle of success that came to govern contemporary baseball. It became apparent that even the Yankees could not win *every* year, and seasoned rooters tipped their cap to the new breed of ballclubs threatening to take control.

For example, when 21-year-old Red Sox rookie Billy Rohr carried a no-hitter into the ninth inning at Yankee Stadium on his major league debut in April 1967, the home crowd cheered him on despite ancient enmity. When Yankee stalwart Elston Howard broke up the no-no bid with one strike remaining, the small crowd jeered its hero.

Nobody had ever twirled a no-hitter in their first major league start, and the knowledgeable Stadium patrons knew a good story when they saw one, Red Sox-led or otherwise. "That is the first time in my life I have ever made a base hit and been booed," said Howard. Rohr recovered to induce another fly ball from Charlie Smith, completing a superb one-hitter.

While Yankee *fans* were rational about their team's humanity, the actual players wearing those heavy pinstripes struggled to compute the demise of their power. Entire swathes of the New York roster had never witnessed a competitive Boston ballclub, and trading places with the perennial doormat did not sit well with some Yankee players. That deep-seated animosity often spilled over into violence.

For instance, when Joe Foy, a New York-born third baseman, homered for the Red Sox during a game at Yankee Stadium in June 1967, pinstriped pitcher Thad Tillotson drilled him in the head with a pitch the following day. Lonborg retaliated for Boston, hitting Tillotson in the shoulder when he came to bat. A mass brawl ensued on the field as both dugouts emptied and punches were exchanged.

Petrocelli of the Red Sox and Pepitone of the Yankees traded blows. Boston centre fielder Reggie Smith threw Tillotson to the ground, highlighting the donnybrook with an iconic vignette. NYPD officers flooded the field, pulling the teams apart so play could resume. Tillotson then beaned Lonborg, who in turn hit Dick Howser. Such was the personal manifestation of this timeless grudge during a high-octane era.

A few weeks after the brawl, Boston traded for Howard, who concluded a prestigious run with the Yankees. Elston won four

World Series rings with New York and also became the first African American to be voted American League MVP. Howard was the first black star in Yankees history, and his brilliant contributions helped change attitudes in the Bronx.

Elston was shocked when Yankees manager Ralph Houk informed him of the trade. Howard seriously considered retiring instead of reporting to Boston, but he eventually joined the Red Sox and played a strong mentoring role as they pushed for an unlikely pennant.

When Ellie returned to Yankee Stadium for the first time as an opposing player, clad incongruously in Red Sox garb, the crowd gave him a fantastic ovation. That surely made amends for the earlier playful jeers, but seeing a Yankee legend in Red Sox garb spoke to a changing dynamic that underpinned an altogether more hostile era ahead.

Boston eventually beat Detroit and Minnesota to the 1967 flag, clinching the American League crown by one game. A mere half-game in the 1966 standings prevented the Red Sox from becoming the first team in major league history to go from worst to first in consecutive seasons. Nevertheless, those hometown heroes settled for legendary status in Beantown, which embraced the Red Sox like never before.

From the trenches of dejection, fans returned to Fenway in unprecedented numbers, breaking the team's all-time attendance record. Crowds were up 113% year-on-year, pushing beyond 1.7 million in total. They watched an exciting brand of baseball, aligned with the technicolour smiles of baby boom America. For so long a sleeping giant of American sport, the Red Sox rose from their slumber. The team's free-spirited milieu was thoroughly intoxicating.

"For millions of Americans, 1967 remains an unforgettable year," wrote Bill Reynolds in *Lost Summer*. "For some it brings back visions of Vietnam or Sgt. Pepper, but for baseball fans, it will forever be remembered as the summer that the impossible happened - the Red Sox won their first pennant in 21 years."

Feverish pleas for a first *world* championship since 1918 died painfully, however, when St Louis prevailed in seven games. Cardinals ace Bob Gibson became the only pitcher ever to hit a home run in Game 7 of the World Series, while old foe Maris - dumped by the Yankees a year earlier - came back to haunt Boston with 10 hits and 7 RBI throughout the Fall Classic.

As if to embolden the pain, St Louis was presented with an *actual trophy* in the Fenway clubhouse after clinching the final out. Taking inspiration from other major sports leagues, MLB introduced a team award to complement individual championship rings in time for the 1967 Series. St Louis was the first recipient, setting a tone for future aspirations, while the Red Sox could only dream about one day needing a trophy room.

Later christened The Commissioner's Trophy, that sparkling gold chalice became a physical manifestation of baseball success and Boston's pursuit thereof. Yaz did not get to hoist the grail in 1967, nor in any other season, but the Red Sox were back after the ride of his life. Restocked with belief and freshly invigorated, Boston was determined to avenge years of oppression. The *fight* was back, perhaps most importantly, and never before had it been so needed as in the age of beanballs and brawls to come.

CHAPTER SEVEN

Class Warfare

Boston had loathed New York since time began, and Red Sox fans had disliked the Yankees for decades, but something changed in the late-1960s. Hatred, genuine *hatred*, was felt between the warring enemies. They could not stand each other, and a more even playing field added to the drama, which was played out in personal feuds of entertaining longevity.

Unlike ephemeral rivalries that fizzled out elsewhere, the Yankees-Red Sox quarrel sustained for generations. It came alive in the technicolour of modernity, throbbing with bitterness. As America came of age, its most intense baseball dispute transcended sports. The distaste between Boston and New York became personal, and millions watched on in fascination as cable television beamed the drama into living rooms across the land.

In this regard, few protagonists disliked each other more than Thurman Munson and Carlton Fisk, two exceptional catchers who went to war throughout the 1970s. Munson, the Yankees' captain, and Fisk, the Red Sox' leader, came to personify the wild discord between New York and Boston. Under their aegis, the rivalry morphed into a new stratosphere, laced with acerbity and vitriol. The pair of transcendent backstops set the tone for decades to come, and their legacy is still felt today.

Munson had a cup of coffee with the Yankees in 1969 before taking over full-time in 1970. The rough Ohioan hit .302 that year and became the first catcher ever to win American League Rookie of the Year honours. Such an accolade should have distinguished him as the premier backstop in all of baseball. However, shortly thereafter, Boston had Fisk, a handsome media darling, and Cincinnati had Johnny Bench, arguably the greatest ever to don a mask. Munson was never embraced by the mainstream in quite the same way, and that indignation led to snarling frustration on his part.

Fisk matched Munson's Rookie of the Year feat in 1972, then won the 1973 American League All-Star vote in a landslide to start at catcher. Munson loathed Fisk's apparent omnipotence, believing it to be a media creation swallowed by lazy fans. Fisk disliked Munson's pandering to Yankee mythology, viewing it as outmoded piety. Genuine detest bristled between the pair, and neither player missed an opportunity to disrespect the other.

Indeed, Thurman *was* one of the most prideful Yankees of all-time, and some say that distinction offered a sneering arrogance to his game. There was a commanding mystique about the Yankees, even as the world titles dried up somewhat. Their name, logo and heritage were synonymous with glory, and Munson wore that pinstriped heart on his sleeve, almost as visible as the messy moustache.

Laidback and self-assured, the smiling Fisk embodied everything that Munson and the Yankees resented about the modern game. Undoubtedly a fierce competitor with a phenomenal will to win, Fisk apportioned time to commercials and longform interviews despite never winning the World Series. *Sports Illustrated* put Carlton on its famous cover twice, while Munson was rarely honoured. Fisk was the star of tomorrow, coolly chiselled in latter-day celebrity, and that gnawed at pinstriped dignitaries, who failed to keep up for once.

Thurman felt slighted, and the Yankees struggled to adjust as baseball evolved into a megawatt industry surrounding the diamond. After triumphing in the 1962 World Series, the Bombers endured a barren run of 15 years, their longest drought since 1901-1923. The demise and departure of legendary players drove the Yankees towards a crossroads, and unlike in previous eras, the franchise struggled to decide on a cogent direction.

⚾⚾⚾

In 1964, Columbia Broadcasting System (CBS) bought an 80% stake in the Yankees for $11.2 million and duly presided over the team's first losing season in 40 years. The media network took full control by 1966, installing corporate functionary Michael Burke as president and CEO of the ballclub. Rival teams protested the takeover, fearing the $500 million revenues of CBS may make the Yankees untouchable. However, dystopian predictions of monopoly never came to pass as the global conglomerate swallowed Yankee mystique almost entirely.

During a period of exponential growth for CBS, a big league baseball team was just the latest fad in which it wanted to dabble. Already a powerhouse of radio, television and entertainment, CBS added a toy company, record label and film production arm to its portfolio in the 1960s. It even bought Fender, the famous guitar manufacturer, paying more for musical instruments than for the fabled New York Yankees. Alas, CBS had little long-term interest in MLB, and the franchise suffered as a result.

Contrary to later portrayals, Burke was a progressive president, introducing new colour schemes, revitalising marketing efforts and renovating Yankee Stadium. Lee MacPhail was hired as general manager, and he generally had bright ideas about streamlining the New York farm system, but a lack of available talent thwarted his efforts.

As basketball and football soared in popularity, baseball suddenly had competition for the best high school and college athletes. The introduction of an amateur draft in 1965 regulated that market even further, protecting impressionable prospects from extravagant chequebooks. Teams had to get creative when scouting, signing and developing young players. More than ever before, they also had to wait their turn.

New York got a new National League team in 1962 as Casey Stengel agreed to manage the upstart Mets. Playing in Queens, the colourful ballclub lost 120 games in its first season, followed by 111, 109, 112, 95, 101 and 89-loss campaigns. Through their first seven seasons, the Mets lost 66% of their games. Then, in 1969, they went out and won the World Series, outdrawing the moribund Yankees and shocking the baseball world. The Big Apple was suddenly up for grabs, and Bronx Bombers no longer had exclusive autonomy in those battles.

A mild disgruntlement came to define the Yankees, who chased the illustrious burden of their own history just as much as the present-day pennant. Boston stoked the flames with Machiavellian intent, revelling in its identity as anathema to everything by which the Yankees abided, while the Mets were a whirlwind of irresistible *action*. Nouveau riche ballclubs saw their chance to agitate and tease the once impenetrable goliath. A whole new landscape opened up on baseball's horizon.

⚾⚾⚾

MLB expanded in the 1960s, adding teams in Anaheim, Washington, Houston, New York, Kansas City, Seattle, Montreal and San Diego. A divisional system was devised with the winners of each league subset advancing to an expanded playoff scenario. Bundled together in the American League East, the Yankees and Red Sox competed in an even tighter space, causing unbelievable friction, especially between Munson and Fisk.

Divisional play was introduced in 1969, but neither Boston nor New York won the AL East flag until 1975, somewhat remarkably. The Red Sox came close a number of times, only to blow their chances in agonising fashion. The new format turned a mirror on both teams' growing ineptitude.

In 1972, for instance, Boston engaged Detroit in a fascinating war for the division title, eventually finishing second by half a game. Thanks to labour disputes and a subsequently unbalanced schedule, Boston played 155 games while Detroit played 156. The teams met for a three-game series to close the season, and in the opening game, a baserunning blunder by Sox shortstop Luis Aparicio helped the Tigers to victory.

Down 1-0 in the third inning, Tommy Harper and Aparicio singled with one out, bringing Yastrzemski to the plate. Yaz smashed a likely triple, scoring Harper and inviting Aparicio to follow in behind with the go-ahead run. Usually a skilled baserunner, Aparicio tripped over third base and rolled into foul territory, killing the rally. Stranded between second and third, Yastrzemski was tagged out attempting to retreat. Reggie Smith struck out, Boston lost 4-1, and Detroit won the following day, too, advancing to the American League playoffs.

The Red Sox were truly pissed off at this point, and those dynamics of anger, resentment and exasperation converged against the Yankees at Fenway Park on 1st August 1973, culminating in one of the most infamous brawls in baseball history.

With the score knotted a 2-2, Munson led off the ninth inning with a double to left field. A Graig Nettles groundout pushed him to third before Felipe Alou was walked intentionally so Boston could face Gene Michael, the ninth-place hitter who finished the season with a .225 batting average.

In repost, Yankees manager Ralph Houk called for a suicide squeeze play. Munson broke for home as if attempting to steal, but Michael missed the bunt attempt, leaving Thurman out to dry. Fisk corralled the ball and positioned himself to tag the onrushing Munson. Thurman picked up speed before barrelling into Fisk, who held on to the ball, recording the out and flipping Munson over his shoulder. Thurman jumped to his feet and punched Fisk in the face. Michael also landed a blow as both benches cleared. Fisk and Munson were both ejected from the game, which Boston won on a walk-off single by Mario Guerrero.

The tide was changing, and the 1970s Red Sox seemed less inclined to stand pat and watch the Yankees walk all over their dreams. Young stars like Dwight Evans, Fred Lynn and Bill Lee meshed with the old guard of Yastrzemski, Petrocelli and Luis Tiant to form a certain kind of magic. There was a fearlessness about the Red Sox, while the Yankees seemed out of touch.

Boston won the pennant again in 1975, defeating Oakland in the modern playoff format to face Cincinnati in a legendary World Series. Fisk hit a famous walk-off home run in Game 6, waving the ball fair as it joyously clanked off the left field foul pole, but Cincinnati prevailed in the seventh game.

Once baseball's definitive superpower, the Red Sox won three pennants in 55 years after selling Babe Ruth. Each time, they lost the subsequent World Series in seven games. Heartbreak became a recurring experience in New England as many questioned whether the Sox would *ever* win it all in their lifetime. Some never lived to see it happen as the drought reached epic proportions. Others merely gave up, shunning baseball out of desperate self-defence.

No matter how exciting they looked in spring, the Red Sox were bound to the same outcome in autumn. Regardless of how convincing they seemed in summer, the star-crossed heroes mourned in winter. The rhythm of Red Sox failure came to punctuate Boston, and agonising defeat became a way of life.

Some fans found the annual heartache strangely *affirming*, a reassuring token of normality, but others became sick of the anguish. Such was the bittersweet enchantment of Boston Red Sox baseball, and for generations the panacea remained painfully out of reach.

Fisk's iconic home run etched his legacy into the game's eternal fabric. Carlton had a signature moment that distinguished his *individual* abilities, whereas Thurman worked hard to deliver success for his *team*. Pudge cared about image whereas The Walrus scrapped for rings. Fisk yearned for headline glory while Munson fought to restore pride in the Yankee pinstripes. Rarely had two men playing the same position been so incompatible.

Thurman found an ally in George Steinbrenner, a swashbuckling entrepreneur who bought the Yankees from CBS for $10 million in 1973 and promised to rekindle former glories in the Bronx. "We plan on absentee ownership as far as the Yankees are concerned," said Steinbrenner at a media briefing following the sale. "I'll stick to building ships and let the baseball people run the team."

Contradicting himself almost immediately, Steinbrenner introduced a strict personal appearance policy, forbidding his players from growing beards and forcing them to keep their hair short. "There are ballplayers, and then there are Yankees," said The Boss, whose determination to win was matched only by his willingness to spend enormous amounts of money in pursuit of success.

When imposing ace Catfish Hunter found a loophole in his Oakland A's contract in 1975, arbitrator Peter Seitz declared him a free agent. Hunter duly signed a five-year contract with the Yankees, who blew away the field with a $3.35 million salary offer.

The reserve clause - which effectively bound baseball players to one team for life barring a trade or retirement - was subsequently abolished, heralding the era of free agency, in which players sold their services to the highest bidder. This was a boon for the filthy rich Yankees, who transformed a stale roster with George's bottomless pit of cash.

Reggie Jackson, the game's brightest star, became a free agent following the 1976 season, shortly after the Yankees were swept by Cincinnati in the World Series. Desperate to save face, Steinbrenner set his heart on landing the slugger and pulled out all the stops, flying Jackson to New York for negotiations and chauffeuring him to complimentary meals. The Yankees eventually signed Reggie to a five-year deal paying $2.96 million. The baseball economy had changed forever.

With fresh superstars in tow, New York won the World Series in 1977, its first crown in 15 years. Once again, the Dodgers were defeated in a famous Fall Classic, cursing the Yankees as in times of yore. Jackson hit three home runs on three pitches in Game 6, earning his famous Mr October nickname as the Yankees clinched the 21st world championship in franchise history. George had a taste of success, and he liked it very much.

Fashioned in his image, the Yankees became a corporate machine, cast in stark contrast to the bohemian Red Sox. It was a struggle of rich against comparatively poor, cold-blooded capitalism against idealistic socialism, and stout imperialism against quaint romanticism. The Yankees were your boss. The Red Sox were your neighbour. There was little to unite the two except the interconnected surge of predictable success and recurring failure. They were two distinct planets in a complicated solar system.

Steinbrenner demanded greatness from every employee, right down to the groundskeeper and the clubhouse attendants. "Winning is the most important thing in my life after breathing," he once said. "Breathing first, winning next."

In his first 23 seasons at the helm, George changed managers 20 times, bordering megalomania in his micromanagement of staff. Billy Martin, a passionate Yankee, was fired and rehired on five different occasions, while Dick Howser, Bob Lemon, Gene Michael and Lou Piniella all had multiple tours of duty.

"The first time George fires you, it is very traumatic," Yankees public relations czar Harvey Greene once said. "The three or four times after that, it's like, great: I've got the rest of the day off!"

The 1978 season became a microcosm of the Yankees under Steinbrenner's command. Dubbed The Bronx Zoo, that incarnation of the team was characterised by internal conflict and soap opera storylines. Despite interminable chaos and intractable disagreement, the team thrived on a sense of injustice and disrespect, which eventually coalesced into a historic postseason drive.

Encapsulating the fury of subjugated Bronx neighbourhoods, the Yankees became a vehicle for regional pride. Plagued by poverty, inequality and racial tensions, the Yankees' home borough fell into disrepair as frustrations mounted. Arson became a symbolic tool of protest against a failing economy and mass urban decay. The Yankees caught fire, too, raging through the American League with outrageous combustibility.

Sparky Lyle, the Yankees' closer, had been dominant in 1977, winning the American League Cy Young Award after maintaining a 2.17 ERA through 72 relief appearances. Nevertheless, during the winter, Steinbrenner went out and signed Goose Gossage, another relief ace, giving him a larger salary than Lyle's. Despite talk of a late-inning rotation and forming a potent one-two punch at the end of games, Gossage was favoured in the big spots. Lyle went from "Cy Young to Sayonara," as Nettles put it. There was no place for sentiment on the modern Yankees.

Such resentment was replicated throughout the team. Players, coaches and executives seemed almost inhuman to Steinbrenner, who moved them about like bishops and knights in a game of championship chess.

Meanwhile, Martin and Jackson, manager and slugger, endured a tumultuous relationship that destabilised the Yankees' efforts. Martin disapproved of Jackson's swashbuckling style, while Jackson was turned off by Martin's verbose rabblerousing. The pair even came to blows at one point in the dugout at Fenway Park, embarrassing the organisation before a national television audience.

In this regard, Martin gradually lost control of his players, a victim of eroding respect. At one point, Mickey Rivers was benched for a lack of hustle in the outfield, while an alcohol-fuelled brawl aboard an airplane brought shame on the Yankees. Boston developed a strong division lead, adding to the cauldron of anger. New York was destroyed by its own explosive potential.

The Yankees were savaged by a barbaric tabloid press, as Rupert Murdoch's *New York Post* fought the *New York Daily News* in a sensationalist war of controversy and sleaze. The tabloids became embroiled in a race to the bottom, seeking salacious stories to splash across the back pages. The Yankees filled notebooks with their incendiary daily drama, and the resultant culture of backstabbing set the club ablaze.

In July, for instance, Martin instructed Jackson to lay down a sacrifice bunt in a game against Kansas City. Jackson failed to get the bunt down in his first attempt, at which point the sign was taken off. Perhaps out of spite, Reggie continued to show bunt, eventually striking out. Martin removed him from the game and suspended him for a week.

Steinbrenner sided with Jackson, flabbergasted that a guy who launched three home runs in one World Series game mere months before would be asked to lay down a sacrifice bunt. "The two of them deserve each other," Martin told the press of his star and his owner. "One is a born liar. The other is convicted."

This was a reference to illegal contributions made by Steinbrenner to Richard Nixon's presidential campaign in 1974. George duly began shopping for a managerial replacement, attempting to broker a trade for White Sox skipper Bob Lemon, who was subsequently fired by Chicago. The day after his controversial remarks, Martin resigned for health reasons at a tearful press conference, jumping before he was pushed. Lemon replaced him in the hot seat.

However, just five days into Lemon's tenure, the Yankees announced that, effective from the 1980 season, Martin would return as manager, at which point Lemon would move upstairs into an executive role. Steinbrenner regretted his ousting of Martin, but aides somehow convinced him that Lemon deserved at least a year in charge. Chaos reigned supreme.

A stooge in the love-hate triangle of George, Reggie and Billy, Lemon quietly led the Yankees to one of the greatest comebacks in baseball history to finish the 1978 campaign. Boston enjoyed a 14.5-game lead over New York in late-July, but the Yankees surged under Lemon's command, reducing the deficit to four games by early-September, just in time for a four-game series at Fenway.

In baseball's answer to the Boston Massacre, New York won all four games, sweeping the series by a combined score of 42-9. The Yankees annihilated their stunned rivals, outhitting them

67-21 and moving into a tie for first place in the embryonic AL East.

"Forget any other games these two teams have ever played," wrote Mike Vaccaro of the series in *Emperors and Idiots*. "The four that would forever be known as 'The Boston Massacre' live on, and will continue to live on, as a permanent symbol of what this rivalry was for eighty-five long summers. The Yankees walked into Fenway Park and rifled the place, robbing Boston of a pennant that had been all but ceded to them months earlier."

In fact, both teams jostled for pole position until the season's momentous climax. The demands of excellence were exhausting. Entering their final game of the season, New York held a one-game lead in the division. Cleveland won said game, offering a reprieve to the Red Sox. In turn, Boston beat Toronto to draw even in the standings with a 99-63 record, identical to that of the Yankees. A one-game playoff was arranged for the following day, and a coin toss selected Fenway as the venue.

Just one win separated the Red Sox or Yankees from the American League Championship Series, where Kansas City lurked with eyes on the pennant. A crowd of 32,925 crammed into the old yard on Yawkey Way for a Monday afternoon showcase. Ron Guidry, a precocious young ace, started for the Yankees while Mike Torrez, a wily veteran, got the ball for Boston. Tension filled the air.

Yastrzemski parked a solo homer in the second and Rice tacked on a further run in the sixth, giving Boston an 85% win probability, per Baseball-Reference.com. That is when the Yankees rallied.

Nettles flew out to lead off the seventh before Chris Chambliss and Roy White lined consecutive singles, putting two runners aboard. Torrez recovered to induce another fly ball from Jim Spencer, hauling the Red Sox within seven outs of a postseason berth. Bucky Dent, the ninth-place hitter, stepped to the plate with a batting average in the .240s. Ahead 2-0, Boston was in command.

A spindly shortstop, Dent was on the Yankees' roster for his glove, not his bat. In six major league seasons to that point, the quiet guy from Savannah, Georgia had mustered just 22 home runs, less than four per season on average.

Amid a raucous Fenway crowd, batting with two outs and two on, Dent flirted with *automatic out* status. Given a stronger bench and a healthier roster, Lemon may well have pinch-hit for Dent. Instead, Bucky wrote his otherwise forgotten name into the record books, a villain for all-time.

Opening the plate appearance, Torrez threw a ball before Dent fouled a pitch off his foot, bringing Yankee trainer Gene Monahan from the dugout for assistance. Hobbled and pressured, Dent settled back in, crouching over the plate in an awkward stance. The crowd buzzed expectantly, sensing victory for the Red Sox. Torrez came set, kicked, and delivered a fastball that tailed back across the plate.

Boom.

Dent connected with the pitch and lofted a high fly ball to left field. Yastrzemski chased helplessly, a miniscule figure peering up at the huge outfield wall, begging for it to grow, yearning for it to keep the ball in play. The wind did not cooperate, however, blowing Dent's pop fly over the Green Monster.

Going.

Going.

Gone.

Yastrzemski doubled over in pain. A shattered pall settled over Fenway Park. The Yankees were ahead, 3-2. It was Groundhog Day in New England.

Rivers followed with a walk, knocking Torrez from the game. Munson drove him in with a double off reliever Bob Stanley, who also surrendered a bomb to Jackson in the eighth. Boston rallied with RBI singles from Yastrzemski and Lynn, but Gossage gritted his teeth and closed the door on a 5-4 win. Once an ocean of opportunity, the Red Sox' season was over.

Duly buoyed, the Yankees beat Kansas City en route to a World Series rematch with the Dodgers. Down 2-0 in *that* Series, New

York came roaring back to win yet another world title in six games.

Guidry and Jim Beattie pitched excellently, while Jackson came up clutch with 2 home runs, 8 RBI and a 1.196 OPS against Los Angeles. However, Dent was named World Series MVP as a remarkable season received its exclamation point. The Yankees celebrated the most improbable championship in their history.

⚾⚾⚾

The Yankee family, and indeed the wider galaxy of Major League Baseball, was devasted in August 1979 when Munson, the very embodiment of pinstriped pride, died tragically in an airplane accident at Akron-Canton Regional Airport.

Aged 32, midway through his eleventh season with the Yankees, Munson had so much more to give. Steinbrenner adored his catcher, a fellow Ohioan, making him the Yankees' first captain since Gehrig. Like Lou, Thurman was often surrounded by brighter stars and flashier teammates, but he was the guts and glue that held everything together. He was hard-bitten ballast aboard the pinstriped yacht, and without his hustle, the Yankees' corporate malaise may have continued.

With a loving family at home in Canton, Ohio, Munson learned to fly so he could visit them more on off-days during the season. The catcher bought a Cessna Citation I/SP jet, enjoying the freedom that came with a pilot's licence.

On the fateful afternoon of 2nd August 1979, Munson practiced take-offs and landings with Jerry Anderson, a close friend, and Dave Hall, his fight instructor. Three touch-and-go landings were completed on Runway 23 of the municipal airport, but a fourth ended in disaster. Munson did not extend the landing flaps and allowed the jet to sink too low. With increased engine power, the plane clipped a tree and fell short of Runway 19, striking another tree stump and bursting into flames.

Hall and Anderson both survived, albeit with severe burns. Munson suffered a broken neck and died of asphyxiation due to the inhalation of superheated air and toxic substances. America's reluctant lionheart was taken before his time.

A day after losing their heart and soul, the Yankees began a four-game series with Baltimore in the Bronx. Baseball hardly matters in such harrowing contexts, but led by Steinbrenner, the classy ballclub honoured its passionate captain with beautiful subtlety.

Steinbrenner paid Munson's salary to Diana, Thurman's widow, in perpetuity. The Yankees retired Munson's number 15 and placed a poignant inscription from The Boss in Monument Park, the treasure trove of history beyond centre field at the fabled yard. Munson's locker was never reassigned, remaining empty as a lasting tribute until the Stadium closed in 2008.

The entire team attended Munson's funeral in Canton on 6th August, regardless of the pressing major league schedule. "If we do not get back in time, we will forfeit the game," said Steinbrenner of a contest against the Orioles that very same night. The team *did* return in time, quite remarkably, travelling almost 1,000 miles in a heartbreaking day then recovering from a 4-0 deficit through six innings to win 5-4.

Bobby Murcer parked a three-run shot as Yankee Stadium shook to its foundations. He then won the game in walk-off fashion with a two-run single, catharsis masquerading as a base hit. Just hours earlier, Murcer delivered a eulogy as his closest friend was buried. He then came through with 5 RBI, hauling the Yankees to victory. Rarely has baseball experienced a more emotional moment.

Thurman would never be forgotten, but he would always be missed. Though inconsequential in the wider sphere of life, the rivalry also lost something when Munson passed away. Only one non-Yankees player sent a personal note to Diana expressing sympathy after Thurman's death: Carlton Fisk. Even the Red Sox missed the tough-as-nails catcher, who personified their frustration in a hectic baseball age.

After losing Munson, their competitive compass, the Yankees endured something of an institutional crisis throughout the 1980s and early-1990s. A further pennant was secured in 1981, but the Dodgers were far stronger in the World Series, beating their recurring nemesis at long last.

"I want to sincerely apologise to the people of New York and to fans of the New York Yankees everywhere for the performance of the Yankee team in the World Series," wrote Steinbrenner in a statement. "I also want to assure you that we will be at work immediately to prepare for 1982."

In the lexicon of global sports, how many teams feel the need to *apologise* for not winning the ultimate prize for which they compete? Real Madrid is perhaps the only club that comes close to the New York Yankees in this regard. Even Manchester United and the Los Angeles Lakers take more pragmatic approaches. Even the Montreal Canadiens have accepted the laws of competitive probability. The Yankees, meanwhile, expected greatness. They still do. Anything less than a World Series title is deemed a failure.

By that calculus, the Bombers failed a whole lot in the 1980s. When lucrative free agent signings like Dave Winfield and Don Baylor did not perform at ungodly levels, Steinbrenner grew frustrated, meddling in day-to-day operations more than ever before. Managers came and went with alarming regularity, and even the omnipotent Yogi Berra was discarded mercilessly.

New York actually scored more runs than any major league team throughout the decade, but its pitching was frequently suspect. Dave Righetti no-hit the Red Sox in 1983, and Guidry was excellent until his arm exploded, but the Yankees could not get enough pitching to compete for a sustained period. New York even won 97 games in 1985, but a ring was not forthcoming.

Their struggles in the 1980s were personified by Don Mattingly, a handsome first baseman who enjoyed a cult following across the country. Mattingly was the consummate ballplayer, doing everything well in a fluid style of innate mastery. He exemplified Midwestern hustle, working to the point of perspiration to hone a tormenting craft. That there was no crowning reward for years of such daunting toil endures as a great sadness of modern baseball. Even Yankee *haters* wanted them to win one for Don.

Despite claiming a batting title, an MVP award, nine Gold Gloves and making six All-Star teams, Mattingly played in just one postseason series throughout his career. The Yankees lost that ALDS matchup to Seattle, denying Donnie Baseball a shot at reaching the World Series.

Mattingly hit .307 through a 14-year career, collecting 2,153 hits with 222 home runs and 442 doubles. His number 23 was retired by the Yankees and *The Simpsons* even immortalised the moustachioed messiah in one of the show's most popular episodes. Still, Mattingly never had a shot at winning it all, and his lack of a World Series ring is one of the most poignant vignettes of 1980s sports.

Mattingly debuted in 1982, when the Yankees were defending American League champions. He retired in 1995 due to chronic back problems, a year before the Bombers beat Atlanta to reclaim the world championship. That spell in between - 14 seasons of stagnant frustration - encapsulated Mattingly's career. It also encompassed the Yankees' longest absence from the postseason in 60 years.

Even the Bronx Bombers have down times, and even the greatest must sometimes lose. Life is more about recovering from setbacks than it is about celebrating victories, and even the Yankees' magic potion occasionally ran dry.

🥎🥎🥎

CHAPTER EIGHT

The Curse

The Red Sox emerged from their own prolonged slumber midway through the 1980s to compete for a world championship. Led by mechanical third baseman Wade Boggs, who fought Mattingly hard for batting titles and acclaim, the Red Sox became serious contenders again. Roger Clemens, a flame-throwing ace, also rose to dominance as Boston jumped ahead of Steinbrenner's faltering stars in the American League arms race.

In 1986, the Red Sox embarked on another of the randomly miraculous seasons they seem to author periodically. Clemens struck out 20 Seattle Mariners at Fenway in an April contest, establishing a hallowed major league record en route to a 24-win season and the first of seven career Cy Young Awards. No Red Sox pitcher had won that many games since 1949.

Boggs hit .357 in 1986, claiming a second consecutive batting title and the third of his career. He successfully defended the hitting crown in 1987 and 1988, too, as Boston fell in love with the suspicious gamer, who religiously ate a whole chicken before every ballgame in a strange recurring ritual.

In Clemens and Boggs, Boston had the best pure hitter and the best power pitcher in baseball. Meanwhile, Jim Rice and Dwight Evans still produced at solid levels, and Dennis 'Oil Can' Boyd complemented Clemens in an exciting one-two punch of young phenom hurlers.

The Red Sox won 95 games in 1986, their best tally since Bucky Dent crushed their dreams. For once, the Yankees could not keep up, finishing in second place to Boston for the first time since 1904, back when they were known as the Highlanders. Magic twinkled through the air at Fenway Park.

Boston beat the California Angels in a seesaw American League Championship Series, catapulted to victory by a famous home run from Dave Henderson. Meanwhile, in the National League playoffs, Houston was defeated by the Mets, who embarked on another magic carpet ride after years of mediocrity.

For Yankees fans, then, 1986 culminated in the ultimate nightmare: Red Sox versus Mets for the world championship. At least one of their subservient victims would seize the day and climb from the squalor of inferiority. Either the annoying upstart neighbour or the ancient gnarled nemesis would emerge victorious. Oh, to be a fly on the wall in the Steinbrenner residence during that World Series.

Boston won the first two games in New York before the Mets stormed back to even the series at Fenway. Behind the stellar pitching of Bruce Hurst, the Red Sox won Game 5 to edge within one victory of their first world title in 68 years. Shea Stadium, less than 10 miles from the tormenting Bronx, figured to be the venue for the ultimate sporting catharsis. Then the roof fell in, just as it always did for the Boston Red Sox.

Clemens pitched seven innings of gutsy ball in Game 6, holding the Mets to four hits and two runs. He carried a no-hitter into the fifth and retired the side in order to finish the seventh inning. At that point, Boston led, 3-2. Still, Roger developed a blister on his right middle finger, and his pitch count stood at 135 with six outs remaining. When Henderson reached second base with one out in the eighth, Sox manager John McNamara sent young Mike Greenwell to pinch-hit for Clemens, removing his ace from the game. Greenwell struck out and Henderson was stranded in scoring position.

Relieving Roger, Boston closer Calvin Schiraldi was called upon for a six-out save. He flirted with danger, struggling for command in the most intense situation of his career. New York cobbled together a rally when Lee Mazzilli singled and Lenny Dykstra beat out an attempted sacrifice bunt. A *genuine* sacrifice moved the runners into scoring position, and a Gary Carter fly out allowed the tagging Mazzilli to level the score at three. Just like that, Clemens' hard work was undone.

Neither team scored in the ninth inning, but Boston came storming back with a stunning repost in the tenth. Henderson clobbered another home run, putting the Sox ahead 4-3, before Boggs spanked a two-out double. Marty Barrett singled him in, and Boston took a two-run lead into the bottom half of the inning. If the Red Sox could record three outs before the Mets scored two runs, they would be world champions at last. The impossible seemed probable.

When Schiraldi retired Wally Backman and Keith Hernandez on seven pitches, and subsequently got ahead of Gary Carter, the Red Sox were two strikes away from destiny. Champagne was wheeled into the visiting clubhouse and a Shea Stadium videoboard congratulated Boston prematurely. They had a 99% likelihood of winning the ballgame, and the World Series, according to Baseball-Reference.com. As everyone knew, that had not happened since 1918.

But Carter singled to spark feint hope. Then Kevin Mitchell singled as well. Digging deep, Schiraldi ran the count to 0-2 on Ray Knight, putting Boston one strike away from ecstasy. Still alive, Knight fought off an inside pitch from Schiraldi, dumping a single to right-centre that scored Carter. Mitchell moved to third on the play and Schiraldi was replaced by Bob Stanley, who duly uncorked a disastrous wild pitch while facing Mookie Wilson. Mitchell scored, tying the score at five as Shea came unglued. Knight moved to second on the play, remaining alert even as the baseball universe shook around him.

Wilson saw nine pitches, producing a fine at-bat. He chopped the tenth pitch down the first base line, a routine groundball to Bill Buckner, a solid player with sound, instinctive fundamentals. From millions of contenders, that groundball became the most infamous in baseball history. Its fate altered lives forever.

At 36, Buckner was in the 18th year of a solid major league career that saw him top 2,700 career hits. However, his knees routinely betrayed him, and McNamara typically used Dave Stapleton as a late-inning defensive replacement throughout 1986. Sentiment won out on this occasion, though, and the Boston manager wanted his respected veteran to be on the field for the final out of a World Series clincher. Stapleton stayed on the bench.

Banged up and stiff, Buckner approached Wilson's groundball awkwardly, failing to crouch and set properly over the ball. He did not put his mitt down in the textbook position - as he had done thousands of times before - and the ball scooted through his legs and into sporting infamy. Wilson was safe at first while Knight raced around third to score the winning run. One strike away from glory, Boston had blown it again.

"One wild pitch. One error by first baseman Bill Buckner. One pitch away," rued Montville in a hastily rewritten column for the *Boston Globe*. "Pandemonium landed as if it were a giddy disease. The Mets gave curtain call after curtain call, handshake after handshake, while the Red Sox walked off the field with the dumbstruck look of accident victims. The worst. The absolute worst."

The deciding Game 7, played two days later, is often described as a foregone conclusion. The karmic forces of Red Sox baseball spawned a narrative that, with Buckner's immortal error, the entire season collapsed. In fact, there was still a ballgame to be played between two teams of 25 players. Boston even took a 3-0 lead into the sixth inning of *that* one, only to capitulate yet again.

The Mets took advantage of a team that gave them innumerable chances to come back from the dead, winning Game 7 by a score of 8-5. Once again, ecstasy for New York was analogous with agony for Boston. The Mets even wore pinstripes, as if to rub it in, and a whole new generation was left to question whether the Red Sox truly *were* beyond help.

Evil forces seemed inexorably influential, stifling progress for Boston whenever glory came near. That sentiment became supercharged in the ensuing decades as conspiracy theories infected the team's soul. The Red Sox almost became an outgrowth of their own incompetence rather than the author of its progress. It became increasingly difficult to distinguish the baseball team from the hysteria that engulfed its failures.

⚾⚾⚾

In 1990, eloquent *Globe* reporter Dan Shaughnessy connected the dots, publishing a book about the Red Sox' interminable championship drought entitled *The Curse of the Bambino*. Shaughnessy's opus funnelled Boston's ghoulish calamities towards one narrative: that the sale of Babe Ruth altered the destiny of this team forever and doomed it to eternal failure.

Shaughnessy retraced the infamous course of Red Sox history, arguing that such a surfeit of pain and misfortune did not befall any other professional sports team in the world. The degree to which Boston baseball elicited heartache could not be mere coincidence, Shaughnessy asserted. Something else was at play. The team was cursed.

Those World Series defeats in 1946, 1967, 1975 and 1986? They were the karmic consequences of selling the greatest player who ever lived, according to Shaughnessy. Bucky Dent and Bill Buckner? Blame Harry Frazee, he said. No world championship in 50, 60 and then 70 years? Yeah, that is the Babe's ghost, omnipotent in the currency of deciding winners.

The Curse took on a life of its own, becoming a definitive part of Red Sox lore. Yankee fans chanted "1918!" at any given opportunity, while Boston fans retaliated with "Yankees suck!" t-shirts that became so common as to border cliché. One hardcore punk named Ray LeMoine made close to $500,000 shifting those bootlegged shirts, which sold like hotcakes on the streets around Fenway.

In some New England high schools, Shaughnessy's book became required reading, the ultimate explainer of the region's hardball infatuation, while every film starring Ben Affleck, Matt Damon or Mark Wahlberg seemed to reference the hex.

Thoroughly imbued into the culture of Red Sox fandom, the curse actually *enriched* what it meant to associate with Boston baseball. There was a nobility in rooting for the underdog and an identity to be found in the harrowing quest for that elusive championship. The literary nucleus of America, Boston came to almost romanticise failure, wearing each heartbreaking loss like a badge of honour or a warped token of toughness.

This sense of comradeship through blind faith created a bubble of *otherness* around the Boston Red Sox that encouraged devotion from the frustrated and forgotten. This community, known as Red Sox Nation, swelled in size, spreading across the country, beckoning likeminded people to the green nirvana of Fenway Park.

By losing so frequently, in such agonising fashion, when victory seemed so close, the Red Sox distinguished themselves from every other sports franchise. The absence of success was not necessarily appealing, but the uncommon crusade to end the infamous drought gave the Red Sox more purpose and meaning than just about any baseball team on earth.

"Weeks. Seasons. Years. Decades. Centuries," wrote
Shaughnessy. "They come. They go. The Red Sox are forever.
The Red Sox still don't win the World Series. The Curse
continues."

As the chief instigators of said curse, the powerful Yankees
became a focus of intense loathing throughout the land. Broad
and energetic, Red Sox Nation needed somewhere to direct its
virulent passion, and the Bronx Bombers were an ideal target.

The timeless dichotomy of a blue-collar populace revolting
against the pinstriped corporation took on new meaning. The
rivalry became deeply intense, tinged with sheer hatred.
Shaughnessy stoked a fire that burned for a generation, and
modern baseball was dominated by the power struggle he helped
articulate. Nothing else seemed to matter.

⚾⚾⚾

In reality, the concept of a curse steering the Red Sox to disaster
was incredibly juvenile. The very act of selling Babe Ruth did not
catalyse decades of hard luck and hurtful failure in and of itself,
but the *strategic philosophy* that inspired such a transaction
definitely did.

Put simply, getting rid of Ruth was a nonsensical move of
questionable motivation, and that propensity to make
harebrained decisions was never exorcised from the Fenway
offices.

The Red Sox lost not because of ancient yin yang, but more
accurately because of managerial myopia, overt racism, chronic
cronyism and individual errors fashioned by the cauldron of
self-fulfilling doom created by all of the above.

Owned for 44 seasons by Tom Yawkey, an insular businessman
of capricious desires, the Red Sox represented an old country
club well into the 1970s. They were male, pale and stale. More
pertinently, they were deliberately obtuse with regard to
integration and innovation, falling behind their rivals as a
consequence.

In 1945, when a local councillor threatened to ban Sunday
baseball in Boston unless Negro League players were given a

chance to showcase their talents, the Red Sox set up a farcical trial of appeasement. A spindly infielder named Jackie Robinson was among a group of African American players who were invited to work out at Fenway, but the ballclub drafted in high school pitchers to throw batting practice in a display of insouciant disrespect.

According to *42 Faith* by Ed Henry of Fox News, Red Sox top scout Hugh Duffy was impressed by Robinson's skill but powerless to do anything about it. "Too bad he's the wrong colour," Duffy concluded, according to the book. White skin was a prerequisite of acceptance in Boston, and those who failed the primeval test were summarily discarded.

Robinson and his fellow ballplayers were even subjected to racial epithets during their Fenway trial. "Get those niggers off the field!" came the cry, according to one sportswriter present. Ed Henry says that such a grim pronouncement was made by a Red Sox executive, perhaps general manager Eddie Collins or Yawkey himself. Such racism impaired the judgment of key evaluators, stunting the team's growth on many occasions.

Dismissed by Boston, Robinson eventually signed with the brave Brooklyn Dodgers, breaking the colour barrier in modern Major League Baseball en route to a Hall of Fame career. Robinson debuted with the Dodgers in 1947, winning Rookie of the Year honours and subsequently starring as an MVP, World Series champion and six-time All-Star. The Red Sox could have benefitted from those skills, if not for disgusting prejudice.

Robinson later branded Yawkey "one of the most bigoted guys in baseball," a fitting explanation of the team's stagnation. Yawkey even served on an owners' committee that kept an internal memo rationalising a segregated league. His was an overt brand of discrimination, and the Red Sox' resultant apartheid saw them miss innumerable opportunities for enrichment.

A couple of years later, in 1949, Boston scout George Digby agreed a deal in principle to sign a 17-year-old outfielder named Willie Mays for $4,500 from the Birmingham Black Barons, a Negro League team in Alabama. However, Yawkey and Joe Cronin - the new Red Sox general manager - nixed the deal, refusing to sign a black player.

At minimal cost, the Red Sox could have had Jackie Robinson at second base, Willie Mays in centre field and Ted Williams in left for a good portion of their respective careers. That trio combined to hit 1,318 career home runs. All of them could have been in a Boston uniform, powering the Red Sox to a slew of world championships. Alas, Mays joined the Giants, carving a legacy as one of the greatest ballplayers of all-time in New York and San Francisco. Meanwhile, Boston finished 19 games out of first place *on average* throughout Mays' 22-year career, winning just one AL pennant in that span.

The Red Sox never signed a black player until Pumpsie Green in 1959, twelve years after Robinson debuted. They were the last major league team to integrate, doing so more than a year after Detroit, the final holdout beside Boston. Such unwillingness to embrace the evolving landscape of American society plagued the Red Sox, who repeatedly shot themselves in the foot.

Contrary to most mainstream recitals, the team's noxious history of racial intolerance does not stop with Pumpsie Green, however. The Red Sox never signed a black *free agent* until Billy Hatcher in 1992, more than 16 years after the system was introduced. During that time, Boston passed on premier black free agents such as Reggie Jackson, Joe Morgan, Dave Winfield, Bobby Bonds, Rod Carew, Tim Raines, Willie Randolph, Andre Dawson, Rickey Henderson and Darryl Strawberry. For a team with many holes on its roster, that seems very odd in retrospect.

Even after signing Hatcher, the Red Sox never seriously competed for marquee superstars like Albert Belle, Kenny Lofton or *Barry* Bonds when they hit the open market in the mid-1990s. It was almost as if those guys were absent from the war room whiteboard each winter. It was almost as if they were excluded.

Mo Vaughn was a beloved black centrepiece who graduated through the Boston farm system in the 1990s, bridging eras and rekindling excitement. Yet even Vaughn, the 1995 MVP, was allowed to leave via free agency amid repeated disagreements with management. He often complained of feeling underappreciated and misunderstood, especially by Duquette, who never embraced the slugger. It is now clear that Vaughn was the victim of implicit racism throughout his Boston tenure.

The Red Sox *did* eventually acquire black stars with greater regularity, after multiple changes of personnel, and that is when they began to win. Black and ethnic minority players were eventually pivotal in breaking the curse and building a dynasty. The sad reality is that, if those guys played during any other era in the previous 90 years, the Boston Red Sox would probably have shunned them due to their skin colour.

A street outside Fenway Park was renamed to honour Yawkey after his death in 1976, but that privilege was revoked in 2018 when the city of Boston cited his racist transgressions while reverting to the original Jersey Street moniker. Unfortunately, such a quick fix could not be made to the Red Sox almanac, which was eternally besmirched by managerial prejudice upheld in Yawkey's image.

⚾⚾⚾

Boston languished behind the curve in baseball operations, too. Jean Yawkey, Tom's widow, headed a family foundation that owned the Red Sox until 2002. The Yawkey trust was prone to narrow-minded favouritism and outright nepotism, hiring long-time allies from a small talent pool. Paranoia hampered the team's development, and inept stasis derailed the Fenway front office.

Former Sox scrub Haywood Sullivan, a trusted Yawkey confidant, was general manager from 1977 until 1984. Though manager Don Zimmer is often blamed for the epic collapse of 1978, resulting in Dent's pop fly home run, Sullivan mindlessly traded away key veterans such as Bernie Carbo, Fergie Jenkins and Reggie Cleveland as clubhouse morale imploded.

Following that fateful campaign, Sullivan then allowed Luis Tiant, a beloved Red Sox pitcher, to join the dreaded Yankees as a free agent. He further angered Boston fans by dumping the extroverted Bill Lee for reasons that defied logic. Sullivan dismantled a strong roster without outlining a clear strategy for replenishment, and his egotistical stubbornness rubbed diehards the wrong way. Many stopped listening, while others tuned out altogether.

Things got even worse in the offseason of 1980, when Sullivan failed to mail contract offers to core stars Lynn and Fisk, expediting their free agency and ultimately losing their services. Lynn was traded cheaply to California while Fisk signed with the White Sox. The duo combined to make a further seven All-Star appearances before retiring, not so much playing out the string as continuing their excellence elsewhere.

Lynn and Fisk were not minor league castoffs or spring training invitees on the big league roster bubble. They were bona fide stars who held the Red Sox together. Heck, Lynn *led the team* with an 8.6 WAR in 1979, while Fisk was still productive despite the customary bruises of a veteran catcher. Sullivan's failure to mail contracts to either player, wilfully tampering with franchise cornerstones, amounted to a dereliction of duty. Haywood wanted to avenge personal grievances more than he wanted the Red Sox to win. In the game's history, it is difficult to identify a baseball man more unfit for his respective occupation.

On the whole, Boston seemed allergic to the prevailing trend of free agency, preferring to develop its own players instead. However, the franchise also routinely failed to draft with the nimble efficiency of a serial winner, debasing that entire paradigm. Sullivan even picked his own son, Marc, in the second round of the 1979 draft, despite most observers considering him a late-round selection at best. Alas, when the farm system dried up predictably, the Red Sox receded into mediocrity.

Despite holding a slew of high-value draft picks across multiple eras, the Red Sox whiffed on future stars like Ted Simmons, Rick Sutcliffe, Rafael Palmeiro, Tino Martinez, Torii Hunter, CC Sabathia and Adam Wainwright. Sure, plenty of other teams failed to pick those players as well, but the Red Sox seemed to throw darts at the board while blindfolded.

Fenway contributed to the malaise, too. With its huge left field wall plonked just 310 feet from home plate, a succession of Red Sox general managers were seduced by the idea of acquiring righthanded sluggers to take advantage of the cosy dimensions. While logical to some extent, Boston kingmakers became obsessed with this method of building a ballclub. A string of burly sluggers made the Red Sox one-dimensional: big, slow and lumbering. That worked at Fenway, but half of the team's games were played on the road. Oh, and the small matter of pitching was rarely addressed, either.

For generations, the Red Sox tried to beat their opponents using the same method: hitting the ball over the left field wall. They lacked the fundamental small ball acumen and situational hitting of successful teams, while the notion of a stolen base was almost folly in New England.

Elsewhere, rival organisations were ahead of the curve, pushing baseball towards its age of enlightenment in the 1960s and 1970s. Earl Weaver brought success to Baltimore, placing emphasis on stellar defence and reliable pitching. Former Boston skipper Dick Williams struck gold in Oakland, where his Swingin' A's played with dynamic verve. And Sparky Anderson built The Big Red Machine in Cincinnati, redefining small ball with great situational hitting and speed on the basepaths.

By comparison, Boston became an outmoded ruin of diluted baseball potential. The team achieved sporadic success, peppering its general incompetence with occasional peaks of unsustainable hedonism. However, the Red Sox lacked a consistent thread from one botched experiment to the next, and lessons learned from each failure were thrown in the dumpster as each doomed executive cleared his desk.

Amid a messy power struggle, Sullivan was replaced by Lou Gorman in 1984. A Rhode Island native, Gorman made a promising start to his dream job, acquiring players like Henderson and Schiraldi en route to the 1986 pennant. However, Gorman became something of a laughingstock as time moved on, the physical embodiment of Boston's befuddling myopia. As desperation for a world championship crystallised, Gorman made kamikaze trades hoping to put his team over the top. They usually backfired.

In 1988, for instance, the Red Sox dealt Curt Schilling, a young farmhand, and Brady Anderson, a rookie outfielder, to Baltimore for veteran pitcher Mike Boddiker. The deal did not move the needle for the Red Sox, who were swept by Oakland in the playoffs. Schilling later matured into an all-time great with Philadelphia and Arizona before returning to Boston expensively in 2004. Anderson was a three-time All-Star who hit 50 home runs in 1996. Meanwhile, Boddiker made just 82 starts for the Red Sox and washed out of baseball within five years of the deal.

Late in the 1990 season, repeating that flagrant ineptitude, Boston traded Jeff Bagwell, a promising prospect, to Houston for Larry Andersen, a *reliever*. Andersen made 15 appearances for the Red Sox, who were swept by Oakland yet again in the ALCS. Bagwell spent 15 *years* in Houston, hitting 449 home runs, winning Rookie of the Year and MVP honours, and eventually having his number retired en route to the Hall of Fame.

Red Sox fans watched in disbelief as their team routinely made such horrific decisions. Players changed. Executives came and went. Managers were hired and fired. But still, the years passed and the champagne lay stagnant in a Fenway Park cellar. The shadow of George Herman Ruth loomed over everything, and there was no escaping the fatalistic gloom.

The deal-breaker for many, though, was the loss of Wade Boggs to the Yankees. The definitive icon of Boston baseball in the 1980s, Boggs hit above .300 for 10 straight seasons. Heck, he hit above *.360* four times in that stretch, winning the hearts of Red Sox fans across New England.

When the third baseman slumped to a .259 average in 1992 - his age-34 season - the Red Sox let his contract expire, presumably figuring a precipitous decline was about to unfold. Boggs signed with the Yankees, a once unthinkable notion, and then hit above .300 in four consecutive seasons, peaking at .342. He also won two Gold Gloves in the Bronx and helped the Yankees clinch the 1996 World Series, their first title in 18 years.

Boggs famously rode a police horse around the Yankee Stadium field while celebrating what became the only world championship of his career. The sight of a Red Sox folk hero exulting in pinstripes, a champion once discarded, was difficult for Boston fans to stomach. It was a microcosm of the rivalry: relentless, jarring and overwhelmingly one-sided. The Red Sox could not resist their own grotesque karma.

Continuing the trend, Boston did not re-sign Clemens following the 1996 season, saying goodbye to the dominant ace who had three Cy Young Awards, two 20-strikeout games and 192 wins - joint with Young for the most in franchise history - on a glittering resume. Despite posting a 3.63 ERA and leading the league with 257 strikeouts in 1996, Clemens was undervalued by

125

the Red Sox at the age of 33. They offered him a contract extension but never approached his true market value in terms of monetary commitment. Roger was rightly miffed, and he looked elsewhere for respect and commitment.

Typically error-prone and short-sighted, new Boston general manager Dan Duquette remarked that he hoped to keep Clemens in Boston during the "twilight of his career." Roger duly pitched for another 11 seasons, winning four more Cy Young Awards and claiming the pitching Triple Crown in consecutive seasons. Clemens spent two years in Toronto, rejuvenating his approach, before being traded to the Yankees, with whom he won two World Series rings and reached the prestigious 300-win club.

In Boggs and Clemens, the Red Sox could have locked down two era-defining stars for their entire careers. Boston could have benefited from league-leading performance on both sides of the ball while marketing a famous duo to new-age fans. Roger's 300th win and 4,000th strikeout could have come in a Red Sox jersey, just as Boggs' 3,000th hit could have thrilled New England. Alas, those marquee moments happened elsewhere in the AL East, reinforcing the Red Sox' profound stupidity.

For more than a century, this potent mix of intransigence, intolerance and ineptitude thwarted the progress of Boston baseball. Few teams in world sports have traded, neglected, overlooked and underappreciated so many world class superstars as the Red Sox. The wreckage is strangely absurd and almost unrealistic in scope. Deeper analysis creates more layers of morbidity.

Even a cursory review of Red Sox history reveals a litany of missed opportunities. Between 1916 and 1990, Boston rejected, dumped or sold Tris Speaker, Babe Ruth, Willie Mays, Jackie Robinson, Roger Clemens, Curt Schilling and Jeff Bagwell, a septet that combined to produce 639.9 wins above replacement elsewhere. That is the equivalent of dismissing five Mickey Mantles.

Elsewhere, the Red Sox failed to keep Boggs, Fisk, Lynn, Waite Hoyt, Eddie Cicotte, Red Ruffing, Reggie Smith, *Carl* Mays and Dennis Eckersley. Those guys delivered a further 332.2 wins above replacement away from Boston. Such value is identical to having Barry Bonds, Sandy Koufax and Alex Rodriguez for their whole careers. *Poof* – gone in the blink of an eye.

Accordingly, while the media attributed Boston's championship drought to superstition and bad luck, repeated front office meltdowns were more accurately to blame. Shaughnessy's curse was a compelling allegory of New England despondency, but it works better as a hyperbolic ode to Red Sox fandom than it does as logical rationale for decades of baseball incompetence.

By contrast, the Yankees have acquired, signed, embraced, developed and extended more megastars than any team in baseball. From the Babe himself in times of yore through Munson, Catfish and Reggie, onto Mattingly in the contemporary age, New York honed a clinical instinct for finalising deals and attracting stars. They knew who they were and they pursued that mission with zeal. There was little deviation from the course.

The Yankees spared no expense while building one juggernaut after another. The Red Sox, meanwhile, were invariably cheap, hesitant and worried about hypotheticals. That cosmology caused a perfect storm in the AL East, and Boston routinely fell victim to the resultant devastation.

⚾⚾⚾

CHAPTER NINE

The Core Four

While the Red Sox seemingly did everything to ruin their own future in the 1990s, the Yankees doubled down on their promise to field a championship-calibre team every single year. It did not always work out, but the sentiment was certainly there. The Yankees became a fully functioning All-Star team.

In a bid to cajole success from his expensively assembled galaxy, George Steinbrenner bordered narcissistic paranoia. He made outlandish public statements and discarded personnel with capricious ease. He micromanaged projects and demanded insight on rival organisations. He spent an ungodly amount of money and yearned for the boldest dreams. Yet the more George tried to barge his way to a world championship, the further it slipped away.

Winfield became a particular focus of Steinbrenner's ire. In 1989, the outfielder sued the Yankees for failing to contribute $300,000 to his charitable foundation, as per a contract agreement. Steinbrenner was infuriated, dubbing Winfield *Mr May* for his perceived underperformance.

Waging a deranged war against his chosen scapegoat, The Boss paid gambler Howard Spira $40,000 to "dig up dirt" on Winfield. Midway through the 1990 season, commissioner Fay Vincent banned Steinbrenner permanently from day-to-day management of the Yankees as a result. George was mortified.

Ironically, the lack of maniacal meddling allowed the Yankees' front office to implement a strategic overhaul that delivered the team's next great dynasty. Gene Michael assumed a leading role in baseball operations during Steinbrenner's suspension, and the former Yankees shortstop placed an emphasis on youth.

Whereas Steinbrenner typically gutted the farm system to acquire ageing stars, Michael hoarded prospects like the cherished currency they became as baseball evolved. In their owner's absence, the Yankees stitched together a new core of sustainable stars. With vision and patience, Michael laid the foundations for another pinstriped empire.

Mariano Rivera, a raw pitcher, was signed as a 21-year-old lottery ticket out of Panama in February 1990. Jorge Posada, an overlooked catcher, and Andy Pettitte, a fine southpaw, were drafted a few months later. Bernie Williams, a sleek centre fielder, debuted in 1991, while Derek Jeter, a spindly shortstop from Kalamazoo, Michigan, was selected sixth overall in the 1992 draft.

Those five players, likely discarded as trade chips in Steinbrenner's traditional business model, formed a core that delivered greatness to the Bronx well into the twenty-first century. With a combined career WAR of 271.2 in pinstripes, the legendary quintet became arguably the greatest combination of teammates in baseball history. When all was said and done, they had 23 World Series rings between them.

Jeter became a transcendent leader, taking his place alongside Ruth, Gehrig, DiMaggio and Mantle in that sacred pantheon of pinstriped greatness. Rivera became the greatest closer ever to hold a baseball, transforming the game's tactical machinations by dominating out of the bullpen. Pettitte became a reliable ace, especially in big games, wily enough to finesse his way out of trouble and keep his team in contention. Posada became the next great Yankees catcher, the bedrock of their success, a beating heart of passion and fire. And Williams became an understated linchpin, often overlooked but quietly reigning as one of the finest centre fielders in team history.

When lucrative contracts with cumbersome free agents did not work out, the Yankees still had a sustainable foundation on which to rely. They still had a versatile nucleus capable of growing organically into a superpower. They still had a concise framework around which to add complementary pieces en route to the World Series.

Even The Boss acknowledged the remarkable reconstruction completed by his staffers. George returned to the managerial coalface in 1993, his suspension reversed, and he became a backseat driver, occasionally chastising and instructing but otherwise leaving navigation to those more qualified than himself. Michael remained general manager until 1995 before Bob Watson - the first black GM to win a World Series - and then Brian Cashman formulated an uber team. For all his breathless pontificating and snarling desire to win, it took removing Steinbrenner from the equation to kickstart the Yankees' resurgence. And boy was there a resurgence.

Following Boggs' epic horse ride and the world championship of 1996, the Bombers embarked on another dominant run as their young core matured into greatness. Managed by the inspirational Joe Torre, New York won three straight World Series titles between 1998 and 2000, giving them four in five years. They also won the pennant in 2001 and 2003, appearing in six of eight Fall Classics either side of the millennium. When all was said and done, the Yankees had 26 titles. Boston was still waiting for its first since 1918.

⚾⚾⚾

Jeter quickly emerged as the face of baseball, a princely icon defining the game's commercialisation. He won five World Series rings, enough to encrust an entire hand with diamonds, rubies and emerald stones. He played in 14 All-Star Games, won five Gold Gloves, and was voted Rookie of the Year in 1996. Few could match Jeter's austere productivity, and he played the role of transformative baseball hero with understated genius.

As a kid, Derek fell in love with the Yankees, watching games with his grandma, a passionate fan. Possessed of extraordinary determination, Jeter was destined to become a big league ballplayer. When schoolteachers asked young Derek about his future career aspirations, he always had a succinct reply: he was going to play shortstop for the New York Yankees.

Of course, millions of kids share that dream. In the same way that rich businessmen experiencing a mid-life crisis yearn to become president, young kids besotted with baseball dream of roaming the dirt between second and third for their favourite team. Few actually *achieve* those dreams, but Derek Jeter did. He had a rare penchant for controlling his own future.

In the 1992 amateur draft, the Kalamazoo kid somehow fell to the Yankees, picking sixth overall in the first round. Houston, Cleveland, Montreal, Baltimore and Cincinnati passed on the chance to sign a boy who became one of the greatest ballplayers who ever lived. The Yankees grabbed their chance, as if by destiny, and Jeter spent the next 22 years in their organisation.

One year during spring training, back when Jeter was a fated prospect, the great Mattingly taught him vital lessons in Yankee decorum. When Jeter strolled casually off a practice diamond one day, Donnie Baseball took him aside and reiterated the importance of setting a strong example by hustling relentlessly, even when the training facility was empty. From that day forward, Jeter ran on and off the field at all times, assuming the mantle of Yankee leadership. Mattingly was impressed with the precocious kid, who grasped the magnitude of his own responsibility.

In fact, the schoolyard dreamer proceeded to play more games for the New York Yankees than anybody else who ever laced a pair of cleats. Morphing into a national icon with hit after opposite-field hit, Jeter embodied the modern American Dream, and the Yankees were blessed to have him.

Derek ventured to bat for his beloved team on more than 12,000 occasions. While wearing that heritage-drenched uniform, he never once carried himself with anything less than tranquil humility. In 2003, the sacred Yankee captaincy was bestowed upon Jeter, a sequestered honour that capped his greatness. The thread of tradition was passed to Derek, who weaved a masterpiece with minimalistic poise.

"He represents all that is good about a leader," said Steinbrenner when reviving the illustrious captaincy. "I'm a great believer in history, and I look at all the other leaders down through Yankee history, and Jeter is right there with them. I told him I want him to be the type of cavalry officer who can sit in the saddle. You can't be a leader unless you sit in the saddle. I think he can."

Of course, just as Williams opposed DiMaggio and as Fisk rivalled Munson, Boston mustered a handsome shortstop of its own to challenge Jeter's majesty. A superstitious sage on the baseball field, Nomar Garciappara set the game alight after winning Rookie of the Year honours in 1997. Some felt he was better than Jeter, rekindling the classic squabbles and timeless debates of yesteryear. Some felt he could lead Boston to salvation, cracking the code where so many forebears had failed.

Beloved by Red Sox fans, Nomar hit .306 in his debut campaign before improving that mark in three subsequent seasons, reaching .357 in 1999 and .372 in 2000. No righthanded hitter ever produced a higher batting average in the post-war era, and the media was quick to narrate a rivalry between Jeter and Garciaparra, fuelling the ancient antagonism of their teams.

A third gifted shortstop created a triangle of fascination as baseball tried to recover from labour strife that ravaged the 1994 season. Out in Seattle, far away from the mainstream glare, Alex Rodriguez staked his own claim as baseball's definitive star. Regularly topping 40 home runs in a season, then 50, all while hitting around .300, the enigma known as A-Rod transformed the shortstop position, building on the legacy of Cal Ripken Jr. to recalibrate traditional perception.

Typically reserved for small, nimble athletes whose glove spoke louder than their bat, shortstop became a glamour position akin to centre field. Tall, gangly and regal, Rodriguez bestrode the infield like a prized gazelle, all languid arms and flowing legs. He altered the game forever, along with his more respected contemporaries to the east, and there was no greater constellation in the modern realm of baseball.

Jeter emerged from the holy triumvirate as superior by virtue of the Yankees' willingness to build a juggernaut around him. Steinbrenner sanctioned relentless aggression in free agency, willing his executives to do anything and everything to sign the best players, often contrary to logic. In stark contrast, the Mariners flittered between strategies while the Red Sox devalued yet another star. Jeter was The Chosen One, and irritation trickled through the American League as he won a stream of titles.

A-Rod eventually moved from Seattle to Texas, where his exorbitant 10-year, $252 million contract left little flexibility for a mid-market team to construct a winning ballclub. Similarly, in Boston, Garciaparra became preoccupied with his own self-worth, focusing on securing big contract extensions that never materialised to save face in the personal shortstop soap opera.

As his rivals fought with their ballclubs to gain long-term trust and security, Jeter concentrated on winning. Sure, Derek eventually signed his own 10-year deal before the 2001 season, netting $189 million, and his endorsement portfolio grew with every waking hour, but the only metric of success that motivated

Jeter was World Series championships. The same cannot necessarily be said for Rodriguez and Garciaparra.

❖❖❖

While much was written about the Yankees' Core Four, and while the shortstop saga became a recurring subplot, Boston had a tremendous opportunity of its own to capitalise on the emergence of Garciaparra, whose skill was undeniable. Prior to the 1998 season, the Red Sox also added Pedro Martínez, a livewire ace, in a deal with Montreal, creating a two-pronged attack that figured to compete for multiple championships.

However, despite possessing such generational talents, the Red Sox still adhered to a boom-or-bust model when constructing their rosters. All too often, the latter outweighed the former, causing incessant second-guessing and plenty of sleepless nights.

With greater managerial foresight, the Red Sox could have welcomed the new millennium with a starting rotation featuring Clemens, Martínez and Schilling, arguably the three toughest pitchers of their generation. Bagwell and Garciaparra could have shared an infield, augmenting the lockdown rotation, with Vaughn serving as a full-time designated hitter.

Regardless of their riches, even the Yankees would have struggled to topple such a roster. It would have been the most exciting team in franchise history, and Boston could have become a perennial World Series favourite. Instead, the 1999 Red Sox featured journeyman like Mark Portugal and Bret Saberhagen, Mike Stanley and José Offerman, John Valentin and Lou Merloni. They could have been great, but instead they were only good. Another opportunity seemed set to drip away.

In this regard, genuine commitment to winning as judged by free agency dollars was never forthcoming in Boston as New York pulled away. In 1996, the Yankees spent $52 million on player salaries while the Red Sox spent $39 million. Boston tried to keep up, especially after a change of ownership, but that chasm widened considerably over a relatively short period of time. By 2003, the Yankees' payroll spiralled to $152 million with the Red Sox languishing at a mere $99 million. New York spent 42% more than Boston on player salaries, an accurate reflection of the teams' divergent philosophies.

In modernity, the Yankees' brand morphed into a glamorous consumer product in its own right. Spurred by affinity with burgeoning hip hop culture and the team's perennial success, the interlocking NY logo became almost a cultural cliché around the world. The Yankees' famous cap became the go-to headwear for people of all ages, backgrounds, nationalities and interests, filling the team's coffers and feeding a relentless cycle of revenue and triumph.

Such was the sudden ubiquity of Yankees merchandise around the globe, many people were not even aware that the logo belonged to a baseball team. Synonymity with New York, all glitz and glamour, became a real asset for the Yankees in this regard, providing them with an iconic base from which to develop a commercial empire.

Suitably, the Yankees were also one of the first major league teams to develop an expansive internet presence at this time. David Bowie, a British popstar, played an instrumental role in building the team's first real website, which featured revenue-generating tools beyond the kin of more traditional teams. Soon, everyone replicated the model, which became a latter-day prerequisite. Regardless of the topic, people looked to the Yankees for inspiration.

At the confluence of such exemplary marketing and relentless on-field success, the Yankees also drew exceptional attendances to their home games, leading the American League for 13 straight years in one stretch. They remain the only major league team ever to draw more than 4 million spectators in a single season *four separate times*. In turn, that public appreciation swelled their budget, fuelling the envious churning of success.

In 1999, the Yankees looked to capitalise on that bedrock of attention by creating their very own television network, blazing a trail and creating what ultimately became the brightest jewel in their branding crown. When fully established, the Yankees Entertainment and Sports Network (YES) gave the team complete leverage over its own broadcasting rights at a time when that market exploded. The YES Network future-proofed the Yankees' recurring quest for glory.

Generating upwards of $100 million for the team every year, then stretching to $200 million, then soaring over $300 million, YES became the most lucrative regional sports network in America. Coupled with domination of the merchandise, cyberspace and attendance sectors, this resource gave the team unparalleled fiscal flexibility when constructing a ballclub each winter. Every year, the Yankees seemed to add a big free agent, be it David Cone or Mike Mussina, Jason Giambi or Hideki Matsui. The American League chased Steinbrenner and his invincible credit card. There was only one winner.

◡◡◡

To combat pinstriped hegemony, midway through the 1990s MLB introduced one wildcard entry to the postseason per league. All division winners naturally qualified for the playoffs, but from 1995, so did the second-place team with the best record in each league.

The Red Sox became the biggest beneficiaries of this system, relying on it for postseason admittance as the Yankees won 10 division titles in 11 seasons between 1996 and 2006. Boston won five wildcard berths in that span, appearing in the same postseason lotteries as its rival for the first time in history. Emotional shootouts became an October possibility, and both fanbases experienced new echelons of jubilation and dread.

Pedro Martínez was superhuman in 1999, producing a season for the ages. With fearless confidence and a supreme blend of pitches, the Dominican sported a 2.07 ERA and a 0.923 WHIP amid an epidemic of illegal performance-enhancing drugs across the league. His was arguably the most dominant peak in baseball history, and Boston rode the waves of momentum caused by Pedromania.

Martínez recorded 313 strikeouts and won 23 games in 1999. He even started a historic All-Star Game at Fenway Park that year, striking out five of the six batters he faced. Those batters were Sammy Sosa, Larry Walker, Mark McGwire, Bagwell and Barry Larkin. Three of those guys are now in the Hall of Fame, while the quintet combined for 342.3 career WAR. By way of reference, Babe Ruth and Ty Cobb combined for 333.5 career

WAR. Rarely had fans seen such a display of extreme pitching talent as that authored by Pedro.

In September, amid a chase for the playoffs, Martínez started against the Yankees before 55,239 spectators in the Bronx. Lithe and sharp, Pedro pitched a complete game with 17 strikeouts. No pitcher had ever struck out that many New York Yankees in a single game. No opponent had ever scared the pinstriped institution so much.

The Bombers mustered just one hit - a Chili Davis home run - off Martínez on that occasion, and the 5-foot-11 ace threw 80 of his 120 pitches for strikes en route to a near-perfect game. In the expansive annals of baseball history, the Yankees had never been manhandled in such a derogatory fashion, and certainly not in their own yard. Dignitaries scratched their heads, unaccustomed to such flagrant rebellion. This was not meant to happen in baseball's autonomous citadel.

Pedro Martínez did not care about reputations, however, and his one-man revolution threw a stick of dynamite into the traditional Red Sox-Yankees ballad. Pedro did everything in his power to win, and that was a refreshing boost for his success-starved franchise. Boston dared to believe whenever Martínez took the mound, and that fizzy faith grew with each masterpiece.

The Yankees remained a defiant powerhouse, however, and they recovered to win 98 games and defeat wildcard-winning Boston in the 1999 ALCS. The Red Sox thumped Clemens in Game 3 at Fenway, inspiring derogatory chants and sparking a classic rivalry with Martínez, while Game 4 was remembered for a blown call by umpire Tim Tschida on a phantom tag of José Offerman by Yankees infielder Chuck Knoblauch.

New York already led 9-2 by that point, but Red Sox manager Jimy Williams was incensed. When a close call went against Nomar an inning later, Williams stormed the field and started a riot. After the game, a handsome Yankee win, Steinbrenner accused Williams of "inciting" the Fenway crowd, which littered the field with debris. "When Georgie Porgie speaks, I don't listen," said Williams in repost. "I didn't incite the fans. The situation incited the fans. I'm a manager of a major league team. Standing up for the team is one of my responsibilities."

Seemingly impervious to the war of words, New York secured the 1999 pennant in five games. The Yankees got tremendous pitching from Pettitte and Orlando 'El Duque' Hernández, who allowed just three earned runs in 15 innings of high-octane domination. Facing its nemesis in a postseason *series* for the first time, Boston came up short. Indignation coursed through the water at Fenway, which was once again the scene of another team's party.

"Red Sox fans have become alarmingly paranoid, finding monsters underneath the bed almost every night," wrote Shaughnessy in an update of his curse handbook. "It's a hard way to live, but it's the price one pays to follow a 100-year-old franchise that has become part of American sports folklore."

Joe Torre's team beat Atlanta in the subsequent World Series, but things were getting tighter between the Yankees and Red Sox. The composite boxscore from that 1999 ALCS shows a 23-21 scoreline in favour of New York, but Boston outhit the Yanks 54-42. If not for an error-prone defence and a nagging lack of *situational* hitting, the Red Sox could have seriously challenged. They were improving, however, one step at a time. Something *different* was brewing in New England. Those efforts just required verification.

⚾⚾⚾

Martínez was arguably even better in 2000, *lowering* his ERA to 1.74 and *reducing* his WHIP to 0.737. Boston stayed close in the divisional race, but New York swatted away the Red Sox' advances whenever threatened, teasing and tantalising with frustrating autonomy.

The Yankees' roster underwent a subtle makeover as Brian Cashman plugged gaps before they appeared. Veterans like Dwight Gooden, David Justice, Glenallen Hill and José Canseco were welded to the precocious core, giving Torre enough ammunition to keep his team spluttering along.

In June, the Yankees trounced Boston by a score of 22-1 at Fenway. The game was fairly tight until the eighth inning before the Bombers unleashed fury on their raw rivals by scoring 16 runs before the final six outs were recorded. New York remained just a notch ahead, just a bit more refined. Theirs was a calm assurance, and Red Sox frustrations reached a critical mass.

While Boston bristled with indignant rage, another rivalry occupied Yankee rooters: their civic shouting match with the crosstown Mets. With the modern introduction of interleague play during the regular season, matchups between the New York nemeses became more frequent. For instance, on 8th July 2000, the two teams played a rare day-night doubleheader at two different stadiums. That had not happened in the major leagues since 1903, and the Yankees won both games by identical 4-2 scores. They always did rise to the occasion.

Growing in fervour, the Yankees-Mets rivalry was less intense than previous New York baseball combinations, but the simultaneous pennant races of 2000 brought the feud to life. The city was aglow with baseball fever, and millions were intrigued to see whether the upstart Mets could topple the dynastic Yanks.

Established in 1962, the Mets were fashioned from historic residues of the departed Dodgers and Giants, who left for California. The Mets initially struggled to generate a fanbase beyond their home borough of Queens, but several Long Island counties and western New York enclaves came to identify with the team's counterculture. The Bronx, Manhattan, Staten Island and New Jersey remained devout Yankee territories, but occasional Mets success scattered enough seeds to make things feisty.

With impervious belief, the 2000 Yankees weathered a September swoon to finish 87-74 and take the division flag by two-and-a-half-games from Boston, whose learning curve continued. Across town, the Mets posted a 94-68 record, good enough to capture a wildcard berth. Managed by Bobby Valentine and driven by the mercurial talents of superstar catcher Mike Piazza, the Mets played with a carefree energy that started conversations and raised eyebrows. They were relevant again, and that made Gotham all the more passionate.

Relying on heart more than skill and guts more than talent, the Yankees navigated through choppy waters to beat Oakland and Seattle in the playoffs. Showing nerve and poise, the Mets knocked off Barry Bonds and the Giants before thumping St Louis to win their first pennant since Buckner's notorious error.

"Now there will be a resumption of that ancient New York tradition: the Subway Series," wrote George Vecsey in the *New York Times*. "Fasten your seatbelts, it's going to be a bumpy ride."

In reality, though, the first interborough World Series for 44 years was rather anticlimactic, save for an infamous incident where Clemens threw the barrel of a broken bat in the general direction of Piazza as he scampered down the first baseline in Game 2. Tempers flared amid one of the most bizarre episodes in Fall Classic history, but when play resumed, the Yankees eked out a 6-5 victory to take a 2-0 lead in the Series.

Clemens had bad memories of Shea Stadium from the 1986 debacle, when the Mets broke his heart as a Red Sox prodigy. Incidentally, the Mets called on members of that championship team to throw ceremonial first pitches during the 2000 Series, but revenge was sweet for Roger as the Yankees emerged on top.

When it mattered most, Torre's warhorses delivered, driving the Yankees to success in five games. They knew that failing to beat the Mets would shame the organisation and invalidate years of glory. Somehow, they found deeper reserves of determination to power a satisfying triumph. Somehow, they found a way.

Paul O'Neill hit .474 in the Series. Tino Martinez hit .364. Jeter hit .409 with two home runs, while Bernie Williams and Scott Brosius came up with clutch hits. The Yankees became the first team to win three consecutive World Series titles since the 1972-1974 Oakland Athletics. They did it with great timing and learned wisdom, and the Big Apple was most assuredly theirs.

"We beat a great team," said a teary Steinbrenner during the clubhouse celebrations. "It was the battle of New York, and it was a great one to win. They showed me as much heart as any team I've ever had."

Millions of fans flooded the Canyon of Heroes to celebrate the Yankees' threepeat. Kids skipped school to join the parade. Workers hurled shredded paper from office windows, creating a tickertape effect. Revellers partied from dawn until dusk as the Yankees made good on their yearly promise of glory. Meanwhile, forlorn Mets fans trudged through the debris of broken dreams. Now they knew how Bostonians felt all those years ago.

⚾⚾⚾

The offseason connecting 2000 and 2001 was transformational for the Yankees, who sensed a minimisation of their power despite hoisting another title. David Cone, a key contributor to their formative dynasty, joined the Red Sox in free agency, attempting to prolong his career at the age of 38. Once an understated ace, Cone compiled a 6.91 ERA in 2000, figuring his time was up in the Bronx. When the Yankees signed prize free agent Mike Mussina to a six-year, $88.5 million contract, Cone looked elsewhere for offers, and Boston gave him a chance.

Upon returning to Yankee Stadium for the first time in rival red, Cone received a standing ovation regardless of his garb, a show of class from the New York fans who appreciated his toil in pinstripes. Cone won four World Series rings with the Yankees and also threw a legendary perfect game in 1999. He was one of the most understated cogs in the Yankees' latest dynasty, but true baseball fans knew his value.

Indeed, the rivalry often authors such nuanced expressions of respect. Boston denizens also gave Joe Torre an ovation when he made a comeback from cancer surgery in May 1999, for example. Some things are more important than baseball, and that credo became the game's defining ethos later in a 2001 season of unbearable heartache.

Still, vitriol percolated anew following the Yankees' dynastic resurgence. After beating Mussina in one rivalry game, Martínez spoke for Red Sox Nation when asked about the supposed hex placed upon his team. "I don't believe in damn curses," said the firebrand hurler. "Wake up the Bambino and have me face him. Maybe I'll drill him in the ass." Martínez never won another game all season.

By contrast, Cone and Mussina were altogether more dignified when facing off on 2nd September 2001 at Fenway. Mussina came within one strike of a perfect game before Carl Everett blooped a single to left-centre, sparing Red Sox blushes.

Mussina settled for a one-hit, 13-strikeout masterpiece, while Cone tossed a pristine game of his own, pitching into the ninth inning of a scoreless contest. New York finally got to Cone with a game-winning double from Enrique Wilson, but it was refreshing to see the veteran compete at an elite level once again.

Just over a week after that legendary encounter, baseball paled into relative insignificance as America suffered one of the darkest tragedies in its modern history. On the morning of 11th September 2001, four airplanes set for east-to-west coast domestic journeys - including two that departed Boston's Logan International Airport - were hijacked by terrorists intent on destruction. Two of the jets were redirected to New York, colliding with the twin towers of the World Trade Center in a symbolic attack on American power.

Both towers subsequently collapsed, killing thousands of innocent civilians. The third hijacked plane crashed into the Pentagon, headquarters of the US Department of Defense, in Arlington County, Virginia. The fourth jet, flown towards Washington D.C., crashed into a field in Pennsylvania after brave passengers thwarted the hijackers.

In total, 2,996 people died in the coordinated attacks, while more than 6,000 sustained injuries. Mental and economic side effects were felt for generations to come, while deaths related to asbestos exposure from the blasts continue to mount. New York was wounded like never before, yet proud defiance simmered through the world's preeminent metropolis. The Big Apple would not be defeated.

A fitting metaphor for life, mirroring its ups, downs and daily unpredictability, baseball became a cohesive vehicle for that municipal affection. *The Yankees* became an avatar of national determination. Once loathed and hated across the land, those hallowed pinstripes became a symbol of strength, hope and renewal. The whole country rooted for New York and its definitive team. Never before had Steinbrenner's men received such universal goodwill.

Yankee players and officials visited Ground Zero in the immediate aftermath of the attacks. They also spent time in hospitals and recovery centres, emergency service stations and community hubs. They comforted citizens in the darkest moments of their lives, hearing stories of departed loved ones and shattered dreams. Then they went back out onto the diamond and embodied that spirit with class.

After a week of mourning and soul-searching, the Yankees resumed play in Chicago, where White Sox fans unfurled banners supporting New York. Similarly, in Boston, even Red Sox fans proclaimed their love for the city that never sleeps, holding supportive signs and singing along to Sinatra's *New York, New York.*

For perhaps the first time in their existence, the New York Yankees were America's team. They always had the largest fanbase, but more people hated them than loved them. Yet for once, nobody would have begrudged them winning the World Series in 2001. It would have been a symbolic triumph for the country. In the mundane machinations of everyday life, it was almost as if victory for the Yankees correlated with defeat for Al-Qaeda. Baseball became a portal to national healing.

The Yankees won 95 games in the 2001 regular season, capturing another division title and inspiring thoughts of a juggernaut run through October. However, Oakland won the first two games of a tense ALDS as the Yankees fell one game from elimination. New York hauled a 1-0 lead in the seventh inning of Game 3, setting the stage for an iconic intervention from Jeter.

Oakland's Terence Long dumped a double down the right field line, encouraging Jeremy Giambi to chug around the bases from first. Shane Spencer retrieved the ball but uncorked a wild relay throw that missed cut-off man Tino Martinez. Leaden-footed, Giambi rounded third as the ball trickled up the first base line. Jeter instinctively ranged across the infield, far from his shortstop berth, to intercept the ball and shovel it to Posada, who applied a tag just in time. Giambi was out at the plate, and a new clip joined the go-to montage of baseball incredulity.

New York won that fateful game 1-0 and The Flip was duly etched into baseball lore as one of the greatest examples of Jeter's preternatural ability. Rightly inspired, the Yankees won the remaining two games against Oakland before dispatching 116-win Seattle in the Championship Series. Their magical momentum was back again.

Alfonso Soriano came up with a crucial hit in Game 4 of the ALCS, the Yankee star lofting a two-run walk-off homer into the right-centre field abyss. Such an inspired intervention motivated New York as the Yankees went to the World Series for the fourth straight year and a fifth year in six. Arizona stood between Gotham and salvation.

Set against a backdrop of cultural healing and newfound togetherness, the 2001 Fall Classic was quite possibly the greatest ever played. Rarely had Yankee Stadium throbbed with such energy and raw emotion, and rarely had the Yankees faced such stout competition for the world title.

An expansion team formed in 1998, the Diamondbacks possessed an immortal one-two punch at the front of their starting rotation. Aged 34 and 37, respectively, Schilling and Randy Johnson were brutally dominant in 2001, using guts, guile and gritted teeth to power a postseason run.

Schilling won 22 games while Johnson won 21. Schilling had a 2.98 ERA while Johnson lay at 2.49. Schilling struck out 293 batters while Johnson struck out 372, including a record-tying 20 in one game. The duo was totally overpowering.

Together, Schilling and Johnson combined to throw more than 500 innings in the regular season, practically hauling Arizona to a division crown ahead of San Francisco and Los Angeles. The Diamondbacks then beat St Louis and Atlanta in the postseason, confirming a World Series date with the Yankees.

The dual aces began the Fall Classic in dazzling form, holding New York to just one run through the first two games. It seemed so *easy*, almost like a video game where you artificially boost pitchers' attributes. Heading back to the Bronx for Game 3, down 2-0, the Yankees needed a little magic. That is exactly what they got as President George W Bush threw the ceremonial first pitch at Yankee Stadium.

Regardless of political inclination and personal grievances, people were moved by the sight of a US President standing on an open field, exposed to 55,820 people in an enclosed space at the heart of a city that had been terrorised less than three weeks earlier.

A big baseball fan and minority owner of the Texas Rangers, Bush appreciated the magnitude of this moment. Wearing a bulletproof vest, he warmed up underneath the stands, heeding advice from Jeter. "You better throw from the mound," said Jeter. "Don't bounce it, they'll boo you." Bush did *not* bounce it. He threw a dart from the mound, earning applause on a night when the Yankees came storming back to life with a 2-1 win.

"I had never had such an adrenaline rush as when I finally made it to the mound," said Bush years later. "I've been to conventions and rallies and speeches, but I've never felt anything so powerful and emotions so strong. The collective will of the crowd was so evident."

Amid such defiant yearning, Game 4 was arguably the greatest World Series contest of all-time. Hurt and wounded, the Yankees came back from the brink of defeat to win in storybook fashion. Even today, it remains impossible to watch the highlights without trembling with goosebumps.

Nursing a 3-1 lead with six outs remaining, Arizona manager Bob Brenly turned to his closer, Byung-hyun Kim, hoping to press home the advantage. The Korean struck out the side in the eighth as New York gawped at a major deficit in the series. Things were a little different in the ninth, however, as O'Neill lined a one-out single to spark hope. But when Bernie Williams struck out, the Diamondbacks were one out from victory.

Tino Martinez, a beloved slugger, strode to the plate representing the Yankees' last chance. With a quirky submarine delivery, Kim poured a pitch over the heart of the plate, thigh-high and hittable. Martinez lashed at the ball, sending it high and far towards right-centre field. Cast against a still black sky, a white dot soared in a smooth parabola, landing with aplomb in the bleachers, transformed into a whirring maelstrom of contorted limbs. The game was tied, and Yankee Stadium shook like never before.

The Yankees turned to Mariano Rivera, their relief ace, to keep Arizona at bay in the tenth. Then, somewhat remarkably, Arizona used Kim for a third inning of work as the clock ticked beyond midnight. The Stadium scoreboard flashed with a famous message: "Welcome to November baseball."

With two outs, Jeter battled through a nine-pitch at bat before slicing a 3-2 slider towards the short right field porch. As if propelled by a gust of wind and driven by pleading New York hearts, the ball cleared the outfield wall and landed on the front row of seats, clinching an immortal win for the Yankees and evening the World Series at two games apiece.

For the first time in baseball history, a home run was hit in the eleventh month of the year. The season was pushed back due to the terrorist attacks, giving Derek Jeter a chance to become Mr November, a tongue-in-cheek memento from a game for the ages. New York exulted in the gritty determination of its ballclub, and the Yankees rose from their slumber.

The following night, Game 5 was peppered with similar magic. In harsh symmetry, Arizona once again handed a two-run lead to Kim in the ninth inning, and once again he coughed it up amid bedlam in the Bronx.

With the Yankees down 2-0, Posada led off the home ninth with a double before Kim retired Shane Spencer and Chuck Knoblauch. Scott Brosius, a veteran third baseman, then skied a two-run homer to left, tying the game and rocking the ancient ballpark to its core. To quote the great Yogi Berra, it was déjà vu all over again. Logic lost all meaning.

The Yankees won Game 5 in 12 innings when Soriano shot a walk-off single to right field. Knoblauch came around to score the winning run, beating the throw home to put the Yankees one win away from a fourth consecutive world title. A more exhilarating comeback was hard to find in the catacombs of baseball history.

Alas, in unorthodox fashion, the Yankees never closed the deal. With New York one win from glory, the series reverted to Phoenix, where the Diamondbacks lined up Johnson and Schilling to pitch two crucial games. Arizona won Game 6 in blowout fashion, thumping the Yankees 15-2 to force a do-or-die decider at Bank One Ballpark.

If the 2001 World Series was the ultimate baseball masterpiece, Game 7 was a study of intense human emotion all of its own. Clemens got the ball for New York, matching Schilling step-for-step before 49,589 enrapt fans. Across America, almost 72 million people caught a glimpse of the game on television. Even more watched around the world, including here in England, as baseball reached a universal apex.

Rising to the occasion, Arizona scored first in the sixth inning, but the Yankees answered back with an RBI single from Tino. When Soriano took Schilling deep to lead off the eighth, New York eked out a 2-1 lead. Rivera dominated in the bottom half of the eighth, dragging the exhausted Yankees within three outs of another crown.

With brazen rebellion, the upstart Diamondbacks did not lie down, however. Mark Grace singled to lead off the home ninth as the sellout crowd made a deafening din. David Dellucci pinch-ran for Grace and was safe at second base when Damian Miller's bunt coaxed a throwing error from Rivera.

Jay Bell bunted into a forceout before Tony Womack lined a game-tying doubled to right field. Wayward and ruffled, Rivera then hit Craig Counsell with a pitch before Luis Gonzalez blooped a walk-off, series-clinching single over a drawn-in Yankee infield and into the shallow outfield of fate. Arizona had toppled the pinstriped galaxy.

Buster Olney, a national baseball writer for the *New York Times*, later published a book about the Yankees' dominant run with a specific focus on the 2001 World Series, which heralded the start of a subtle decline. *The Last Night of the Yankee Dynasty* delved inside the team's expiring mystique and spoke to the nation's shock whenever the Yankees *did not* win it all. Some kids grew up thinking that was impossible, and they learned the hard way that life can be tough.

Indeed, Yankee defeat became increasingly common in the 2000s as historic roles were reversed. The Yankees got a taste of their own medicine as rival teams caught up with and even surpassed their tired business model. The great Steinbrenner dollar lost value in a coming age of statistical efficiency, and the tectonic plates of baseball power shifted beyond recognition.

⚾⚾⚾

CHAPTER TEN

A Baseball Revolution

The Yankees' impenetrable success and exorbitant spending in the 1990s changed Major League Baseball forever. As per the laws of evolution, rival organisations were left to concoct ever more creative ways of remaining competitive. In this regard, the Yankees inspired their own downfall as the underlings caught up.

In smaller markets, avoiding humiliation by the Yanks meant finding undervalued assets and creating new formulas for success. In this regard, the rise of advanced analytics transformed the sporting landscape, and Oakland became the epicentre of a statistical revolution.

Once a powerhouse, the advent of free agency gutted the Athletics during Charlie Finley's 1970s denouement. Oakland lost Reggie Jackson, Catfish Hunter, Rollie Fingers and other stars in quick succession as Finley fell out of love with baseball. Fans stopped visiting the Coliseum as success dried up. A change of focus was needed, and that is just what the Athletics got.

Under the fresh ownership of Water A Haas Jr., the Athletics were revitalised throughout the 1980s. Roy Eisenhardt left a secure job at a plush Bay Area law firm to become president of the team, and he brought a bright Harvard law graduate named Sandy Alderson with him, creating an unorthodox hierarchy. A Dartmouth alum with no formal background in baseball, Alderson was promoted to general manager within two years, and his aggressive brand of leadership drove the organisation forward.

While free agency robbed Oakland of its best players, it also drove salaries into a range that mid-market teams struggled to reach, creating a two-pronged impact. Haas, Eisenhardt and Alderson could never compete with Steinbrenner for big ticket stars. They did not have the cash. Accordingly, Oakland focused on regenerating from within, developing elite prospects like Mark McGwire, José Canseco and Walt Weiss. Those guys won three consecutive Rookie of the Year awards from 1986, vindicating the team's plan.

McGwire and Canseco became known as the Bash Brothers, slamming prodigious home runs and sparking a new era of Athletics baseball. Still, Alderson knew that moon blasts alone did not win championships. Oakland finished below .500 in each of Sandy's first three seasons. That is when he hired Tony La Russa to be his manager, embracing a bold strategic vision.

A master strategist, La Russa was stigmatised by traditional fans and writers who said he overmanaged his teams. Indeed, La Russa took a finickity approach to bullpen strategy, often using left-handed relievers to face just one batter. At that point in baseball history, such techniques were alien, and veteran observers thought La Russa was crazy. In the end, he was not just *ahead* of the curve. He *drew* the curve, and everybody else struggled to keep up.

Whereas old school managers followed their gut when controlling a bullpen, Tony confirmed or denied his hunches by using data, specifically platoon splits and historical game logs. La Russa was the first manager to obsess over potential matchups and hypothetical game sequences through a statistical prism before each game. Such preparedness gave him an intense focus during games, allowing Oakland to squeeze maximum performance from its players.

"Sometimes, he stayed awake to work things out," Buzz Bissinger wrote of La Russa in *Three Nights in August.* "Find an answer in the seeming absence of any, pick a situation apart and put it back together and pick it apart and put it back together again. Beneath his taciturn exterior was an optimist, someone convinced that if you thought about something hard enough, grinded through it enough, examined every possible alternative enough, it could be fixed."

Alderson was intrigued by La Russa's research habits, and he embraced them himself, poring over analytical dossiers before making big decisions. A baseball neophyte, Alderson figured that his lack of specialist knowledge compared to rival general managers could actually be a *positive.* Sandy had a less prejudiced view of the game than many of his contemporaries, uncoloured by personal experience, and he was therefore more inclined to trust objective data over subjective opinion. Such an approach delivered success in the coming century, with statistics replacing sunflower seeds as the fuel of baseball victory.

Blazing a trail, Alderson was one of the first baseball executives to realise that dollars spent in the front office could be more effective than those spent on the field. As ownership gradually cut costs, Oakland could not compete for marquee free agents, but it *could* be first in line to mop up Ivy League graduates each summer. Those bright minds held the key to baseball's future, and the A's turned them loose in a quest to bridge the chasm.

In this regard, Alderson recruited exceptionally well, stocking his front office with rebellious intellectuals like Billy Beane, a former player with an economics degree from the University of California San Diego, and JP Ricciardi, a perceptive evaluator of talent. A rigorous mentor, Alderson tasked these staffers with devising innovative methods of player evaluation, attempting to break new ground and redress the imbalance of MLB's distorted economy. In short, Oakland became a laboratory of baseball's future, with scholars working on a vaccine long into the night.

Sandy introduced Beane, Ricciardi and others to the work of Bill James, a leading proponent of new-age baseball thinking. Working nights at a pork and beans factory in Kansas, James honed a searing passion for sport into iconoclastic writing that was often acerbic. A reluctant Svengali, James ranked ballplayers using obscure metrics and frequently ridiculed major league teams for moves that jarred with his algebraic rationale. Much of James' early work nourished an underground cult and little else besides, but Alderson encouraged his disruptive executives to keep abreast of the sabermetric zeitgeist. He thought it would be useful one day.

Meanwhile, out on the diamond, away from the grimy den of thirtysomething number-crunchers, Oakland won three straight pennants between 1988 and 1990. La Russa's men were beaten comprehensively in two of their three World Series appearances, but they did sweep San Francisco in 1989, clinching a sweet title against their local rivals.

La Russa left for St Louis in 1996, and McGwire joined him a year later. Canseco had already toured the American League by that point, wearing out his welcome in multiple cities, while older guys like Rickey Henderson and Dave Stewart played out the string. Alderson switched jobs himself in 1998, joining the commissioner's office, but his data-driven bloodline continued to upset the odds.

Filling Sandy's void, Oakland promoted Beane to general manager. In turn, Beane made Ricciardi director of player personnel, while Paul DePodesta, another data zealot, was plucked from Cleveland to turbocharge the Athletics' plan. DePodesta had an economics degree from Harvard, and his was a steadfast belief in Jamesian dogma.

Together, the trailblazing trio built on Alderson's foundation, taking Oakland's innovative blueprint to its logical endpoint. Their success revolutionised baseball, and we are still analysing the fallout. Never before had the game's internal wiring been so disrupted by a group of seditious dreamers. The Athletics sparked a rebellion, and rival teams had no choice but to join the insurgency.

ﷺﷺﷺ

In 1998, when Beane first gained control as Athletics general manager, he spent $22 million on player salaries while the Yankees spent $65 million. By 2003, the disparity reached triple digits, with Oakland spending $50 million in contrast to New York's $152 million. They were playing different games.

In 2003, the Yankees paid more to four players – Jeter, Mussina, Williams and Raul Mondesi – than Oakland paid to its entire 40-man roster. Theoretically, the A's should have finished last every single year, but Beane, a former player with a fiery competitive instinct, could not allow that to happen, and it did not.

Rather than lurking in the cellar where their budget belonged, Oakland won the American League West in 2000, 2002 and 2003, frequently making the postseason against all odds. The A's won 91 games in 2000. They improved to 102 wins a year later, while the 2002 season yielded 103 victories. Oakland even won 20 consecutive games in the latter campaign, establishing an American League record.

Despite having the third-smallest budget in Major League Baseball, no team won more games than the 2002 Athletics. Despite spending 68% less than the Yankees on player salaries that year, Oakland won the same amount of games. Despite an operating income of just $6.6 million, the Athletics outperformed organisations with double and triple their revenue. Something big was happening in major league front offices. Something *new*. The Yankees became victims of their own success.

Tasked with constructing a successful major league team with a miniscule budget, Beane delved back to the very basics when searching for a way to beat Steinbrenner. He asked the simplest yet most overlooked question of all: how do you win baseball games? He found that the answer was very different to the prevailing culture of contemporary MLB.

Inspired by Alderson's daydreams, Beane embarked on an exhaustive study to decode this ancient game. Rather than relying on the gut instinct of scouts and the colourful opinions of crusty veterans, Beane advocated an aggressive brand of sabermetrics, fully embracing James' ideology. Billy also studied the Wall Street strategies of billionaire Warren Buffet, tweaking his modus operandi to fit a baseball template.

In explicit terms, sabermetric dogma holds that granular statistics such as on-base percentage (OBP) and on-base-plus slugging percentage (OPS) are far more predictive of true value, in the sense of winning baseball games, than a muscular body or a cannon arm.

Whereas big market teams signed players who performed well in traditional counting stats like home runs and RBI, Oakland took advantage of such ignorant munificence, hoovering up the best players as judged by obscure analytical measures that actually indicated team success.

To win baseball games, a team must score more runs than its opponent. To score runs, said team must first turn hitters into baserunners. Sabermetrics held that the mere act of repeatedly getting on base via any means available was the most undervalued commodity in baseball. More aesthetically pleasing factors were comparatively unimportant.

Walks were not sexy and they did not sell jerseys in the team store, but from a logical endpoint of scoring runs and winning games, they were just as valuable as a line drive single. The latter improved a player's batting average, correlating to higher pay in the warped marketplace of baseball. The former caused no discernible uptick in any of the core statistics acknowledged by the mainstream, creating a pool of undervalued players. Oakland fished in those mystical waters, constructing one of the most efficient baseball teams of all-time.

Rather than courting home runs, a costly stock, Beane focused on pitches-per-plate appearance, a relatively overlooked ingredient of runs. Rather than lusting over RBI, an inflated bond, Beane mined the markets of secondary average, a vague metric cooked up by James. Rather than pining over strikeouts, a flawed indicator of pitching prowess, Beane respected WHIP, more closely aligned with actual skill. Billy did not even watch his team play live, lest he form sentimental opinions that would undermine the objective evaluation framework. He was married to big data.

Above all else, Beane worshipped at the altar of OBP. He was first to that particular party, and he had first dibs at the lavish buffet. More corpulent foes had larger plates, but Billy had greater nutritional wisdom with which to fashion a healthier meal. Under his command, even the poorest team never starved.

In 2002, David Justice, a former star who caught on with the Yankees, embodied the market inefficiency while playing for the A's. Steinbrenner paid half of Justice's remaining $7 million salary just to offload him to Oakland, where he led the team with a .376 OBP at the age of 36. By contrast, Jeter earned more than *double* Justice's salary but got on base *less*, his .373 OBP representing a vast overpayment according to sabermetricians.

Oakland repeated this concept over and over again. They paid Scott Hatteberg $900,000 to get on base at a .374 clip, also more than Jeter and a host of overpaid stars around the league. They paid Miguel Tejada less than $4 million to win the MVP Award and they paid Barry Zito $295,000 to claim Cy Young honours.

A regular season juggernaut, the Athletics never quite figured out how to win in the postseason, however. Oakland lost by three games to two in the ALDS in *four straight years*. Still, Billy Beane changed the conversation with regard to competitive balance in professional sports. Oakland played a different game, and teams in larger markets were intrigued.

At first, richer teams did not know exactly *how* Beane was constructing a winner, but they knew he was on to *something*. Paranoid and confused, big market teams pillaged Oakland, signing its best players in free agency as if that were the antidote.

The Yankees gave $120 million to Jason Giambi. The Red Sox spent $31 million on Johnny Damon. The Cardinals inked Jason Isringhausen for $27 million. Oakland did not flinch, scouring the market for undervalued and underappreciated replacements, sticking to its blueprint with a revolving cast of misfits.

Despite losing three of their best players, the A's actually won more games in 2002 than they did in 2001. The more those richer teams spent on imperfect free agents, the further Oakland delved into the game's analytical underground, finding new ways to win an unfair game.

The aforementioned Michael Lewis published a bestselling book about the 2002 Athletics that altered baseball forever. *Moneyball* worked as a small market manifesto for success, and its application transformed global business beyond mere sport.

"At the bottom of the Oakland experiment was a willingness to rethink baseball," wrote Lewis in the preface to his bestseller. "A baseball team, of all things, was at the centre of a story about the possibilities - and the limits - of reason in human affairs. Baseball, of all things, was an example of how an unscientific culture responds, or fails to respond, to the scientific method."

Lewis' revelations blew the lid off commerce around the world. Oakland's ethos was soon replicated throughout professional sports, and variations of Moneyball delivered championships across the country, just not for the Athletics.

Beane's success, and Lewis' portrayal thereof, made the dream of becoming a major league general manager newly accessible. Although Beane played professionally, his revolutionary embrace of academia penetrated walls and led to an influx of nerds in decision-making positions throughout baseball. Even as a kid from the UK, that appealed to me years later, and the aspiration seemed *attainable*. I wanted to be one of those nerds, and *Moneyball* encouraged the dream.

In 2002, amid baseball's statistical awakening, the Yawkey Trust finally sold the Boston Red Sox for $660 million. New England Sports Ventures, the purchasing consortium, was headed by John W Henry, a serial investor who believed wholeheartedly in the analytical revolution sweeping big business in the United States.

Henry's eponymous investment firm made a fortune by pioneering the use of statistical analysis to drive objective trading decisions on soybean products. Henry devised a system of evaluation that precluded human emotion, automating the investment process in coherence with market trends, governed by data. His algorithm produced $2.4 billion in wealth, allowing the cerebral Henry to dabble in luxurious pursuits.

A boyhood Cardinals fan who worshipped Stan Musial, Henry hungered to own a baseball team. He purchased the minor league Tuscon Toros in 1989 and later invested in the West Palm Beach Tropics. Most notably, Henry bought shares in the Yankees - reportedly equating to 1% - in 1991. Let it never be forgotten, therefore, that George Steinbrenner's stylistic antithesis was once his minority partner.

Henry progressed to buy the Florida Marlins for $158 million in 1999. He never got around to selling those Yankee shares, however, causing consternation in some quarters. When Henry bought the Red Sox three years later, with more than a little engineering from commissioner Bud Selig, he briefly owned pieces of three major league teams, a sign of his conflicted priorities.

Naturally, after gaining control of the Red Sox, Henry was keen to implement his soybean strategy in Boston. Henry appreciated the success of Beane in Oakland, and he yearned to implant such flagrant iconoclasm at Fenway Park. Perhaps data, science and mathematics held the answer to an eight-decade championship drought. John Henry believed that the repost to Babe Ruth's ghost lay in a calculator, and he set out to prove it.

When Oakland was eliminated from the 2002 postseason by Minnesota, Henry approached Beane and entered discussions about the vacant general manager post in Boston. Duquette was fired immediately after the new owners took office, and Henry was so impressed by Beane's success that he wanted to make Billy the best-paid executive in the history of North American sports while transplanting the driving ethos from Oakland to Boston.

The Red Sox offered Beane a five-year contract worth $12.5 million to spearhead their baseball operations department. Beane seriously considered the offer, at one point tentatively agreeing. However, he ultimately rejected the lure of a big market budget in favour of continuing his resuscitation project in Oakland.

Henry was disappointed but perhaps not surprised. Nevertheless, he remained utterly convinced that sabermetrics held the key to success in Boston, and he set about recreating Beane in the aggregate, rather like Oakland did when trying to replace Giambi, Damon and Isringhausen.

With a clear avatar of their ideal general manager in mind - young, innovative and nerdy - the Red Sox turned their attention to Ricciardi, a Massachusetts native who ran the Blue Jays' front office after graduating from the lair of Beane and Alderson. Toronto signed Ricciardi to a five-year extension, however, scuppering a potential homecoming for the analytically-minded exec.

Deviating from their script, Boston asked New York for permission to interview Gene Michael, but Steinbrenner declined the request. After completing due diligence on a number of other candidates, the Red Sox eventually homed in on a 28-year-old assistant already working in their own front office. Henry found his spirit animal lurking in the basement.

A Yale graduate with visionary intelligence, Theo Epstein grew up in suburban Brookline, a 10-minute drive from Fenway. The Red Sox were in his blood, and he dreamed of one day leading his boyhood team to elusive glory.

Looking for a start out of college, Epstein worked in public relations with the Baltimore Orioles, striking up a strong rapport with player development czar Larry Lucchino. When Lucchino was hired by the Padres, Epstein moved to San Diego with him, becoming a linchpin between marketing, ticket sales and baseball operations.

Lucchino saw great potential in Epstein, who completed a law degree at night school after his boss said it would aid his progression. Theo worked tirelessly, spending long hours at the ballpark. When he was not pushing season tickets, Epstein devised complex statistical models and tinkered with detailed scouting reports that impressed Lucchino. Theo also studied the work of James and Beane, refining his baseball ideology.

Despite a middling payroll, San Diego won the National League pennant in 1998, a testament to the team's overhauled operation. The Padres spent $15 million less than Atlanta, the NL's most liberal spenders that year, but still managed to oust the Braves in a tight championship series. Of course, the Yankees crushed San Diego's dreams in the subsequent Fall Classic, but Epstein continued to rise through the Padres' ranks, eventually becoming director of baseball operations.

Meanwhile, upon taking office in Boston, Henry and Werner were keen to find a reliable club president with day-to-day autonomy. Henry appreciated Lucchino's reputation as a builder of great teams and even greater ballparks, and those attributes meshed nicely with the Red Sox' revitalisation plan.

Lucchino was in charge of the Orioles when Camden Yards opened its gates, and he later influenced the design of Petco Park in San Diego. Both stadiums were outrageously successful, and Henry thirsted for a similar vibe at Fenway. Lucchino was subsequently headhunted to join the Boston renaissance, and he brought Epstein with him as a baseball operations figurehead.

For years, Lucchino groomed Epstein for general manager stardom, waiting for the right moment to elevate his protégé. When Beane rejected the Red Sox, Larry broached Theo's name for the top position. Epstein's time arrived, and in November 2002, the Red Sox made him the youngest general manager in baseball history.

"We concluded that the right person was right before our eyes," Lucchino said at an introductory press conference. "We believe this franchise will benefit from a new structure and fresh philosophies."

Epstein believed in a hybrid approach to baseball operations, blending the best advice of scouts with the finest cutting-edge analytics. In Boston, he assembled a front office that meshed the two warring factions of baseball evaluation, synthesising a contemporary formula for success.

Jed Hoyer, a graduate of Wesleyan University, became assistant general manager aged 29. Ben Cherrington, an academic star at Amherst, formed part of the managerial nucleus as director of player development aged 28. Bill James himself, the godfather of baseball's statistical enlightenment, was ushered into the mainstream, joining the Red Sox as a consultant. There was even room for Bill Lajoie, a traditional baseball lifer who was a special assistant to Epstein aged 69. Theo ticked every box.

Without a playoff berth since 1999, Boston faced the 2003 season with an altered focus. Epstein and his lieutenants scanned the market for value, runs and players who got on base rather than for smiles, muscles and megawatt names that sold tickets.

Bill Mueller was signed as a free agent. He duly won the batting title in his first season with the Red Sox. Kevin Millar was claimed off waivers as the Marlins attempted to sell him to the Chunichi Dragons of Japan. He hit 25 home runs with 96 RBI as an introduction to Boston, a discarded asset turned profitable.

And then there was David Ortiz, a big-bodied slugger whose natural game had been restrained through six frustrating years in Minnesota. The Twins wanted Ortiz to hit for a higher average and put the ball in play rather than unleash his power. Minnesota eventually released Ortiz, who was one of the most undervalued players in baseball history. Epstein signed the future Hall of Famer for $1.25 million. Few baseball investments have ever been more profitable.

For once, the Red Sox made shrewd acquisitions rather than shooting themselves in the foot with questionable decisions. Notoriously cynical, the Boston media resented the team's shopping for inexpensive additions, and unenlightened talking heads questioned its approach. The Red Sox were looking in the bargain bucket, some complained, and besides, none of these guys could play defence to any spectacular standard. Heck, where did they all fit together on the diamond?

Mueller became the third baseman, Millar played first, and Ortiz was inserted as the full-time designated hitter. With a much larger budget and a far bigger crumple zone, Theo implemented a refinement of Beane's philosophy in Boston, caring not for subjective opinions but for data-driven dogma. The results were legendary, as the Red Sox took impartial evaluation to whole new levels.

Although subsequent films and books sugar-coated the Boston renaissance, Theo and his bosses did not have it all their own way in the first instance. For example, Epstein received a crash course in pinstriped frustration during the winter of 2002-03 as New York beat him to the signature of a prized international free agent. The heartache of boyhood percolated anew.

While pitching for the Cuban national team against Baltimore in a 1999 exhibition, José Contreras struck out 10 major league hitters and tossed eight shutout innings. Big league scouts fawned over his potential, and Contreras defected in 2002, making himself available to the highest big league bidder.

Steinbrenner felt embarrassed by the Yankees' failure in the 2001 World Series, especially given the goodwill afforded to his team around the country. Despite authoring a run of incredible greatness, general manager Brian Cashman found himself on the hot seat. Only in the Bronx could a guy win four straight pennants and still have to fight for his job.

New York looked to the international market for reinforcements, signing Hideki Matsui, a legendary slugger with the Tokyo Giants of Japan, to a three-year, $21 million contract. However, George was still not satisfied. "Lose Contreras and you're done," The Boss told his baseball operations staff. The Yankees duly inked the 31-year-old hurler to a four-year, $32 million pact, much to the annoyance of fans in other cities around the country.

In particular, Epstein loved the idea of pairing Contreras with Martínez at the front of his starting rotation. The Boston front office hatched an elaborate plan to land Contreras, even travelling to Nicaragua for negotiations and renting out an entire hotel to prevent the Yankees from getting near their target.

When New York topped Boston's bid at the last moment, signing Contreras from under the Red Sox' nose, Epstein smashed up his hotel room in a fit of anger. Back in America, the *New York Times* reached out to Lucchino for his comments on the Contreras deal. He initially declined their requests before unleashing one of the most memorable quotes in modern baseball history. "The evil empire extends its tentacles even into Latin America," said Lucchino, full of bitterness. And just like that, new coals were added to the fire.

The 2003 Red Sox scored 961 runs, a terrific improvement on the previous season. They led the majors in almost every offensive category, including batting average and OBP. Most impressively, Theo's powerhouse recorded a .491 team slugging percentage, smashing a hallowed mark held by the sacred Yankees of 1927.

Boston won 95 games, the most they had managed since 1986, when Epstein watched Buckner's gaffe from behind the couch as a heartbroken fan. Still, somewhat remarkably, the Yankees won even more games, clinching another AL East title with a 101-61 record. New York had an innate sixth sense for what was needed to topple everybody else, and once again, Boston settled for the wildcard.

When the Yankees beat Minnesota and the Red Sox defeated Beane's Oakland in the 2003 postseason, the two warring factions met in a poignant ALCS that captured the global imagination. This time, it was war, and the combatants dealt with heightened emotions like never before.

Beginning in 2001, MLB adopted an unbalanced schedule, meaning the Yankees and Red Sox played 18 or 19 times in the regular season each year, intensifying their feud. With a pennant at stake in 2003, Boston and New York duly became the first teams to play each other 25 times or more in a single season. Familiarity breeds contempt, and the rivalry entered a new stratosphere.

"It's bigger than the World Series when we play them," said Red Sox lifer Johnny Pesky on many occasions. Indeed, the ancient baseball bloodlust transcended sports during this era, and the game has never quite recovered from those dizzying peaks of passion.

The first two games of the 2003 ALCS were split in the Bronx before the series switched to Boston. Clemens faced Martínez in a Saturday afternoon matinee at Fenway Park in Game 3. A worldwide television audience of millions watched as hatred boiled over.

In the fourth inning, Yankees leading 3-2, Martínez hit New York right fielder Karim Garcia with a wild pitch near the batter's head. Garcia was livid, peering at Martínez and muttering his disdain. Martínez maintained an indomitable façade on the mound, gawping blankly into an incensed Yankees dugout. The spark was lit.

When Jorge Posada barked at Pedro, the pitcher pointed to his head and then at the Yankees' catcher, insinuating a further beanball was forthcoming. Several Yankees players spilled from the dugout to confront Martínez, while home plate umpire Alfonso Marquez warned both teams against inciting violence.

Never one to back down, Clemens promptly returned to work and threw a high fastball to Manny Ramírez, who charged the mound. The pitch was not inside, nor did it come especially close to hitting Ramírez, but the benches and bullpens emptied regardless, sparking a mass brawl. An infamous vignette of the fight saw Don Zimmer, the Yankees' 72-year-old bench coach, charge Martínez aggressively. Pedro sidestepped the attack and threw Zimmer to the ground. The rivalry had never experienced a more classless nadir.

The game endured a 13-minute delay, during which a heavy police presence was deployed and all beer sales were stopped at Fenway. Remarkably, nobody was ejected from the game. Clemens and Martínez pitched into the late innings, creating the fine spectacle everyone wished to see.

With a 4-3 lead heading to the bottom of the ninth, New York turned to Mariano Rivera, the indomitable closer. However, before he could get to work, another brawl broke out, this time in the Yankees' bullpen, where a Fenway groundskeeper cheered a double play turned by the Red Sox to end the previous half-inning.

Yankee reliever Jeff Nelson took exception to the boisterous bias, and a fight unfurled involving Nelson and Garcia, who hopped the right field fence to get involved. The Red Sox employee was eventually taken to hospital, where "cleat marks" were found on his body, according to a team statement. Storm clouds gathered over the ancient duel.

Respectful ribbing turned nasty, and the rivalry's overall tenor descended into anarchy. Rivera locked down the final three outs, putting the Yankees ahead 2-1 in the series, but the war continued in verbal format long after Game 3 finished.

"Karim Garcia, who is Karim Garcia?" asked Martínez when questioned by the media. "I have no respect for that guy. I don't have anything to prove to that guy. He needs to be forcing himself to come up to where I am, to my level.

"When you talk about Jeter, Bernie Williams, Paul O'Neill, guys like that, you really tip your hat. That, you can understand. But guys like Karim Garcia? So what? Who are you? Who are you, Karim Garcia, to try to test Pedro Martínez, a proven player for ten years? That's what I don't understand. Why would I hit Karim Garcia?"

Meanwhile, Red Sox spokesman Charles Steinberg exacerbated tensions with misplaced hyperbole. "The Red Sox are terribly concerned and distressed about the attack on our employee," said Steinberg, whose choice of words was tribal and sensationalist.

In repost, Yankees president Randy Levine was incensed. "Someone from the Red Sox organisation should be on the phone right now apologising to George Steinbrenner and Joe Torre and every player in here," he said. "It's pathetic. It outrages me."

"That's a disgrace," said Boston reliever Scott Williamson, fighting fire with fire. "You've got kids out there, so for that to happen, it's very upsetting. If you're having a bad day, don't take it out on the groundskeeper."

Laced with bitterness and shrouded in anger, the series continued to capture the imagination of baseball fans around the world. Boston evened the series behind the gentlemanly Tim

Wakefield, only for New York to claim Game 5 on a clutch two-run double by Garcia.

Kevin Millar rallied his Red Sox teammates behind a Boston-against-the-world mantra of "cowboy up," which became a slogan for the team's unceasing determination through adversity. The bravado was fragile, however, and fear lurked beneath the veneer of defiance.

Heading back to the Bronx, raucously baying for blood, the Yankees needed to win just one of two games to clinch a sixth pennant in eight years. Alas, the Red Sox fought back strong in Game 6, edging a rollercoaster contest 9-6 to earn a do-or-die capper.

Through six games, the series' composite boxscore was locked at 24-24. After playing 25 games from Opening Day through to winter, the Yankees held a 13-12 advantage over Boston. Something had to give. There could only be one winner.

The Florida Marlins awaited in the World Series having infamously defeated the Chicago Cubs in seven games to clinch the National League pennant. Without a world championship since 1908, the Cubs took a 3-0 lead into the eighth inning of Game 6 against Florida, edging within five outs of a rare trip to the Fall Classic, only to blow it in macabre fashion.

When Marlins infielder Luis Castillo hit a ball down the left field line, Cubs outfielder Moisés Alou liked his chances of corralling another important out. Even though the ball swung foul, Alou attempted to make a play, scaling the Wrigley Field wall only to have his reach upended by a group of fans who yearned for a souvenir.

Steve Bartman, the most prominent fan, knocked the ball away from Alou, who reacted angrily. When the Marlins erupted to score eight unanswered runs, Bartman had to be ushered out of the ballpark for his own safety. The Cubs' interminable wait continued.

A night after the Marlins clinched their NL crown, 56,279 fans crammed into Yankee Stadium to watch Clemens fight Martínez in Game 7 of the ALCS. A rabid atmosphere engulfed the field, every play greeted with vociferous approval or dejection. A tenser contest was barely imaginable.

After completing his pre-game warm-ups in the Yankee bullpen, Clemens took a trip to Monument Park, where he rubbed the plaque of Babe Ruth for good luck, as if invoking the curse. Such storylines added to the drama, which ebbed and flowed before a stunning crescendo.

Boston drew first blood, touching Clemens for three runs in the second inning. Trot Nixon parked a two-run homer before a throwing error by third baseman Enrique Wilson allowed Jason Varitek to score. Clemens struggled to command his pitches and was replaced by Mike Mussina after just three innings of work. New Yorkers looked at each other confusedly, attempting to deal with the unfamiliar pain of mounting humiliation.

The Red Sox tacked on another run in the fourth as Kevin Millar went deep. The Yankees finally got to Pedro in the fifth and seventh, however, clawing back single runs in each inning to cut their deficit to 4-2. Nevertheless, Martínez pointed to the sky after striking out Soriano to end the seventh, his signature sign-off at the end of each outing. After throwing exactly 100 pitches, Pedro thought his night was done. The whole world thought so, too, except for Red Sox manager Grady Little, who asked Martínez to stay in the game.

When Ortiz homered off David Wells in the eighth, Boston restored its three-run lead. Refocusing on the fly and tuning back into the game after mentally checking out, Pedro got Nick Johnson to pop out leading off the home eighth. The Red Sox were five defensive outs from a trip to the World Series.

The Yankees' comeback started with Jeter, as was so often the case. Derek doubled to right field and was quickly driven in by Bernie Williams, who lined a single up the middle. Boston had multiple relievers warming in the bullpen, Williamson and Mike Timlin ready to replace the tiring Martínez. Meanwhile, southpaw Alan Embree also prepared to possibly face Matsui, a powerful lefty hitter.

With a 5-3 lead, one out and a runner on first in the eighth inning, Little made a trip to the mound, presumably to thank Pedro for his sterling effort and to finally hand the game over to his bullpen. However, after a passionate conversation, Little returned to the dugout, leaving Martínez in the game despite his pitch count sitting at 115.

Matsui ripped a ground-rule double to right, putting runners at second and third for Posada. The recipient of Martínez' taunts earlier in the season, Jorge exacted revenge, lofting a flair to shallow centre field, scoring both runners, tying the score at five and knocking Pedro from the ballgame. Yankee Stadium quaked uncontrollably.

Embree and Timlin managed to tightrope out of danger before a comparatively normal ninth inning passed without incident. Rivera was exceptional in relief, working three masterful innings for New York. Boston mustered just two hits off Rivera, who worked a scoreless ninth, tenth and eleventh with the season on the line. After 48 pitches, his night was likely done, however, placing pressure on the Yankees to pounce, and that is exactly what they did.

An unpredictable knuckleballer, Tim Wakefield retired the Yankees in order in the tenth, earning another inning of work. The Red Sox bullpen had been pretty terrible all season long, so Little's reticence to rely on it was perhaps understandable. Nevertheless, that weakness was eventually exploited as a new hero etched his name in the annals of Yankee greatness.

In the Fox broadcast booth, Joe Buck and Tim McCarver were joined somewhat randomly by Bret Boone, an infielder with the Seattle Mariners. *Aaron* Boone, Bret's younger brother, led off the Yankees' eleventh, a .125 batting average in the ALCS inspiring little confidence.

If broadcasters on radio and television were even slightly late returning from commercial breaks, they would have missed one of the most dramatic moments in baseball history. Wakefield's first pitch was a flat knuckleball that bubbled into the strike zone at 69 mph. Boone almost jumped out of his shoes, swatting the ball high and deep to left field.

Charting a mesmeric contour, kissing the autumnal night sky, the baseball found ground in a chaotic vortex of limbs beyond the outfield wall. That confounding white sphere, arching through the taut playoff din, represented broken hearts and giddy utopia all at once. When eventually it came to rest, trampled by a gyrating ocean of euphoria, the New York Yankees had won the pennant again, while Boston could only mourn another impossible defeat.

Bucky Dent had a modern accomplice. Aaron Boone was the latest effigy of Red Sox heartache, while Grady Little joined Buckner in the Boston house of horrors, another pale ghost in the cramped closet. Everything was different about the 2003 Red Sox, until it was not. Old habits trumped new thinking, and Theo went back to the drawing board as New York went to the big dance.

For the second time in three years, the Yankees lost the 2003 World Series to an expansion team. Led by Josh Beckett, a 23-year-old starlet, the Florida Marlins triumphed in six games over New York, much to the annoyance of Steinbrenner and the Yankee cognoscenti.

A confident flamethrower from Texas, the cradle of power pitchers, Beckett started twice in the World Series, silencing a vaunted New York lineup. In Game 3, Beckett pitched into the eighth inning before the Marlins bullpen blew the game. He returned on short rest to start Game 6, a potential clincher for the upstart Marlins. Ice trickled through his veins.

In the 100th World Series game played at Yankee Stadium, Beckett joined an exclusive echelon of players who have thwarted the evil empire. With 55,773 fans in attendance, the youngster fired a complete game shutout on 107 pitches to secure the world championship. Incredulity bathed New York.

A Yankees lineup featuring Jeter and Williams, Matsui and Posada, Giambi and Soriano mustered just five hits all night. Only two runners progressed beyond first base. The $152 million megateam was beaten by the $49 million 10-year-old, and a crisis brewed on River Avenue.

For the first time since 1964-1976, the Yankees lost in consecutive World Series appearances. After the Boone blast, prolonging Boston's pain, the Fall Classic seemed almost anticlimactic. The Yankees froze in the limelight, frustrating fans who measured success by world championships alone. The competition finally caught up, and even Steinbrenner saw his influence diminished.

In the eight seasons between 1996 and 2003, the Yankees won seven division titles, six American League pennants and four World Series championships. Only in the Bronx could that be considered an underperformance, but Yankee officials rued those missed opportunities, cognisant of the win-now credo governed by the heroes of yesteryear.

According to the stewards of pinstriped greatness, the Yankees should have won six world championships in that span. Losing to the Diamondbacks and Marlins was embarrassing and, therefore, entering the winter of 2003-04, general manager Cashman was forced to double down in pursuit of glory.

The exacting standards of the world's most successful sports team drove him forward, inspiring an offseason of unprecedented domination. If 2003 was explosive, 2004 was cataclysmic. That entire season became a line of demarcation in the advance of modern sports. It became the yardstick by which all future baseball stories were measured.

CHAPTER ELEVEN

2004

The Yankees and Red Sox both lost the final game of their respective seasons in 2003, and a similar sense of failure permeated the Bronx and Boston as October flipped to November.

In the championship-or-bust climate of AL East baseball, both teams were determined to improve over the winter. In fact, they went toe-to-toe for some of the most talented players of a generation, trading blows and plotting for glory. It was Texas hold 'em through a sabermetric prism. Both teams went all-in.

The Red Sox fired Grady Little quicker than you could say *Pedro*, replacing the beleaguered skipper with Terry Francona, whose infectious personality was emblematic of a culture change at Fenway Park. Francona had the bubbly charisma and nimble street smarts to protect his players from external pressure while inspiring them to achieve greatness. He was a breath of fresh air.

Next, Epstein went shopping for an ace to support Martínez at the front of Boston's rotation. Out west, the Diamondbacks toiled through an identity crisis following their radical triumph over the Yankees in 2001. Schilling, one of their two superstar hurlers, was dangled as trade bait as Arizona eyed a rebuild. To the Boston front office, he seemed an ideal conduit to postseason endurance.

Aged 37, Schilling wanted to compete for a couple more world championships before retiring. Accordingly, the salty veteran told Diamondbacks ownership that he would only accept a trade to one of two big market teams: the Philadelphia Phillies or the New York Yankees, ballclubs with rabid fanbases that demanded success. That changed, however, when Epstein and a bunch of Red Sox executives scarified their Thanksgiving plans to visit Schilling at his family home.

Over turkey and football, a deal was agreed. Convinced by Epstein's authentic pursuit of history, Schilling accepted a trade to Boston, agreeing a two-year, $25.5 million contract extension with a third-year option in the process. Schilling milked his role as proposed Red Sox saviour, negotiating a personal bonus of

$2.5 million that would activate if Boston won a championship during his tenure. "I want to be a part of bringing the first World Series in modern history to Boston," the ace said of his seismic cross-country trek. "And hopefully more than one."

After adding an ace, Epstein pursued a closer to fix the chronically challenged Red Sox bullpen. In 2003, Boston tried a closer-by-committee model, following the sabermetric ethos that a team's best reliever should pitch in the most high-impact situations rather than being saved arbitrarily for the ninth inning alone. That experiment ended in disaster, and Epstein was not about to replicate the drama.

Keith Foulke led the American League in saves in 2003, another Billy Beane reclamation project that worked a treat in Oakland. The Red Sox swooped in as Foulke became a free agent, signing him to a three-year contract to rival Mariano Rivera late in tense games against the Yankees.

While Boston fortified its pitching staff, Steinbrenner lost three cornerstones of his own rotation, destabilising the Yankees' reliable core. After winning 21 games in 2003, Pettitte signed with the Astros as a free agent, keen to play closer to his Texas home. Despite announcing his retirement following a 17-win season in 2003, Clemens joined Pettitte in Houston, signing a one-year deal that sparked yet another renaissance for The Rocket. And finally, Wells agreed to free agent terms with San Diego as New York searched for a genuine ace.

Pettitte, Clemens and Wells accounted for 53 of the Yankees' 101 wins in 2003, more than half the team's output. As a dominant triumvirate, albeit one of increasing age, they were never truly replaced, and that created problems down the road for New York.

In particular, the trio had serious acumen in postseason play, possessing the nous to navigate tough lineups. That lack of frontline leadership eventually proved fatal for the Yankees, who ran out of mystique in October.

⚾⚾⚾

The Texas Rangers found themselves in a similar situation to Arizona as the 2004 season rolled into view. Flailing in the

standings and sinking into debt, general manager John Hart
tried to move his own star, much as the Diamondbacks did with
Schilling. However, Alex Rodriguez was in a different orbit
altogether. Trading the prime-age shortstop would alter the
baseball landscape forever.

In seven years with Seattle, A-Rod established himself as one of
the most exhilarating five-tool players in living memory.
Rodriguez won a batting title in 1996, hitting .358. He topped 40
home runs in three successive seasons, becoming a consistent
power threat. And he also stole bases with great efficiency,
joining the exclusive 40-40 club in 1998.

After the 2000 season, Rodriguez became a prized free agent,
eventually signing with Texas, a surprise bidder lurking in the
American League basement. Texas signed A-Rod to a 10-year,
$252 million deal, the most lucrative contract in sports history.
Quite where they expected to find the money, god alone knows,
and panic set in before the ink even dried.

Rodriguez' deal did not just *break* the record for the most
expensive baseball contract of all-time; it *shattered* all previous
contenders. Texas promised A-Rod $63 million more than any
team had ever granted *any* player. In 2001 alone, the Rangers
gave Rodriguez $22 million, a quarter of their entire payroll.
Such an arrangement was deeply unsustainable for a franchise
that went bankrupt within the next decade.

A-Rod spent three seasons in Texas, tearing up the record books
in relative anonymity. He hit 52 home runs with a .318 batting
average in 2001. He *improved* to 57 homers a year later, driving
in 142 runs, before adding a further 47 bombs en route to his
first MVP award in 2003.

From a statistical perspective, Rodriguez was clearly the best
player to emerge from the much-hyped shortstop triad featuring
Jeter and Garciaparra. Between 1997 - the first year all three
guys were big league regulars - and 2003, A-Rod produced 53.4
WAR. Nomar came second at 38.4, with Jeter a close third at
34.8.

In all measurable aspects of the boxscore, Rodriguez was
unchallenged as the best shortstop. Still, Jeter played in six
World Series by 2003, winning four rings. Nomar and A-Rod
only went to seven *postseasons* combined in the same

timeframe, mustering no championships and losing to Jeter's Yankees three times. Derek had an intangible greatness that transcended analytics. He was a predatory winner, and his contemporaries still had a lot to learn in that regard.

Nevertheless, Rodriguez had 345 career round-trippers by the age of 27. That is when Texas surrendered to fiscal logic and sought to move Rodriguez and his paralysing contract. Hart met with A-Rod to discuss a realistic exit strategy. Rodriguez duly supplied a list of teams to which he would accept a trade. The Yankees and Red Sox featured prominently, and Rangers personnel tried to make a connection.

When seeking relief from albatross contracts, most teams turn to the Yankees, a franchise whose gross domestic product dwarfs that of small nations. Hart engaged Cashman in conversations around Rodriguez, but the Yankees had minimal interest. Jeter was their shortstop and their captain. Hell, he was the *face of baseball* entirely, and nothing would erode that stature. The Yankees did not explicitly *need* Rodriguez, so Cashman passed on the opportunity.

After checking New York off his list, Hart moved on to Boston, the second-richest team, discussing A-Rod with Epstein, who saw an opportunity to transform his star-crossed franchise for all eternity. Perhaps not since Babe Ruth himself had such a talented player become available at a prime age. Bringing Alex Rodriguez to Boston would redress the dark karmic forces that conspired to doom the Red Sox for almost a century. Theo knew he had to find a way of making it happen.

Firstly, Boston had to make room for A-Rod, and Epstein worked on multiple deals to reset his roster. In return for Rodriguez, Texas would receive mercurial outfielder Manny Ramírez and Jon Lester, then a 19-year-old pitching prospect, from Boston. Meanwhile, to clear space at shortstop and replace Manny, the Red Sox would send Garciaparra to the White Sox for a package headlined by Magglio Ordóñez, a lively left fielder.

The respective deals were agreed in principle at the 2003 winter meetings in New Orleans. Epstein and Hoyer visited Francona in his hotel room at 03:00 am to show him a mock lineup card featuring Rodriguez, Ordóñez and Ortiz, surely the most devastating combination in baseball. Francona danced around his room semi-naked.

In 2003, Ramírez and Garciaparra combined for 65 home runs, 209 RBI and a .386 OBP. By comparison, Rodriguez and Ordóñez mashed 76 home runs with 217 RBI and a .388 OBP. The likely improvement was subtle but real. In a division decided by fractions, such upgrades were the difference between success and failure. Besides, A-Rod was two years younger than Nomar, whose prime seemed to be over. Adding Rodriguez would therefore extend the Red Sox' window of contention.

Moreover, by most metrics, A-Rod was the best *defensive* shortstop in baseball among qualifiers between 1996 and 2003. In fact, it was not even especially close. According to FanGraphs, Rodriguez had a defensive WAR of 37.9 in those eight seasons before landing on the trade block. The next-best defensive shortstop over that period, Édgar Rentería, only managed a 25.6 mark in the same category. As for Garciaparra? Well, he ranked 18th among qualifiers with a 5.5 defensive WAR. Epstein knew that could be fatal.

Moving Ramírez and Garciaparra also figured to improve the Red Sox' clubhouse culture. Though a distinguished artisan at the plate, Ramírez was unendingly eccentric. He regularly demanded to be traded from Boston, suffering momentary changes of heart after signing a lucrative free agent contract. Meanwhile, Garciaparra grew resentful as the Red Sox found new stars, and the shortstop's ceaseless wrangling over a contract extension became a distracting soap opera.

The blockbuster seemed to be a slam dunk success for Epstein and his team. Even as the New England Patriots compiled a 14-2 record en route to success in Super Bowl XXXVIII, Boston sports fans were preoccupied with the hot stove action emanating from Fenway Park. The hometown club was finally getting even with those damn Yankees, and that was appointment television. Even Millar, an *active player*, said he preferred A-Rod to Nomar when asked during an interview. Loyal fans could barely contain their excitement.

However, Red Sox ownership was not particularly enamoured of A-Rod's contract, which still had seven years and $179 million outstanding. Rather than suck it up and make a commitment to improving its team, Boston tried to renegotiate Rodriguez' deal. That is when things got weird.

A-Rod was willing to accept the trade and restructure his contract so the Red Sox could remain competitive in building a team around him. However, the MLB Players' Association scuppered such a deal, fearing the precedent that might be set by its star member voluntarily reducing his salary.

Major League Baseball duly granted a 72-hour negotiating window in which an agreeable proposition would have to be made. The deal ultimately died as the Red Sox failed to stump up the cash required to acquire Rodriguez. The eventual difference in negotiations was $12 million, less than Boston gave to Byung-Hyun Kim, Ramiro Mendoza, Brian Daubach and Ellis Burks combined in 2004. Epstein was rightly disappointed.

For all intents and purposes, it appeared that A-Rod would remain in Texas, continuing his assault on the record books away from the limelight. Then Aaron Boone decided to play some pickup basketball to alleviate boredom in January 2004, violating his contract. The Yankees' hero third baseman tore his anterior cruciate knee ligament in the process, putting New York in a bind just weeks before spring training.

The Yankees had no backup with experience as a regular third baseman. Utilitymen like Miguel Cairo and Enrique Wilson could man the hot corner in a pinch, but the prospect of defending a pennant with such a deficient infield lacked validity. Yankee management was pissed, and Boone was released from his broken contract.

With a little imagination, Hart sensed an opportunity to re-engage Cashman on Rodriguez, who he foresaw shifting to third base in a hypothetical Yankee infield that would be one of the greatest ever assembled. Texas asked for Alfonso Soriano plus a high-level prospect in return. The Yankees drew up a list of young players they were willing to include in such a deal. Robinson Canó, a future star, was on that list, but the Rangers selected Joaquín Arias, who wound up playing just 474 games in an eight-year big league career. Canó became an eight-time All-Star and two-time Gold Glover with more than 2,500 career hits. Fortune favoured the bold.

With the framework of a trade in place, the Rangers agreed to pay $67 million of A-Rod's remaining salary. Rodriguez, a lover of baseball history, yearned to wear pinstripes in the megawatt metropolis, and he duly accepted a move to third base, deferring to Jeter's reverential status. MLB approved the deal, which was also accepted by the Players' Association. Just like that, Alex Rodriguez was a Yankee.

A lavish press conference was arranged in the Bronx, attended by more than 300 media members. As team captain, Jeter played a rather awkward and contrived role on the stage, helping Rodriguez into a pristine jersey bearing the number 13. "I almost felt like I had one foot in a Red Sox uniform," said A-Rod. Tensions were ramped up a notch in the everlasting rivalry.

Just like Clemens and Boggs, Ruffing and Pennock, Hoyt and Ruth, Alex Rodriguez joined the exclusive club of Red Sox icons embraced by Yankee mystique. Unlike his fellow converters, however, Rodriguez did not even play a single game for the Red Sox before crossing the Rubicon. Once again, Boston disowned a legitimate superstar on the cusp of his prime, and even John Henry was not immune to the virus.

While adding A-Rod and Ordóñez would have represented a considerable upgrade for the Red Sox, replacing Boone with Rodriguez was a *monumental* improvement for the Yankees. According to FanGraphs, A-Rod was worth 9.2 WAR in 2003, whereas Boone weighed in at 2.1 WAR. The Yankees won 101 games *and then* added such a game-changing force. No expense was spared in their pursuit of domination.

For the first time in 90 years, a reigning MVP was traded. The team that picked him up was the reigning American League champion. For Red Sox fans, this was viewed as Babe Ruth 2.0, New York profiting from Boston's profligacy yet again. Losing the pennant in such gut-wrenching fashion was painful enough. Losing Alex Rodriguez to the greedy pinstripes added insult to injury.

⚾⚾⚾

Shaughnessy's curse took on a life of its own after Boone's blast and A-Rod's move to the Bronx. A segment of Red Sox fans glorified their own ineptitude, finding identity in the Jobian prophecy of Boston baseball.

Paul Giorgio, an avid Red Sox fan, sought advice on exorcising the curse from a Buddhist holy man in Tibet. He was told to climb Mount Everest and place a Red Sox cap at the summit while burning a Yankees cap at the base. That is just what Giorgio did.

Elsewhere, father Guido Sarducci, a fictional priest of *Saturday Night Live* fame, was hired to sprinkle holy water on the Green Monster. Former Red Sox pitcher Bill Lee suggested exhuming the body of Ruth and transporting it to Fenway so the team could publicly apoligise for trading him. Even singer Jimmy Buffett devised a comical curse-busting show, bringing a Bambino impersonator onstage with a witch doctor while performing a concert at Fenway.

A musical was produced telling the story of Red Sox futility. Somewhere, Harry Frazee smiled. Divers searched for a piano that Ruth once pushed into a pond in Sudbury, Massachusetts. Apparently, resuscitating a musical instrument was the antidote to decades of sporting futility. One graffiti artist even amended a street sign on Storrow Drive, Boston, so that it read 'Reverse the Curse' rather than 'Reverse Curve.' Beantown was gripped by baseball paranoia.

Every game between the Red Sox and Yankees felt like a monumental clash of cultures. A sellout crowd gathered in Fort Myers for the first rivalry game of 2004, a spring training encounter in the second week of March. Commemorative pin badges sold for $15. Stalls hawked t-shirts saying *I don't brake for Yankee fans*. The Red Sox rejected hundreds of requests for media credentials. The Grapefruit League had never seen anything like it. And, oh yeah, the Yankees won, as they always seemed to do, by a score of 4-0. Seasons change, players come and go, but New York typically emerges on top.

Behind the scenes, life was not all smooth sailing for Joe Torre and his team, however. In fact, the Yankee institution was rocked by unsettling revelations and worrying underperformance. Something was just not right in the Bronx. Cracks were forming in the battleship.

Late in 2003, Jason Giambi and Gary Sheffield, two Yankee sluggers, were implicated by FBI officials investigating the Bay Area Laboratory Co-operative (BALCO), which supplied illegal anabolic steroids to professional athletes. The *San Francisco Chronicle* reported that Giambi and Sheffield obtained performance-enhancing drugs from Greg Anderson, a personal trainer connected to BALCO. Barry Bonds, baseball's single-season home run king, was the headline name atop the BALCO scandal, but the Yankees' brand was sullied, too.

A federal investigation was launched into doping throughout professional sports. According to the *Chronicle*, in his grand jury testimony, Giambi admitted to using several different steroids during the winter months between 2001 and 2003. He also admitted injecting himself with human growth hormone, believed to enhance muscle-twitch reflexes and, by extension, to aid performance at the plate.

While Giambi later made a public apology to baseball fans around the world, Sheffield pleaded ignorance with regard to his own alleged transgressions. Sheffield admitted using a testosterone-based cream supplied by Bonds while the pair trained together, but he insisted that he did not know it was an illegal steroid at the time.

In the absence of drug testing, a steroid wildfire ripped through baseball in the late-1990s and early-2000s. Mark McGwire relied on chemical enhancement to top Maris' illustrious single season home run record, just as Bonds likely injected his way past Big Mac. The MLB Players' Association had little historical interest in agreeing to the random drug testing of its members, but the whispers rolled into vociferous protests in 2003, threatening a public relations meltdown.

Accordingly, sparse testing was rolled out without attached punishments. At this time, baseball viewed steroid abuse more as a lifestyle problem than as a scurrilous illegality. Not until the BALCO boys entered court was heat truly applied. A deal was agreed to roll out experimental urine testing for banned steroids in 2003 and 2004. If more than 5% of tests returned positive in either year, penalties would be introduced immediately.

During the 2003 season, MLB said that between five and seven percent of 1,438 anonymous tests were positive, triggering the penalty structure for real. Years later, the *New York Times* reported that David Ortiz and Manny Ramírez were among those who tested positive, eroding any moral high ground Red Sox Nation felt it had. Indeed, the most intense chapters of this storied rivalry coincided with baseball's steroid shame, and that can never be ignored.

A former Yankee *and* Red Sock, José Canseco published *Juiced* in 2005, and his autobiography-turned-expose blew the lid off illegal performance enhancement in baseball. Bitter at the demise of his promising career, Canseco luxuriated in a self-styled role as the steroid king of MLB. José took personal credit for introducing scores of teammates to PEDs, sharing scandalous anecdotes about injecting teammates in stadiums across the league.

Canseco outed McGwire, Giambi and Rafael Palmeiro as steroids cheats, while accusing Roger Clemens and other legends of his generation. Iván Rodríguez and Juan González were also mentioned by Canseco in relation to doping, shattering the game and sparking major upheaval.

The dust had barely settled on Canseco's bombshell when *Chronicle* journalists Mark Fainaru-Wada and Lance Williams published their own book, *Game of Shadows*, detailing the BALCO years and baseball's wider steroid shame. The original news-breakers expanded their investigation and presented damning evidence of cheating by Bonds, Sheffield, Giambi, Benito Santiago and athletes from other sports.

Former Senator George Mitchell was commissioned to investigate the use of performance-enhancing drugs in MLB, and when finally delivered in 2007, his damning report later implicated players on either side of the Yankees-Red Sox divide, including Clemens, Canseco, Pettitte, Justice, Knoblauch, Vaughn, Kevin Brown and Éric Gagne.

However, Mitchell was an active director of the Red Sox at the time of his involvement, immediately undermining the authenticity of his investigation. The Yankees almost became the focus of his report, whether by design or through coincidence, and there was always a pang of hypocrisy to the way Yankee cheaters were vilified yet Red Sox dopers became airbrushed media darlings.

Much of the steroid fiasco was in the future, though, as the 2004 season began. Giambi and Sheffield were jeered lustily, and rightfully so, but of greater consequence to Torre was the way in which his team flopped out of the gate. The traditional Yankee lustre was nowhere to be seen.

Boston won six of the first seven games against New York in 2004, dropping the Yankees to 8-11 in late-April. A-Rod was underwhelming, driving in just seven runs in his first 23 games. The Yankee pitching rotation looked old and inadequate with no discernible ace. And even the omnipotent Jeter was booed at Yankee Stadium amid a torrid 0-for-32 slump, the worst of his career.

The addition of Rodriguez seemed to alter the Yankee dogma of yesteryear. Here was a guy accustomed to playing for himself, padding out statistics in the American League cellar. The Yankees' dynasty was fashioned in an entirely different style, with veteran altruism trumping individual egotism. New York rued the retirement of veteran stalwarts like O'Neill, Tino and Cone. Meanwhile, the frosty relationship between Rodriguez and Jeter did little to help team chemistry.

By comparison, the Red Sox coalesced into an eccentric bunch of free-spirited grinders, anathema in every way to the Yankee corporation. In contrast to Grady Little's authoritarian approach, and to Torre's stiff grandiosity, Francona embraced the looseness of his clubhouse, which united across cultural divides using elaborate hairstyles that jarred with the Yankees' strict facial hair policy.

Johnny Damon had a Jesus-like mane. Bronson Arroyo sported blonde cornrows. Manny grew dreadlocks and Ortiz unleashed an afro. Millar attempted a goatee, Gabe Kapler shaved his head entirely, and Pedro hid behind the most dreadful Jheri curls of his career. "We are not the cowboys anymore," said Damon, the apparent leader of this bearded rabble. "We are just the idiots this year."

And, just like that, the Boston Red Sox became the team of blue-collar dreamers around the world. A tone was set, and this became more than baseball. This was good against evil, wealth against effort, interns against ownership. Something changed when Alex Rodriguez wound up in pinstripes. It sparked a rebellion that cracked the code for Boston, one battle at a time.

As summer approached, Boston slumped terribly, playing awful defence amid a disastrous June swoon. Through 75 games, Millar made five errors, splitting time between first base and right field. Mueller was even worse at third, committing seven errors as the Red Sox butchered their own efficiency. Fighting fires, New York also found its stride and managed to edge ahead. Natural order was apparently restored in the AL East, and traditional fatalism simmered through Red Sox Nation.

The teams' contrasting fortunes clashed symbolically at Yankee Stadium on 1st July 2004. A lengthy war unfurled on the sacred turf as the Yankees and Red Sox were locked at 3-3 through nine innings. With each torturous out, the game took on new meaning, as if setting the tone for drama to come.

In the top of the twelfth, Boston advanced a runner to third base with two outs, threatening to eke ahead. Tanyon Sturtze pitched to Trot Nixon, and the Yankees needed a jolt of inspiration. Jeter, their superlative captain, rose to the occasion yet again.

When Nixon sliced a pop fly down the left field line, Jeter ran from his shortstop domain with carefree abandon, tracking the ball with selfless intent. After ranging far from his natural territory, Jeter caught the ball before it landed in foul ground, a stunning play of incredible determination.

Propelled by momentum, Jeter tumbled over the perimeter wall and crashed into the stands, colliding with hard seats and a sea of bodies. Yankee Stadium erupted with approval, inspired by the competitive instinct of Number 2.

Jeter emerged from the stands battered, bruised and bloodied. A gash formed under his right eye, the symbol of a warrior willing to do anything for the betterment of his team. In stark contrast, the television cameras sought Garciaparra, Boston's own shortstop, sat passively on the Red Sox bench, injured and disconnected from his ballclub. The dichotomy was startling.

Boston notched a run in the thirteenth, but the Yankees responded with two shortly thereafter, backup catcher John Flaherty cranking a walk-off single to immortalise Jeter's play as a rabble-rousing signature. Conversely, Garciaparra morphed into a pantomime villain, frequent injuries and unshakeable obstinance making him a pariah on the 2004 Red Sox. Baseball's shortstop trinity had its first premature casualty.

In relentless fashion, the Yankees grasped divisional supremacy and kept pulling away, claiming a seven-game lead by the All-Star break. When the season resumed after the midsummer festivities, New York extended its advantage to nine-and-a-half games over Boston as Red Sox fans lit up talk radio with epic rants about their team's apparent failure to meet expectations.

Under pressure, the Red Sox became determined to avoid humiliation and minimise embarrassment more than anything else. After a promising 17-8 start, Boston went 35-36 in its next 71 games, culminating in another defeat to the Yankees on 23rd July. They remained more than a converted touchdown out of first place.

Everything changed on 24th July, however, as Red Sox history reached a turning point. Ominous weather swept through Boston, delaying the latest rivalry duel by an hour. Red Sox executives wanted to postpone the game, citing a likely slump at the turnstiles, but senior Boston players were adamant that the contest would be played. They were tired of losing to the Yankees and sick of chasing their own shadows. The time had come for genuine change.

Arroyo got the ball for Boston against Sturtze for New York. The Yankees took an early lead, as they always seemed to do, before Arroyo drilled Rodriguez with a pitch in the third inning. Rightfully pissed, A-Rod voiced his displeasure to the rookie hurler as he walked towards first base, barking "fuck you" at Arroyo.

Jason Varitek, the Red Sox' gritty catcher, intervened in the war of words, stepping into Rodriguez' space. "We don't throw at .260 hitters," Varitek allegedly explained to the Yankees' star. A-Rod duly beckoned Varitek to take a swipe and, as any serious Yankees fan will tell you, the Red Sox captain refused to take off his mask in a rather cowardly mismatch.

Nevertheless, Varitek stuffed his mitt into A-Rod's face, an iconic vignette of the ancient power struggle between Boston and New York. A mass brawl engulfed the field as pent-up tension erupted. Punches were thrown and shoves were exchanged. In particular, Red Sox hatred for the Yankee establishment was clear for all to see.

Rodriguez and Varitek were ejected from the game. Arroyo somehow stayed on the mound, pitching into the middle innings. The Yankees eventually knocked him out in a six-run sixth, taking a 9-4 lead, before Boston mounted a valiant comeback.

The Red Sox scored four in their sixth before New York tacked on an insurance run. When Rivera took the ball with a 10-8 lead in the ninth, the game's conclusion seemed cliché. However, Boston found new reserves of faith deep within, and something changed in the city's approach.

Drinking in the last chance saloon, Nomar doubled to lead off the ninth before Nixon flew out. Millar laced an RBI single to right, making it a one-run game, before Mueller cranked a two-run, walk-off homer into the Red Sox' bullpen. A different noise emanated from Fenway Park. This was the start of something special.

Before surrendering that bomb to Mueller, Rivera had faced 320 Red Sox batters over 10 years, including postseason play. Only three of those plate appearances - 0.9% - had resulted in a home run. Boston *had* beaten Rivera before, but never in such emphatic fashion. Every time they faced Mariano, it was a merciless grind and a humiliating war, so to finally hang a significant blown save on the legendary closer was transformative. It was the moment Boston knew it could beat *anybody*.

Harnessing the momentum, Epstein went all-in, pushing every chip he had to the centre of the table. Moments before the 31st July trade deadline, Boston executed two trades that altered the course of baseball history, fixing flaws on its roster before they became fatal. Epstein traded minor leaguer Henri Stanley to the Dodgers for outfielder Dave Roberts, improving his bench. The major move, though, was a severing of ties with Garciaparra.

Brave and fearless, Epstein pulled the trigger on an elaborate four-team deal that sent Nomar and prospect Matt Murton to the Cubs. Boston's return was underwhelming for a star-hungry fanbase: Doug Mientkiewicz from Minnesota and Orlando Cabrera from Montreal. Talk radio imploded, and Epstein was on the hot seat.

While unsexy, when viewed through a sabermetric prism, adding Roberts, Mientkiewicz and Cabrera solved two major deficiencies in the Red Sox' ecosystem: speed and defence, those old familiar defects. Mientkiewicz was a gold glover at first base, a veritable picking machine, while Cabrera won the same accolade at shortstop for his slick-fielding athleticism. A veteran speedster, Roberts had topped 40 stolen bases in consecutive seasons, and his smallball acumen gave Boston a new dimension.

Though complicated for more traditional fans to decipher, these were modern moves by a progressive general manager who mastered the correlation between statistics and scouting. Roberts, Mientkiewicz and Cabrera also improved the clubhouse culture at Fenway, replacing the poisonous individuality of Garciaparra with a team-centric gusto that burnished the Sox' intent.

Garciappara was undoubtedly one of the greatest players of his era. He gave the Red Sox nine great years, notching 1,281 hits, 178 home runs, a .323 batting average and a .370 OBP. A five-time All-Star with Boston, Nomar won two batting titles and became the team's most beloved hero since Ted Williams.

Between 1996, his debut year, and 2003, his Boston swansong, Garciappara logged 38.5 wins above replacement. Only 15 players in the major leagues performed better across that span. At least eight of those guys were later implicated in steroid scandals, illustrating the outstanding magnitude of Nomar's pure skill.

"We lost a great player, but we made our club more functional," said Epstein in a press call after the deadline day trade. "We were not going to win a World Series with our defence."

For once, logic prevailed in the Red Sox' front office. Marrying data and clubhouse intelligence, Theo made moves that would have frightened his predecessors. By doing so, he gave Boston the best possible chance to win.

In repost, the Yankees chased Randy Johnson, who was shopped at the deadline by a flailing Arizona. When the asking price was too steep even for New York, Cashman acquired Esteban Loaiza from the White Sox instead. José Contreras - the guy who once made Epstein trash his hotel room - went to Chicago in exchange, an expensive bust in the unfolding drama.

Loaiza was atrocious with the Yankees, sporting an 8.50 ERA in six starts before being banished to the bullpen. Indeed, after failing to replace Clemens, Pettitte and Wells, New York had a dismal rotation that threatened to derail its progress. Javier Vazquez ended the season with a 4.91 ERA. Jon Lieber had a 4.33 mark. Mike Mussina was at 4.59 and Kevin Brown looked semi-respectable at 4.09. Only Orlando Hernández finished the season with a sub-4.00 ERA, putting tremendous pressure on the Yankees' offence.

Holes began to appear on that side of the ball, too, as injuries and age crept up on New York. Giambi missed time with a benign tumour and was not the same player upon his return. A slew of mundane veterans filled the black hole at first base, including John Olerud, Tony Clark and Travis Lee, while utility players like Cairo, Wilson, Rubén Sierra and Kenny Lofton played a little too much than was originally planned.

Still, the Yankees held on to a dwindling lead in the AL East, finding ways to win when it mattered most. This was a creaking cruise liner about to sink, though, and Captain Jeter and shipmate A-Rod could only quell the tide for so long. Choppy waters tested pinstriped resolve, and the pressure became unbearable.

⚾⚾⚾

On 31st August 2004, during a game against Anaheim, Manny Ramírez cranked a foul ball down the right field line at Fenway, where it smashed into the mouth of Lee Gavin, a 16-year-old boy sat in Section 9, Box 95, Row AA. Gavin lost two teeth thanks to the Ramírez rocket, leaving the ballpark in an ambulance.

Reporters soon discovered that Gavin - one of 35,040 people in attendance - lived in a Sudbury farmhouse that once belonged to Babe Ruth. Yes, the same farmhouse where Ruth once tipped the aforementioned piano into a pond. This was a yarn ripped straight from the Shaughnessian playbook of contrived deduction, and the media lapped it up.

That very night, the Yankees lost 22-0 to Cleveland, the worst defeat in franchise history. Some claimed the curse was broken right there, the bloodied face of a kid who lived in the Bambino's crib symbolic of Boston's resurgence. However, despite drawing close, the Red Sox could not topple the Yankees, who won 101 games *in a down year* to clinch the division. Boston dominated the wildcard race yet again, underlining the exceptional *otherness* of these distinct powerhouses. They were above and beyond every other franchise.

Nevertheless, within that exclusive fight, Boston still felt a sense of powerlessness in the face of Yankee omnipotence. "What can I say?" a bedraggled Pedro once thought aloud. "I just tip my hat and call the Yankees my daddy." The scene was duly set for another October battle.

Boston swept Anaheim in the 2004 ALDS, a two-run, walk-off, series-clinching home run from Ortiz setting the tone for future heroics. Meanwhile, the Yankees had little trouble defeating Minnesota in their own first round matchup, clinching in four games as Rodriguez and Matsui came alive with batting averages over .400.

After fighting their way through 19 regular season games like Rocky Balboa and Ivan Drago, the Red Sox and Yankees duly assembled for another tilt at the pennant. Twelve months after Little's brain cramp and Boone's blast, Boston and New York renewed hostilities for a trip to the World Series. The symmetry was poetic.

With Yankee Stadium crying out for an ace, Mussina opposed Schilling in Game 1, pitching a perfect game through six innings. Down 8-0, Boston jumped all over Mussina in the seventh and edged within one run in the eighth, only for Bernie Williams to lash a two-run double that put the game beyond the Red Sox' reach. Midway through the contest, Mariano Rivera returned from a family funeral in Panama, rushing from the airport to the bullpen. He later recorded an emotional four-out save as the Yankees won, 10-7.

Game 2 was an unlikely pitching duel between Martínez and Lieber, a 34-year-old veteran who stunk in the regular season.

The Yankees scored in the first on a Sheffield single before Lieber blanked Boston for seven innings, yielding just three hits and one run. Martínez coughed up a two-run homer to Olerud in the sixth, from which the Red Sox never recovered, losing 3-1 and falling into a two-game hole.

If the first two contests were disappointing, Game 3 was downright *humiliating* for Boston, whose season was placed on life support in degrading fashion. The Yankees scored 19 runs on 22 hits at Fenway, establishing a new postseason record in their remarkable history. There seemed no end to the vicious bullying.

Rodriguez went 3-for-5 with a home run. Matsui went 5-for-6 with *two home runs.* Bernie went 4-for-6 with three RBI. The famous green scoreboard rotated with tiring predictability as demeaning New York chants punctuated the night. The final score was 19-8, Yankees. Boston was dead. The funeral was scheduled for the following day.

In the history of Major League Baseball, no team had ever recovered from a 3-0 deficit to win a postseason series. Across the four major North American sports, such a comeback had occurred just twice, accomplished by the 1942 Toronto Maple Leafs and the 1975 New York Islanders of the NHL, respectively. The 2004 Boston Red Sox appeared to lack the energy, ability and fortitude to join that exclusive group. There was little tangible *hope* of a priceless resurrection.

After decades of defeat and years of persecution at the hands of New York, Game 3 of the 2004 ALCS was the final straw for some Red Sox fans. After Ruth and Dent, Buckner and Boggs, Clemens and Boone, Contreras and A-Rod, a 19-8 playoff loss *at home* represented the ultimate nadir. Boston seemed utterly powerless to the march of Yankee domination. The Red Sox ran out of ideas.

"Might as well have been 19-18," wrote Shaughnessy in the *Boston Globe,* making one last reference to Ruth before the season reached a merciless conclusion. "For the 86th consecutive autumn, the Red Sox are not going to win the World Series."

Shaughnessy engaged in conversation with Millar during batting practice on the Fenway field prior to Game 4, a likely Yankee clincher. Millar took exception to Shaughnessy's branding the

Red Sox as "embarrassing," unleashing a famous soliloquy that became a rallying cry for the entire team. "What's embarrassing?" asked Millar. "It happens. It's baseball. But let me tell you: don't let us win today. We got Pedro going tomorrow, Schilling the next night, and anything can happen in a Game Seven."

Millar be damned, the Yankees kept rolling towards their destiny. Facing Derek Lowe, Rodriguez clubbed a two-run homer in the third inning of Game 4, hauling his team ahead. The Red Sox fought back to take a 3-2 lead but immediately coughed it up, Williams and Clark delivering key hits to put the Yankees ahead, 4-3.

New York guarded that lead before passing the game to Rivera for a potential six-out save. When The Sandman navigated his way past Ramírez, Ortiz, Varitek and Nixon in the eighth, the Yankees were three defensive outs away from winning a seventh pennant in nine years. They were three outs away from vanquishing the Red Sox amid their greatest hype for a generation, extinguishing once and for all any notion of AL East equality.

More people had walked on the moon than had scored an earned run off Rivera in the postseason. The Red Sox viewed that almost as a personal challenge, coming alive at the last possible moment. They were determined to make a statement, and that meant beating the world's most formidable pitcher in the process.

Leading off the home ninth, Millar worked a five-pitch walk as Fenway throbbed with tension. Dave Roberts, the bit-part speedster acquired at the trade deadline, replaced Millar as a pinch-runner and promptly stole second base by a hair, creating a huge swing in momentum towards Boston. Rivera appeared distracted, and Mueller - his personal kryptonite - thumped a single up the middle that sent the closer sprawling across the mound. Roberts rounded third and scored the tying run, suspending the Yankees' celebrations.

Rivera worked around further danger to send Game 4 into extra innings. Neither team mustered a run in the tenth or eleventh, and the Yankees went quietly to open the twelfth. The clock ticked past 01:00 am in Boston as Ortiz trudged from the dugout for his sixth plate appearance of the night. Ramírez stood on first after greeting pitcher Paul Quantrill with a base hit. An exhausted crowd begged for mercy. Red Sox Nation yearned to fight another day.

Quantrill struggled to find the plate, running the count to two balls and one strike on Ortiz. His fourth offering, an 88-mph fastball, tailed into the wheelhouse of Boston's definitive slugger. Ortiz uncoiled and hammered the baseball to right field, far and deep. Sheffield gave chase, but the ball landed in the Yankees' bullpen, a two-run, walk-off blast that averted a sweep.

Even well after midnight, Fenway was full to the brim with hopeful romantics. The stands pulsed with relief and jubilation as Ortiz was mobbed by his teammates at home plate. *Dirty Water*, the Red Sox' victory song, rocked through the public address system. Boston was not dead after all. Certainly not yet, and perhaps not *ever*. The Red Sox toppled the greatest closer who ever lived to extend their shot at glory. A whole new series opened up before them.

A duel between Martínez and Mussina, Game 5 started at 17:11 pm local time on a Monday evening, barely 16 hours after the end of Game 4. America was engrossed by the emerging storyline, and baseball fans around the world tuned in to see if Boston could delay its own funeral yet again.

Remarkably, the fifth game was longer, in time and innings played, than the marathon contest ended by Ortiz' homer. Each team used seven pitchers, who laboured for almost six hours in a game of unending intrigue. Adrenaline replaced energy at the extremes of sporting exertion.

Boston scored twice in the first inning of Game 5. Ortiz laced an RBI single to right field, picking up where he left off earlier that morning. New York chipped away in the second and went ahead, 4-2, in the sixth on a three-run double by Jeter, but Boston would not check out.

Leading off the home eighth, once again six outs from elimination, Ortiz skied a prodigious home run off Tom Gordon, trimming the deficit to 4-3. Millar followed with another walk and Nixon singled to centre field, putting runners at first and third with a raucous crowd sensing drama.

Torre turned to Rivera again in his timeless October tic, but Marino yielded a sacrifice fly to Varitek, tying the game. For the second consecutive night, the invincible closer blew a crucial save, although this disaster was largely authored by Gordon, a former Red Sock. Noted Sox fan Stephen King once wrote a novel called *The Girl Who Loved Tom Gordon*. The crowd at Fenway loved him more than ever, though, as a glimmer of hope presented itself.

Foulke recorded two quick outs in the Yankee ninth before walking Sierra. Clark then thwacked a 1-2 pitch down the right field line, destined for trouble. Sierra raced around the bases, heading for home as Kapler prepared to field the ball, which took a wicked bounce and landed over the wall for a ground-rule double. Sierra had to stop at third base, his likely run a figment of Bronx imagination. Foulke induced a foul popup from Cairo to stop the threat and maintain the 4-4 tie. These things did not usually happen to the Boston Red Sox.

Neither team threatened much after that until the bottom of the fourteenth inning. Wild and worrying, Loaiza sandwiched two walks around two swinging strikeouts in that frame, facing Ortiz with Damon on second and Ramírez on first. As the clock struck 11:00 pm, the Yankees and Red Sox had spent 11 of their previous 27 waking hours locked in mortal combat on the Fenway diamond. These guys were sick of the sight of each other, and Ortiz once again took matters into his own hands.

Loaiza laboured mightily against a formidable rival, throwing nine pitches, six of which were fouled off heroically. His tenth pitch, high and tight, was difficult to hit, but Ortiz found a way, *any* way, of making contact. Big Papi fought off the fastball, straining every sinew to dump a flair into centre field. Damon scored the winning run on a second straight walk-off from Ortiz. "He can keep on running to New York," barked Joe Buck on the Fox broadcast. "Game Six, tomorrow night."

Disbelief infused Fenway Park, whose denizens were shocked at the Yankee capitulation occurring before their very eyes. Boston stayed alive, almost inexplicably, as the series shifted cities. Pressure mounted on the Bronx Bombers, whose cabal of stars resembled a black hole of unfulfilled promise. The winningest franchise in sports contemplated the most unlikely defeat of all-time.

In pre-series media briefings, Schilling made headlines with anti-Yankee barbs and grandiose self-promotion. "I'm not sure I can think of any scenario more enjoyable than making 55,000 people from New York shut up," said the Red Sox' ace. In Game 6, he got another chance to do just that, and millions watched on with bated breath.

However, Schilling was hobbled by a torn tendon sheath in his right ankle that caused intense pain as he drove from the mound towards home plate in his delivery. The injury occurred in the ALDS and contributed to a sub-par outing in Game 1 against the Yankees. That old New England staple of dread and doubt crept in once again, and diehards wondered whether they were just being teed up for the Red Sox' annual implosion.

Schilling was in trouble, but his promise to bring a world championship to Boston loomed large against the October sky. Nothing would stop him pitching in an elimination game before a vociferous Yankee Stadium crowd with a chance to even the series. Schilling turned to experimental surgery in a bid to take the mound, pushing the boundaries of modern physiology.

Dr William Morgan, team doctor for the Red Sox, devised an elaborate procedure to stabilise the peroneus brevis tendon, which moved untethered over the lateral malleolus, creating severe pain when Schilling pitched. By placing three sutures through the skin, acting as a pathway to the tendon, Dr Morgan found that he could create a temporary barrier that would allow Schilling to pitch. Never before had a small human tendon been the subject of so many prayers.

The procedure had never been attempted before, and Morgan practiced hastily on a cadaver. Schilling went under the knife 30 hours before his potential Game 6 start. The Red Sox were still down 3-1 in the series at that point, on the cusp of probable elimination, but Schilling put his body on the line, nevertheless. Stitched up and stiff, the workhorse found a way to pitch following Ortiz' heroics. Then he went out onto the most sacred diamond of all and hurled the game of his life.

Schilling threw seven innings of one-run ball, gritting his teeth and relying on pure heart and instinct. The Yankees struck out just four times against Schilling, who struggled to generate maximum velocity, but the sheer depth of his yearning was truly transformative. Schilling got by with fire and brimstone, carrying the dreams of a Nation on his shoulders.

Varitek came through with a two-out RBI single in the fourth, opening the scoring, before unsung second baseman Mark Bellhorn lofted a fly ball to left field with two runners aboard. A fan in the bleachers attempted to catch the ball, which fell back onto the field. Umpire Jim Joyce missed the interference and signalled that the ball was still in play. Francona ran onto the field to challenge the call, which was eventually overturned after the umpires huddled for a discussion. Just like that, Bellhorn had a storybook home run and the Red Sox had a 4-0 lead. This suddenly felt like their year.

In previous eras, dominated by the curse, such calls would not have been overturned. Shaughnessy seemed destined to write a column lamenting the blown call that cost Boston a run as New York won by the thinnest margin. However, the kismet of this prolonged rivalry was shifting. For the first time in generations, perhaps *forever*, the Red Sox had genuine momentum against their nemesis. Pinstriped panic set in.

Schilling gave up a solo shot to Williams in the seventh, nudging the score to 4-1, but he recovered to finish the inning smartly. As the stitches in his ankle came undone through the repetitive force of pitching, blood poured through Schilling's sock. This became an iconic symbol of Boston's determination, a literal red sock bleeding with the hopes, dreams and determination of New England. Television cameras zoomed in on Schilling's butchered ankle, crafting his legacy as the ultimate baseball warrior.

By contrast, the Yankees grew desperate, sensing impending disaster and attempting wildly to halt its progress. Jeter doubled home Cairo in the eighth as a rally formed against Arroyo, pitching in relief of Schilling. However, another overturned call confirmed the Red Sox' apparent destiny.

Alex Rodriguez came to the plate as the tying run, Yankee Stadium pleading nervously for salvation. A-Rod hit a slow roller up the first base line, drawing Millar off the bag while Arroyo fielded the ball awkwardly. Attempting to avoid an inevitable tag, Rodriguez swiped at Arroyo's glove, knocking the ball loose into foul territory. Jeter scored and Rodriguez moved to second.

However, once again, Francona emerged from the dugout, fighting for his team. The contrast to Grady Little was chilling. A number of Red Sox players were confused as to how Rodriguez was called safe when his transgression was so obvious. Francona encouraged the umpires to huddle once again, and they subsequently reversed the call, wiping a run from the scoreboard and calling Rodriguez out.

Apoplectic and indignant, the Yankee Stadium crowd erupted viciously. Fans threw baseballs and garbage onto the field as Francona waved his players into the dugout. Riot police were drafted in and perched on the field to restore order. A cacophony of boos rained down in the Bronx as baseball's ancient ecosystem of success was brutally dismantled.

There was lyrical symmetry to the fact that Rodriguez, one of the brightest stars in baseball, resorted to cheating in order to compete with the team he almost joined. The sight of his feigned incredulity gave America a prescient insight into A-Rod's immorality, while the whiny protests of Joe Torre spoke to a $182 million baseball team that ran out of power.

Arroyo retired Sheffield to finish the eighth before Foulke worked around two walks to lock down the win. The 26th team in baseball postseason history to face a 3-0 series deficit, Boston became the first to force a Game 7. The chasm was erased, the inferiority crushed. One game remained. A game for all time.

⚾⚾⚾

Including overhyped spring training exhibitions, the Yankees and Red Sox had played 55 games in the 20 months between March 2003 and October 2004. For the second time in the same timeframe, the 56th game would also decide the winner of the American League pennant. Out of ideas, the Yankees called on Bucky Dent to throw out the ceremonial first pitch before the 2004 decider, hoping to summon the curse. Mystique and aura were dead, and New York relied on mythical ghosts for preservation.

Prior to Game 6, a group of Red Sox players drank small shots of Jack Daniel's whiskey in a symbolic bonding exercise. The trend continued before Game 7. They had come too far to throw the series away, even by their own morbid standards, so no ritual was off limits. Ortiz cranked a two-run homer in the first and Damon skied a grand slam in the second, gifting Boston an oxymoronic 6-0 lead it would never relinquish. Apparently, they were not too drunk, after all. Meanwhile, the Bronx readied itself for a monumental hangover.

Perhaps The Babe himself, cold beyond the grave, would have been more use than the frozen Yankee stars in Game 7. Jeter, Rodriguez and Sheffield mustered one measly single in 12 combined at-bats as Lowe pitched six stellar innings for Boston. New York approached its nadir.

The Yankees scored a run in the third and two in the seventh, but the Red Sox tacked on two in the fourth and single runs in the eighth and ninth to master their own destiny. Damon went deep again and wound up with 6 RBI on the night, etching his name deeper into Boston sports history. The serene progression of Game 7 belied the city's psychology.

When Embree induced a ground ball from Sierra shortly after midnight, braggadocious second baseman Pokey Reese fired the ball to Mientkiewicz, who recorded the final out. The Boston Red Sox won, 10-3, clinching the American League pennant and completing the greatest comeback in the history of sports.

So often celebrated as champions, the New York Yankees looked on in stunned disbelief, the biggest chokers in the annals of baseball history. Goliath ran out of time, magic and strength while David, embodied by the eponymous Ortiz, ascended to hardball heaven. It was the only fitting way for Boston to master the formula, by humiliating New York simultaneously. Most devout rooters could scarcely believe their eyes.

In a display of timeless class, the first thing Torre did after returning to his office was place a call to the visiting clubhouse, where he asked to speak with Wakefield, the scapegoat of yesteryear. "I'm happy for you," Torre said, magnanimous in defeat. "You deserve this. Good things happen to good people."

Indeed, over 75,000 of those people spilled onto the streets of Boston to celebrate the Red Sox' triumph over the Yankees. It would not have been the same had Boston beat Minnesota, say, or Tampa. These were the *New York Yankees*, the schoolyard bully, and they had just been shamed before a global audience.

"Forevermore, the date goes down in the New England calendar as an official no school, no work, no mail delivery holiday in Red Sox Nation," wrote Dan Shaughnessy in his Game 7 recap. "Mark it down. Oct. 20. It will always be the day Sox citizens were liberated from eight decades of torment and torture at the hands of the Yankees and their fans. Boston baseball's Bastille Day."

Indeed, back in Beantown, an impromptu party took shape in the early hours of an immortal morning. A small contingent of fans became unruly and overzealous, damaging property and overturning cars. Attempting to disperse the crowd, Boston police fired a pepper spray projectile into the mob, striking 21-year-old journalism student Victoria Snelgrove in the eye. Snelgrove began to bleed excessively as ambulances struggled to navigate the baying crowds. She died 12 hours later in hospital.

The Boston Police Department accepted full responsibility for Snelgrove's death. An autopsy stated that the projectile opened a three-quarter-inch hole in the bone behind her eye, breaking it into nine pieces and ultimately damaging the brain. Baseball barely mattered in the context of such a tragedy, but the Red Sox honoured Snelgrove's legacy by bringing home the elusive title for which she hungered.

⚾⚾⚾

From a position of retrospect, the 2004 World Series is typically dismissed as a foregone conclusion, a mere add-on for the rampant Red Sox. However, the National League champion St Louis Cardinals were a formidable foe, and of course they thwarted Boston in 1946 and 1967, creating historic anxiety for Red Sox Nation.

During the 2004 regular season, St Louis won 105 games, seven more than Boston. Managed by Tony La Russa, the Cardinals possessed a thunderous lineup led by Albert Pujols, who hit .331 with 46 home runs and 123 RBI. Jim Edmonds also topped 40 bombs, while Scott Rolen, Édgar Rentería and Reggie Sanders added depth to a multifaceted offence.

Nevertheless, Boston appeared irrepressible, rolling to a monumental sweep almost inexorably. The 100th World Series of all-time was a poetic mismatch, and another annoying ghoul was excommunicated from The Hub.

The Red Sox outscored the Cardinals 24-12 and outhit them 39-24. Boston even made four errors in each of the first two games, contrary to Epstein's defensive plan, but the Red Sox seemed invincible, winning where previously they would have lost.

Ortiz, Damon and Bellhorn all hit further home runs against St Louis, adding to their October canon, while Mueller got on base more often than he made out in the Fall Classic. Ramírez had a .500 OBP, too, eventually winning series MVP honours from a pool of worthy candidates.

In contrast, the fearsome trio of Pujols, Rolen and Edmonds managed just six hits and one RBI in 45 Series at-bats. St Louis hit .190 as a team throughout the World Series and managed just two home runs in four games, both by Larry Walker. The redbirds had their wings clipped, and there was little recourse to positivity therefrom.

On 23rd October 2004, a crisp Saturday night, Carl Yastrzemski threw out the ceremonial first pitch as Fenway hosted its first World Series game in 18 years. Boston's starter for Game 1? Why, Tim Wakefield, of course. Just 373 days after crying at his Yankee Stadium locker, everyone's favourite knuckleballer was back on top of the world. The Red Sox won a slugfest, 11-9, prolonging their autumnal dream.

Stitched up and pumped with antibiotics, Schilling answered the call once again in Game 2, hobbling to the mound and giving Francona six courageous innings of four-hit ball. Cabrera, Varitek and Bellhorn came up clutch, knocking in all of the runs in a 6-2 Red Sox victory. With two wins down and two to go, Boston could smell redemption. This time, it would not be denied.

Prior to Game 3, Stan Musial threw out the first pitch at Busch Stadium, a moving moment for John Henry, who worshipped The Man during his pomp. For once unperturbed by such ghosts of heartbreaks past, Martínez threw seven shutout innings, striking out six Cardinals and allowing just three hits. Manny backed his fellow Dominican with a memorable home run, and Boston closed out a 4-1 victory, secured the most important win of Pedro's career.

Quite remarkably, after 86 years of ardent misfortune and last-gasp capitulation, the Boston Red Sox never trailed once throughout the entire 2004 World Series. Game 4, the fateful clincher, was played on 28th October beneath a lunar eclipse at Busch. A crimson moon welcomed the first Red Sox world championship since 1918. Shakespeare overpowered Shaughnessy.

The Cardinals' last hope resided in the hands of Rentería, who shuffled to the plate with two outs in the bottom of the ninth inning, his team down 3-0. Rentería famously won Game 7 of the 1997 World Series for Florida with a walk-off single, but even his enchanted October bat met a superior destiny this time around. When the Colombian shortstop flailed at one pitch miserably, Buck unleashed another immortal call: "Back to Foulke! Red Sox fans have longed to hear it: the Boston Red Sox are world champions."

Catharsis.

From Portland, Maine to Providence, Rhode Island, tears trickled down wrinkled cheeks. From Worcester, Massachusetts to Waterbury, Connecticut, champagne sprayed across living rooms and through taverns. And from Manchester, New Hampshire to Burlington, Vermont, forlorn navy caps with little red B's lay on the gravestones of loved ones who never lived to see it happen.

After so much waiting, so much hoping and so much pain, the Boston Red Sox exorcised the ghost of George Herman Ruth, pulled the plug on Yankee domination and overturned decades of hurt authored by St Louis. All in the space of a few October weeks.

The World Series triumph came eight months after the Patriots won Super Bowl XXXVII, making Boston the first city to hold both trophies in the same year since Pittsburgh in 1979. So often the bridesmaid, Boston finally got hitched. A cult took shape around the world.

The day after Game 4, the *Boston Globe* more than doubled its daily print run to 1.2 million copies. They still sold out. A parade was held the following day, attended by more than 3 million people in Boston. For comparison, around 2 million attended the funeral of Pope John Paul II in Rome, while 1 million paid their respects in London when Princess Diana passed away. This mattered. *The Red Sox* mattered. Few had seen anything like it.

People scaled traffic lights and hung from bridges, straining to get a peek of their immortal warriors. Confetti rained down as a city exhaled. One fan even handed a sign to Ramírez, riding a victory duck boat towards the Charles river. "Jeter is playing golf today," it read. "This is better!"

Everybody wanted a piece of the 2004 Red Sox. President Bush phoned John Henry from the White House, offering his congratulations. *Sports Illustrated* named the entire team its Sportsman of the Year, a rare honour. Dozens of books and a handful of movies were given the green light, celebrating one of the most transcendent sports teams ever assembled.

One of those aforementioned movies, a documentary called *Faith Rewarded*, was picked up by Five here in Britain as Red Sox Fever swept the globe. That was the film I stumbled across late one night as a kid. I have been intoxicated by the storyline ever since.

In sports, there are few more common creatures than the Red Sox fan whose rooting genesis lies in 2004. I was part of that bandwagon. There was something so relatable about the Idiots and their curse-busting crusade, and sweet diversion from everyday life could be found in their success.

As a Tranmere Rovers fan, I subconsciously associated with the lovable loser narrative, while basking vicariously in the glow of a purgative world championship seemed like an ideal way to begin life as a baseball rooter. "All literary men are Red Sox fans," said John Cheever, a famed novelist. "To be a Yankee fan in a literate society is to endanger your life."

Indeed, as an introverted kid obsessed with words, the Red Sox appealed to me on a philosophical level. The Boston legends of 2004 were my baseball ushers. They took my ticket, showed me to the correct seat and fetched cold beverages as I watched the drama unfold. That magical team and its remarkable achievements sparked passion in my soul, and the growth of obsession was automatic from there.

With grand imagination and unquestionable commitment, I was set for a life of Red Sox adoration. I felt emboldened by their success and enlivened by my association with it. The Red Sox' rustic road to domination appealed to my soul, and the thought of sharing that onward journey was incredibly exciting.

"Baseball, it is said, is only a game. True. And the Grand Canyon is only a hole in Arizona. Not all holes, or games, are created equal." – George Will

PART THREE

A Baseball Memoir

CHAPTER TWELVE

Life on the Red Sox Bandwagon

When Opening Day came to Fenway Park in 2005, the Yankees were in town, naturally. New York was forced to watch as Boston celebrated its ultimate triumph, a gift of lyrical symmetry. The Red Sox received their World Series rings in a lavish ceremony, and the Yankees showed their class by applauding from the visitors' dugout. However, the YES Network refused to broadcast the presentation, a sign of residual bitterness and frustration.

That undercurrent percolated throughout an unusual season, which saw New York and Boston finish with identical records of 95-67. The Yankees were crowned division champions by virtue of a better head-to-head record, while the Red Sox settled for their customary wildcard spot.

Neither team carried any magic into the postseason, though, as years of intense October drama finally took its toll. Lethargic and disorientated, Boston was swept by the White Sox in the ALDS. Indignant and unwieldy, New York also lost at that stage, falling to the Angels by three games to two.

Seemingly exhausted, Theo Epstein, the most beloved architect of Boston glee, resigned after the 2005 season, rejecting a three-year, $4.5 million contract extension. Epstein resented the way Red Sox ownership tried to capitalise on its newfound success, and he decided to take a sabbatical.

Theo had strong beliefs about how to construct a winning baseball team. The Red Sox should build organically for sustainable success, he argued, replenishing their farm system and focusing on the development of homegrown talent. Conversely, Larry Lucchino - the bullish club president - and Tom Werner - a part-owner whose background was in television - were similarly stubborn in their belief that Boston should pursue expensive free agents to appease a growing fanbase. The impasse ended when Epstein quit.

The prodigy never lost contact with his front office, however, and indeed he was reinstated just three months later. The Red Sox made some notable moves in his absence, though, trading star prospects Hanley Ramírez and Aníbal Sánchez along with a slew of lesser assets to Florida for Josh Beckett, the Yankee killer, and Mike Lowell, a Yankee reject who transformed his career in Beantown.

As ever, the Yankees sought to outshine their rivals by making a controversial free agent acquisition. Just days before Christmas in 2005, barely a year after leading the blue-collar plot to topple them, Johnny Damon signed for the Bronx Bombers. Cherished as the aesthetic leader of a sacrosanct Red Sox team, Damon once said there was "no way" he could ever play for the Yankees. However, Johnny defected when Brian Cashman offered him a four-year contract paying $52 million. Jesus Christ became Pontius Pilate.

Cutting his hair and shaving his beard to comply with Yankee policy, Damon sold his soul for personal gain, at least according to Boston sports fans. The chief Idiot joined Boggs and Clemens as *personae non gratae* in Red Sox Nation. The 2004 miracle received an uncomfortable footnote.

Damon played a key role in a notorious five-game Yankee sweep at Fenway in August 2006, all but ending the Red Sox' season. New York clung to a one-and-a-half-game lead in the AL East going into the much-hyped series, extended abnormally due to postponements earlier in the season. That lead was six-and-a-half games when the Yankees left town, evoking memories of the 1978 massacre.

"More than 35,000 sad souls had shuffled out of Fenway Park by 5:00 pm on Monday," wrote Tyler Kepner for the *New York Times*. "There were seagulls circling the centre field bleachers then, but they might as well have been buzzards. In 75 punishing hours, the Yankees had pounded their rivals into little more than a carcass."

The Red Sox eventually slumped to a third-place finish in 2006. At 86-76, Boston missed the playoffs for the first time since 2002. Meanwhile, the Yankees won their ninth straight division title before Detroit brushed them aside in the ALDS.

Joe Torre infamously dropped a slumping A-Rod to eighth in his batting order during that series as controversy simmered through the Bronx. Rodriguez topped 2,000 career hits and 450 lifetime home runs midway through the regular season, but a prolonged playoff slump saw Torre relegate him to his lowest lineup position in a decade.

Rooted in arrogance and sprinkled with vainglory, the marriage between A-Rod and New York never truly thrived. Rodriguez was forthright about his desire to join the Red Sox before that immortal trade was nixed, while repeated media faux pas eroded what little credit he built up with Yankee fans and teammates. When A-Rod underperformed at the plate, it did not take long for management to resent the exorbitant contract afforded to him.

Indeed, the entire Yankee organisation approached a historic crossroads. Without a world championship since 2000, pressure mounted on Torre, who grew increasingly impatient with the petulant stars assembled for him. Cashman was embroiled in a power struggle of his own as executive factions in Tampa, close to the ageing Steinbrenner, sought to exert control. Meanwhile, ground was broken on a new, ultra-modern Yankee Stadium just across the street from the sacred cathedral of sports as a halcyon age drew to a close. The Yankees struggled to define their new identity.

Defending against institutional meltdown, Steinbrenner ceded day-to-day autonomy in 2007 amid deteriorating health. George entrusted his sons, Hal and Hank, to run Yankee Global Enterprises. Hal, an introverted academic, took control of the Yankees, whose win-now credo was tamed somewhat by his ascension.

"An incrementalist, Hal wasn't ready to make bold changes or quash the Yank's pursuit of pricey stars," wrote Bob Klapisch and Paul Solotaroff in their book *Inside the Empire*. "They were winning their division and printing money at the gate, even after their flameouts in the playoffs. But he was a businessman who believed in data sets and the efficiencies of thrift. When he ran the numbers at season's end, he saw nothing to suggest that spending $200 million was a passkey to a title."

Indeed, despite Clemens returning for a final tour of duty aged 44, the Yankees failed to win their division in 2007, a startling wakeup call for the transitional regime. For the first time in 12 years, Boston won the AL East, powered by a homegrown core in Epstein's promised vision. Forever *chased*, the next-gen

Steinbrenners had some catching up to do. The Red Sox were becoming the yardstick of model franchises, and New York flailed in their wake.

By 2007, many of Epstein's fated prospects had graduated to big league stardom, making Boston the envy of North American sports. Kevin Youkilis, an on-base machine, made first base his own; Dustin Pedroia, a scrappy baller, won Rookie of the Year honours at second; and Jacoby Ellsbury, a lightning quick outfielder, also made a terrific introduction. Then there was Jon Lester and Jonathan Papelbon, transformative arms in a solid pitching staff.

Boston swept the Angels in the 2007 ALDS but fell behind, three games to one, against Cleveland in a subsequent joust for the pennant. Conjuring inspiration from nowhere, the Red Sox then outscored the Indians 30-5 over the next three games, winning them all to earn another fabled trip to the World Series.

Despite unprecedented momentum, the Rockies were no match for Boston, which swept the Fall Classic in clinical fashion. Without a world championship for 86 years, the Red Sox won two in four seasons. While 2004 was tinged with historic desperation, the second title shone as Epstein's magnus opus. The guy was invincible, and I lauded his ethos.

❦❦❦

Like millions of people who fell in love with the Red Sox after their 2004 heroics, I thoroughly enjoyed the 2007 season and its euphoric climax. If breaking the curse attracted innumerable bandwagon fans, winning a subsequent title consolidated their love. Boston baseball ardour spread like wildfire.

In 2002, the average attendance at Red Sox road games was 30,925, fifth in Major League Baseball. By 2007, that figure rose to 38,642, tops in baseball and a 25% increase. Across America, people associated with this team like never before, and that manifested in constant attention.

Media networks offered wall-to-wall Red Sox coverage. Merchandisers could not produce hats and hoodies and shirts fast enough to meet demand. Schilling became involved in politics, stumping for George W Bush during the presidential election, while makeover show *Queer Eye for the Straight Guy* turned the entire team into a focus of reality television.

Even here in Bromborough, my quiet village across the pond, local sports stores acknowledged a peak in baseball interest. JJB Sports sold a range of MLB caps, and my parents bought me a Red Sox one that I wore in perpetuity. That hat got so faded and battered through use, we had to replace it within six months. It meant everything to me, even if my hairline never quite recovered.

Never before had so many people around the world associated as fans of the Boston Red Sox. At one time, passing such a potentially heart-breaking affiliation from one generation to the next was almost taboo. Fathers were reluctant to subject their kids to decades of sporting hardship and humiliation. However, 2004 changed everything, and being a Red Sox fan became cool, hip and edgy.

"It's like following an unknown band through thick and thin, watching them blow up and sell-out stadiums, then being angry because they hit the big time," wrote old school Red Sox fan Bill Simmons. Indeed, a sense of resentment spread among the Boston sports vanguard. *We sat through four years of Tom Brunansky for this, fuck you!*

Entrepreneurs of every type knew that, to sell *anything* in 2004, the secret was to stick a Red Sox logo on its masthead. From newspaper editors and book publishers to movie producers, apparel hawkers and small-time artists – *everyone* tried to cash in on the fad, legally or otherwise.

Of the 870 unique potential matchup combinations in Major League Baseball, a staggering 13% of all ESPN *Sunday Night Baseball* games between 2005 and 2014 were Yankees-Red Sox contests. Fans of other teams ridiculed such a trend, growing tired of the same regurgitation, but ratings were abnormally high for those games and big business reacted accordingly.

At Fenway, ticket prices were hiked every single year between 1996 and 2007. They also increased annually between 2009 and 2011, then again from 2014 through 2020. From $15 in 1996, the average ticket price for a Red Sox home game soared to $123 by 2020, a 720% rise that changed the demographics of Red Sox fandom.

Playing to this swift gentrification, ownership revamped and expanded the selection of luxury suites at the old ballpark, tying corporate clients into 10-year commitments. Annual Red Sox revenues from each suite rocketed from around $200,000 in 2007 to over $1 million today. The team now has 52 suites, making money hand over fist.

Thanks to shrewd marketing and expert redevelopment, Fenway was always full. In fact, for 820 consecutive games between May 2003 and April 2013, not a single seat was spare at a Red Sox home game. The longest home sellout streak in sports history looked engineered at certain points, but booming interest in Boston baseball was undeniably genuine.

A season ticket waiting list held more than 7,500 names. The Red Sox formalised Red Sox Nation, selling packages complete with identity cards and store discounts. Jerry Remy was even elected president of the group, which had governors in multiple states. I wanted to establish a UK chapter, but my emails were never answered.

"Red Sox Nation? What a bunch of bullshit that is," said Hank Steinbrenner, suitably riled, in 2008. "That was a creation of the Red Sox and ESPN, which is filled with Red Sox fans. Go anywhere in America and you won't see Red Sox hats and jackets, you will see Yankee hats and jackets. This is a Yankee country, and we are going to put the Yankees back on top and restore the universe to order."

In response, John Henry inducted Hank *into* Red Sox Nation, a satirical jab that poured gasoline on the fire. The Yankee partner received a membership card by post, complete with an array of giveaways, including a hat personally signed by David Ortiz. Such was the baseball landscape as 2007 flipped to 2008.

In reality, though, the Red Sox were becoming exactly what their hardcore fanbase loathed. With gimmicks and gadgets, capitalism and consumerism, Boston baseball was transformed from rustic roots into a hyperactive circus. The Red Sox were becoming something anathema to their soul. They were becoming the Yankees.

They had the television network. They had the expensive payroll. They had the fanbase and the media attention, the celebrity fans and the lofty arrogance. They even had the World Series titles, ranging far from the trough of conventional despair. Their transformation was complete, leaving some to mourn the loss of innocence.

In the first seven years of John Henry's ownership, Red Sox revenues increased annually, from $171 million in 2002 to $269 million in 2008. Some of that money was pumped back into the machine, while Fenway Sports Group also branched out into other areas, purchasing a NASCAR team and launching a sports marketing division that featured basketball star LeBron James as a client.

The market was flooded with Red Sox regalia, most of which was unlicensed. You could buy Green Monster seats and Fenway Park dirt. You could buy Big Papi cufflinks and commemorative *Coca-Cola* cans featuring the Red Sox' emblem. I even recall Jonny Gould gifting Josh Chetwynd a Red Sox bottle opener for his birthday one year, with Joe Castiglione's immortal World Series call greeting every beer. The world went mad for anything and everything related to the Boston Red Sox. I have never known a frenzy like it.

A suitably besotted fan, I ate it up, consuming anything and everything related to the Red Sox and to baseball. I played in the street, pretending to be Manny. I wrote about Ortiz in school essays, confusing my teachers. And I listened to Neil Diamond and the Dropkick Murphys on an endless loop, embracing the self-indulgent soundtrack of a glorious age.

I did not own a green jersey or a pink hat, those signature trinkets of bandwagon ignorance, but I did luxuriate in the newfound symmetry of Red Sox success. There was something ever so romantic about the curse and its eventual demise. I piggybacked on decades of baseball devastation, enjoying indirectly the purifying glow of two world championships.

In 2007, I was 13 years old and, quite frankly, good times never seemed so good. The Boston Red Sox were champions of baseball, and I was their biggest fan anywhere in England. That passion seemed eternal as baseball overtook football in my hierarchy of religious fixation. It was impossible to foresee a day where that faith would not exist, and I did not want such a day to rise.

I have no problem admitting my bandwagon genesis as a baseball fan because it happened organically, not through cunning selection. I was a naïve, sports-obsessed kid who saw a documentary telling the most unbelievable story from America, and I fell in love with its main protagonists.

Unlike the fully-grown adults who mistakenly asked why the Fenway crowd booed Youkilis, I did not consciously *choose* to be a Red Sox fan. It just sort of happened. My discovery of the sport was drenched in serendipity, and there seemed something *charismatic* about the Red Sox, so they became my team. There was not much more to it than that. Some intricate conception would be far more interesting, but this is not a work of fiction, and I see little wrong with my rooting chronology.

Moreover, my embryonic love of baseball was anathema to the society in which I lived. Accordingly, there was no historic or traditional lineage to inherit with regard to fandom. I never spoke to a fellow baseball fan in England for perhaps the first six or seven years of my fandom. I discovered the Red Sox in isolation and, quite frankly, nobody was even interested in my obsession. There was no deceitful scheme underpinning my matriculation. I made a heartfelt acquaintance that bloomed into love.

The difference between your traditional Red Sox bandwagoner and me is that I actually developed a full-blooded passion for the team that grew organically. I devoted years of my life to studying the team's history. I could differentiate between Devern Hansack and Wily Mo Pena. I acknowledged that *El Guapo* was a relief pitcher, not a Venezuelan drug lord. And I knew that Smoky Joe Wood was not a brand of cigars. I was a real fan, pure and simple. I took pride in my baseball awareness.

My baseball library grew by the week. I spent hours each day immersed in another world, reading on the stairs or in my bedroom about this wonderful sport and its beguiling heritage. My fertile brain became a repository of random baseball trivia, and my vocabulary grew as a pleasant consequence of the unceasing quest for hardball knowledge.

Without the necessary cash to buy mlb.tv, I relied on Channel Five and Gameday for my fix of live action. The latter, a graphic-based simulator, did not even support video when I first started watching. I literally stayed awake until four in the morning staring at my computer screen, where faceless cartoons re-enacted the events of random midsummer games in static morbidity. Still, it was baseball, and I felt part of something great.

My knowledge, interest and passion were turbocharged by the 2007 World Series. As always, *Baseball on Five* carried the entire series live, in the depths of British night, and I watched every single pitch in rapt appreciation. There was a beautiful stillness to those moments that I have never managed to replicate, and there is still a sepia tinge to my fond reminiscence.

Such was my baseball intoxication, and perhaps my baseball *alienation*, I decided to write a book about life as a Red Sox fan in the UK. I was barely a teenager, but a precocious desire and a rare ability collided in my head. This felt like my calling in life, and I was single-minded in the pursuit of creative expression.

I began to type and type and type, working on a British imitation of *Faithful* by King and O'Nan. I was utterly convinced, and entirely deluded, that publishers in my homeland would be interested in a baseball book. When written by a pubescent adolescent, those miniscule odds dwindled to nothing.

I did not care, though, because I had unbounding love for the subject and a natural passion for the craft. I wanted to be a baseball writer from the earliest age and, in the end, that is just what I became. Nobody was going to stop me, nor would they halt my love for the Boston Red Sox. The force of emotion conquered all.

⚾⚾⚾

CHAPTER THIRTEEN

The Olde Towne Team

In my childhood home, a clunky old computer occupied one corner of the living room. As one of six children, my time on the device was limited. Mum acted like a strict cyber referee, timing our usage to ensure everybody got a turn. The standard allowance was half an hour each, which did not leave much room for experimentation.

My sister spent hours chatting to her friends on MSN, the virtual chatroom. My younger brother watched wrestling videos and cartoons, studying stars like John Cena. I wrote a book about baseball. The ecology of our family was entirely random.

In the winter of 2007, bleeding into the spring of 2008 and beyond, I developed an efficient routine for following Major League Baseball from afar. Unlike today, I could not rely on social media for instant news and opinion. As such, I bookmarked all of the esteemed baseball websites and consumed them daily in the same rotation.

I began keeping a baseball diary on Microsoft Word, jotting down the latest news, and that quickly morphed into a mammoth manuscript about my addiction. I decided to chronicle the 2008 season in fine detail and publish the resultant book. I was young and naïve enough to believe my own dreams.

In hindsight, the entire project was fatally flawed. Here was a British teen writing about the Boston Red Sox in pretty mundane fashion. The monotony of a baseball season requires short and sharp analysis, but my early writing style resembled a stream of baseball consciousness.

Moreover, I followed the Red Sox in painful isolation, so the story was not exactly compelling. Whereas *Faithful* shared experiences from the ballpark, effectively giving readers a season ticket on the first base side, my diary was littered with references to Gameday, MLB Trade Rumours and *Baseball on Five*. I lived in a different world.

However, writing that failed book was one of the most important and rewarding experiences of my formative years. It helped broaden my vocabulary and it sharpened my desire to become a professional writer. I was 13 years old and writing every day. When it was not my turn on the computer, I read, awaiting an opportunity to write. That is crucial in the development of self-awareness and pivotal in the expression of linguistic flair. That is crucial in the honing of intelligence and important in becoming a well-rounded human being. That is the best advice I can ever give to anybody who wants to become a writer: just *write*, because life is too short to get caught planning.

I gave the book a grand working title - *The Olde Towne Team: Life as a UK Boston Red Sox Maniac* - and stuck at it every single day. Accordingly, the 2008 Red Sox hold a special place in my heart, and I have rarely encountered such a rollercoaster of emotions as created by that season.

Years later, I was diagnosed with obsessive-compulsive disorder (OCD) amid a mental health crisis. The classic associations of OCD focus on the ritualistic aspects of obsession, usually portrayed through tampering with light switches and excessive cleanliness. However, there are different *kinds* of OCD, and I have traditionally struggled with the mammoth surplus of creative ideas that it generates.

Somebody with OCD can only attain happiness or satisfaction after the completion of certain tasks, typically in a cyclical fashion. That cycle never ends, however, resulting in anxiety and often leading to further mental health struggles. Looking back, deciding to record every detail about an American baseball team for more than 12 months was symptomatic of that disorder. Writing *The Olde Towne Team* was a towering *manifestation* of OCD, not just an idea formed by it.

Every single day, and often multiple *times* per day, I sat at the rickety living room computer and wrote about baseball. If I did not check the boxscore immediately after waking up, the day became a disaster. If I did not get all of my thoughts and feelings about a game down on paper, anxiety built. If somebody else used the computer while a major baseball story broke, agitation manifested itself in worry and sulking. I was entirely hooked on the Boston Red Sox.

Indeed, that was a fertile period in my wider self-discovery. New to high school, I was quickly confronted by my own *otherness*. I attended South Wirral, a rough and rugged school for the working class. Few people liked to read or write there, and fewer still knew that baseball existed. I was a social alien, more comfortable in my own company - in my own lyrical fantasies - than in a wider group of hyper peers. I belonged to a different stratum of existence, adrift and unmoored from my own base of fulfilment. There was nobody like me, and not in a good way.

Following baseball religiously from England was exceedingly difficult. I struggled with the time difference, unable to watch enough games, and that fed demoralising cycles of separation and loneliness. The financial struggles of my family also added to the challenge, scuppering progress and enhancing frustration. My passion often seemed incompatible with the outside world, and I was left to improvise in pursuit of satisfaction.

Our small family home, rented from a local authority, was fitted with a pre-paid electricity meter rather than with a standard monthly tariff system. When our credit ran out, somebody had to take a key to the local shop, load additional supplies onto it, then return home to feed the machine. In the meantime, our house lay in cold darkness.

Every day, the electricity cut out at some point, usually while I was writing my manuscript or watching a crucial Red Sox rally on Gameday. That pre-paid meter became an occupational hazard, not just an occasional annoyance, and I rewrote innumerable sections of the book from scratch.

A similar arrangement plagued our internet connection. As a large family on the breadline, luxuries such as wi-fi often came last in the hierarchy of needs. First, we had to eat. Then, we had to keep the electricity and gas ticking over. Paying the internet bill was not a necessity, and so our connection was frequently severed, putting me out of action for days at a time.

Often, when there was no money to immediately reconnect us to the grid, I relied on Bromborough library and the computers at school for baseball sustenance. People probably wondered why I was so irate or elated scrolling through obscure sports websites, but my fixation was too strong to suppress.

I also learned the hard way about backing up files and protecting a computer. Late in the season, when my book had grown to gargantuan proportions, our PC imploded due to a virus. I remember crying angrily as all logical solutions did not work.

Jay, a distant relative, took the computer away and fixed it, but I was out of action, and more importantly *out of touch with America*, for more than a week. The manuscript was somehow recovered, but I had a lot of catching up to do. I wrote in fast-forward, breathlessly pursuing the remote heroes of my imagination.

⚾⚾⚾

The 2008 Red Sox, my central protagonists, were fun to watch. The second championship, achieved in Theo's vision, gave Boston an even greater belief in homegrown talent, which flowed throughout the roster. Francona still points to the 2008 squad as his best in Boston, and I wholeheartedly concur as a sentimental fan who enjoyed every minute.

Youkilis, Pedroia and Ellsbury were particularly awesome, while Lester became an ace. In the bullpen, Manny Delcarmen complemented Papelbon, forming a one-two punch of fearsome power. Perplexingly, Ortiz and Ramírez suffered down years by their own lofty standards in 2008. Nevertheless, I enjoyed watching their charismatic friendship. Meanwhile, less heralded veterans like Lowell, JD Drew and Coco Crisp performed strongly, keeping the Red Sox on course for success.

By contrast, in their final season at the original Yankee Stadium, the Bronx Bombers resembled a parody of their former selves. Torre left to manage the Dodgers, while Rodriguez opted out of his contract during the 2007 World Series and later received a 10-year, $275 million extension that rocked the pinstriped boat.

At first, Yankees ownership refused to negotiate with A-Rod, seeing his power play as an act of betrayal. Rodriguez issued a public apology and restated his desire to remain in the Bronx. Amid a tidal wave of bad publicity and chronic mistakes, A-Rod's mere presence became an eye-rolling melodrama.

The Yankees were seemingly caught between eras. Bernie Williams was gone, while Posada and Giambi dealt with recurring injuries. Ageing veterans like Damon and Bobby Abreu were solid if unspectacular as a new crop of Baby Bombers tried to emerge under the management of Joe Girardi.

Robinson Canó, the languid prospect once offered to Texas for A-Rod, became the second baseman. Melky Cabrera, a whirlwind of energy, made his debut in the outfield. Joba Chamberlain, a precocious flamethrower, carved a special place in the bullpen. Still, the Yankees failed to address chronic deficiencies in their starting rotation, which crumbled to dust over a period of many years.

Andy Pettitte was ineffective at 36. Carl Pavano was a disaster at 32. Mike Mussina won 20 games in 2008 but retired prematurely. Chien-Ming Wang became entangled in a web of injuries and underperformance. The search for 27 outs each day became a protracted saga.

New York experimented with a range of mediocre starters, guys with names like Darrell Rasner, Sidney Ponson and Dan Giese. Even Ian Kennedy, a prized prospect, never amounted to much as the Yankees faded to a third-place finish in 2008. Their glory days were most assuredly over, and it was time for new blood. Reinforcements took longer to arrive than in previous eras, though, as baseball experienced a period of immense change.

Surprisingly, Boston had a new nemesis in the AL East: Tampa Bay, the division's perpetual doormat. Prior to the 2008 season, team owner Stuart Sternberg renamed his ballclub, dropping the *Devil Rays* moniker in favour of the more optimistic *Rays*. Complete with new uniforms and a refreshing rebrand, the exorcism seemed to work as Tampa Bay competed for the division.

An expansion team born in 1998, Tampa Bay had never enjoyed a single winning season. In fact, in their first 10 years of existence, the Rays lost at least 91 games *every single year*. Through 2007, their all-time record was 645-972, while Tampa Bay typically finished 34 games out of first place *on average*.

However, managed by Joe Maddon, an enthusiastic sage, the 2008 Rays caught lightning in a bottle. Using advanced analytics to compensate for budgetary deficiencies, Tampa Bay assembled a unique roster full of homegrown talent. Losing so much gave the Rays serious ammunition in the draft, and young general manager Andrew Friedman slowly built a team capable of competing with the mightier foes in Boston and New York.

Evan Longoria became a star at third base. Carl Crawford dazzled in the outfield. Melvin Upton Jr showed glimpses of greatness. Tampa Bay also nurtured versatile stars like Ben Zobrist and Rocco Baldelli, but its pitching staff was particularly dangerous.

With an emphasis on developing elite arms, Tampa Bay had a formidable rotation in 2008 led by a three-headed monster. At 26, James Shields emerged as an ace, broad and dominant. He was supported by two 24-year-old workhorses: Matt Garza, a rabble-rousing enigma, and Scott Kazmir, an astute lefty. David Price, another uber prospect, debuted late in the season aged 22, adding to the plethora of young pitching talent that carried the Rays into contention.

A June brawl at Fenway spoke to the general indignation surrounding Tampa Bay's surge. When Shields hit Crisp with a pitch, the Red Sox outfielder charged the mound, sparking a benches-clearing fight for the ages. Genuine punches, the rarest commodity in any baseball brawl, were actually exchanged, and eight players were subsequently suspended.

As midsummer rolled around, then, the Red Sox faced a legitimate dilemma: they were better than the Yankees, but the Rays would not go away. Suitably perplexed, Epstein set about reshaping his roster, just as he did in 2004. Once again, the Boston general manager showed no mercy in trading away a fan favourite to spark a reaction. I was absolutely crushed.

Manny Ramírez was my first baseball hero. Dreadlocked and insouciant, he swaggered about the field with breathtaking ease. Eccentric and frustrating, he became one of the greatest righthanded hitters in baseball history. It was bewitching to watch him hit, and from an early age I worshiped him as a baseball savant.

However, Manny's off-field travails were a ubiquitous subplot in Boston, a permanent caveat to his on-field greatness. Ramírez lived in his own unique bubble, one of inane nihilism that permitted stupendous acts of stupidity. After many years, the persona wore thin, and some began to question whether Ramírez did more bad than good.

Manny slipped inside Fenway's Green Monster to make phone calls mid-game. Manny strangely sold used barbecuing equipment on eBay despite earning more than $200 million in his career. Manny failed to run out ground balls and made stunning errors in the outfield, living up to his class clown caricature. For many years, he was a law unto himself, using home runs as currency for impunity. It was just Manny Being Manny, and there was little anybody could do to discipline him.

Capricious and impatient, Ramírez frequently demanded to be traded by the Red Sox. Boston was too overbearing, he complained, and the grass always seemed greener on the other side. Manny even asked Henry to explore possible deals during their *first meeting* in 2002. The guy was uncontrollable.

Nevertheless, Ramírez was a major part of the Red Sox' success. Manny produced six straight seasons with at least 30 home runs and 100 RBI for Boston. Signed for eight years and $160 million by Duquette following the 2000 season, he topped out at 43 dingers in 2004 and contributed 144 RBI in 2005. Ramírez consistently hit above .300, as well, making him a premier force at the plate.

Manny struggled in 2007, however, failing to break the 100-RBI plateau for the first time in a decade. His 20 home runs were also the fewest he had managed since 1994. To borrow a phrase from Dan Duquette, Ramírez was entering the twilight of a remarkable career, and despite frequent postseason heroics, Epstein questioned whether the Red Sox could carry such a declining asset into their bright future.

In fairness, Manny performed strongly to open 2008, his age-36 season. Through 100 games with Boston, he hit .299 with 20 home runs, 68 RBI and a .926 OPS. Ramírez launched his 500th career home run against Baltimore in May, but discontent brewed behind the scenes. He was living on borrowed time.

A dugout altercation with teammate Youkilis did not look good, while Ramírez later fought with Jack McCormick, the team's 64-year-old travelling secretary. Manny pushed McCormick to the ground amid a confrontation and was later fined $15,000 by the team. In hindsight, we were likely seeing the effects of 'roid rage in Ramírez, who became a malcontent.

As the 2008 trade deadline came into view, rumours swirled about Epstein's desire to dump Ramírez, and I was suitably upset. He was my favourite player, after all. I had never known the Red Sox without him, just as bygone kids had never known the Red Sox without Nomar, Roger or Wade.

On deadline day, I distinctly remember being forced to endure a family trip to Liverpool. Roaming around the Albert Dock, I was displeased and agitated. I just wanted to be at home, refreshing MLB Trade Rumours and writing my thoughts on the unfolding saga. I did not have a mobile phone, nor did Twitter exist as the go-to news-breaking behemoth for baseball writers around the world. Tension grew.

Fortunately, we returned home about an hour before the deadline and Manny was still a Red Sock. Lulled into a false sense of security, I was duly sucker-punched when the fatal news landed shortly after 9:00 pm GMT. The Red Sox traded Ramírez to the Dodgers in a three-team deal that brought Jason Bay to Boston from Pittsburgh. Emotional and sensitive, I struggled to see the logic in such a deal. Here is what I wrote in *The Olde Towne Team:*

"That was one of the weirdest and worst five minutes of my life as the baseball world was turned on its head in a matter of seconds.

A trade has come absolutely out of nowhere and, after eight years, the great Manny Ramírez is out of Boston.

This trade could not have been worse as far as we are concerned. We ate $7 million of Manny's contract for 2008, sent him to LA and sent Craig Hansen and Brandon Moss to Pittsburgh. All we got in return was an overrated outfielder in Jason Bay.

I am so, so sad that Manny Ramírez, my all-time favourite ballplayer, has gone forever. Theo, you really have messed this one up bud!

Gone are our two best prospects who we have been nurturing for years, and gone is the best cleanup hitter in the club's history - all for Jason Bay? Well done Theo, now we face a huge battle just to gain a wildcard berth."

My writing style has thankfully improved since I was 13, but a small part of my heart is still yet to recover. Manny Ramírez will always patrol left field in the Fenway Park of my mind. A more mystifying ballplayer is yet to swing a bat.

⚾⚾⚾

Manny was incredible for the rest of 2008, powering the Dodgers with insatiable productivity. He hit .396 with 17 home runs, 53 RBI and a 1.232 OPS in 53 games for Los Angeles. Wearing the number 99, Ramírez inspired the cult of Mannywood, carrying Torre's Dodgers to a lengthy playoff run.

Meanwhile, Jason Bay was far better than I envisaged in Boston. Finishing the 2008 season, he hit .293 with 9 home runs, 37 RBI and a .897 OPS in 49 games. Good? Sure. But *Manny Ramírez* good? Nowhere near.

Contrary to my fears, the Red Sox *did* manage to secure a wildcard berth, beating the Yankees and Twins to a playoff spot. Tampa Bay won the AL East with a startling 97-65 record, but through all the turmoil, Boston came in close behind at 95-67. Meanwhile, the Yankees missed the postseason for the first time since 1993.

The Rays beat Chicago while Boston beat Anaheim in the first playoff round, and a tantalising ALCS was duly secured between the trendy foes. I was pumped, following along in the wee hours of British fall. A happy ending to my book remained within reach.

The Red Sox took Game 1 but lost Game 2 in walk-off fashion at Tropicana Field. With fine pitching, Tampa Bay stifled Boston and won the next two games at Fenway, claiming a 3-1 series lead and reading the Red Sox' last rites. After chronicling the team's exploits for a year, I was extremely anxious. It all looked set to end in disaster, and there was nothing I could do to help.

Through six-and-a-half innings of Game 5, one win away from glory, Tampa Bay built an ominous 7-0 lead on the road. Down to their final seven outs, the Red Sox finally snatched a run on an RBI single by Pedroia. It still seemed too late, but then Ortiz, that old October magician, thumped a three-run homer to slash the deficit to 7-4. It was almost like old times.

Much maligned, Drew, another of my favourite players, slashed a two-run shot in the eighth, hauling Boston within one run of survival at 7-6. Crisp then laced a single to right, scoring Mark Kotsay and tying the game in remarkable style. In the ninth, Drew came up huge again, winning the contest with a walk-off single.

The baseball world was stunned as the Red Sox completed the second-biggest single-game comeback in postseason history. Not since Game 4 of the 1929 World Series - almost 80 years prior - had a team overturned a seven-run deficit in the playoffs. No team had ever produced such theatrics when facing elimination, and I lived through every pitch as an authentic rooter. My adrenaline crashed through the roof.

Beckett duelled Shields in Game 6, back in the gruesome environs of Tropicana Field. Boston won 4-2 as Youkilis and Varitek went yard. Ortiz had another key hit, adding to his incredible legacy, and the Red Sox forced a decisive Game 7.

That game was carried live by Five here in the UK. At the pinnacle of Red Sox infatuation, I stayed awake on a scary Sunday night to watch it. First pitch was at 01:09 am GMT. I was 14 years old and totally beholden to a Major League Baseball team to moderate my mood.

The Red Sox scored first in Game 7, a Pedroia home run setting the tone nicely. However, after that, Garza was masterful for Tampa Bay, allowing just one further hit in seven innings of nimble work. In repost, Lester fought valiantly, pitching seven innings of his own, but the Rays tacked on single runs in the fourth, fifth and seventh to go ahead, 3-1.

Sensing history, Tampa Bay turned to Price, the heralded phenom, with two outs in the eighth. He pitched spectacularly in relief, extinguishing Red Sox hope with clinical proficiency. Alas, there was no incredulous comeback or death-defying resurgence this time. We were left to suck it up.

I remember watching through gritted teeth and watery eyes as Price navigated his way through the ninth inning. The noise emanating from Tropicana Field, that neon hub of nightmares, was sickening.

When Jed Lowrie poked a groundball to second baseman Akinori Iwamura at 04:40 am, the most intense season of my baseball life died with sudden horror. For added poignancy, Iwamura took the ball to second base himself, standing on the bag to record an unassisted forceout that won the pennant for Tampa Bay.

I slumped to the floor, choking back tears. The notion of *tomorrow* was wiped from my world, and I have never felt sporting pain like it. There is no crying in baseball, or so the adage goes, but I bawled uncontrollably. Lest anyone argue that bandwagoners do not hurt the same as diehards.

Somehow, I managed to quell the agony enough to type a few thoughts into my instantly anachronistic season diary. Here is what I wrote:

"The 2008 Boston Red Sox are history as the phenomenal comeback fell short and Matt Garza pitched the Rays to the first World Series in their short history.

It was absolutely shattering as I watched the slow death of our playoff dreams, painful pitch after painful pitch. It was the most drastically awful game I have ever watched during my short rooting days.

All those sleepless nights and endless hours in front of a computer. All the blood, sweat and tears count for nothing as Matt Garza threw seven innings of two-hit ball to earn himself the 2008 American League Championship Series Most Valuable Player Award.

Jon Lester was good, but not good enough for a Game Seven, and the mistakes he made were punished severely. What makes it more painful is the fact that it was so close all game long and we wasted a couple of great chances to pull one more rabbit out of the hat.

After eight months of brilliance, controversy, adversity and a sheer adrenaline rush, it all came crashing down in the horrible confines of Tropicana Field. Watching the Rays embrace in a huge pile on the infield rug knocked me sick, and the sight of Joe Maddon holding aloft the American League Championship trophy almost gave me seizures.

Why couldn't we just get that base hit when we needed it, or that perfect pitch at the perfect time? I suppose coming from 3-1 down against one of the best young, energetic, enthusiastic teams in the game, facing their two best pitchers in the hostile dome was just a little too much to ask, even for the greatest franchise in the history of Major League Baseball, the Boston Red Sox."

⚾⚾⚾

All season long, I lived in fantastic delusion, believing that publishers would show interest in my Red Sox book. That belief lacked pragmatic validity for a number of reasons, but the lack of a fairytale ending all but curtailed the project prematurely.

Still, I approached a slew of publishers, sending them an unwieldy manuscript of 799 pages, 265,000 words and 1.4 million characters. The naivety is quite incredible, looking back, but I'm exceptionally proud of that book, which acted as the greatest tool of experimentation as I found my writing voice.

The rejection slips came in thick and fast. I collected them in a folder. Some editors did not even bother to respond. I proposed a harebrained idea, but it was one wrapped in extreme passion, love and enjoyment. Unfortunately, there was no market for such wild scribblings. At least not at the time.

I even sent the manuscript to Craig W Thomas, whose *Roads to Redemption* made such a lasting impression on me. Craig kindly responded with a postcard and subsequent letter, sharing advice that made sense only years later.

My writing lacked the gravity that comes with age and experience, Craig explained, but merely having the inspiration and motivation to tackle such a project was rare for a raw teenager. Craig congratulated me on writing a book, and he taught me that, regardless of whether it was published commercially, such an achievement was not to be devalued.

Of course, nobody touched the book as a commercial asset, and it has lay dormant on an old laptop for more than 10 years. It is littered with errors, mistakes and oversights, but I'm nostalgic about the process of writing such a diary. I'm nostalgic about the *old* Boston Red Sox, back before everything got so complicated. It was the most enriching journey, and learning to express my emotions was exceedingly valuable.

Such a skill became very useful in the years ahead, as times changed and as emotions drifted away. What happened next defied foretelling, but my world was thrown into utter chaos with a series of business transactions. My love affair with the Boston Red Sox ran out of steam, and the consequences were earth-shattering. I'm still picking up the pieces, more than a decade later.

❧❧❧

CHAPTER FOURTEEN

Betrayal

Amid the march of modern capitalism, ruthless and unforgiving, *Baseball on Five* was cut following the 2008 World Series, won by Philadelphia over the Rays. A downturn in the British economy put Five in a bind, and its late-night sports package was pruned amid cost-cutting measures.

I was plunged into something amounting to trauma. A dull ache of regret nagged at my heart. A sudden pang of sadness gnawed at my soul. A debilitating emptiness trickled through my blood. So many questions raced through my mind. How? Why? What next? It was a time of immeasurable sorrow, the Red Sox' playoff defeat compounded by the loss of my only connection to live baseball coverage.

"The economy was bad at the time, and I believe Five wasn't doing great," Josh Chetwynd explained years later. "There were cheaper ways to programme late nights and I think they were driven by that, which is sad as the baseball show was its longest running programme.

"I remember going to visit my family in the US just before Christmas in 2008 and being told that there were just some details that needed to be worked out, but that the show was coming back. Within a few days of being in the States, I was told the show was done. It was a huge kick in the guts to all of us. Very, very sad times."

Amid rumour and counter-rumour, snipe and counter-snipe, Jonny Gould emerged with an open letter to the baseball-loving masses, confirming the show's unfortunate demise in a piece of prose that still makes my heart sink:

"Welcome, fellow baseball nuts. God, I'm going to miss saying that. I'm sure most of you have heard the rumours. Five TV have ended their association with our beloved sport, or at least they have not committed to another season of Baseball on Five *every Wednesday and Sunday night.*

The rumours have been many and mixed, and I'm sorry that I'm not in a position to fully clarify the situation for you. What I can tell you is that if this is the end, it has been one hell of a ride.

Understandably, many of our hardcore viewers are pretty pissed off with Five, but remember they have made a 12-year commitment and for that alone we should all be very grateful.

So what's next? Well first and foremost, the movers and shakers in UK baseball are still committed to finding a home for baseball on UK television. There is no guarantee as to when or even if that will happen, but we are committed to keeping the baseball family intact.

To that end, we are continuing the fantasy league this season regardless of whether my baseball TV career has legs. So get your fantasy caps on tilt because it's time to play ball!

Baseball – it's a hardcore thing!!

Jonny Gould

Just like that, it was all over. Baseball *did* return to British television, with BT Sport broadcasting many games per week, but viewers had to pay for the privilege. The lack of a studio presence, and the resultant loss of intimacy, left a void that was never filled. My family could not afford such a premium television package, so my ties with live baseball were cut.

Indeed, the 2009 season was a time of constant upheaval. The proliferation of social media became readily apparent, diluting the experience of fandom to 140 characters. The Red Sox introduced a new logo and uniforms, neither of which were particularly impressive. Then they were swept in the ALDS by Anaheim, all but ending an era of incessant competition.

Throughout the season, I struggled to keep abreast of developments in Boston. Not yet earning any money, and therefore unable to penetrate paywalls, I did not watch a single game live. My interest waned as the magic lost its sheen. Gould and Chetwynd briefly returned on BBC radio, broadcasting a ballgame every Sunday, but even that arrangement was eventually nixed as my baseball obsession began to fall apart.

The Yankees opened their new home in 2009, a $2.3 billion imitation of the original yard rising 300 metres across East 161st Street. Hal and Hank sanctioned a lavish spending spree to construct a winning ballclub fit for the new Stadium, which was designed to eke every penny out of humble Yankee fans.

In 2008, New York missed the playoffs for the first time in 16 years, and management was keen to avoid a repeat in their new digs. Bulldog ace CC Sabathia was signed to a seven-year, $161 million contract, replacing Mussina, who retired. AJ Burnett, another gutsy starter, received a five-year deal paying $82.5 million, adding another stubborn presence. Pettitte then signed another one-year, $5.5 million pact, rounding out a stellar rotation.

In the field, Giambi was out as the Yankees declined an option in his contract. Cashman duly signed Mark Teixeira, a marquee first baseman, for eight years at $180 million. On-base machine Nick Swisher was also acquired in a trade with the White Sox, giving manager Joe Girardi a plethora of tools with which to build a winner.

Sporting a $201 million payroll, the 2009 Yankees lost their first eight games against the Red Sox, stoking pinstriped paranoia. New York founds its stride soon enough, though, storming back to split the season series 9-9. Slamming the ball out of their new ballpark, the Yankees won 103 games in total, eight more than Boston, en route to the division flag. Jeter broke Gehrig's all-time franchise record for hits in September, setting the scene for another vintage run at the October mountain.

The Yankees swept Minnesota in typical first round fashion before outlasting the Angels in a topsy-turvy ALCS. Rodriguez finally delivered in the playoffs, answering his critics with a string of clutch hits, while Sabathia did what the Steinbrenners paid him to do: win big games.

New York faced Philadelphia in the 2009 World Series, emerging victorious in six games. Aged 37, old friend Pedro Martínez resurfaced with the Phillies, pitching twice in the Fall Classic amid a torrent of abuse. The Yankees beat Pedro both times, hanging a 6.30 series ERA on the veteran and hastening his retirement. Meanwhile, Hideki Matsui was superhuman against Philly, hitting .615 and slugging 1.385 in 14 plate appearances while launching three crucial home runs.

Rivera induced the final out, as ever, getting Shane Victorino to flail at a trademark cutter, beating a groundball to Canó. When the languid second baseman whirled a throw to Teixeira, the Yankees secured their 27th World Series championship of all-time. The House That Jeter Built saw its first coronation.

I do not recall watching or listening to the 2009 World Series, but I *do* remember shaking my head in disbelief when learning that the Yankees were back on top. However, distanced from live coverage, my bearings began to change and my passion was less intense. Then, in October 2010, with one shocking announcement, my affiliation with Boston baseball was consigned to history. The final nail was hammered into my Red Sox coffin, and I was powerless to stop it.

To my eternal agony, John Henry and Tom Werner bought Liverpool FC, my ultimate nemesis, for £300 million, vowing to rekindle glory at Anfield. The Red Sox, my baseball dream, duly became linked to Liverpool, my football nightmare. For a British lad hardwired to obey the omnipotence of soccer, there was only one winner. I was no longer a Red Sox fan.

The dreadful news was conveyed by *Daybreak*, a short-lived breakfast show on ITV. Aged 16, I was preparing for another day at high school as the bombshell was dropped. My response was fittingly childish but deeply emotive. In my head alone, this felt like the most flagrant betrayal, and John Henry became my chief antagonist.

At school, awash with Liverpool fans, I was teased and goaded. Many acquaintances knew I was a Red Sox fan and Liverpool hater, and their queries about my future allegiances were loaded with sarcasm. A few close friends asked about my bedroom, the de facto Red Sox shrine, and I felt embarrassed. Upon returning home, I ransacked the room, smashing photos and tossing souvenirs. Then came the tears of unquenchable rage.

More than anything, I was sad. Deeply and unshakably sad. The thought of contributing to the success of Liverpool, a club I wanted to see lose, was deeply unsettling. From an ethical standpoint, I could not bring myself to buy a Red Sox hat or hoodie knowing that those dollars would trickle into the empire of Henry and Werner, whose redistribution to Liverpool would improve an organisation I yearned to destroy.

Guided by tribal tradition, I could not be complicit in the existence and growth of Liverpool Football Club, which correlated inextricably with the demise of Tranmere Rovers, my ultimate sporting faith. By virtue of common ownership, rooting for the Boston Red Sox achieved that nefarious end, furnishing Fenway Sports Group with the resources and credibility to rebuild a football team I wanted to fail.

"I want to express how incredibly proud and humbled we are to be confirmed as the new owners of Liverpool FC," said Henry in a statement. "We regard our role as that of stewards for the club with a primary focus on returning the club to greatness on and off the field for the long-term. We are committed first and foremost to winning."

I listened to my values, though they squawked in childish indignation, and I abandoned all association with the Red Sox. Never would I knowingly aid the growth of a cancerous tumour, and that is just what Liverpool FC is to my dearest identity. It was a difficult time, awash with hurt, but I stood by my decision. The sense of pride was great, even if the heartache was greater.

∾∾∾

Changing allegiance to a sports team is sacrilege in modern society. People change jobs and religions, file for divorces and move to new homes, but they never stop rooting for their favourite clubs. To do so, and to *admit* to doing so, is to tarnish one's reputation beyond reclaim. The stakes are *that* high.

In any one year, 30% of British workers change occupation. In the same timeframe, more than 27 million people either convert to or leave Christianity. Meanwhile, in the United States, there is one divorce every 13 seconds, while the average person will typically change accommodation 11 times in their life.

However, our sporting values belong to an altogether more sacred pantheon of emotion. Those loyalties are an appendage of family, forming bonds that last a lifetime. Those optics are wrought by civic affiliation, anchoring people to their hometowns where else they may stray. Those beliefs are entwined with our precious sense of self, affirming our suspicions and underpinning our confidence. Disowning the predetermined faith is taboo of the highest order, because sporting fandom is non-refundable.

But what happens if, like me, you are not assigned a baseball team at birth? What happens if, like me, you are raised thousands of miles away from the nearest major league ballpark? *Then* what happens if the team with which you eventually fall in love jumps in bed with an organisation you despise? How do you reconcile those disparate poles?

Alas, there was no sense of familial obligation binding me to the Red Sox when Henry and Werner bought Liverpool. My love of baseball was an individual endeavour, and I owed nobody an apology for feeling disenfranchised. There *was* a familial obligation to Tranmere Rovers, and - by extension - there was a hereditary intolerance of Liverpool. For me, the logic was clear. I had to end my affiliation with the Red Sox.

In hindsight, perhaps I acted foolishly, more like a petulant brat than a calm academic. John Henry does not know who I am, and nor does he care. The *Boston Red Sox* do not know who I am, and losing my support is of little consequence to a team worth $3.2 billion. However, something deep within compelled me to act. My own ethical arithmetic said there was little choice but to leap, and so I handed back my key to a conflicted Red Sox Nation.

The kangaroo court of public opinion may brand me immature, disloyal, or just plain stupid, and I'm ready for that. I claimed to be the most rabid Red Sox fan in Britain, but a miniscule third division soccer team with average attendances of 6,000 was more important? What a joke. I professed to love Boston but fled over grievances with another city on another continent? Erm, okay. I celebrated a world championship with this team but did not stick around when things got tough? Way to go.

I never wanted this to happen. Soccer faded into the background when I discovered baseball. America's national pastime is infinitely greater as a sport. However, even as baseball became my favourite game, the allegiance to Tranmere Rovers remained omnipotent. It remained the driving force in every sphere of my life, and I obeyed its associated demands.

Rooted in family heritage and societal pride, that identity was my most definitive characteristic. Penetrating layer after layer of homespun propaganda was impossible. Loving Tranmere was ingrained in my makeup, and loathing Liverpool came as a natural by-product. I was brainwashed, conditioned and indoctrinated. The Red Sox had to go, and so I got rid of them.

჻჻჻

What is so bad about Liverpool FC?

I have been asked that question on innumerable occasions. However, to make such an inquiry is to misunderstand the essence of sporting affiliation. I dislike Liverpool just as any fan of any team in any sport dislikes the rival of said team. That is how this works.

Football is bound by tribal instinct, tethered to geographical gravity and communal pride. In this regard, the distinction between Liverpool, a big city, and Wirral, a medium-sized borough, holds the key to discord between football supporters on either side of the river.

Birkenhead, the largest conurbation in Wirral, is known colloquially as the one-eyed city. Why? Well, there are a number of theories, but the most logical explanation is derived from the town constantly glancing sideways, watching its mighty neighbour thrive through hegemony.

Once a powerhouse of 1800s affluence, Birkenhead would have been a *real* city if commerce, wealth and industry were not funnelled to Liverpool. For instance, apart from Trafalgar Square in London, Hamilton Square in Birkenhead contains the most Grade I listed buildings in one municipal square anywhere in England, a testament to the town's historic significance. The slights and snubs coalesce over time, however, and a wry resentment is imbued into the Wirral psyche.

Despite resting two miles apart, Liverpool and Birkenhead are very different places. City versus town. Comparatively rich versus comparatively poor. Regenerated commercial hub versus derelict forgotten afterthought. A sense of resentment suffuses Wirral, where a peninsula mentality of us-against-them helps defend against suppression.

There has long been a temptation to lump Wirral and Liverpool together as one fulcrum of northern emergence. In 2014, the Liverpool City Region Combined Authority was formed, harnessing powers over transport, economic development and regeneration. Wirral became entwined in the Combined Authority, which meshes seven local jurisdictions together under the aegis of Liverpool. The political impact of this scheme is debatable, but the misappropriation of Wirral history and culture amid such an arranged marriage has been stark.

This is a borough of remarkable heritage, heavily influenced by early Viking settlers. Wirralians have their own ethos, values, dialect and ambitions. Merely grouping those traditions with Liverpool - blurring the boundaries of identity, belonging and society - is at best lazy and at worst offensive. We are fiercely independent people, but our idiosyncrasies have been standardised.

Such is the enforced synergy between these two locales, outsiders have come to view them as one united place. People from Liverpool are known as *scousers*, a social identity that has often morphed into derogatory stereotype. Residents of Wirral are often branded as scousers despite their distinct character, principles and history. Frustration festers deep within, even if the outward message is one of neighbourly support and tolerance.

By contrast, some detractors call Wirral arrogant or elitist. Certainly, the borough's western quarter features affluent enclaves such as Hoylake, West Kirby, Thurstaston and Heswall – places of infinite beauty and distinct personality that can be construed as secular, haughty and posh. These rural outposts, scattered along the coast, have contributed to a view of Wirral as aloof, upmarket and luxurious. Accordingly, many scousers refer to Wirralians as 'wools,' a disparaging term that describes anyone hailing from *near* Liverpool but ultimately outside the city itself.

To call somebody a wool is to evoke their *difference* and to highlight their supposed inauthenticity relevant to the mighty metropolis. Woe betide anyone who actually displays pride in their hometown, for it is apparently invalidated by virtue of it *not* being Liverpool.

Without surrendering to woke sensationalism, people from Birkenhead and Wirral endure these subtle forms of prejudice in all walks of life. An inherent sense of inadequacy pervades alumni, whose perceived inferiority manifests in unwanted private jokes and insensitive office banter. As the recipients of nationwide ridicule, scousers should know better, quite frankly, but such behavioural inconsistencies fortify their hyperactive conceit.

Among the misunderstood and misplaced, football is often the most powerful tool of this cultural frustration and the most accessible forum for public revolt. That is particularly true in working class areas, while northern outposts typically harbour deeper sporting passions. Therefore, Birkenhead can be seen as the quintessential rebellion town, and Tranmere Rovers - its predominant football club - is impregnated with greater philosophical meaning as a result.

Johnny King, a legendary Rovers manager, explained the ecology better than anybody else. "Tranmere may never be able to compete with Liverpool or Everton," said King. "They are big liners like the Queen Mary. However, I see Tranmere as a deadly submarine, attacking them silently from beneath with a torpedo."

Indeed, Tranmere rarely play Liverpool on the field. They occupy different leagues and, as we have seen, they operate in different echelons of prestige. Rovers *did* beat Liverpool in World War II exhibitions, but this is otherwise a one-sided rivalry that barely registers on the wider football radar.

The clubs last met competitively in 2001, when Liverpool won 4-2 in a tense FA Cup tie at Prenton Park, Tranmere's home stadium. It was the closest Rovers ever got to toppling their greatest enemy in a meaningful fixture. Too young to attend in person, I remember watching the game on television then recreating the action – albeit with a different outcome – in the street while waiting for my dad to return home.

In the absence of regular games between the two clubs, this feud is therefore played out at grassroots level, usually in the playgrounds, workplaces and pubs of Wirral. Admittedly, the rivalry exists more in the minds of ardent Tranmere fans than it does in the conscience of Liverpool supporters, but the oppressor rarely cares about his or her subject, so such an arrangement seems natural.

Given the sense of stifled individuality on Wirral, and viewing football as a vehicle of social conscience, logic would seem to bestow upon Tranmere Rovers a large fanbase drawn from its immediate catchment area. However, that is not the case, as external greed, selfishness and nonchalance congeal to threaten the club's existence.

Wirral has a population of 330,000 souls while the city of Liverpool is home to 490,000 people. In 2018-19, the average attendance at Tranmere home games was 6,552, compared to 52,983 for Liverpool FC matches. In terms of population, Liverpool is 48% bigger than Wirral, but typical attendances at Anfield are 708% larger than those at Prenton Park. In such a stark dichotomy lies the grand frustration of those tortured few who root for their hometown team, as was the original distinguishing essence of football.

Of course, Everton - *the other club in Liverpool* - exacerbates this problem, too. On average, attendances at Goodison Park are 492% larger than those at Prenton Park. Everton also threatens the existence of Tranmere, but it does so without the self-righteous virtue signalling of Liverpool. Besides, Tranmere beat Everton 3-0 at Goodison Park in 2001, a rare FA Cup triumph that ranks among Rovers' greatest accomplishments. This places Everton in a less stable position from which to exert power over Tranmere. In truth, I struggle to take them seriously.

Returning to the chief antagonist, then, why do people from Wirral so frequently shun Tranmere Rovers and instead support

Liverpool, travelling across the Mersey for sporting entertainment? Well, because Liverpool win and Tranmere do not. Any other argument lacks credibility.

Liverpool has won the English first division championship on 18 occasions. It has won the FA Cup, a prestigious knockout tournament, seven times. On the continent, no British football club has achieved more success, with Liverpool claiming six European Cups, three UEFA Cups and four UEFA Super Cups. From these shores, only Manchester United can compete in terms of silverware and fame.

By contrast, Tranmere has never played in the top division of English football; it has never progressed past the FA Cup quarter-finals; and its record attendance is just 24,424. Rovers have never won a major trophy, and their solitary league title - a regional third division crown - came in 1938, back when Adolf Hitler was named Man of the Year by *Time* magazine. According to mainstream observers, Tranmere is a small club with a sparse history. It is an afterthought, ultimately, and few seem to care.

However, Rovers were formed in 1884 while Liverpool FC was formed in 1892. Therefore, if football finds enchanting purpose in its geography-bound tribalism, somewhere along the line a group of Wirralians corrupted that concept, and I have spent my whole life trying to avenge that infringement.

By rejecting Tranmere and embracing Liverpool, these rebels altered the ecosystem of Merseyside football forever. More pertinently, they encouraged *gloryhunting,* a nefarious phenomenon resting at the heart of my Liverpool intolerance.

Some would say that my grievance lies with Liverpool *fans,* or perhaps more accurately Liverpool *gloryhunters,* rather than with the club itself. Just as Islam should not be condemned for terrorism wrought by an extremist minority of its adherents, a sports club should be appraised independent of its supporters.

Likewise, some would see as contradictory my jumping aboard the Red Sox bandwagon while simultaneously admonishing Liverpool gloryhunters. It can be easy to conflate the two concepts when, in actuality, they are entirely different experiences.

I did not so much *choose* to become a Red Sox fan in 2004 as the team found its way to me. I was 10 years old. The notion of success and failure was foreign in my world. A timid kid from a poor family, I had never *encountered* glory, so how could I knowingly seek it? The Red Sox appeared in my life out of nowhere, the first baseball team I ever knew. Joining their crusade was a spiritual assimilation, immaculate and natural. It was not an engineered campaign.

With regard to fandom, a distinction must also be made here between innocent childhood infatuation and irresponsible adult profiteering. The hero-worshipping child is an understandable phenomenon, but nefarious, *knowing* gloryhunting is often a preserve of adult insecurity. Selecting or changing sporting allegiances to compensate for deficiencies elsewhere - personally, professionally, romantically or otherwise - is a vacuous equalisation of one's own fractured ego. You cannot do it and expect to be respected.

The frustrated sports fan will never find happiness aboard a bandwagon, just as the seasoned alcoholic will never find salvation at the bottom of a bottle. The 'solution' feeds the problem, and there is no way to end the irritable cycle. It all becomes too much, and the individual loses grasp of their own personality.

Of course, we do not live in an authoritarian dystopia, and each individual has the right to make their own decisions. I will never question those liberties, but we must also never suffocate the right to disagree with our peers' choices. There is something egregious about the manufactured pursuit of achievement, and I will always defend myself against such charges.

Wirralians who support Liverpool make a clear, binary choice to do so. By contrast, Englishmen who root for *any* North American sports team face a nuanced, multifaceted predicament that cannot be easily solved or analysed. We must differentiate between planned frontrunning and natural inquisitiveness. A great chasm separates those two concepts, and the latter should never be mistaken for the former.

There are 30 MLB teams of overwhelmingly similar constitution. They are *franchises*, as in agents of the same product. I fell in love with one, not because it won but because it was *different*. Set in 2004 or any other year, that was not gloryhunting. That was organic symbiosis that coincided with a world championship. World Series triumph was not the catalyst of my fandom. It was the medium of discovery and the portal to awakening. Even if the Red Sox lost to St Louis, their redeeming features would have stayed the same in my eyes.

Conversely, at a granular level, aside from the poor optics and general annoyance it creates, *true* gloryhunting has dire consequences for those left behind. The single-minded growth of Liverpool FC directly undermines that of Tranmere Rovers. Such are the laws of football's evolution.

Merely by existing, and by beckoning people to join its movement, Liverpool FC places Tranmere on the endangered species list. They could wipe us off the planet and few people would notice. *We* would notice, though, as genuine Rovers fans, and we will never let that happen.

Life without Tranmere would not be worth living. Therefore, living without Liverpool is the *elixir* that sustains us. Resisting the overtures of Liverpool allows us to survive, even if we continue to be crippled by the big red behemoth.

ससस

Digging deeper, it is important to analyse *why* Liverpool wins so much, positioning itself as the ideal club to support. Just how did Liverpool become so appealing to the masses, and why does its conspicuous mythology remain so abnormally unchallenged?

Well, ambition is the root of all achievement, and this is an area where even I can only commend my tormentor. From the start, Liverpool FC dreamed big and backed those fantasies with consistent action. The club wanted to thrive on a global scale, and it enacted a strategy to that effect. Ambition fed success, which attracted fans, who boosted the club's resources, allowing it to develop a larger stadium and create an endless cycle of glory and growth.

Tranmere, meanwhile, was more concerned with the local landscape. From rudimentary beginnings, Rovers were somewhat myopic in their planning. They joined poorer leagues and settled for imperfect players. They failed to buy upgrades and struggled to compete outside their immediate local region. They were poor and insular, not built for worldwide acclaim. If Liverpool was about commerce, Tranmere was about community. Their mission statements were profoundly different.

Such contrasting philosophies led to a dichotomy of results, success, fan appreciation and fame between Tranmere Rovers and Liverpool FC. Geographical neighbours, the respective clubs quickly came to operate in different galaxies, and any semblance of similarity was discarded long ago.

By 1896-97, Liverpool attracted average home attendances of 12,400 in the first division while Tranmere loitered in obscure regional leagues. Liverpool won its first league title in 1901 as Rovers jostled with Birkenhead FC for supremacy *even within Wirral*.

By the time Tranmere was accepted into the Football League in 1921, Liverpool already had a stranglehold on the local fanbase. Crowds at Anfield soared to more than 38,000 on average by that point, correlating with sustained on-field success, while Tranmere struggled to attract even 7,000 fans on a regular basis.

The tone was set early, then, by the visionaries who ran Liverpool and by the subpar wheeler-dealers who managed Tranmere. Four or five generations of Wirral football fans have subsequently become intoxicated by the romance of Liverpool success, eschewing their hometown club as a pitiful consequence.

To this very day, thousands of Wirral youngsters become Liverpool fans, adhering to the mainstream script and thoughtlessly following the crowd at the expense of their local team. The replica red shirts are so ubiquitous as to desensitise the masses, while an arrogant insouciance towards Tranmere smacks of belittling revisionism.

On the whole, Tranmere is viewed as the annoying younger sibling of Liverpool and Everton, largely forgotten and chronically overlooked. The local press has traditionally failed to cover Tranmere with anything approaching originality. Alas, to many, Rovers became a tiresome afterthought to the Merseyside mega clubs, just as Birkenhead lurks as a misunderstood adjunct of the adored metropolis.

However, Tranmere Rovers has its own beguiling history that is never quite appreciated. Tranmere is the only club with a Norse-Viking name in professional English football, for instance, while Rovers unearthed, refined and gifted to the world a young striker named William Ralph Dean. Later known as Dixie, this raw colt from Birkenhead became one of the greatest forwards ever to lace a pair of boots.

In fact, the three most prolific goalscoring seasons in English first division history were authored by players from Wirral originally discovered by Tranmere Rovers. Pongo Waring joined Dean in that elite scoring echelon, with both stars eventually playing for England.

There is also an implacable *dignity* to Tranmere that deserves greater consideration. Eleven percent of all professional British footballers who died during World War II played for Rovers. Moreover, Tranmere was the first club on Merseyside - and one of the first in England - to hire a black professional footballer, giving a chance to Nigerian student Elkanah Onyeali in 1960.

A font of quirky trivia, Tranmere is the only English football club with three lions on its logo, bringing to life the famous Euro '96 anthem by *Baddiel, Skinner and The Lightning Seeds*. Tranmere is the only British club with a 100% winning record at Highbury, the vaunted home of Arsenal, a global superpower. Rovers were also the first English club to experience foreign ownership, American lawyer Bruce Osterman purchasing the club in 1984.

Interestingly, there are also historic links between Wirral and New York City that are lost under a deluge of Beatlemania and Liverpool love. When designing Central Park in Manhattan, architect Frederick Law Olmstead drew inspiration from Birkenhead Park, the first publicly funded park in the world. Additionally, sandstone from a quarry in Storeton - just 10 minutes from my family home - was used for cladding on the Empire State Building.

These stories never receive the appreciation they deserve. Indeed, many Tranmere facts, figures and phenomena went simply unreported for decades, a trove of untold stories waiting to be explored. I published a concise anthology of those anecdotes and factoids in 2019, and *Planet Prentonia* was just the ninth book ever written about Tranmere Rovers. Meanwhile, Liverpool became press cherubs as the local, national and international media created and maintained a romantic narrative of the club's heritage.

Lauded as a paragon of working class pride, Liverpool positions itself as a socialist football club of the people. Its triumphs are dramatised, and hyperbole washes over a sanctimonious fanbase defined by delusions of grandeur.

Liverpool fans live in the past. They are pious guardians of tradition and culture, but they also incubate myths, harbour falsehoods and hide facts in the most unscrupulous manner possible. They are hypocrites, quite frankly, perpetrating a heroic image that covers a shameful past that is often airbrushed.

Liverpool did not sign a black professional player until 1977. When eventually it did, that player - Howard Gayle, a local lad from Toxteth - endured implicit and explicit racism from all facets of the club, as detailed in *61 Minutes in Munich*, his autobiography:

"The culture at Liverpool dictated that I was expected to just allow it to go over my head and not take things so seriously. But it wasn't in my make-up to let certain words get used without responding forcefully. So I came back at them. It contributed towards me getting the reputation as someone who had an attitude problem: someone who was reluctant to fit in.

"Attitudes towards me were mixed. The majority did not have a problem with a young black male entering an absolutely white environment. But I could sense my presence made some uncomfortable. This presented another problem. Some comments were made by those who I liked, those who did not mean any real harm. But even if I let those comments ride, would it create the impression for those with more entrenched views that it was OK to follow suit?

"I first became aware of intolerant attitudes at Melwood [Liverpool's training complex] through people who didn't realise I was close by and within earshot. Unacceptable phrases were used. It would happen in the canteen at Anfield. It would happen on the bus en route to training or games. Such language was delivered in jest. But I was not laughing.

"The racism was easier to take from the terraces because you reasoned it was down to your performance, you liked to think you were doing something right. Maybe that's naïve. I was abused frequently, whether I played well or badly. When it comes from the people that you work with, though, it hurts."

Such incidents are not isolated in the history of Liverpool FC. Roy Chubby Brown - a notoriously racist comedian banned from British television for his crude humour - once compered the club's Christmas party, telling jokes about the Toxteth race riots. Liverpool never signed an Irish Catholic player until 1979, maintaining divisive Protestant traditions, while John Barnes, one of the club's first black stars, was routinely subjected to abuse throughout the 1980s and 1990s.

Liverpool supporters wrote letters to Barnes telling him not to join the club. Teammates used racist language in Barnes' presence. Perhaps most infamously, bananas were thrown at Barnes on the field, likening him to a monkey. These incidents cannot be forgotten.

Years later, in 2011, Liverpool striker Luis Suárez was banned for eight matches by the Football Association after being found guilty of racially abusing Manchester United defender Patrice Evra. Rather than condemn his actions, Liverpool backed Suárez in public. Prior to a game against Wigan Athletic, the entire Liverpool squad wore t-shirts emblazoned with Suárez' face, an ill-advised symbol of solidarity. Even their manager, club legend Kenny Dalglish, spoke to the media wearing the insensitive garment. Liverpool then released a garbled statement contesting the judgment, adding insult to injury:

"Liverpool Football Club is very surprised and disappointed with the decision of the Football Association commission to find Luis Suárez guilty of the charges against him.

We find it extraordinary that Luis can be found guilty on the word of Patrice Evra alone when no-one else on the field of play – including Evra's own Manchester United teammates and all the match officials – heard the alleged conversation between the two players in a crowded Kop goalmouth while a corner kick was about to be taken.

It seems incredible to us that a player of mixed heritage should be accused and found guilty in the way he has based on the evidence presented. We do not recognise the way in which Luis Suárez has been characterised."

This refusal to accept the truth, and such attempts to influence facts, strikes at the heart of my disapproval of Liverpool FC. The club is simply incapable of seeing itself as anything other than a victim in almost every aspect of cultural operation. It even refused to use the word *racism* in relation to Suárez. When you strip back the bluster, however, Liverpool FC is more often the perpetrator of intolerance than it is the recipient. Their fans will never admit it, though, and attempts to discuss such topics typically end with lectures of bitter mythology.

For example, Liverpool fans played a pioneering role in the advent and growth of football hooliganism, which plagued the British game in the 1970s and 1980s. Around this time, gangs of likeminded youths, disenfranchised from everyday society, gathered at football matches to find a sense of identity. Angry and petulant, they resorted to violence and mayhem as weapons of rebellion, with organised fights between rival *firms* – terrace parlance for gangs – becoming a centrepiece of the matchday experience.

These firms adhered to a worrying counterculture centred on hedonism, train travel, music and fashion. Known as *casuals*, hooligans did not just arrive at the stadium and decide to fight. Rather, belonging to such a group offered a distinct way of life, complete with a carefully curated wardrobe, endless amounts of alcohol, and excursions planned with military precision.

Liverpool had a greater influence on nascent casual culture than any other club in world football. Perennially successful, Liverpool competed on all fronts, becoming a force in Europe. As Liverpool fans followed their club around the continent - playing games in France, Italy, Spain, Germany and beyond -

they returned with the latest styles and most popular brands from each locale, influencing nationwide tastes.

Discovered, embraced and promoted by Liverpool casuals, brands such as Lacoste, Sergio Tacchini, Benetton, Fila and Stone Island became popular among British football fans. The radical change in dress fooled domestic police officers, who associated the archetypal football hooligan with a skinhead and Dr Martens boots. Liverpool blazed a trail on the terraces, and it was not always pretty.

While such contributions to football fashion may appear quaint and idiosyncratic, the actions of those fans bedecked in designer clothes was ultimately shameful. More importantly, hooliganism stunted the progress of English football - commercially, structurally and culturally - and brought shame on our nation. Hooliganism dumped football back a few generations on these shores while rival countries took giant leaps forward.

In 1985, football violence reached its grim nadir when Liverpool played Juventus in the European Cup final at Heysel Stadium in Brussels, Belgium. Before the game kicked-off, rival fans exchanged barbs on the terraces, where they were segregated by a vacant concrete area. Perhaps provoked, Liverpool fans nevertheless went beyond the pale, breaching fences, ploughing through the neutral zone and chasing Juventus fans in nightmarish fashion.

Attempting to escape the barrage, many Juventus supporters turned around and ran up the terraces, seeking relief. A concrete wall retained crowds at the back of the stand, and as fans rushed towards it, those people already stood in front of the wall were crushed horrifically. Amid incredible pressure, the wall collapsed, killing 39 people and injuring 600. Most of the victims were Italian Juventus fans.

Amid protracted legal wrangles, 14 Liverpool fans were found guilty of manslaughter. Each was sentenced to three years in prison. UEFA, European football's governing body, banned all English club from its competitions indefinitely. The ban was not overturned for five years, while Liverpool did not return to European competition until 1991-92.

During the ban, some of the finest teams in English football history were denied their chance to compete on the biggest stages. More pertinently, our national reputation was destroyed by overzealous Liverpool hooligans. That pales in comparison to the pain inflicted on those Italian families, however. Their voice has rarely been respected.

When Juventus played Liverpool at Anfield in 2005, the clubs' first meeting since the disaster, attempts at reconciliation were inadequate. A group of supporters from both clubs approached the travelling Juventus fans carrying a banner with slogans of memory and friendship. Hundreds of Juventus fans turned their backs in protest, snubbing the belated tokenism.

Crumbling and ageing, Heysel was not a suitable venue for such a monumental final, and several top officials were also sanctioned for their negligence in bringing the game to Belgium. Policing at the final was also insufficient for such a large spectacle. Nevertheless, Liverpool's role in one of the most harrowing tragedies ever to befall a European football match cannot be ignored. Some may want to conveniently forget such uncomfortable truths, but I'm not among that number.

Of course, as desired by the pro-Liverpool media, the Heysel disaster is rarely discussed in conventional circles. BBC News published an article in 2015 branding it *English football's forgotten tragedy*. To the more discerning eye, though, the actions of Liverpool fans in Belgium were so appalling as to anger. Is it really so difficult to understand why I do not want any association with this football club?

❧❧❧

Regardless of allegiances, one catastrophe unites all football fans in mourning. The Hillsborough disaster - a stadium crush that killed 96 Liverpool fans at their FA Cup semi-final against Nottingham Forest in 1989 - exists beyond the sphere of partisan point-scoring. It unifies our spirt and transcends our affiliations.

Nobody should ever go to watch a sporting event and not return home. The excitement of an FA Cup semi-final only heightens the poignant dichotomy of emotion. Mums and dads, brothers and sons, sisters and daughters woke that morning with giddy anticipation for the day ahead. That life was forever altered by grave mistakes in stadium management is eternally heartbreaking. It remains the most shameful chapter in English football history.

Shortly before kick-off at Hillsborough, dense crowds formed inside and outside the Leppings Lane End, allocated to Liverpool supporters. Attempting to ease the congestion, the police match commander, chief superintendent David Duckenfield, ordered an exit gate to be opened. Seeking space in which to breathe, fans moved through the gate, an influx that could not be contained within the decrepit grandstand.

Amid a devastating crush, dozens perished and hundreds were injured. The Leppings Lane End featured a high perimeter fence separating fans from the pitch, and this proved a fatal hurdle for many. Supporters clambered onto the field for relief, while heroic acts of bravery and comradeship also saved lives in imminent danger.

Following the disaster, culpable police officers concocted false stories that were reported by a sensationalist tabloid press. Citing doctored witness statements and unsubstantiated sources, *The Sun* wrongly blamed the tragedy on hooliganism and drunkenness among Liverpool fans. Margaret Thatcher's aggressive Conservative government was complicit in a shameful coverup, but the city of Liverpool fought long and hard to clear its name.

Finally, in 2016, after interminable campaigning, a second coroner's inquest ruled that the supporters were unlawfully killed due to grossly negligent failures by police and ambulance personnel to deliver on their duty of care. Duckenfield faced criminal trial for 95 counts of manslaughter - the 96th victim, Anthony Bland, died almost four years after the disaster, beyond a controversial cut-off point for legal retribution - but was controversially acquitted in 2019.

No wound is etched deeper into the emotional psyche of Merseyside than that created by Hillsborough. Most local families know somebody directly or indirectly affected by the disaster, which is the worst in British sporting history. The way in which our local area has come together, regardless of club allegiances, to attain criminal justice, makes me proud. It is a paragon of belief in the face of adversity, and we can all gleam important lessons from the campaign.

In the aftermath of the tragedy, Tranmere held a memorial service at Prenton Park, attended by Liverpool players and officials. The ceremony was exceptionally poignant, with flowers and scarves draped over the goalposts in a display of solidarity. Rovers have also embraced the passionate fight to shun *The Sun*, banning representatives of the newspaper from attending club events.

In British culture, very few things transcend the sanctity of one's footballing faith. Yet ultimately, we all share a love for this beautiful game, and indeed for the beguiling wonder of sports more generally. That should never result in unlawful death, and that should never be grist for political engineering.

The Hillsborough disaster rests in a human echelon, not in a biased echo chamber of sporting partisanship. Injustice to one group of football fans is injustice to *all* football fans, and we must never let rivalries dilute that sense of moral camaraderie in the winds of injustice.

⚾⚾⚾

As a kid, abhorring Liverpool FC was my defence mechanism against schoolyard hectoring. The vast majority of my peers were Liverpool fans, and I was often the lone Tranmere fan in various settings. The constant teasing and squabbling took its toll, and I actively rooted for the demise of my nemesis. In fact, you could say I cheered for two teams: Tranmere, and whoever was playing Liverpool.

The sense of entitlement among Liverpool fans is bewildering. They have a distorted worldview that portrays their football club as omnipotent, quite literally seeing the game through rose-tinted glasses. This chronic absence of reality when supporting a top level club is bizarre. It is anathema to my core values.

When Premier League fans moan about perceived hardships, rest assured that they are not really hardships at all. Woe betide the Arsenal manager who loses two games in a row, for instance, and god forbid Chelsea endures a season without silverware. Such narrow-minded arrogance makes football an instrument of success rather than a metaphor for humanity. It strips the meaning from sport and exposes its thorough pointlessness.

Somewhere along the way, the essence of fandom was disorientated in this capitalist vacuum. Glory became the defining characteristic and cash became the ultimate prize. Merely representing a region barely seems to matter anymore, beyond what said region can provide in terms of pounds and dollars. We see this as sports teams move from one city to another, and we see this as people select their athletic allegiances based on championships and payroll rather than family and geography.

According to sports business website Spotrac, Liverpool paid Mohamed Salah £200,000 per week during the 2019-20 season. They have 12 players who earn more than £400,000 every month. The club's annual wage bill is £263 million. By contrast, Tranmere's highest earner makes just over £2,000 per week, while Rovers' yearly payroll hovers around £3.5 million. Tranmere could afford to pay Salah for 122 days, so long as they employed *nobody else*. *That* is why I cannot relate to Premier League football. It lacks any basis in reality.

The things that make football great - pride, identity, belonging, civic achievement - are diluted or destroyed by supporting a team from out of town. Of course, everybody has a right to make their own decisions and to form their unique opinions, but mine says that football ceases to be *football* when its local authenticity is removed. It becomes entertainment, a universal product on a clinical stage, and a travelling circus of obfuscated meaning.

We castigate large companies that import raw materials from China, lamenting how globalisation bankrupts the local farmer, but what about the football behemoth thwarting the hometown underdog? What about Liverpool FC killing Tranmere Rovers?

Critics may say I'm just bitter, that Liverpool is simply a successful business with excellent skills in recruitment, marketing and public relations. It has built a powerful brand that is loved around the world, and I'm just indignant at its inexorable growth.

Well, that is partly true, I guess. Liverpool has undoubtedly hired great people and pushed all the right buttons in developing a fantastic commercial base. The club has even played preseason friendlies against Tranmere to boost Rovers' budget and spread goodwill. However, the careless ways in which it does so leaves a bitter taste in the mouth of those who do not subscribe to the red mantra.

For example, Liverpool has a retail shop in the heart of Birkenhead town centre. Tranmere Rovers does not. This is an affront dressed as sound marketing, strategic business development masking subtle exploitation. For Liverpool, this is just one of many shops globally. However, the success of such shops, and indeed the efficiency of such territorial invasion, makes it impossible for Tranmere and other small clubs to compete.

We would love to sell merchandise in our own town centre, but the price is too steep, driven upwards by the wealthy elite and its endless stream of cash. How can we ever compete if the *tools* of competition are locked in a room we cannot enter? There is a huge gulf in resources between lower league clubs and the Premier League elite. Pretty soon, that chasm will give rise to an irreversible monopoly. When that finally happens, football as we loved it will die a shameful death, and there will be nothing to gift our grandkids.

⚾⚾⚾

I can forgive the reader for detecting a hint of hypocrisy in my writing so far. Here is a guy complaining about people from out of town supporting Liverpool, yet he follows baseball teams on *another continent*? Strange. Here is a guy dispelling gloryhunters who chase success, but he became a Red Sox fan after the 2004 World Series? Odd.

Here is a guy lambasting Liverpool for spending exorbitant amounts of money on players, but he once cheered for a baseball franchise that did the same? Bizarre. Here is a guy scolding Liverpool for its poor record on race relations, yet he once rooted for the Red Sox, the last of all MLB teams to integrate? Dumb. Here is a guy writing about betrayal, yet he himself disowned those same Red Sox when John Henry bought something he did not like? Cute.

Well, my situation is a little different, ladies and gentlemen. I'm British. The conventional apparatus of baseball allegiance – determined by locality, incubated by exposure and regulated by family tradition – was never afforded to me. I had to forge my own path in North American sports. There was no roadmap to follow.

My dad did not grow up rooting for a particular team, and nor did my grandad. Nobody in my entire family tree knew what baseball even was, so inheriting a team simply never happened. You cannot bequeath something that does not exist. It was therefore impossible for me to naturally receive a baseball religion.

Likewise, the Liverpool Trojans are the closest ballclub to my home. Perhaps I should root for them, following the logic of this book, but the standard of British baseball is comparatively abysmal to that of traditional powerhouses. We are not talking *third division to Premier League* difference here. We are talking *earth to mars* difference. It is barely worth considering. It is barely the same sport.

Besides, I love Major League Baseball, and I have a right to identify with one of its teams, just as others have a right to support a top tier football club if they so desire. Some people may not like my rationale, but it is exactly that: *my* rationale. Everyone has a different heart, and this book is not a manifesto for outward change but rather an instruction manual for inner peace.

I will never dispute claims that fans on the ground who attend games each night, living and breathing with every pitch, are more authentic rooters than me. If we are handing out medals for real world engagement, I'm unlikely to win one. However, physical detachment does not exclusively curtail or instinctively diminish emotional passion. I'm just as capable of rooting for a big league baseball team as anybody else on the planet. The internet now provides certain tools that help such transatlantic obsessions, and I will feverishly defend my right to create bespoke baseball experiences without fear of ridicule.

Returning to the central point of this argument - my disdain for and rejection of the Boston Red Sox once they entered symbiosis with Liverpool FC - it is difficult to find a suitable comparison in North American sports with which to illustrate my predicament. The best I can do relies on independent league baseball and subsequent affiliation with a major league conglomerate.

Imagine, for a moment, that you are a rabid fan of the Sugar Land Skeeters, one of the most famous independent baseball teams in America. You have seen Roger Clemens wear your beloved uniform, and you live and die with every pitch, keeping season tickets at Constellation Field. There is no alternative to your Skeeters, and you loathe the Houston Astros and Texas Rangers, big league organisations from the same state that barely acknowledge your team's existence.

One day, you wake up to the frightening news that those Astros have *purchased* the Skeeters and co-opted them into the Houston major league system. Once a proud independent team representing a historic, overlooked city, the Sugar Land *Astros* are now just another Triple-A farm club, one more generic vehicle of player development, complete with new uniforms, altered logos and garbled business objectives.

What would *you* do? How would *you* react? Perhaps you would continue rooting for the Skeeters as their identity changes and as they become a tool of Astros propaganda. Or maybe you would stand up for yourself, fight for your principles, and defend the originality of your hometown by severing ties.

There are obvious differences between this hypothetical concept and my personal experience. Liverpool FC and the Boston Red Sox play different sports and operate in entirely different leagues. There is very limited mutuality between the organisations. Still, what little mutuality *does* exist is too much for me to bear, such is the extent of my feeling.

Some will blame my own pessimism for creating such a dramatic situation. They will point out potential *positives* of the shared ownership, such as Henry and Werner spending time on Merseyside, likely opening an office here. Theoretically, opportunities to meet them and pitch for that dream job working for the Red Sox became more realistic because of the

Liverpool takeover. John and Tom may have even made me the Red Sox' head of European operations. Now just imagine *that*.

However, once Liverpool was subsumed into Fenway Sports Group, the Red Sox became a cursory concern for Henry and Werner. The owners split time between England and the US, doing justice to neither team and letting both spiral out of control. In Boston, when such neglect began to affect the standings, loyal employees were thrown under the bus. Even Francona was eventually burned at the stake, a forgotten legend left out in the cold.

"They came in with all these ideas about baseball, but I don't think they love baseball," Francona said in his memoirs. "I think they like baseball. It's revenue, and I know that's their right and their interest because they're owners – and they're good owners. But they don't love the game. It's still more of a toy or hobby for them. It's not in their blood."

Admittedly, my story is rife with logical redundancies. Boycotting the Red Sox because their owners bought something I do not enjoy is akin to boycotting pizza because the fascist Mussolini was once prime minister of Italy. Snubbing the Red Sox because a few executives went to a soccer game is like unfriending your best pal on Facebook because his dad likes a Donald Trump video. Where do we draw the line?

People will scold my bewildering fallacy, and I understand why. The Boston Red Sox are a proud, interdependent organisation in their own right, unburdened from any mere soccer team. I get it. I hear you. There is no counterargument. Alas, some things are just more important than opportunistic profiteering. My personal values encouraged a certain decision, and I stand by the results to this day.

I'm a deeply spiritual, political and philosophical person. Where most see surface actions, I sense motivating morals. I'm concerned with the *process* of events, concepts and institutions, not just mindful of their external *appearance*, tampered optics and calcified marketing spiel. Liverpool Football Club does not mesh with my views, and its sphere of influence should therefore be avoided to negate self-destruction.

For more than five years, a baseball team from Boston, Massachusetts occupied a special place in my world. Living on a different continent, I made incredible sacrifices to follow the Red Sox through feast and famine. My heart pounded for The Olde Towne Team, until it was shattered by unknowing treachery of the highest order.

The Boston Red Sox were my religion, and losing that centre of gravity caused chaos in my universe. Recovering from such a monumental shock was incredibly difficult, and continuing daily life amid such an attack on my constitution was virtually impossible. I was down, out and mired in the sporting wastelands. The love of my life jumped in bed with my dearest foe, and the concept of *tomorrow* lost all appeal in my eyes.

CHAPTER FIFTEEN

The Wilderness

Without a team to root for, I fell out of the baseball loop almost entirely. The daily routine of mining various news sites fell by the wayside, and a general disinterest washed over me. I was disenfranchised, literally and figuratively. There seemed to be no future for me in Major League Baseball.

The occasional internet clip or news feature piqued my interest, but any sustained interest was difficult to achieve. Chetwynd tried valiantly to keep the *Baseball on Five* flame alive, penning blogs and touring radio stations, but the players became unfamiliar as I failed to keep up.

For months, I conflated the loss of Red Sox fandom with the end of my enthusiasm for baseball more generally. I was fed up, wandering the sporting wilderness. There was no playbook for how to cope with such unique dissatisfaction. There was no historical precedent devoid of a catastrophic conclusion. There was no guidance on how to act or where to turn. I was lost.

In hindsight, the most natural reaction would have been to become a Yankees fan. What better way to rebel against John Henry and the Red Sox than by ditching them for their biggest rival? Alas, the supposed taboo of Yankee fandom had been stitched into my psyche by that point. I had been thoroughly brainwashed, and rooting for the Bombers still seemed somehow wrong.

One day during the resultant malaise, Nath returned from a local video game shop with a battered copy of *MLB 07: The Show*. It was the first baseball game we ever laid hands on, and playing it put a smile back on my face. More importantly, while flicking through the various ballclub logos one day, the notion of choosing another team to root for, hitherto forbidden, presented itself with exciting vigour. FSG hurt me enough by defecting to Liverpool, and I decided it would not continue to cast a shadow over my passions. I would not wallow in baseball victimhood forever. It was time to get back on the horse and ride again.

Contrary to my obsessive-compulsive nature, the method I chose to select a new baseball rooting interest was laughably unscientific. I sat down for perhaps half an hour and scanned a few webpages before settling on a team in kneejerk chaos. I randomly decided to become a fan of the Los Angeles Dodgers.

At a subliminal level, the pristine white uniform with classy blue trimmings reminded me of Tranmere, while the sandy abyss of Dodger Stadium always captivated me. There was an intrigue to the Dodgers, one of baseball's most historic franchises, and I was vaguely excited to be part of it.

Of course, I picked perhaps the worst possible time to become a Dodgers fan. The San Francisco Giants - a mortal enemy - won the World Series in 2010. They repeated the trick in 2012 and 2014. Meanwhile, the Dodgers struggled through an institutional crisis that made them a laughingstock. I showed up with woozy optimism, but veteran diehards were not in the mood.

In October 2009, it was announced that Frank McCourt and Jamie McCourt - owner and CEO of the Dodgers, respectively - would separate after almost 30 years of marriage. Amid the resulting divorce, the team was plunged into financial difficulty, filing for bankruptcy protection. MLB intervened, appointing a representative to oversee daily operations at Chavez Ravine. McCourt agreed to put the Dodgers up for sale, but one of the most famous sports teams in the world teetered on the brink of meltdown.

Naturally, such a woeful downturn coincided with my interest in the Dodgers. Hell, why not? My misfortune seemed unshakeable. To be honest, though, even amid such dire circumstances, I thoroughly enjoyed the 2011 season, characterised by stunning dysfunctionality. It was a nice transition for a recovering Red Sox addict.

Remarkably, I never watched a single Dodgers game live during my brief interest in the team. In hindsight, rooting for a west coast franchise was highly impractical. First pitch was usually after 03:00 am here in Britain, and games often stretched into the early breakfast hours. Insomnia was a morbid consequence of such fandom, and even I struggled to find the required stamina.

Still, I read extensively about Dodgers history, appreciating the legacy of Jackie Robinson even more. I enjoyed the work of Vin Scully, whose loquacious musings were a tailormade accompaniment to the national pastime. There was something so pure and pleasing about the Dodgers, something so *refined*. They reminded me of summer afternoons and heady days of indulgence. An elegance characterised Dodgers baseball, and the team's unalloyed beauty reflected the genius of human taste.

In particular, I associated with the distinct averageness of those 2011 Dodgers. Their quirky route to mediocrity was also redolent of Tranmere. At 26, outfielder Matt Kemp had the best season of his career, hitting 39 home runs and stealing 40 bases. His efforts were matched by Clayton Kershaw, a 23-year-old ace who was virtually unhittable. Kershaw went 21-5 in 2011 with 248 strikeouts and a 0.977 WHIP. Together, Matt and Clayton were the twin terrors of a Dodgers generation. The melding of their skill was a sight to behold.

Alas, Kemp and Kershaw were surrounded by failing veterans and overhyped youngsters. Rod Barajas was the starting catcher at 35. Jamey Carroll was the second baseman at 37. Juan Uribe hit .204 at third base. Meanwhile, fading prospects like James Loney, Andre Ethier, Dee Gordon and Tony Gwynn Jr. struggled to meet expectations.

Managed by Yankee martyr Don Mattingly, the team was constructed by Ned Colletti, a well-meaning executive whose traditional approach was borderline comical. Working within severe financial constraints, Colletti built an imperfect team that was actually intriguing to watch. He was the last general manager to put his gut before his calculator.

The 2011 Dodgers spent $103 million on payroll, less than eleven other clubs, and they finished with an 82-79 record. Arizona won the division as Los Angeles missed the playoffs for a second straight year. The Dodgers were the definition of *mediocre,* but they piqued a morbid curiosity within me. They were decidedly *human,* fiscal chaos included, and I liked the potential resurrection buried within such a moribund institution.

However, things changed quickly at Chavez Ravine, and an ethos of winning at all costs was implanted by a new regime. Such reckless capitalism was anathema to the Dodgers I knew, descended from the working class neighbourhoods of Brooklyn. Everything changed in the blink of an eye, leaving me without a baseball team once again.

Inarguably, the Dodgers needed new ownership. Frank McCourt starved the franchise of resources in the dying embers of his premiership, and the organisation fell into disrepair. Dodger Stadium needed a facelift, broadcast deals needed to be agreed, and the farm system needed to be replenished. However, the way in which Guggenheim Baseball Management - the eventual winning bidder - made those changes was ever so slightly disconcerting. The group lost my support almost immediately by failing to understand the cultural texture of their acquisition.

Almost overnight, the Dodgers became a lucrative organisation steeped in financial freedom. That was partly exciting, of course, but it also felt somewhat contrived. At least to me, anyway. My blue-collar sensibilities jarred with the insecure posturing of Los Angeles, and I never swallowed the glitzy sales pitch. It was far too fast and far too *fake*. I needed a dose of reality.

⚾⚾⚾

Meanwhile, in the sweet throes of karma, the 2011 Red Sox became the first team in major league history to hold a nine-game lead in September and fail to make the playoffs. Boston went 7-20 in the final month, capitulating in gross fashion. The Sox even blew a ninth-inning lead against Baltimore on the season's final day, while the Rays enjoyed a walk-off win over the Yankees to clinch a wildcard berth.

As the season went up in flames, Josh Beckett could often be found in the clubhouse on days he was not pitching, drinking beer, eating fried chicken and playing video games. Jon Lester and John Lackey, colleagues in the starting rotation, also participated in the clique, which was partly blamed for the Red Sox' poor play.

Francona lost control of his team and, shortly thereafter, lost his job entirely. Epstein also left Boston in the offseason, agreeing a five-year contract worth $18.5 million to spearhead the Chicago Cubs' baseball operations department.

"Football legend Bill Walsh used to say that coaches and executives should seek change after 10 years with the same team," Epstein wrote in a farewell letter printed by the *Boston Globe*. "This idea resonated with me. Although I tried my best to fight it, I couldn't escape the conclusion that both the Red Sox and I would benefit from a change."

Ben Cherington became the Red Sox' general manager while Bobby Valentine took over in the dugout. Much maligned, Valentine was never truly embraced by the team's veteran core. He lasted just one season at the helm, marred by chronic injuries, in-fighting, clubhouse mutiny and public relations nightmares. His 2012 Red Sox lost 93 games, their worst season in 47 years, and they were saddled with poisonous egos that ran astray.

For example, Carl Crawford was signed by Epstein to a seven-year, $142 million contract in December 2010, only to produce the worst season of his career in 2011. Crawford appeared in just 31 games throughout the 2012 campaign, as well, inciting volcanic tantrums across Red Sox Nation. Once a potent threat with Tampa Bay, stealing more than 50 bases five separate times, Crawford broke down in Boston, suffering one injury after another. Epstein was duly criticised for the worst signing of his tenure, and people questioned whether the protégé had lost his magic touch.

With five-and-a-half years remaining on his exorbitant deal, Crawford looked finished as the force we once knew. The Red Sox appeared to be burdened with a degenerating outfielder who could not handle the bellicose Boston media. Throw in Beckett, a law unto himself, and Adrián González, a star who resented Valentine's management, and the Red Sox were set for long-term mediocrity. At least until the Dodgers intervened with reckless intent, bailing them out to my eternal chagrin.

Fronted by Magic Johnson, a beloved Lakers basketball player, Guggenheim bought the Dodgers for $2.15 billion in March 2012. No sports team had ever sold for more. The group was keen to make an immediate impact, and it did so with a number of high-profile trades and international signings.

The most controversial trade of all - that which defined a generation in Major League Baseball - was consummated with the Red Sox. *Because of course it was.* The deal left me flabbergasted, and not in a positive sense, as the Dodgers essentially helped the Red Sox retool for a fresh championship run while binding themselves with restrictive contracts and noxious personalities.

Mired in crisis, Boston sent González, Beckett, Crawford and Nick Punto to Los Angeles, along with $11 million, in return for Loney, Rubby De La Rosa, Jerry Sands and two middling prospects. The Dodgers agreed to cover $258 million of the $270 million owed to the cabal of malcontents joining them. The Red Sox could scarcely believe their luck.

A very good first baseman, González regularly topped 30 home runs and 100 RBI in his formative years with San Diego. Boston acquired the Mexican in a December 2010 trade and promptly gave him a seven-year contract extension worth $154 million. González performed spectacularly for the Red Sox, hitting .338 with 27 home runs, 117 RBI and a .410 OBP in 2011. He got off to a great start in 2012, too, and the Dodgers yearned for his services.

Loney was a fine defensive first baseman for Los Angeles, but the new regime wanted a superstar at the position. Moreover, the Dodgers have strong cultural ties to Mexico, bound by geography and the symbolic rise of pitcher Fernando Valenzuela in the 1980s. Ownership appreciated the commercial importance of attracting stars from the region, inspiring new fans to watch games and buy jerseys. A marketing dream, González was therefore pivotal to the blockbuster trade, and the Dodgers facilitated a Red Sox salary dump of monumental proportions just to get him.

There is a direct, if subconscious, correlation between the Dodgers rescuing the Red Sox and my interest in the team evaporating. I never consciously decided to boycott the Dodgers because they added bad blood from Boston. I just gradually drifted away from the team, almost as quickly as it ceased being the ballclub I knew.

In particular, there was something unquenchably discombobulating about Beckett and Crawford in Dodger blue. It just never quite felt right. *Contrived*, almost, as if somehow artificial and vacuous. The Dodgers became unrecognisable to me, and any slight emotional connection I had to the team was swiftly truncated.

Los Angeles missed the playoffs in 2012 then proceeded to acquire even more superstars on inflated salaries, hoping to crack the code artificially. Zack Greinke got $147 million. Hyun-jin Ryu got $36 million out of South Korea after the Dodgers paid $25.7 million just to *negotiate* with him. Then there was Yasiel Puig, a Cuban amateur who signed for seven years and $42 million despite never playing a professional game.

The Dodgers also granted huge contract extensions to their own homegrown players. Kemp signed for eight years and $160 million. Ethier re-upped for five years and $85 million. Shortly down the road, Kershaw dwarfed everyone with a seven-year, $215 million pact as Los Angeles lost all sense of reality. They spent money like it was soon to be discontinued.

From $95 million on Opening Day 2012, the Dodgers' payroll mushroomed to $216 million twelve months later, a precipitous rise of 127%. By that point, I had lost all interest in the team. There was no long-term vision in any of the Dodgers' dealings, and the team's lack of a gritty soul left me bored.

Such a sudden and drastic change shocked my system. Sure, the Dodgers belong to the upper echelon of big league spenders, and a market like Los Angeles requires bold investment, but the abrupt deluge of reckless spending gushed forth without warning. There was no honeymoon period or gradual transformation. The Dodgers changed course *overnight*, taking the fast-track highway while loyal fans remained on the humble sidewalk.

Again, some will identify a hint of hypocrisy in my actions, and I can only offer minimal defence against such charges. Ultimately, I felt no deep-seated emotional connection to the Los Angeles Dodgers, and my interest in the team was based purely on surface level aesthetics. When those aesthetics changed, there was no basis for long-term infatuation. My philosophical yearning overpowered the optical illusion.

Many people will struggle to understand why the Dodgers' heavy investment in payroll was a bad thing in my mind. Certainly, a willingness to improve the on-field product should be praised, but there was an absurd lack of *authenticity* to the Dodgers' spending. Magic Johnson was like an immature teenager wielding his first credit card.

More pertinently, I'm not sure if they even had that money to spend in the first place. When Guggenheim bought the Dodgers, it did so by borrowing $1.3 billion from the insurance arm of its corporation. Policy holders of Guggenheim Life expected their money to be invested in safe, liquid assets. However, Mark Walter used those premiums to buy a bankrupted baseball team, perhaps the opposite of *safe* and *liquid*.

Guggenheim inherited $412 million of debt from McCourt, while the Dodgers failed to turn a profit in any of the new regimen's first four years in charge. Coupled with more than $1 billion spent on procuring new players; annual payrolls exceeding $300 million; and luxury tax bills surpassing $100 million – well, let's just say the team's financial situation was murky at best and unfeasible at worst.

Walter and his associates even pledged their *personal* wealth to guarantee the insurance investments, an unusual move suggestive of fiscal turmoil. I love baseball, not economics. I rooted for the Dodgers, not for Wall Street. This was all too much, and I had to get out.

While lawful in a heavily regulated industry, Guggenheim's ascension smacked of bourgeois arrogance. The Dodgers effectively became a rented toy of the ultrarich, bought and sold with somebody else's Monopoly money. That did not sit well with me, and the megawatt makeover of a banal team left a bitter taste in my mouth. I became a free agent fan, but I was not necessarily available to the highest bidder.

I wanted to be engaged on an intellectual and philosophical level, not just placated with showcase commerce and vague celebrity imitation. In hindsight, then, the Dodgers - or more accurately, the *Guggenheim* Dodgers - are quite possibly the major league team that is *least* compatible with my worldview. I'm a pauper and they are plutocrats. It was never likely to work.

Our relationship made little sense, and it was suitably fleeting. I was a Dodgers 'fan' from the summer of 2011 until the autumn of 2012. There were no playoff games during that span. There was 168 wins and 155 losses. I rooted for the Dodgers during one of the worst stretches in their history. There are few regrets on my part, although I do have *some* happy memories stowed away for darker days ahead.

❧❧❧

In the summer of 2013, I was 18 years old and focused on the future. After gaining strong high school grades, particularly in English, I was in the process of completing my A-Level exams, attempting to earn a place at university to study journalism.

Determined to live my extreme dream as a professional baseball writer, I began taking voluntary roles to gain experience. In 2011, I covered the AA North Division as a beat reporter for the British Baseball Federation. They gave me a £50 honorarium for the trouble. I also started my own baseball blog, complete with a woeful design, and promoted articles on social media, that newfangled tool of empowerment.

I understood the importance of a university degree in turbocharging a journalism career. However, struggling with worsening anxiety, I heaped enormous pressure on myself to perform well in the A-Level exams. I worried about anything and everything. I wallpapered my bedroom with notes and reminders, tips and research. I started cramming for June tests in February, awash with paranoia. I did not trust my own ability.

The obsessive-compulsive brain is hyperactive. It literally never stops spinning notions, creating projects, connecting concepts and analysing opportunities. That often slides into pessimistic or even fatalistic thinking, as the worst possible outcome in any situation presents itself with irresistible noise. But if channelled correctly into a creative endeavour, the obsessive-compulsive brain is capable of extreme talent and unknowing genius.

In the murky depths of intelligentsia, that which made me unique - obsessive determination, tireless organisation and relentless scheming - also pushed me closer to capitulation. I needed an outlet for my frustration and relief from the endless *thinking*. Of course, the distractions I built - reading, writing, attempting to become a journalist - relied *intrinsically* on thinking, and to great excess. Such is the illogical cycle of OCD.

Accordingly, while studying Excel weighted averages as part of my IT coursework, I stumbled across an incredible idea: creating the ultimate spreadsheet to identify the Major League Baseball team most suited to my tastes, values, preferences and desires.

Speaking to detailed analysis and requiring immense skill, the concept excited me greatly. I was breathless and distracted. My legs bounced uncontrollably with nervous impatience as I sat at the bedroom desk, building a monolithic spreadsheet of destiny. A grand vision formed in my uncontrollable mind, and chasing it helped me overcome the sluggishness of baseball alienation.

At first, I rushed my school studies each day to play around with the spreadsheet. Then, with the exams looming, my priorities shifted, and I was totally hooked on this beguiling side project. I stopped revising entirely, surrendering to the obsessive urge for baseball purification. My eyes burned from the glare of a thousand formulas, and my thoughts were refracted by hardball hysteria.

Granting omnipotence to mathematics, I felt like Billy Beane, mining data to find innovative answers to age-old problems. My bedroom became a private Moneyball laboratory, dedicated to isolating the most fitting baseball team for a neurotic Englishman to support. I doubt anybody else in the world has attempted such a crazy investigation. I doubt many people have even *contemplated* it.

As a first step, I brainstormed every conceivable *aspect* of a major league team, from logos, uniforms, ballparks and championships to revenue, location, culture and fanbases. I even listed more granular data points relating to salaries, attendances, farm systems, city crime rates and social media followers. I was particularly keen to assess which teams played the most day games, making them more accessible to British audiences. A whole new world opened up with each click.

After finalising the overarching criteria for my experiment - ranging into hundreds of unique determinants - I evaluated my preference for each data point then applied weighted averages to consolidate that infrastructure. The result? By evaluating each team in each category, inputting the relevant data, my weighted formula would spit out a leaderboard of major league teams most suited to my wants, needs and desires.

With the little money I could muster from blogging and writing, I purchased mlb.tv for the first time. I planned to watch at least one game of each team, assessing the broadcasters and getting a feel for the culture of each club. This was a novel brainwave that rekindled my dormant passion for baseball, and the game writhed through my body once again.

I developed an unhealthy routine while on study leave from school, staying awake through the night watching baseball on my laptop while typing into The Spreadsheet. Pretty soon, that damn Excel document was the governing force in my life. I barely thought about anything else, exams included. Something had to give.

I wrote to all 29 eligible MLB franchises asking for a synopsis of why they should become my eternal team. Only one organisation, the Cleveland Indians, replied, receiving a huge boost in the embryonic rankings. Nevertheless, while studying the Chicago Cubs later in the process, everything seemed to click into place. Subjective feeling defeated objective mathematics, and a once-complicated decision became clear.

Aesthetically, the Cubs had always captivated me. The friendly confines of Wrigley Field, matched with the team's chronic inability to win a world championship, appealed to me on a visceral level. There was just something endlessly poetic about the Chicago Cubs, and as a lyrical bard, I could not resist their haunting storyline.

Rooting for such a star-crossed franchise in 2013 was analogous with supporting the Red Sox in 2001. Steeped in tradition and defined by the romantic fumes of failure, both teams were cut from the same cloth. Historic ballpark. Rabid fanbase. Intoxicating heritage. Routine failure. I was ensnared once again.

While Boston went 86 years without a World Series title, Chicago's beleaguered north side hearkened back even further to 1908 in search of a baseball championship. While Boston blamed the curse of Babe Ruth, Chicago cited a billy goat as grist for recurring ineptitude. Yes, a billy goat. Please hear me out.

In a former life, the Cubs were once a relative baseball powerhouse, winning nine National League pennants and two

World Series titles between 1876 and 1908. A relatable team, the Cubs enjoyed a special bond with their fans, who mobilised entire neighbourhoods in baseball fascination. If the Red Sox were an extension of family, the Cubs were an outgrowth of fraternal recreation. They were variations of the same theme, vaguely linked together in style and substance.

One pillar of the local community, William Sianis, reached to the extremities of superstition when attempting to help the Cubs win. Proprietor of the Billy Goat Tavern, a local watering hole, Sianis kept a literal goat as a pet-turned-mascot. Believing it brought the team good fortune, Sianis took the goat to Cubs games at Wrigley Field. Baseball bordered religion for Sianis, and friends enjoyed his boundless passion.

Accordingly, when the barkeep and his goat were refused entry to a World Series game against Detroit in 1945, Sianis was enraged. A loyal fan rejected amid potential glory, Sianis proclaimed the Cubs would never win another Fall Classic. Some say he even sent a telegram to PK Wrigley, the team owner, articulating his decree. It presaged 70 years of recurring heartbreak.

Of course, Sianis was not a baseball god, and his angry words did not actually alter the course of Chicago Cubs history. However, just as the Bambino hex became a convenient crutch for frustrated Red Sox fans, the billy goat theorem grew in popularity with each Cubs implosion. It attempted to explain the inexplicable, albeit in ludicrous terms.

Sianis died in 1970, and the Cubs did not even *appear* in the World Series again during his lifetime. In fact, the team's championship drought became the longest in North American sports history, stretching from the age of telegrams to the dawn of smartphones. Some people questioned the damn goat. Perhaps it *was* supernatural after all.

The *style* of Cubs failure was even more astounding than its longevity. In 1969, for example, the Cubs built a nine-and-a-half-game divisional lead in late-August, only to finish eight games back amid a disastrous collapse. Then in 1984, they reached the NLCS only to lose the decisive fifth game when Leon Durham made a fatal error at first base. Durham preceded Buckner in baseball's pit of anguish.

The Cubs enjoying postseason play was akin to astronomers enjoying a total solar eclipse - it happened very rarely. Red Sox fans thought they had a hard life, snatching defeat from the cusp of victory, but Cubs fans looked at them enviously. At least Boston came *close* to success during its fallow spell. Chicago barely registered on the radar.

While analysing the Cubs for my spreadsheet investigation, I happened upon the most remarkable documentary of their plight. Part of the ESPN *30 for 30* series, *Catching Hell* romanticised the team's failure and focused on its most unfortunate victim, the aforementioned Steve Bartman. I was struck by the grim juxtapositions of Cubs fandom, and the team's existence was about much more than baseball.

Of course, Bartman was a diehard Cubs fan. The kind of fan who listened to play-by-play commentary through headphones while actually sat in the ballpark. He rooted for his team with tremendous passion, and he yearned to see the Cubs win it all.

In 2003, that dream seemed more attainable than ever before. Headlined by Sammy Sosa, a fine slugger, and Kerry Wood, a fearless pitcher, the Cubs won their first division title in 14 years. They then beat Atlanta in the playoffs and progressed to the NLCS, building a 3-2 series lead over Florida at the precipice of salvation.

The Cubs were one win away from reaching their first World Series since 1945, back when Sianis' goat was denied entry. Game 6, potentially historic, was held at Wrigley Field, where thousands of revellers were locked out. One lucky fan *did* manage to score a ticket, however. Steve Bartman had to be there when his team won the pennant.

As giddy excitement buzzed through the ancient yard, the Cubs carried a 3-0 lead into the eighth inning. Sceptics began to believe. Cynics began to pray. There was hope for kids and pensioners alike. The unthinkable seemed *likely*. When Mike Mordecai flew out to left field, the Cubs were five defensive outs away from the Fall Classic. An insurmountable lead, surely. Even by Cubs standards.

Juan Pierre doubled for the Marlins, sparking hope. Then Luis Castillo produced a fantastic at-bat, seeing seven pitches and running the count full against Cubs ace Mark Prior. A pure hitter with great bat control, Castillo was in self-preservation mode, just trying to make contact and stay alive. The Cubs still had a 95% win expectancy, according to Baseball-Reference.com. That is when the goat bleated.

On the eighth pitch of his plate appearance, Castillo poked a high fly to left field. Slicing towards the foul line, the ball looked to be in play. Cubs outfielder Moisés Alou ranged to his right, chasing the ball with serious intent. Alou scaled the perimeter wall separating the field from fans sat in foul territory. He had a potential play, a potential second out of the inning. However, his path to the ball was impeded by a forest of outstretched hands. While a few fans lunged for the baseball, Steve Bartman had the decisive touch, knocking it away from Alou, who was incensed.

With a potential huge out becoming just another foul ball, Castillo lived to see a further pitch. Prior walked him, bringing the tying run to the plate. Florida then unleashed a storm that stunned Wrigley, scoring eight unanswered runs to win the game and even the series. Bartman had to be removed from the premises for his own safety.

The Cubs took an early lead in Game 7, only for a shaky bullpen to cough it up as usual. Nobody remembers that, though, because in the dramatic hues of pop culture, the season died when the geeky human resources assistant in a green turtleneck thwarted Moisés Alou.

Florida won the deciding game, 9-6, then toppled the Yankees to clinch the world championship. For a 95th consecutive winter, the Cubs put their champagne back on ice, awaiting elusive glory. For one fan, though, the human cost was even more torturous. Bartman was rarely seen in public, let alone at Wrigley, ever again. He became the ultimate avatar of Cubs capitulation, a metonym for destruction when all seemed glorious.

Before eviscerating a mere fan, few stopped to remember that the Cubs lost three consecutive games after leading the NLCS 3-1. Fewer still stopped to realise that Bartman never laced a pair of cleats or made a definitive trade. He was not a player, owner, coach or executive. His impact on Cubs history was at once miniscule and seismic. Such is the bewildering contradiction of

Chicago sports psychology, and such is the unforgiving finality of baseball heartache.

I was enthralled by *Catching Hell* and the story it dramatised. The testimony of diehard fans put a lump in my throat. The palpable dream, shared by millions, stirred my soul. This stuff was deep. This stuff *mattered*.

For some strange reason, I found the concept of championship droughts transfixing. There was a substance to these teams, I thought. They had a gravity and purpose in a world of ephemeral feeling. They were more than mere logos and corporate shells. They *meant* something, and that is rare these days.

When teams crisscross the country, chasing profit as corporate franchises, it is difficult to discern meaning in their existence. If not to shower a specific city with joy and pride, then what is the point of playing at all? After spending time in Oakland, Los Angeles and Las Vegas, do the Raiders *matter* anymore, beyond surface entertainment? After hopscotching between Cleveland, Los Angeles and St Louis, do the Rams carry *significance* these days, other than at the bank? And where will the Chargers move next, when ownership becomes bored of California?

From loyal fandom and ceaseless yearning comes a strong identity that simply is not present in more successful towns. Hardcore fans bristled, but defeat was the Cubs' elixir. The more they lost, the more people were engrossed. That is very disconcerting in and of itself, although there is little point fighting the concept. The Cubs were not *the Cubs* unless they lost. America expected them to fail.

There is something brilliant about that contradiction, something unique, daring and uplifting about getting up off the canvas so many times. That paradox between annual agony and a fanbase of such size and passion never ceased to amaze me. It is the genesis of meaning. It is the accelerator of definition. It is the closest thing to love sports can truly muster.

In this regard, it struck me that the Chicago Cubs were the most purposeful sports team on earth at that particular time. Not the best or richest or most famous, but definitely the most *purposeful*. No team carried such a dense weight of communal hope, and no team was burdened with over a century of dreams, derived from the heart of millions around the world.

Eddie Vedder, the face of Pearl Jam, is a passionate Cubs booster. He once penned a beautiful song about the team and its loyal rooters. The opening lines perfectly capture the essence of Cubs devotion:

> *"Don't let anyone say that it's just a game,*
> *For I've seen other teams and it's never the same.*
> *When you're born in Chicago,*
> *You're blessed and you're healed,*
> *The first time you walk into Wrigley Field."*

I wanted to be part of that cult. I wanted to associate with something larger than myself and invest in a long-term experience. I wanted to earn any potential euphoria by driving the bandwagon rather than by merely jumping aboard. I wanted to feel the interminable thirst.

To that end, I abandoned The Spreadsheet and fell into a state of quasi Cubs fandom. I stayed awake until 06:00 am watching meaningless games against the Athletics in Oakland. I bought a Starlin Castro shirsey and obsessed over series with the Cardinals. I found pleasure in the Cubs' ecological standing as second tier spenders. The Cubs were a sleeping giant, big enough to compete but no so big as to suffocate on their own largesse. They were the ideal *companion*.

Another famous Cubs song, penned by folk icon Steve Goodman, reduced me to tears. *A Dying Cub Fan's Last Request* speaks to the beautiful futility of north side baseball, and it became the anthem of my fandom:

> *"Do they still play the blues in Chicago,*
> *When baseball season rolls around?*
> *When the snow melts away,*
> *Do the Cubbies still play,*
> *In their ivy-covered burial ground?*
>
> *When I was a boy, they were my pride and joy,*
> *But now they only bring fatigue*
> *To the home of the brave,*
> *The land of the free,*
> *And the doormat of the National League."*

To me, there was a cosmic inevitability about the Cubs one day winning it all, and that was somehow reaffirming. Such was my misguided belief, I even started saving in a sealed moneybox for whenever the Cubs won the pennant. If they ever managed to topple their demons, I wanted to be present as a witness. I wanted to shower in the glee and feel the cathartic release. I wanted to *experience* the north side's exorcism, among the most celebrated in human history.

A Cubs world championship was the last great sports story of our time, lingering in tantalising potentiality. I needed to be involved somehow. I needed to chronicle the rise. The poetry was irresistible, and so I joined the crusade. There was a sense of obligation buried somewhere in my soul. To a traditional baseball guy like me, rooting for the Cubs just seemed *right*, and I was determined to give it a shot.

⚾⚾⚾

Just as in Boston, the Cubs' championship drought actually had more to do with dysfunctional ownership and archaic strategy than with billy goats and supernatural curses. The Cubs just never seemed to find the pieces they needed to win, and repeated failures in leadership prolonged their downfall.

In 1916, William Wrigley, the famous chewing gum magnate, bought a minority stake in the team. As his eponymous brand grew in stature, he increased his Cubs stock, becoming majority owner in 1921. The team was transferred to his sole control by 1925, presaging decades of substandard hereditary ownership.

William died in 1932, leaving his son, Phillip, to oversee the family empire. A well-meaning chap, Phillip *tried* to modernise the Cubs, but he did so in a rather haphazard and inconsistent manner. The team was always second to the chewing gum machine, and that bothered loyal fans who grew frustrated across decades of stagnation.

While other teams embraced the advent of floodlit night games, Wrigley resisted the innovation. The first big league evening game took place in 1935, but the Cubs did not embrace the trend until 1988, passing on innumerable opportunities for growth. They were the last MLB team to play home games under lights, and some say the gruelling schedule of days games drained the

Cubs, especially during the summer, putting them at an instant disadvantage.

Paradoxically, Wrigley was all too happy to meddle in on-field affairs. In 1961, he abolished the traditional field management structure in favour of a doomed system known as The College of Coaches. Essentially, a raft of coaches took turns managing the team, rotating in and out. The resultant lack of leadership torpedoed the Cubs, who squandered the best years of legendary players like Ernie Banks, Ron Santo and Billy Williams.

When Phillip Wrigley died in 1977, his family had presided over 61 years of fruitless Chicago Cubs baseball. Phillip's son, William Wrigley III, inherited ownership of the team, but his plans were derailed as financial uncertainty plagued the family business. When William's mother died a few months after he took charge of the Cubs, a large estate tax bill put pressure on the family. Most of William's money was tied up in baseball and chewing gum ventures, to a point where paying his dues required selling the Cubs.

In 1981, the Chicago Tribune Company - a large media conglomerate housing papers like *The Chicago Tribune* and *The Daily News* - bought the team for $21.1 million. The sale included Wrigley Field and all of the Cubs' mounting debts. A fresh dawn approached Chicago's north side.

Concurrently, the advent of free agency, coupled with increased television coverage and marketing opportunities, transformed Major League Baseball from genteel pastime to big business. Family ownership decreased as financial clout became a key requirement for sustained competition. In this regard, Cubs fans hoped the Tribune Company would bankroll their dreams. Such a fantasy never quite materialised, however, as the baseball team became just another spoke in the corporate wheel.

Dallas Green, an adept general manager, was immediately hired to transform the Cubs, but his insurgent ideas often irritated corporation functionaries. Green returned the team to postseason play for the first time in almost 40 years, only to be fired before momentum could flourish into success.

The Tribune Company cared more about maximising profits than about winning ballgames. For example, Greg Maddux, the

Cubs' ace, won the Cy Young Award in 1992 following a 20-win season only to be shunned by management. Rather than building around him, attempting to capitalise on a generational talent, ownership let him to leave via free agency. Maddux signed a five-year, $28 million contract with Atlanta en route to 355 career victories and a place in the Hall of Fame. The Cubs struggled on with subpar journeymen, failing to replicate with an *entire rotation* what Maddux routinely produced alone.

"Then-general manager Larry Himes, one of the all-time nefarious names in Cubs history, gave Maddux a competitive offer," wrote Jon Greenberg for ESPN. "But he couldn't close the deal. Himes treated Maddux like a very good pitcher, rather than a future legend. It was the kind of ordinary thinking that kept this major-market team a minor factor all those years."

Naturally, then, the 1990s were a disaster for the Cubs, who made just one postseason appearance in the entire decade. The Tribune Company faced pressure from fans, who remained loyal, selling out Wrigley Field to watch a chronically underwhelming product.

The 1994 appointment of Andy MacPhail as president rekindled competitive instincts and instilled fresh hope in Wrigleyville, however. MacPhail led the Minnesota Twins to two world championships before joining the Cubs, where he managed to convince the corporation to loosen the purse strings. Along with Jim Hendry, MacPhail built the team that lost agonisingly in 2003, but sustained success was never forthcoming.

Hendry assumed overall control following the 2006 season, delivering successive division titles, yet progressing beyond the first round of playoff games proved difficult. The Tribune Company spent more money in the new millennium, harnessing stars like Sosa, Prior, Wood and Derrek Lee. Yankees playoff hero Alfonso Soriano was later signed to an eight-year, $136 million contract that defined an expectant era. Still, no World Series title arrived, causing consternation in the corridors of power.

Over several decades, the Cubs adhered to numerous different paradigms, but all roads led to the same despondency. They toyed with benefactor models and tried corporate funding, but hypothetical talent was routinely derailed by human imperfection. Each heartbreaking loss evoked spontaneous overcorrection, resulting in wayward oscillation between confidence and despair. Finding the right blend of ideas became a generational challenge, and Cubs fans were put through the ringer.

For instance, when shifting digital and economic landscapes hit businesses hard in the late-1990s, north side baseball fell into a perilous state of uncertainty. As the internet became ubiquitous, newspapers faced a bleak future, putting the Tribune Company on shaky ground. Once lucrative, conventional newspaper advertising was gutted as investors spent their marketing dollars with Google and emerging social networks instead. A key revenue pipeline was diverted, forcing the giants of legacy media to adapt or die.

When advertisers turned digital, the Tribune Company subsequently privatised amid rising debts. Its business model became outdated as a general economic downturn meshed with the ruin of traditional media. Debts spiralled to $13 billion, symbolic of a *boom or bust* culture that led to a market crash. The Cubs became an irrelevant luxury on a complicated balance sheet.

In December 2008, the Tribune Company filed for bankruptcy protection and was forced to sell Cubs stock to balance the books. Investment bonds billionaire Tom Ricketts purchased 95% of the team, plus Wrigley Field and a quarter of Comcast SportsNet Chicago, for $900 million. He was ratified as majority owner in October 2009, heralding another fresh start for a weary institution.

A lifelong Cubs fan, Ricketts took a blank canvas approach to building a winner on the north side. A century of ineptitude showed that a new philosophy was needed, and Ricketts razed the organisation to its foundations. With grand intent, he vowed to rebuild the Chicago Cubs into a modern powerhouse fit for long-term domination. For once, it actually worked.

Early in Ricketts' reign, Major League Baseball became a vast money-making enterprise defined by lucrative media deals, plush luxury boxes and stadiums optimised for capitalist spending. The Cubs, by contrast, were a tired neighbourhood baseball team defined by community spirit, sentimentalised defeat and a quaint ballpark that did not actually do much. Tom Ricketts changed that, setting the team on course for prosperity.

Conducting a thorough diagnosis, the new owner learned that, for many years, the Cubs had been left behind in terms of baseball operations. Rather like the fatigued ballpark, the Cubs' front office failed to keep up with the dawning domination of analytics in baseball evaluation. For too long, the Cubs had been a static adjunct of chewing gum companies and newspaper conglomerates rather than a thriving entity of their own accord. This resulted in cronyism, nepotism and a country club vibe that was incompatible with success.

Ricketts appreciated that, in order to reverse decades of neglect, he first had to address the Cubs' creaking infrastructure - literally and figuratively. In this regard, he referred to the John Henry playbook for revitalising an ancient ruin of a baseball team into a contemporary juggernaut. The similarities between Boston and Chicago were uncanny.

Just as the Red Sox redeveloped Fenway - transforming it into a revenue-generating tourist attraction with pricey tours and seats on the iconic left field wall - Ricketts embarked on a similar scheme at Wrigley, spending $575 million to renovate the ballpark and introduce new income streams from increased advertising and a giant videoboard.

The Cubs also pursued the creation of their own television network, just as the Red Sox did with NESN. Meanwhile, a $99 million spring training facility opened up new avenues for player development and sports science enrichment as the Cubs embraced fresh thinking.

Ricketts even robbed Henry's general manager, pushing his imitation to the extreme. The incoming owner knew that one man was better qualified than anybody in baseball to exorcise the Cubs' laissez-faire culture and instil a thriving heart of world class decision-making. In one of the great happy coincidences of sports, that man just happened to become available when Ricketts needed him most. It was almost like a bad Hollywood movie.

The protégé who brought *two* world championships to Boston and laid the foundation for a third, Theo Epstein left his boyhood club in 2011, agreeing a long-term deal to become the

Cubs' president of baseball operations. Baseball's chief curse-buster found his ultimate challenge.

"Baseball is better with tradition and history," said Epstein at a Wrigley press conference announcing his arrival. "Baseball is better with fans who care. Baseball is better with parks like this one, and it's better during the day. And baseball is best of all when you win. Ultimately, that is why I'm here."

Epstein's legacy in Boston became complicated as the team lost its identity. Late in his reign, the Red Sox struggled to deliver tangible returns on phenomenal investment, and fans questioned moves that deviated from the plan for sustainable success.

Julio Lugo did not pan out. Daisuke Matsuzaka was a $103 million bust. JD Drew was routinely scolded for underperformance. Then Epstein brought in Crawford, whose $142 million deal defined *kneejerk reaction*.

When the Red Sox capitulated down the stretch in 2011, Theo saw the writing on the wall. With senior players rebelling in the clubhouse and expensive stars failing to meet expectations, Epstein knew that change was needed. The task of replacing Francona, a beleaguered manager, seemed ominous, while a sparse Boston farm system did not bode well for the immediate future.

Epstein knew the honeymoon was over. His halo was slipping, submerged in doubt by questionable transactions and devolving clubhouse culture. Frustrated by ownership meddling and tired of surging expectations, the boy wonder looked for an exit strategy. The Chicago Cubs offered an ideal solution.

Theo duly came to Chicago as genius, saviour, messiah and hero. He managed to deliver on those expectations where countless others had failed. Upon entering office, Epstein analysed the baseball landscape and recognised several trends. He then weaved that intelligence into his blueprint, giving the Cubs a huge likelihood of success.

Epstein designed his front office in trailblazing fashion, hiring Jed Hoyer from San Diego to be the Cubs' general manger. Once a rising star of the Fenway think tank, Hoyer spent two years in charge of the Padres before becoming Theo's righthand man in Chicago. Together, they built an empire in Wrigleyville, decoding historic misconceptions en route to breaking another hex.

Due to increased luxury tax penalties, teams were becoming reticent to sign veteran stars to enormous contracts, favouring homegrown talent instead. Farm system graduates were younger, cheaper and more controllable. It therefore became desirable to build from within and then supplement with a few splashes of external quality rather than saddling a clubhouse with expensive egos hooked on past performance.

By building a cost-effective core of foundational players, the Cubs would eventually be in a handsome position - financially and culturally - to supplement that hub with expensive external free agents. The resultant blend of youth and experience, excitement and accomplishment, figured to put them over the edge and deliver the Holy Grail. Theo analysed the black box from the Red Sox' demise and vowed never to make the same mistakes again.

This philosophy placed huge emphasis on the stockpiling of minor league prospects. In turn, as the chief mode of gathering such commodities, the amateur draft became a key focus for teams. A race to the bottom ensued, with franchises vying for the worst record and, thus, the best draft position each year.

In modern baseball, finishing .500 was the worst possible outcome for a team. Those who flirted with averageness in mid-season often dumped assets at the trade deadline, hoping to swap veterans for prospects while falling further back in the standings to recoup more impactful draft picks. This process, known as *tanking*, hit the game like an epidemic, and the Cubs mastered the art.

Epstein and Hoyer knew that, to get better, the Cubs first had to get worse. Short-term pain led to long-term gain in the contemporary environment, and the dynamic duo devised a daring plan to that end. The Cubs lost 101 games in Epstein's first season. It was their worst campaign since 1966. They lost 96 games in 2013 and 89 games in 2014. Some casual fans were perplexed, seeing only the immediate results, but down on the farm, Theo built a monster.

Epstein and Hoyer traded every depreciating asset they had in return for future value, either in the form of prospects or draft picks. Veterans like Reed Johnson, Geovany Soto, Ryan Dempster, Matt Garza and Soriano were swapped for younger pieces as the Cubs replenished their core. Long-term strategy replaced short-term calamity in Wrigleyville, and the Cubs finally saw light at the end of an ancient tunnel.

Theo moulded his ethos around young cornerstones like Anthony Rizzo and Starlin Castro, eyeing a distant window of contention. Ironically, Rizzo was drafted by Epstein for the Red Sox in 2007 and subsequently flipped to Hoyer in San Diego as part of the original package for Adrián González. Once reunited, Theo and Jed acquired Rizzo *again* in their first significant Cubs deal, solidifying a de facto captain at first base for years to come.

The Cubs also drafted well, converting their first round picks into future stars like Kris Bryant and Albert Almora while mining the international market for transformative pieces such as Gleyber Torres and Jorge Soler.

For the first time in more than a century, Epstein became an efficient conduit between Cubs ownership and baseball operations, between the overarching business plan and the on-field product. Rather than stifling progress and deviating from the script, Theo quietly tinkered with his creation, timing it to coincide with Ricketts' commercial revitalisation project.

The utopian vision figured to make the Cubs world champions by 2016. At that point, a renovated Wrigley would be home to a sustainable team of handpicked stars and elite farm system graduates. Theo would have great payroll flexibility due to lucrative broadcast deals and enhanced revenue streams. The Cubs would be set for *perennial attempts* at conquering the October summit, not just singular kamikaze missions. Such an experience had not occurred in the north side for almost a century, and whole generations thought it was impossible. Theo wanted to prove those doubters wrong.

In theory, The Plan was mesmeric. There was a magnetism to Epstein, Hoyer and their long-term vision. For once, Cubs fans lived in the future tense, pining for the next great prospect to arrive and focusing more on minor league boxscores than major league defeats.

In reality, getting through those barren months and years required immense faith. It was tough. I remember watching Darwin Barney hit .208. I remember watching Nate Schierholtz hit cleanup. I remember terrible players like Brian Bogusevic, Julio Borbón and JC Boscán receiving big league playing time.

Nevertheless, it was uplifting to watch the Cubs' transformation from forgotten underdog to burgeoning superpower. The interaction of Ricketts, Epstein and Hoyer was incredible, and their process inspired me to begin writing about baseball again.

When the Cubs added Joe Maddon - perhaps the smartest manager in baseball - following the 2014 season, there had never been more expected of a 73-win ballclub. The dreams of my inner baseball geek became reality, and I chronicled the rise at *Cubs Insider*, a humble blog operated by Evan Altman. It was fun to reignite that passion.

My debut article for *Cubs Insider* was an expose of my own defection from Los Angeles to Chicago. Cubs fans welcomed me with open arms, and I made several friendships with north siders that survive to this day. Once again, I apologise to anyone who feels betrayed by my subsequent actions. It was never my intention to have things end how they did.

Indeed, by the time Theo and Jed delivered on those incredible demands, I was no longer a pious worshipper of *Eamus Catuli*. The sands of time, and the march of professionalism, eroded my childlike love for MLB, and even the Cubs could not change that.

The closer I came to achieving my baseball writing dream, the more I saw the game change before my eyes. The more I delved beyond baseball's layer of innocent fandom, the deeper I became ingrained in its money-making network. The less I watched baseball for pleasure, the more I found other things stimulating.

The business of baseball, cold and unforgiving, demanded maturity. The industry of baseball journalism, transparent and competitive, required impartiality. There was little time to be a Theo Epstein fanboy. I had to go to work, and those sacrifices took a great toll on my mind.

CHAPTER SIXTEEN

No Cheering in the Press Box

In 1973, esteemed baseball writer Jerome Holtzman published a book chronicling the lives of the best sports journalists of his generation. Raw and fresh, *No Cheering in the Press Box* turned a spotlight on the writers behind the stories. Its key message of journalistic objectivity was a cardinal rule abided by generations of sportswriters, and an entire industry had been born on its propagation.

If, like me, you wanted to become a professional baseball writer, impartiality was a prerequisite. You rooted for a good story, not for a particular ballclub or player. That was certainly true in more traditional eras, when newspapers were king and when beat writing was the only mode of introduction to a secluded industry. There was no room for teenage meltdowns when covering big league baseball.

Of course, in modernity, far removed from the smoky trains and cliquey card tables of yore, special personalities *have* transcended the restrictive realm, specialising in a team they love. The advent of blogging as a viable profession, backed by pay-per-click advertising and affiliate marketing schemes, made it possible to become an independent baseball writer, covering the game with unconcealed passion.

Bill Simmons, the stereotypical Red Sox fan, pioneered this concept, breaking from the tired player-reporter model to provide a humorous lens of authentic opinion. A poor bartender, Simmons began blogging about Boston sports on an AOL platform in 1997. He wrote with unabashed frat house salt, gaining mass popularity with quirky pop culture references and relatable anecdotes from a fan's perspective. Simmons' column was later picked up by ESPN, and he eventually became a new-age media mogul, amassing millions in personal wealth from outlets such as *The Ringer*.

In this style, modern writers such as Jared Carrabis and Mike Axisa followed Simmons' blueprint, violating Holtzman's credo to great effect. Carrabis is a Red Sox blogger and podcaster for Barstool Sports, and his bias has become part of a complicated act. Likewise, Axisa is one of the most successful independent baseball bloggers of all-time, and his *River Ave Blues* site covered the Yankees with unparalleled detail from a fan's viewpoint.

Though a massive admirer, I could not imitate Carrabis and his blogging peers because of my complicated rooting history and conflicted fandoms. I also lacked the confidence to pull off such a boisterous and demanding act. Nevertheless, from an early age, I was besotted with the idea of covering Major League Baseball, and there just *had* to be a conducive medium out there somewhere.

I wanted to be at the ballpark every day, writing columns in the fading sun. I wanted to work for a respected newspaper and build a strong reputation. I wanted to vote on the Hall of Fame ballot and perhaps be considered for election myself. I wanted to travel back in time, quite frankly, because my dream job was more viable in bygone decades than it ever was during my life.

Indeed, the first professional baseball writer of serious renown was an Englishman. Yes, you may well be shocked, but that is a wonderful fact that cannot be denied. Henry Chadwick was born in the quaint English riviera of Exeter, Devon in 1824 before moving with his family to Brooklyn aged 12. A sportswriter by profession, Chadwick is known as The Father of Baseball, such was his influence on the game's development and burgeoning popularity. Henry's achievements have been a source of great inspiration to me through years of toil in pursuit of similar vocations.

After discovering the game at Elysian Fields one day while covering cricket, Chadwick dedicated his life to baseball's promotion, enhancement and growth. In time, he brainstormed and ushered in new measures that brought sophistication and - inexorably - *professionalism* to the sport. He set baseball on course for mass appreciation, and the game's bewitching beauty did the rest.

Among other innovations, Chadwick is credited with devising the boxscore; using the letter *K* to denote strikeouts; logging player statistics; ending the "bound catch," whereby fielders could retire batters on one bounce; and suggesting the eventual distance of 60 feet 6 inches between home plate and the pitcher's mound.

By day, Chadwick helped redefine the fundamental aspects of baseball. By night, he made strides with the written word. Chadwick edited *The Beadle Dime Baseball Player*, the game's first publicly sold annual. Likewise, Henry oversaw many editions of Albert Spalding's eponymous *Guide*; contributed to the ever-impressive *Reach* annuals; and authored the very first hardback baseball book, *The Game of Baseball*, in 1868.

Chadwick was a scion of early sports journalism, his words shaping the direction of that noble profession and encouraging future greats. We now enjoy the work of so many immortal ink warriors, but it is not unreasonable to conclude that, without Henry Chadwick crossing the Rubicon, baseball writing would have remained a closet hobby for decades. It may never have become a *thing* at all. Chadwick now resides in the Baseball Hall of Fame, a fitting tribute to a remarkable legacy. He is one of just three Brits embronzed in the hardball pantheon.

Accordingly, the road from Wirral, England to Cooperstown, New York seemed impassable, but I was determined to give it a go. Attempting to emulate Chadwick and become the fourth British Hall of Famer was not easy, but I tried. Applying his passion to the modern game, I made many sacrifices to pursue the dream, and foregoing allegiance to any specific team was perhaps the most difficult. I kept asking people for advice and I kept knocking on doors. Soon, they began to open, and soon, I began to develop a name in the industry.

As mentioned previously, in 2011, aged 16, I became involved with the British Baseball Federation, which governs our domestic league structure. I covered the AA North Division as a beat reporter, ringing team managers every Sunday night to hear how they fared. Even Chadwick never reported on the Bolton Robots of Doom or the Newton Aycliffe Spartans, so I was ahead of the curve. At least in my own mind. At least in satirical jest.

I also expanded my baseball blog, writing regularly about major league news and history. A lot of the articles were unrefined and laden with bias, but the small community of British baseball fans on social media offered encouragement. People like Matt Smith of BaseballGB and Mark Blakemore, a similarly passionate fan, encouraged me to keep going. Perhaps they saw some potential in my work.

In 2013, I won the British Baseball Writing Award as the sport's leading journalist in my homeland. I shared the honour with Josh Chetwynd, my *Baseball on Five* hero, and I managed to get some tips from the master himself. The Society for American Baseball Research (SABR) - a renowned think tank that boasts Bill James, Bob Costas, Keith Olbermann, Rob Neyer and John Thorn among alumni - published my award-winning prose amid something of a breakthrough. I was keen to capitalise on this pleasing momentum, even if it seemed rather vacuous and insubstantial.

Later that summer, despite my exam preparation being torpedoed by that damned spreadsheet and the Chicago Cubs, I secured a place to study journalism at Liverpool John Moores University. That figured to be a launching pad to greater things, but worsening mental health robbed me of the opportunity.

Racked by chronic social anxiety and destroyed by acute introversion, the thought of meeting new people on campus petrified me. Stepping outside my comfort zone was an alien concept, and the pressure of becoming an adult reduced me to tears.

I deferred my entry to John Moores, telling friends that I planned to take a gap year. In reality, I was absolutely ruined by psychological turmoil and emotional immaturity. I had no plan at all, devoid of the psychological fortitude demanded by the big bad world. I was totally unprepared for adulthood, and so I became some kind of disgruntled cyborg man-boy, caught between plans and cast adrift in the confusion of it all.

When my self-esteem allowed, I pestered newspaper editors and website managers for freelance writing opportunities. I picked up bits of work here and there, never more than enough to buy a few beers in the pub, but my network gradually expanded and bylines began to roll in.

For one piece, I interviewed Gabe Kapler, a World Series winner with the Red Sox in 2004. I wrote nostalgically about *Baseball on Five*, drawing closer to the guys who made it happen. I also became a baseball columnist for FanSided, the fastest growing sports website in America, earning a few pennies on the side.

In such a competitive industry, there always seemed to be somebody willing to write for free, and that made genuine professional opportunities hard to find. Scores of websites adhered to the same tired model, turning traffic into revenue by way of affiliate marketing links and Google advertising. The *quality* of content barely seemed to matter, and an army of writers - including myself - worked ridiculously hard as volunteers, sold a monetisation dream that never materialised.

The alternative to clickbait and referral schemes was to lock content behind labyrinthine paywalls, requiring readers to purchase a subscription before they could dissect yesterday's boxscore. In August 2013, John Henry bought the *Boston Globe*, once my go-to repository of baseball news, and duly ramped up the newspapers' approach to paid content, making quality journalism inaccessible for vast swathes of loyal readers.

While many media outlets were forced to adopt this model, and while the *Globe* had tinkered with paywall plans before Henry arrived, there was something obnoxious about it all. I thought about the 2013 equivalent of my younger self, holed up in a nondescript bedroom, just trying to read about Jarrod Saltalamacchia and his Red Sox teammates. My family never could have afforded $27 per month for a subscription, and so I never could have kept abreast of developments in Boston. That is a sad realisation.

By purchasing the *Globe*, Henry just happened to control the largest independent organ of Red Sox news in the world. To some, that was at best weird and at worst dangerous. In many respects, the *Globe* was *built* on baseball coverage. Its stable of eloquent and fierce writers - Shaughnessy, Gammons, Montville and Bob Ryan, to name a few - was often among the best in the world. Nevertheless, some insiders worried that, by squeezing the *Globe* into his purview, Henry effectively built a Red Sox propaganda machine.

While such dystopian worries never came to pass, there was a noticeable watering down of criticism from the *Globe* with regard to the Red Sox. For example, down the line, a disparaging anecdote in one of Shaughnessy's columns was suspiciously deleted, some say at Henry's behest. As an ethical journalist and an ardent admirer of the *Globe*, the whole thing did not sit well with me. Fenway Sports Group had designs on a police state, and that violated every rule in the book.

Accordingly, when the Red Sox beat St Louis in the 2013 World Series, clinching a championship *at home* for the first time since 1918, I could not bring myself to write about it. Part of me felt conflicted, as the great Boston sports ballad continued without me, while another part of me felt numb, tired of all the breathless anxiety.

The 2013 Red Sox helped their city heal following horrific bombings at the Boston Marathon, which killed 3 people and injured many more. My heart bled for Beantown, a fundamentally decent place, and I was moved by David Ortiz' expletive-laden speech of defiance on the Fenway diamond in the immediate aftermath.

Still, I remained unmoved by the actual baseball team, and its success did not stir my soul. I was a writer now, not a fan, and the separation dulled my senses. I had a duty to *analyse* now, not just to shout, and doing so while impaired by childish fanaticism was decidedly unappealing. To do my job well, I had to maintain a safe distance from the game, and that is just what I did, muffling my own instincts for the benefit of everybody else.

⚾⚾⚾

The article that changed my life and helped me rediscover my love for baseball was an unpaid exploration of the heart. A lot of articles were back then. I wrote it merely out of passion, to scratch a personal itch, rather than to drive traffic or to earn a lucrative paycheck. There was no foretelling the impact it had on my life. There was no predicting the outcome of my journey.

In 2013, the New York Yankees entered a strategic partnership with Manchester City, an English football club, keen to explore commercial growth. I was intrigued by the possibilities of such an arrangement, hoping it would strengthen the visibility of Major League Baseball in the UK.

The two teams joined forces to create an MLS expansion franchise based in the Bronx. Playing out of Yankee Stadium, New York City FC was a pleasant amalgamation of sporting royalty. The Yankees owned 20% while Manchester City controlled 80%. Analysts tried to decipher what it all meant, and I was right among that pack.

Located an hour from my home, Manchester City posed no immediate threat to Tranmere, so I was interested in the ramifications of their Yankee collaboration. Moreover, as a British baseball blogger, I wanted to explore the City-Yankees relationship in greater detail. More specifically, I wanted to campaign for true mutuality in the arrangement, perhaps with a Manchester Yankees baseball team kickstarting a new era for the sport on these shores.

I saw a genuine opportunity for the Yankees to forge a presence in my homeland, a prerequisite in the fight for MLB games in London, my most fervent fantasy. I decided to write a feature articulating that vision, using New York City FC as a crutch. The response was phenomenal.

Early in the research process, I sent a speculative email to the Yankees' press office, hoping to receive a stock quote about the team's international vision. I referenced the Manchester City project and asked if the Yankees had any further plans to expand throughout Britain. I suggested open days or envoy clinics with popular Yankee players to stimulate interest. In all honesty, I did not expect a reply.

Nevertheless, late one night as I sat down to relax, my phone pinged with an urgent email. I opened the link and saw a message from Cristina Campana, Senior Coordinator of Disabled Services and Guest Relations for the New York Yankees. I was stunned but continued reading excitedly.

Cristina promised to pass my suggestions to relevant personnel within the Yankee behemoth. Furthermore, she commented that, as a Brit, my baseball knowledge had caused quite a stir in the club's offices. As a token gesture, Cristina wanted to send me a hamper of Yankees merchandise. She requested my shirt size and address. I was truly taken aback.

On a number of levels, this was surreal. Firstly, the most powerful sports team on planet earth wanted to send me gifts. Secondly, I had once despised said team while rooting for its main rival. And thirdly, I was a journalist, supposedly impartial, ideally immune to such inducements.

Regardless of morality, something clicked inside my soul, and it all started to make sense. The New York Yankees were defined by class, and I finally saw it for myself. Unicorns suddenly became real, even if others did not believe me. Fiction lost all meaning, because the ultimate story of aspiration came alive in my hands.

In many ways, the Yankees' courtship should have felt wrong. Thinking logically, I should have rejected their offering out of principle, but logic has no power over deep-seated love, stifled or otherwise. I typed a swift response to Cristina, thanking her and confirming my address. A chapter of taboo Yankee appreciation began in earnest.

On Thursday 13th March 2014, a long brown package arrived in the post. It bore a white label, stamped evocatively with the Yankees' fabled top hat emblem. The parcel's origin, labelled tantalisingly, sent a shiver down my spine: *Yankee Stadium, One East 161st St, Bronx, N.Y., 10451.*

Beneath that magical seal lay my address, handwritten for dramatic effect: *Ryan Ferguson, 23 Ashfield Crescent, Bromborough, Wirral, Merseyside, CH62 7ED, United Kingdom.* I was overcome with emotion, struggling to comprehend the chain of events that led to me cradling a gift from the world's most illustrious sporting dynasty. The odds were improbable.

In breathless haste, I tore at the package, carefully remembering to store the label for posterity. I ripped open the box, peering through a window into the champagne-scented, velvet-coated, pinstriped nirvana of baseball glory.

The Yankees sent me one of their famous caps, featuring the sacred interlocking NY logo. They sent me a t-shirt, a pennant, a winter hat, a drinks bottle and a USB stick emblazoned with their signature branding. They even sent me a set of mini Yankees speakers to enrich my listening to games. I gushed uncontrollably.

Cristina included a letter with her parcel, typed on fine paper bearing the Yankees' letterhead. I cherished the message, which read as follows:

Dear Ryan,

Thank you for reaching out to the New York Yankees. We appreciate your interest in our team and baseball! I hope that I may one day be able to help make your visit to Yankee Stadium a pleasant and memorable experience. Enjoy the enclosed items!

Sincerely,
Cristina Campana
Senior Coordinator, Disabled Services and Guest Relations

Spewing historical anecdotes and dizzying platitudes, I tried to explain the magnitude of this team to non-baseball folks like mum and dad. I spoke of Ruth and Gehrig, DiMaggio and Mantle. My family had no idea who those people were, but they were happy for me, nevertheless.

"What about the Cubs?" asked Nath, my younger brother, sensing my defection to a fourth different baseball team in five years. "Well, err..., I'll support them as well," I mumbled, realising the illegitimacy of such a notion as it tumbled from my mouth.

My little brother looked at me with a wry grin. He knew. He always knows. Ryan was a Yankees fan now, and that was a little weird.

⚾⚾⚾

CHAPTER SEVENTEEN

The Derek Jeter Chronicles

I have always been sceptical about religion and supposed acts of divine intervention. To me, the Roman Catholic claiming to be cured of paralysis by washing in the holy waters of Lourdes seems outrageously farfetched. Miracles are difficult to quantify and even more difficult to articulate. Few believe in them.

If not quite miraculous, my intoxicating brush with Yankee mystique held magical properties that defied description. The sudden détente was stunning, even to me. The instant thawing of hostility as the Yankees became the focus of my fascination seemed improbable. Rarely had I experienced such a drastic swing in emotion. I came to believe in a higher fate, even if outright religiosity remained a stretch.

There was no way I could admit to being a Yankees fan. Certainly not publicly, and barely to myself. Some people remembered me as a Red Sox rooter while others knew me as a Cubs fan. Few remembered my private flirtation with the Dodgers, but broaching the subject of pinstriped defection threatened to leave my reputation in tatters, personally and professionally. Nobody wanted to hear such horror stories.

Like many people who experience miracles, I was enveloped by a disconcerting solitude, caught in my own bubble of half-smiles and perpetual doubt. Just as some people claim to be touched by Jesus, transforming their approach to life as a result, I was touched by the implacable aura of New York Yankees baseball, rewriting my DNA. There was a sense of enlightenment that felt uplifting, and relief flooded into my life, but it was almost too strong to corral.

Rather like religious faith itself, I always held a vague *notion* of Yankee class without necessarily believing in it. At various times, I was agnostic and downright hostile to the concept of recurring success creating a culture of sacred greatness in the Bronx. However, through direct experience, the full extent of the Yankees' biblical majesty was revealed to me. I became a believer, accepted into the global faith of pinstriped baseball. That was an incredible feeling.

The Yankees made me a priority, and my perspective changed forever. I was touched by an enchanted force, hitherto apocryphal, that became a driving motivator in my life. I came to worship at the altar of Babe Ruth, that omnipotent hero, even if nobody could ever know. Forbidden lust transformed my outlook.

I'm well aware that my gift box was a small part of the Yankees' commercial kingdom. Anyone can request a 'fan pack' online, and the team dedicates millions of dollars to fan outreach every year, seeking to whet the appetite of naïve seamheads who will then spend even more money on hats, jerseys and tickets over the ensuing decades. I understand that, for the Yankees, this was a miniscule footnote in their grand marketing strategy, but who cares? *Who actually cares?* Some will say I fell for the oldest trick in the sales playbook, but who gives a damn? I certainly do not, and neither should you.

In fact, being wooed and indulged by the New York Yankees was enjoyable. Their offering of gifts is easily the most romantic thing any sports team has ever done for me. It made me feel special, wanted and part of something larger than myself. In short, it worked, just as fine marketing is supposed to do. The Yankees are great at that, too. They know how to impress.

In a world of unrequited sports love, where clubs grow complacent about the support they receive, seeing the most illustrious team of all proactively trying to give something back was refreshing. More than that, it was *cathartic*. Despite hordes of worldwide admirers, the Yankees were still trying to win new fans at a granular level, and that sustained effort dispelled many of my misconceptions about their trademark arrogance.

I began wearing Yankees garb around the house before cautiously testing the waters by donning the cap in town. It felt good, somehow empowering and luxurious, like I had won the lottery. In many ways, I *had* won the lottery, because the New York Yankees wanted me as a fan, and there are few greater honours in sports.

Eager to learn what made the Yankees tick, I began reading tirelessly about the team's history. Famous works by Marty Appel, Jim Bouton, Harvey Frommer, David Halberstam and Richard Ben Cramer opened the pinstriped canon, while modern columns and blogs by Mark Feinsand, Joel Sherman, Sweeny Murti, John Harper and so many others brought the current team to life.

As a lifelong baseball fan, I was always *aware* of the Yankees' unparalleled heritage, but actually getting under the skin of sporting royalty hypnotised me. The Yankees have an aura unlike any other team in any other sport. They transcend mere athletics to occupy an altogether more sacred place in the fabric of global power. The Yankees are America incarnate – big, loud, fearless and proud. Submerging myself in that golden history was an enchanting transformation.

I watched Yankees games on mlb.tv, enthralled by announcer Michael Kay and his mastery of moments. I listened to John Sterling and Suzyn Waldman on WFAN, finally appreciating the atmosphere they create. I read popular blogs like *River Ave Blues* and *Pinstripe Alley*, becoming familiar with the players and understanding their situations. There was no stopping the runaway train of my Yankee infatuation. I lost control of my own heart.

Courting such an illustrious team felt novel, thrilling and exciting. It felt big, meaningful and important. It felt *right*, after so many years in the baseball wilderness, and I see no need to apologise for that inimitable happiness. There was also an inherent symmetry to rooting for the Red Sox' biggest rival in response to John Henry's betrayal. Revenge was sweet, and I ate it cold.

"Rooting for the Yankees is like going to a casino and rooting for the house," comedian Doug Stanhope once said. Well I had the inside track and a world full of chips. There was no way I could lose. Not because of the Steinbrenner checking account, you understand, but because the Yankees filled a void in my heart that had been there for years.

✤✤✤

Before long, a voracious appetite for Yankee success roared up through my soul and tingled through every pore of my body. As ever, the Bombers were ensconced in a pennant race throughout 2014. However, they languished in the chasing pack through midsummer, lurking a handful of games behind Baltimore. Every game mattered immensely, and I was completely hooked.

The 2014 season was dominated by Jeter, whose farewell tour electrified baseball. After 20 years as the Yankees' shortstop, Derek planned to retire when the season ended, gifting it with special meaning. I have rarely experienced anything grander in sports.

From an early age, Jeter served as the dutiful face of baseball, a princely role model in whom people could believe. When the game was besmirched with drug cheats and egomaniacs, Jeter stood as a paragon of comportment, dominating the biggest sports market in the world with stunning ease and natural dexterity.

For two decades, Jeter was the brightest star in the world's preeminent metropolis. New York nurtured within its breast a deep love for him as for Sinatra, Monroe and Lennon in times of yore. He was a classy icon, a glistening role model, and a priceless gift for those prone to hyperbole. He was Derek Jeter, and nobody did it better.

From day one, Jeter appeared preordained for the role, with frosty green eyes, smouldering good looks and an intangible, implacable, largely ineffable aura of supremacy. While wearing that heritage-drenched uniform, he never once carried himself with anything less than tranquil humility, setting an example for millions around the world.

Jeter was the modern steward of Yankee greatness, the heir apparent to Yankee mystique, the incumbent guardian of the illustrious, interlocking NY. His name was etched with gothic majesty alongside those of Ruth, Gehrig and Di Maggio; Maris, Mantle and Berra; Ford, Jackson and Mattingly.

He wore upon his back a defiant, proud and elegant number two, so sensationally evocative when set against a backdrop of pristine pinstripes and cast below the white frieze of Yankee Stadium, his playground, stage and amphitheatre. One day, that would be the last single digit retired by the Yankees.

Jeter bestrode the baseball annals, churning hit after opposite-field hit with that sweet, scything swing, until only five privileged men had more base knocks in all eternity: guys named Speaker, Musial, Aaron, Cobb and Rose.

For more than a decade, Derek was the Yankees' captain, an exclusive honour bestowed upon the finest luminaries of club lore. He was far more than a mere ballplayer, far more than an eternal great. He was a bridge from the era of Tony Gwynn to that of Mike Trout, a certifiable relic of baseball's past but also a gateway to its future.

He was regal, lithe, grace personified. He was opulent, resplendent, youthful charm immortalised. He was a beguiling monument, shimmering like some grand ice sculpture, to the power and permanence of America's dream. I adored Derek Jeter, and his sweet meandering through the troves of baseball history left me somehow enlarged.

Indeed, to an entire generation, Jeter stood forth as the very embodiment of Americana. He rivalled David Beckham, Tiger Woods and LeBron James in endorsing more products than any athlete of the contemporary realm, and he sold more merchandise than anybody ever associated with Major League Baseball.

In typical rectitude, he did not bargain on becoming perhaps the most noble man ever to turn his hand to the game of baseball, but that he became, with awe-inspiring poise and aching mastery of politeness, respect and dignity.

Prior to Jeter's final season, the Yankees spent nearly $500 million rejuvenating the franchise, hoping to assemble a roster capable of returning to the postseason after missing out in 2013. Derek's impending departure inspired one last shot at bygone greatness, and reinforcements were drafted in to lukewarm receptions.

Veteran catcher Brian McCann was signed a few days before Jacoby Ellsbury, a lifelong Red Sock, as Hal Steinbrenner allowed Cashman to splash $238 million in a week. To Red Sox Nation, Ellsbury became the latest disgraced traitor, following in Damon's footsteps from Boston to the Bronx. The Yankees also added Carlos Beltrán via free agency before winning a protracted bidding war for Japanese pitching sensation Masahiro Tanaka, who signed a seven-year contract worth $155 million.

I acknowledge the sanctimony of my lauding the Yankees' expenditure while loathing the Dodgers' revitalisation. However, this is what the Yankees do. Since baseball began, they have spent more money than everybody else. It forms part of their philosophical makeup. It makes them special. By contrast, the Dodgers' spending was unprecedented and reckless. They attempted to *imitate* the Yankees, but in a world where the Yankees already *exist*, why should I settle for second best?

Nevertheless, the Yankees were caught between identities when I became a fan, trying to obey their star-studded heritage even though their traditional methods of roster construction no longer guaranteed success in modern baseball. Cashman and the Yankees became the very antithesis of Epstein and the Cubs. Over time, that disparity was reflected in the standings.

Beltrán and McCann got off to slow starts in 2014, while injuries to Tanaka and a declining CC Sabathia put the Yankees in a bind. As the trade deadline approached, Cashman wanted to blow it all up and rebuild, but with Jeter in situ, that was not a viable option.

Instead, Cashman reshaped his team on the fly with a series of transactions, cobbling together new pieces such as Chase Headley, Martín Prado, Brandon McCarthy, Chris Capuano and Stephen Drew. The frenzied activity resembled one last concerted effort to fashion a competitive team around Jeter. It was a Hail Mary for the captain.

My first experience of in-game Yankee greatness came amid the resultant surge in late-August 2014, when McCann hit a crucial pinch-hit, walk-off home run against the White Sox. "IT IS HIGH... 'N' IT IS FAR... 'N IT IS GAAAHNN!!," howled Sterling. "Yankees win! Yankees win! THUUHH YANKEES WIN!"

I got it. And perhaps more importantly, I *felt* it. Baseball is different in the Bronx, where demands are high and where expectations are stifling. The sense of opulent rejoice when somebody meets those demands and satisfies those expectations is unable to be replicated. It is a wonder to behold.

As the playoff chase unfurled, I found any excuse to write about the Yankees for FanSided. My own blog became littered with Yankee pieces, focusing on their remarkable history and their ubiquitous brand. Fortunately, nobody connected the dots and discovered that I was rooting like hell for them to reach the playoffs, and my life as a secret Yankees fan rolled on.

Despite a $220 million payroll, the 2014 Yankees were fatally flawed. They gave the illusion of competitiveness, lingering at the back of a frenetic wildcard race into September, but they eventually fizzled out of contention, finishing 84-78, their worst showing since 1992.

I felt my own ineptitude affect the Yankees. Aside from the dubious 2007 World Series I enjoyed with the Red Sox, my career as a sports fan was bathed in futility, and by some strange quirk, that miasma held sway no matter which team I rooted for. In many respects, I was a natural-born loser, and even the Yankees could not defy those molecules.

In his final campaign, opposing teams honoured Jeter when the Yankees visited. The Cardinals gave him cufflinks. The Indians gave him a pinstriped guitar. The Astros gave him cowboy boots and a Stetson hat. Detroit gifted Jeter a set of paintings. Anaheim extended a paddleboard. Oakland gave him wine. Throw in a kayak from Tampa Bay, a piece of the Fenway scoreboard from Boston and a bucket of jumbo steamed crabs from Baltimore, and Jeter need a warehouse to store his trinkets.

Many teams donated to Derek's Turn 2 Foundation, which helps children and teenagers avoid drug and alcohol addiction. Even astronauts aboard the International Space Station saluted Jeter, while 7th September was proclaimed Derek Jeter Day by New York City mayor Bill de Blasio. The greatest city in the world stopped to honour its prodigal son. Is there any finer tribute?

To some, it was all a bit much, but I lapped it up. It was my very own crash course in Yankees history. I raced home from Tranmere matches to watch the Yankees on Saturday evenings. I spent hours submerged in my own pinstriped daydreams. When Gatorade released a commercial honouring Jeter to the tune of Frank Sinatra's *My Way*, I cried at the wonder of it all. Derek was just *made* for this story.

After a lifetime of rooting *against* Jeter, I finally appreciated his greatness. After years of admonishing the Yankees, I finally respected their power. After a decade of searching, I finally found my baseball home. It felt raw and it felt real. It felt romantic and it felt rich. It felt *amazing*, quite frankly, and I will not apologise for that satisfaction.

There was no other team that could provide such frequent encounters with magic. There was no other team that could scale such mountainous heights. There was no other team like the New York Yankees, and I was their newest fan.

⚾⚾⚾

Jeter hit .256 in 145 games through the 2014 campaign. At the age of 40, he still played hard every day, even if his dwindling defensive range was occasionally hard to watch. Above all else, Jeter offered *presence* to the Yankees, even as they slipped into mediocrity. He represented a thread to the glory days of yore, and that was enough for me.

Derek played more than 3,000 games for the Yankees, including postseason contests and spring training exhibitions. The Yankees were already eliminated from playoff contention in just *four* of those games, making Jeter's perhaps the most purposeful career in baseball history.

Jeter never played a meaningless game in pinstripes. Not really. In 2008, the Yankees were eliminated with one home game remaining on the schedule, but that game was the final one ever held at old Yankee Stadium, making it *inherently* important. Likewise, in 2014, the Bombers ran out of postseason hope in Jeter's penultimate home game, but the following contest was his last in the famous uniform, giving it sacred meaning.

Just after 6:45 pm ET on Thursday 25th September 2014, then, a rainbow arched over a crimson Bronx sky. It was a parting gift from the baseball gods: Derek's last wish, to play his final home game without a deluge, granted with aplomb.

Ten minutes later, smothered in those hallowed pinstripes and sporting that illustrious cap, Jeter mustered enough strength to hold his emotions at bay and sprint from the first base dugout. He charged towards the most coveted quadrant of dirt anywhere in sports: between second and third bases at Yankee Stadium, the captain's field of dreams.

As fans, we were granted a rare insight into the sweet banality of the game, with television cameras trained solely on Derek as his teammates whirled the ball about the infield in pre-game preparation. The quintessential shortstop scooped a few ground balls, uncorked a few throws, among the last of a storied career spanning two decades and innumerable peaks of drama.

While fielding those pre-game groundballs, Jeter was more animated than usual. He looked up and scanned the seating bowl ensconcing him. He took a moment to admire the sacrosanct frieze and to gaze once more into the bleachers. He took long, exaggerated breaths, kicked at the sleek turf and teetered on the brink of tears. The magnitude of the moment finally felt authentic to Derek and to the watching masses. It was really happening. In a matter of hours, he would ride into the night, never again to don the home whites of his beloved team.

Leading his right field Bleacher Creatures, legendary rooter Bald Vinny Milano initiated one final roll call, with 48,613 lending their tongues to the lusty pronouncement of "DE-REK JEE-TER! DE-REK JEE-TER!"

Amid the cacophony, Nick Markakis, Baltimore's leadoff man, lofted a most unwelcome home run into the second deck in right field, reminding all in attendance that an actual game was to be played and pressing home an often-torturous season for a Yankees club toiling in the Orioles' wake. When Alejandro De Aza followed with a long ball of his own, a little air was let out of The House That Jeter Built as melancholic patrons mourned their own vitality.

In the bottom of the first, Brett Gardner kickstarted the New York revival with a single, bringing Jeter to the plate for the 12,594[th] time in his career. He took three straight balls from Kevin Gausman before the big righty hit the outside corner with a fastball. Then, after a throw to check on Gardner at first, Derek got a pitch he liked, lashing a fat 95-mph fastball out on a line towards left-centre field. The ball streamed through the wet air, propelled by a bellowing, howling, disbelieving crowd willing it to get up, get big and get out.

Watching in my bedroom after midnight, I thought it was gone. More than 3,200 miles away, I stood up, gazing at a fluorescent screen, begging for a fairytale home run. At the last conceivable moment, the ball dived and glanced with a satisfying rip off the outfield wall for a long double that scored Gardner and sent Jeter humming past the immortal Gwynn for 35th place on the all-time two-bag list. Pandemonium.

When an 0-1 pitch from Gausman to McCann got away from Oriole catcher Caleb Joseph, Jeter advanced to third, inspired by rolling waves of goodwill pouring from the grandstand. McCann grounded into a shift yet reached on a Kelly Johnson error, with Jeter sprinting home to score the 1,923rd run of his career. Only 10 men had ever scored more. Even in the waning hours, Derek was still compiling, still adding on, still hitting and scoring and making people cheer, regardless of the standings. He was still Derek Jeter.

In the second, the captain even provided grist for his critics, committing a throwing error on a Johnson grounder. However, on the next play, Jeter charged hard to field a slow roller behind the mound and, with customary panache, fired a dart to first to nab the runner, Jimmy Paredes. Clockwork. Sweet Yankee clockwork.

Following early nerves, Gausman and Hiroki Kuroda settled into an absorbing duel therefrom, trading zeroes through six-and-a-half innings. Jeter grounded out and struck out in subsequent plate appearances, evoking guttural groans from a gathered metropolis. At times, in the quieter moments, one could literally feel the flailing embers of one's childhood drift away. It was a happy moment. It was a sad moment. It was drenched in pathos.

In the seventh, New York loaded the bases for Jeter. How fitting. This felt like The Moment, destined to be replayed on YES for decades to come. Attempting to keep his emotions in check, Derek did not launch a titanic grand slam. Rather, he again grounded to short, where JJ Hardy threw away the ball, allowing two runs to score, gifting the Yankees a 4-2 lead and granting Jeter another RBI, the 1,310th of his career.

McCann added a further run with a sacrifice fly, giving the Yankees a 5-2 lead with which to advance to the top of the ninth inning. Derek Jeter's final inning at home. My final inning of childhood.

Perhaps feeling the tension emanating from thousands of fans chanting, barking and yearning, Yankees reliever David

Robertson lost Markakis to a leadoff walk before striking out De Aza. Then, as the roar of "THANK YOU CAP-TAIN!" grew louder, Adam Jones, immune to pressure, golfed a two-run dinger into the left field seats. 5-4, Yankees.

Robertson struck out Nelson Cruz swinging, bringing the end ever closer. In the dugout, Girardi thought about removing Jeter from the game so he could receive a final ovation, but *something* compelled the beleaguered manager to stay put, and that is just what he did. One out remained, but those party-pooping Orioles could not be restricted. Steve Pearce launched a missile of his own, tying the game and receiving only a cursory glance over the shoulder from an exhausted Jeter, resting on his haunches at short. He knew it was gone. He knew he would have to rise one last time to one last New York occasion. He knew.

José Pirela began the Yankee ninth with a sharp single to left field. Girardi brought in Antoan Richardson to pinch-run. Richardson represented Great Britain in the 2012 World Baseball Classic qualifiers, and he soon scampered his way into the record books, a proud moment for baseball fans across the UK. Gardner bunted the speedster over to second, setting the scene, forming the moment and passing the baton. Derek Jeter did the rest.

For the last time in history, the cashmere voice of Bob Sheppard cut through the New York night. *"Now batting for the Yankees: number two, Derek Jeter. Number two."* From a crouched position near the Yankees' dugout, Derek sprung into life, shot into action and strode to the plate. A shattering applause settled to a respectful, almost mournful hush. This was our last glimpse of the master at work.

Jeter fiddled with the navy guard on his left elbow, dug into the batter's box with slow and deliberate care, and tugged at the brim of his cap. He spun the bat once, twice, thrice, and settled into that old familiar pose. The legs were a little stiffer than in 1995, the posture a little more robotic, but the heart and soul were still there, and so was that elegant, penetrating swing.

On a plump breaking ball from Evan Meek, Derek unleashed a smooth but violent inside-out hack, connecting sweetly and shooting the ball through the right side. Steered by the force of a million New York hearts, the ball grew wings, fluttered past a diving Pearce and rolled into right field. The yell of agreement from Yankee Stadium was immediate. The sense of potential history drenched my British heart. Markakis came up throwing as, all around, eyes bulged with kinetic pride. Richardson, the doting Brit, came hurtling around third to score the winning run in a blaze of his own exertion. Cue delirium. Cue tears. Cue candid overtones of Sinatra. The captain had done it again.

In his final plate appearance at Yankee Stadium, Derek Jeter came through in the grandest way possible. In his final plate appearance as a shortstop, Derek Jeter rolled back the clock. In his final plate appearance wearing those fabled pinstripes, Derek Jeter won the game. There were no more words to be written. There was no more debating his legacy. There was no finer way to depart the biggest stage of all, on top of the baseball world.

For that one moment of mass jubilation, Derek was a kid again, thrashing about the diamond with fire and life and energy. He was free, and it was so poignant to watch. In his final act on familiar ground, Derek Jeter, the princely Yankee icon of our generation, once again proved worthy of his place in that hallowed lineage. He did it, and he did it right. There cannot be anything more to say.

It was all so typically, classically, quintessentially *Jeter*, and I cried into my Yankees hoodie at 03:30 am. It was the end of an era but the start of a lifetime rooting for New York. Jeter's parting gift was my gateway drug. There was no turning back now. I was too emotionally invested.

☾☾☾

Life as a secret Yankees fan was strange, to say the least. Struggling to keep up, my parents still enquired how the Red Sox were doing from time to time. None the wiser, social media friends who knew me as a Cubs fan struck up conversations about Castro and Rizzo. Believing me to be impartial, editors requested articles about the American League pennant race. It was hard not to embellish my writing with pinstriped bias.

Part of me wanted to set the record straight and come clean with the ultimate taboo confession. More than once, I sat down and typed out a tell-all piece, amassing thousands of words before contemplating the ramifications. People do not tend to react well when you change sporting allegiances so often, perhaps understandably, and I shied away from admitting my baseball bigamy.

Living a triple life fed my anxiety. Rather than enjoying my truth, I lived in the context of other people, of strangers I did not know and would never likely meet. When a one-time Red Sox diehard confesses love for the New York Yankees, there is little recourse to respectability. I cared too much about how people would react, fearing rejection and abandonment, and so I kept my emotions bottled up, toiling in restraint. I was a prisoner of my own mind, beholden to an inflated sense of self-importance. I could not find the courage to break free.

Deep down, I knew my defection to the Yankees was wrong, at least in the most common courts of social morality. It was absurd, preposterous and taboo. It was wild, unhinged and unprecedented. It was widely unacceptable, but still I defended my instincts and engaged in conversation with my own demons.

Yes, I began rooting for the richest sports team in the world. And yes, most people who *choose* to follow the Yankees embody the kind of gloryhunting I detest. But my situation was different. My situation had so many moving parts that most people would never appreciate. I simply gave up hope of coming clean.

For so long, I had no natural connection to *any* Major League Baseball team, falling into Red Sox fandom almost by default as a kid. When the New York Yankees came forth and proactively *created* a connection, I was thrilled. Finally, my fandom was underpinned by cogent rationale, even if the bigger picture made little sense.

Besides, when I began rooting for the Yankees, they were pretty terrible. *They lost 78 games in my first season.* In their previous 111 years of existence, the Yankees had only lost more games in a campaign on 19 occasions. My debut therefore ranks among the worst 16% of Yankee seasons *ever*. If I was hunting for glory, there would be a very long wait.

Nevertheless, I knew the enormous potential of this franchise and it inspired extreme passion within me. I wanted to participate in a Yankees world championship more than anything else. It lurked on the distant horizon, a confused possibility, but it always remained an *expectation*. That got me motivated to climb out of bed each morning. That is what *excited* me: the ardent demands, rooted in history, for perpetual success. That is what made the Yankees so special.

There was no greater calling in professional baseball, and I felt the gravitational pull even as an undisclosed rooter. The New York Yankees wanted me to join their timeless crusade for greatness, and I gladly accepted the invitation.

CHAPTER EIGHTEEN

Confessions of a Secret Yankees Fan

In the winter of 2014 and 2015, I consumed more Yankees material than ever before. In the offseason abyss, I watched old Yankee games on YouTube, devouring in retrospect the dynasty years of Joe Torre and his juggernaut. I bought vintage team jackets online and tried to find the courage to wear them. I even thought about getting a Yankees tattoo to consolidate my final choice. I was *that* besotted.

With each passing day, a volcanic passion built inside me. I needed an outlet for that pent-up Yankee dreaming, or else I would implode into psychological meltdown. There had to be a way of articulating my enthusiasm without betraying my reputation. I just had to find it.

Once again, I flirted with the idea of coming clean. I typed an expose of my own deception, ready to tell the world that I was a Yankees fan, but I could never hit publish. I could never send that piece to a newspaper or website because I was so petrified of social and career rejection. I could never admit my own reality.

We are often guilty of living in fantasy worlds of our own creation. Perhaps influenced by reality television and social media, we tend to view our lives in movie form, as if we were the distanced viewer rather than the first-person protagonist. People act in ways that will look good on an Instagram story, rather than being true to their core values. My secret Yankees fandom fell into that category, hidden behind a filter of bullshit pretence.

I turned 20 in October 2014, and I was lost. Sure, I was earning a few pennies from writing, but there seemed to be little direction or authenticity to my life. Socially awkward, I was cooped up in my small bedroom most days, exhausted from inaction. I did not have a healthy lifestyle, drinking at weekends with the few friends I had and staying up through the night to watch baseball. I felt incompatible with the world, destined to become a victim of its unrelenting brutality. I was an immature kid who refused to grow up. Sports and words were my only salvation.

I needed to write about the New York Yankees. That was my compulsion. However, achieving that goal was not straightforward because it would appear strange to outsiders if I suddenly began spewing pinstriped propaganda every day without explanation. A little nuance was needed. A little *imagination.*

Nevertheless, I have to be careful with ideas. Living with OCD, they can very quickly take over my life and strangle the air from my body. Such is the fine line between immense creativity and psychological illness, and such is the difference between genius and insanity.

I thought about creating a pseudonym but concluded that was pointless. I contemplated approaching major Yankees blogs anonymously but decided that was creepy. I even considered building a character called The Secret Yankee Fan, who would report on the team in mysterious ways, but that project stalled in the development stage. It was all too much.

In the end, I settled upon a mechanism that worked for me. The idea grew over a period of weeks, maybe months. As per my obsessive-compulsive trauma, I planned to launch a Yankees media outlet of my own, a standalone brand with its own website, logo, social media platforms and original content. I was inspired by humble blogs such as *Bronx Pinstripes* and *River Ave Blues*, which became vehicles of professionalism for their writers, bridging the gap from hobby to career. I wanted a piece of that pie, too, and so I got to work.

Defining the name, tone and unique selling point of my Yankees project was difficult. I brainstormed ideas for weeks before settling on a recurring concept: a hub of Yankees news for British fans. It seemed somehow fitting.

Indeed, this model had been particularly successful among the UK's growing NFL fanbases. For example, a group of Dallas Cowboys fans launched @UKCowboysFans, a Twitter presence that attracted thousands of likeminded individuals. When the Cowboys played, the sense of community orbiting the brand was great. I wanted to feel that with Yankees baseball.

A similar project among Green Bay Packers fans offered a viable template. Created in 2013, @UKPackers grew to attract more than 10,000 Twitter followers. More importantly, it became the world's largest Packers fan club outside Wisconsin. The group eventually added a blog, Instagram feed, YouTube channel and regular podcasts. I was intrigued. This seemed like an ideal template.

Accordingly, on 19th February 2015, I launched @UKYankeeFans, a Twitter profile allowing me to speak freely about the team. A hub of news, opinion, history, culture and stats, UK Yankee Fans was a passion project, but I had a long-term vision of monetisation and expansion. I wanted to make it a go-to destination for Yankees analysis, ephemera and passion. I wanted to make it a viable force in the world of baseball media.

Behind the comfort of a hastily designed logo, I covered the Yankees anonymously. As spring training began, I retweeted news and offered analysis, all without revealing my identity. I made a few YouTube videos that received more than 250,000 views. People engaged with the brand, following it and creating a sense of kinship. We were all together in the global pinstriped crusade. If only they knew who the founder was.

⚾⚾⚾

A few weeks after launching UK Yankee Fans, I enjoyed a major breakthrough in my baseball writing career. It was not Yankees-related, however. In fact, it was a job covering the sworn enemy and my original love. Yes, somebody wanted to pay me to write about the Boston Red Sox. Strange how things work out, huh?

Operated by a hardworking family, *Yawkey Way Report* is a magazine sold on gamedays at Fenway Park. Made famous by Sly Egidio, the eccentric owner turned salesman, the publication acts as a program for fans at Red Sox games. It treads much the same ground as fanzines here in British football, and I knew that culture well. The opportunity to collaborate seemed logical, and I tried to connect the dots.

Egidio gained popularity while hawking *Boston Baseball*, an earlier Red Sox magazine. His enthusiasm became legendary around the ballpark, but Sly was fired amid chronic disagreements with his boss. Seeking revenge, he started *Yawkey Way Report* and vowed to put his predecessors out of business. A messy war engulfed the streets of Boston.

Printed monthly, *Yawkey Way Report* included a free scorecard and token gift - such as a Red Sox sticker or figurine - with each copy. Putting a dedicated team to work, Egidio ate into the market share of *Boston Baseball*, attracting fans with quality content and free trinkets. Soon, his embryonic magazine earned a strong reputation, growing from strength to strength. It became as much a part of the Fenway experience as paying $50 to park or scribbling on Pesky's Pole.

Jared Carrabis, the aforementioned internet sensation, wrote for *Yawkey Way Report* in his formative years. The magazine became a breeding ground for raw talent, with many of its writers going on to greater things. I had immense respect for those guys, and the magazine was always on my radar. I knew it could be a gamechanger in my career, so I checked in regularly to keep abreast of developments.

In the spring of 2015, *Yawkey Way Report* eyed expansion into the online space. They always had a website, but editor Leigh Vozzella wanted to transform it into an asset through regular blogging. The publication duly advertised a paid role consisting of one print feature and four blog posts per month. I applied, and they gave me a chance. It was a brilliant opportunity.

As a kid, I yearned to one day sit in the press box at Fenway Park and cover the Boston Red Sox for a living. From my bedroom in Britain, I finally got pretty close, authoring work for *Yawkey Way Report* that was read by fans at the ballgames. My dream approached reality, even if telecommuting became a necessary fulcrum.

During the 2015 season, I landed one cover piece: a feature on the Red Sox' lack of a frontline ace. Designed beautifully, my story led the entire publication. People at Fenway, once my cherished field of dreams, read that article and had no idea I lived more than 3,000 miles away. The same people had no idea I was a Yankees fan.

Covering the 2015 Red Sox - a disastrous team that lost 84 games and finished last in the AL East - I found myself rooting for the most hyperbolic stories. I wrote with a searing passion, mourning through words the loss of Boston baseball as I knew it.

That year, corpulent third baseman Pablo Sandoval was a $100 million bust for the Red Sox, posting a .292 OBP in 505 plate appearances. Back as an expensive free agent, Hanley Ramírez was not much better, struggling to stay on the field. Meanwhile, the starting rotation was a shitshow, featuring Wade Miley, Joe Kelly and a degenerating Clay Buchholz. I could barely believe my eyes.

Watching the Red Sox capitulate up close was fun. The talk radio tirades and social media meltdowns were unrelenting. I blogged my way through it all, reporting on the team fairly despite my vested interest. If anything, my complex internal wiring sharpened my scrutiny of the team, yielding fairer analysis as a result. That added balance to the editorial flavour, enhancing *Yawkey Way Report* as a publication.

Nevertheless, I must apologise to anybody who is angered by these revelations after the fact, especially the magazine owners who paid me every month. However, it is the greatest compliment to my professional integrity that nobody noticed I was a rabid Yankees fan covering the Red Sox through gritted teeth. I'm proud of the way I conducted myself, and such a mature approach benefited my career.

Writing for *Yawkey Way Report* gave a certain gravitas to my resume. When pitching to editors, I humblebragged about featuring on the cover of a Red Sox magazine. It was a conversation starter and a door opener. People listened to my proposals.

I pushed the envelope and approached more outlets than ever before with ideas and suggestions. I pestered influencers on social media for tips and advice. I emailed my baseball writing portfolio to newspapers without invitation. I was cheeky and ambitious, daring and invested. My erratic strategy paid off.

Working out of my bedroom, hunched over a rudimentary workstation in the gathering gloom, I struggled with uncertainty, anxiety and feelings of phoniness. The bylines were great, a boon for my ego, but in quieter times, I felt somewhat illegitimate. I was a professional writer, but my own self-doubt told me I was doing it wrong. There had to be a more mature occupation.

People my age were having kids, finishing university degrees and planning weddings. Meanwhile, I was sat in my childhood home writing about baseball. Such decisions do not get you laid very often, and I became a stranger in my own skin. I had daily meltdowns, surrendering to dark anxiety and vowing to quit, but *something* always beckoned me forward. There was usually a flicker of hope that prevented all-out destitution. I'm glad I kept going.

Contrary to those feelings of inadequacy, I made valuable connections by promoting my work on Twitter. People like Nat Coombs, an esteemed television presenter, and Pranav Soneji, a media consultant, put in a good word at various publications and pointed me in the right direction. Josh Chetwynd was also a source of constant inspiration and support, encouraging me to persevere.

In May 2015, I finally made a quantum leap into mainstream baseball reporting. The *Guardian*, a Pulitzer Prize-winning paper, gave me a chance to do some paid freelance work. With almost 3 million followers on Twitter alone, the potential readership was enormous. Tom Lutz, sports editor of the *Guardian*'s US strand, believed in my ability. Or perhaps more accurately, he grew tired of my speculative emails asking for an opportunity.

My first baseball feature for the *Guardian* was about Joe DiMaggio. It focused specifically on his formative years with the San Francisco Seals, but I managed to weave in a few cryptic Yankee references, making myself smile.

I wrote six articles for the *Guardian* in total, swelling with pride every time. I dug up forgotten stories, sharing tales of Sadaharu Oh and chewing tobacco, switch-hitting and The House of David cult. Rounding out 2015, I reported for the *Guardian* on gathering momentum in negotiations to bring MLB games to London. I interviewed Chetwynd during my research, quoting his expertise in my feature. I will always be proud of those pieces, and it was a thrill to represent such an illustrious institution. I pinched myself reading every byline.

⚾⚾⚾

Improved from the previous year but still divorced from traditional expectations, the 2015 Yankees defined frustration. They teetered on the cusp of contention, flattering to deceive, but they never seriously tested Toronto for the division crown.

Shortstop Didi Gregorius was acquired from Arizona to replace Jeter in the offseason, while a bunch of veterans also left New York. Robertson, Kuroda, McCarthy, Ichiro Suzuki and Francisco Cervelli all found new teams as the Yankees got leaner. The winds of change were unbelievably strong.

Dogged by costly long-term contracts, the team still had an older profile, and several established stars enjoyed renaissance campaigns in 2015. At 38, Beltrán hit .276 with 19 home runs and 67 RBI. Just three years younger, Teixeira clubbed 31 home runs, attributing his resurgence to a strict gluten-free diet. A far more liberal eater, McCann also found his power stroke, popping 26 dingers. New York rode the long ball to semi-respectability.

Often stifled by decent pitching, the 2015 Yankees scored just enough runs to carry a dismal starting rotation. Besides Tanaka, who was good but not great, the Yankees cobbled together a slew of wild hurlers like Michael Pineda and Nate Eovaldi. Sabathia battled on at 34, a shadow of his former self, and New York somehow held on in the playoff race, even as Sterling had apoplectic meltdowns in the broadcast booth.

Looking for an edge, the Yankees built a dominant bullpen headlined by homegrown star Dellin Betances and automatic closer Andrew Miller. Girardi hoped to eke a lead from his creaking team through five innings then turn the game over to his relievers, who got the job done with minimal fuss. The formula worked just enough to keep things interesting.

Failing to convince at any point, the Yankees finished 87-75 and settled for a wildcard berth, hosting the Houston Astros in a one-game death match. It was the Astros' first playoff game since 2005. It was the largest crowd for *any* Astros game since 2010. It was a fatal fight against the venerated Yankees, at prime time, in New York City, beneath the twinkling lights, before 50,113 pairs of eyes. It was my first playoff game as a Yankees fan. October just felt different in the Bronx.

To that end, the Astros were supposed to be intimidated. They were supposed to run out of gas. Yet the opposite happened. They were entirely unfazed, and they seized the moment with annoying energy and vitality.

After losing 590 games in the six years between 2009 and 2014, Houston exploded in an orange blur of belief and precocious talent in 2015. Under the studious tutelage of AJ Hinch, the Astros kept playing their intoxicating brand of baseball and kept winning games, even when experts said they could not, and even when the odds laughed in their faces.

On a night when the new Yankee Stadium was loud and hopeful, with fans clapping and chanting like times of yore, the Astros rose to the occasion. The Yankees did not. Houston outfielders Colby Rasmus and Carlos Gomez launched solo homers, while the diminutive José Altuve knocked in another run. Meanwhile, the hosts managed just three hits and manipulated just two men into scoring position. The desperation was palpable.

I watched in my cold bedroom, gawping at mlb.tv on my small iPad as the light went out on another fruitless season in the Bronx. The Astros' remarkable victory was confirmed with three flawless innings from their bullpen, and Houston danced a victory jig on the Stadium infield. The pain was incredible.

The Astros entered the 2015 season with a $70 million payroll, second smallest in the majors. The Yankees, meanwhile, paid their players $219 million, or 212% more than Houston. That the former slayed the latter and advanced to the American League's final four was highly indicative of baseball's changing economic climate. It no longer paid to be the richest guy in the room.

Increasingly, the money a baseball team possessed became less important than the people it employed to spend it. Intellectual firepower within the front office became just as crucial as superstars on the field, and with Jeff Luhnow at the helm, Houston became an exemplar of modern roster construction and data-driven strategy.

The Astros built a literal nerd cave in their front office, stocked with academics such as Sig Mejdal, a former NASA biomathematician who rose to fame in Sam Walker's aforementioned *Fantasyland*. If Moneyball used maths to identify hidden value, Astroball took that analytical output and blended it with science. Houston hauled baseball evaluation into a whole new sphere, and the cradle of modern astronomy became the epicentre of sporting innovation.

The Astros' core of cost-controlled, homegrown talent opened a lengthy window of sustainable opportunity, and their steadfast belief in analytics helped them take advantage. Houston pioneered aggressive defensive shifting, moving its fielders around the diamond on every pitch in accordance with spray charts, heatmaps and batter tendencies. More than any other team, the Astros embraced science, creating a new style of play that jived with the sabermetric doctrine. They went even further than Oakland and Tampa in trusting objective information, and the results were suitably destructive to baseball's status quo.

By contrast, the Yankees were stuck between two philosophical pillars. On one hand, key decision-makers felt obliged to compete, appeasing the legacy of George Steinbrenner, surrendering flexibility for stardom. On the contrary, modern baseball was played in a different financial environment than when The Boss held court. George died in 2010, and a different approach was needed in his absence.

Tighter restrictions on spending made youth movements more conducive with sustainable success than signing superstar veterans. Prospects became more valuable than ever before, and farm systems were scrutinised with searing intensity. The Astros and Cubs were fine prototypes of this strategy, pushing baseball into a post-analytics age. New York was still catching up.

Under Hal Steinbrenner, altogether more pragmatic and sensible than his father, the Yankees tried to honour George's ethos of perpetual success while also transitioning to the new environment. It did not always work, and it was not always pretty.

Perhaps understandably, the Yankees grew tired of paying exorbitant rates of luxury tax on excessive payrolls. Ramped up before the 2003 season, baseball's competitive balance tax acted as a de facto salary cap, penalising teams that spent beyond an agreed threshold. The Yankees were consistently taxed between 17.5% and 50% on every dollar they spent over the luxury tax benchmark. Between 2003 and 2017, the team paid $319.6

million in luxury tax contributions. The Dodgers came closest to that figure but paid less than half of the Yankees' total.

In many respects, then, the luxury tax came to be seen as a Steinbrenner tax. Forever whining about the Yankees' superior financial clout, major league teams implemented the penalty system to encourage parity. Revenue sharing, a sister policy, also clipped the Yankees' wings, as 48% of local net revenues were pooled and distributed among all 30 MLB franchises each year.

A man of numbers and processes, efficiencies and philosophies, Hal Steinbrenner grew tired of helping other teams compete against the Yankees. Division rivals like Tampa Bay and Toronto built rosters with Steinbrenner dollars recouped through revenue sharing. That made little sense to Hal, who mandated austerity measures to control the Yankees' spending and hone its competitive advantages. In a contemporary paradox, the less New York spent on salaries, the more its difference-making resources were distinguished elsewhere. That was difficult for some fans to understand.

You see, when a team drafts and develops a homegrown player, said player is under guaranteed team control for the first six years of his career. Arbitration manages salaries during this period, making farm system graduates the most cost-effective commodity when seeking to build a baseball team under the luxury tax threshold.

As Luhnow and Epstein demonstrated, cramming as many cheap homegrown stars onto a roster was the surest way to remain competitive without committing financial suicide. Associated benefits of coalesced primes and refreshed team culture made this a powerful model adopted by many teams. Those who did not comply were swiftly left behind.

Amid such a paradigm shift, Cashman was eventually ordered to focus more on the farm system than on the major league roster. Signed for $225,000, pitching phenom Luis Severino made his debut in 2015. Prospects such as Gary Sánchez and Aaron Judge progressed through the minor leagues. Ageing veterans saw their contracts expire as the Bronx Bombers shifted focus from today to tomorrow. For the first time in almost three decades, a pinstriped rebuild became the most logical strategy for success.

Of course, when you are the New York Yankees, generating more income than almost any sports team on the planet, competing for the World Series every year and developing a strong farm system need not be mutually exclusive. Some fans became irate at Hal's perceived parsimony. I lurked among that cult for a short period, growing frustrated as the Yankees passed on a stream of elite free agents.

However, short-term pain was necessary for long-term gain, and the Yankees slowly built their next great uber team. The 2015 wildcard game was gut-wrenchingly frustrating, but watching the Yanks in transition was an interesting experience. Dealing with heartache only piqued my desire to see the Yankees win a World Series. I was fully invested, even if the world did not know it yet.

⁂

One man embodied the Yankees' schizophrenic ethos in the 2010s more than anybody else: Alexander Emmanuel Rodriguez, who outstayed his welcome longer than any player in baseball history. From Day 1 in the Bronx, A-Rod was a ticking time bomb, and the timer finally struck zero as a new brand of baseball came of age.

Perpetually admonished, Rodriguez won his third American League MVP award in 2007. Straining to meet extraordinary standards, A-Rod hit 54 home runs for the Yankees that year. He added 156 RBI while batting .314 with a .422 OBP. There was no greater baseball player on the planet.

Despite chronic postseason struggles and huge pinstriped expectations, through the 2008 season, Rodriguez needed just 210 home runs to pass Barry Bonds and establish a new all-time record. A-Rod was 33 with nine years remaining on his contract. He seemed set to rewrite the history books and deliver on his prodigious potential while silencing the critics. He seemed set to be remembered as one of the greatest players who ever lived.

However, if the first half of Rodriguez' career was defined by meteoric surges and melodramatic falls, the closing act was characterised by disgraceful cheating and unprecedented legal battles. Built on dusty diamonds and in packed stadiums, the reputation of an all-time great was destroyed in anti-ageing clinics and sterile courtrooms. A-Rod brought shame on the New York Yankees like few before or since, and it was painful to watch his annihilation.

In 2009, *Sports Illustrated* revealed that Rodriguez tested positive for two anabolic steroids – testosterone and Primobolan – during his 2003 MVP season with the Rangers. Amid the storm, Rodriguez gave an interview to Peter Gammons of ESPN, in which he admitted taking PEDs between 2001 and 2003.

Citing an "enormous amount of pressure to perform" in Texas after signing his 10-year, $252 million contract, Rodriguez described his naïve mistakes and apologised to fans around the world. His reputation was tarnished forever, but many people respected his admittance.

Therefore, when excellent reporting by Tim Elfrink and Gus Garcia-Roberts of the *Miami New Times* uncovered a further steroid scandal circling Rodriguez in 2013, baseball fans felt violated and disrespected. We felt duped - pure and simple. How was this happening again?

Owned by Anthony Bosch, a faux doctor, Biogenesis of America was a boutique health clinic in Coral Gables, Florida. Operating dishonestly behind the practicing certificate of his father, Bosch offered a range of weight loss treatments and hormone replacement therapies to the rich, vain and famous of Vice City. Baseball players enjoyed his services, too.

A cocaine addicted party animal, Bosch built a network of famous major leaguers who relied on him for PEDs. The *Miami New Times* obtained documents from Porter Fisher, a former Biogenesis employee, listing Melky Cabrera, Bartolo Colón and Yasmani Grandal as clients. Each player failed a drugs test in 2012, tempting journalists to join the dots.

Flush with cash and high on his own ego, Bosch felt invincible for a spell, taking his eye off the ball as a result. Partying in dingy clubs and associating with all the wrong people, Bosch became lackadaisical in his approach. Secrets leaked out and documents were left unprotected. A symptom of arrogant neglect, holes appeared in the Biogenesis operation. Those holes eventually sunk the boat.

Later, Elfrink and Garcia-Roberts published a book entitled *Blood Sport* that triggered an earthquake in Major League Baseball. It was to millennials what *Game of Shadows* had been to salty baseball traditionalists. Scarcely have I read a more powerful book laced with such formidable journalism.

Blood Sport described in painstaking detail how Rodriguez cheated for vast portions of his career, from the failed tests of 2003 through to the Biogenesis explosion a decade later. It even presented authentic documents belonging to Bosch, chronicling A-Rod's extensive PED regime. Years of fandom flashed before my eyes reading the book. The scope and scale of evidence was overwhelming.

In 2013, following an MLB investigation, A-Rod was banned for 211 games, which later became one full season after a lengthy appeal process. Rodriguez then fought anyone and everyone in court. He attempted to sue Yankee management for mishandling an injury. He did the same with Major League Baseball and the Players' Association, hoping to overturn the longest PED-related suspension in the game's history. He lost all credibility and created for himself a world of pain. Nobody believed a word he said anymore.

Rodriguez returned from suspension in 2015, aged 39. The Yankees did not really want him around, but they were tied into that godforsaken contract. As Steinbrenner and Cashman eyed their new philosophy, prizing prospects over veterans, A-Rod became a millstone around their necks, stirring controversy and stifling future plans. Management wanted Rodriguez off the team, but it did not want to eat the remaining portion of his contract. An awkward dance ensued.

Defying expectations, Rodriguez forged a renaissance in 2015, playing in 151 games. He hit 33 home runs, his largest total in seven years, and he also topped 2,000 career RBI. In June, A-Rod launched a bomb for his 3,000th career hit. Only Hank Aaron had previously reached both of those sacred landmarks. Such achievements are typically met with immense fanfare, but when it came to Alex Rodriguez, nobody cared anymore. Or at least nobody believed what they were watching.

It was tragic to experience the abnormal dichotomy between *what could have been* and *what was*. The true legacy of A-Rod's cheating can be found in the boos that greeted his greatest accomplishments. I remained silent, although a low-level disgust hummed through my soul. Cheats continued to destroy the grand historicism of baseball, and that damaged its standing within American society.

Entering the 2016 season, Rodriguez was a microcosm of Yankee possibilities. On Opening Day, he needed just 28 home runs to pass Babe Ruth on the all-time list. Yes, *Babe Ruth*. However, there was also a very real prospect that he would implode with advancing age and declining chemical enhancement.

Likewise, a reloaded Yankees team featuring elite closer Aroldis Chapman and my former Cubs favourite Starlin Castro - acquired in a winter trade with Chicago - needed a few lucky breaks to seriously compete. Neither happened, and the fallout was historically transformative as the Yankees demolished their major league roster for the first time in generations.

On 25th July 2016, the Yankees waved a white flag in their flawed attempt at competing while rebuilding. They were buried in fourth place, a 51-48 record killing any hope of a wildcard berth. The wheels fell off with stunning rapidity, and unprecedented change rolled through the Bronx.

Rodriguez and Teixeira ran out of gas and collapsed in a heap. Ellsbury was unrecognisable in pinstripes, and not in a good way. Chase Headley was awful at third base. And the starting rotation was disastrous besides Tanaka and Sabathia.

Cashman recommended the destruction of his own roster. Steinbrenner initially relented but eventually gave the green light after seeing enough. The old Yankee doctrine of fielding a championship-calibre team for every single game was torn asunder. Pioneered by Colonel Ruppert and mastered by King George, the valiant ethos became incompatible with the modern game. It was time for a fresh start.

Sanctioned by Hal, Cashman worked to dispose of major league liabilities in return for minor league assets, expediting the Yankees' rebuild. Chapman was sent to Chicago for Gleyber Torres, the Cubs' uber prospect. Miller was dealt to Cleveland for a package headlined by Clint Frazier, the Indians' top phenom. Beltrán went to Texas for Dillon Tate, the Rangers' first round draft pick in 2015. Cashman even dumped Iván Nova, whose enigmatic act ran out of steam.

In the space of a week, the Yankees' general manager did more to enhance his reputation than he had done in the previous half-decade. Finally unleashed to build the team he wanted, without misguided input from Randy Levine or The Boss, Cashman showed the subtle touch of a genius. Rather like Theo between 2005 and 2008, and again between 2011 and 2016, Brian had a licence to build in his own vision, and he did so to great effect.

In total, Cashman moved five players and welcomed 14 in return at the 2016 trade deadline, a great infusion of talent that remodelled the Yankee farm system as one of the very best in baseball. According to MLB.com, after Cashman's mid-season insurrection, the Yankees had seven of the top 100 prospects in baseball. With four trades in seven days, the team recalibrated its future, and even A-Rod ran out of time as the Bronx Bombers got real.

In early-August, the tumultuous marriage between Rodriguez and the Yankees reached its tipping point after 12 years. Struggling to hit above .200, Rodriguez became a strained anachronism. An OBP below .300 made A-Rod dispensable, while mounting strikeouts frustrated fans and teammates alike.

Betrayed by niggling injuries, Rodriguez had been immobile for years. A full-time designated hitter, the 41-year-old A-Rod was relegated to sparse pinch-hitting duties amid terminal decline. Finally, a press conference was called, perhaps at the subtle urging of Yankee officials, and Rodriguez announced his sudden retirement. After 22 years of chasing ghosts, approval and redemption, A-Rod planned to hang up his cleats within a week. The game had moved on.

"This is a tough day," said Rodriguez, holding back tears. "I love this game, and I love this team. And today, I'm saying goodbye to both. I want to be remembered as someone who tripped and fell a lot, but who kept getting up."

Rodriguez' final game in pinstripes was a rain-soaked affair against the Tampa Bay Rays on 12th August 2016. The Yankees planned a lavish pre-game ceremony for A-Rod, who yearned for the same adoration afforded Bronx idols such as Jeter and Rivera in their final seasons. Symbolically, a huge clap of thunder interrupted the contrived celebration as rain sent people scampering for cover. Satirists all over the world chuckled into their hands. This was the only way it could end.

A-Rod went to bat four times, lofting a bittersweet double for good measure before Joe Girardi let him play third base for the final time. After one out in the ninth, Ronald Torreyes was introduced as a defensive replacement, allowing Rodriguez to enjoy an ovation from the assembled crowd as he walked into the sunset.

A-Rod finished his career with 696 home runs, 2,086 RBI and 3,115 hits. He had a .295 lifetime batting average and 329 stolen bases. Few players had ever produced such a stunning array of mathematical genius, and he still trudged off the field a frozen pariah rather than a worshipped legend. Unease pervaded.

I watched after 04:00 am here in the UK, peering at my laptop in confused purgatory. More than anything, I was saddened by the Alex Rodriguez story. Here was a vulnerable kid thrust into a world of pressure from the earliest age, lavished with millions he did not necessarily want and saddled with expectations unfit for any teenager to bear.

Beneath it all, there was a young guy who just loved to play baseball, and I do believe a certain amount of what Rodriguez says about pressure driving him to PEDs. That is a deeply worrying polemic against a billion-dollar industry that can warp minds and destroy lives. That is an overlooked factor in Alex Rodriguez' mutilation.

We all make mistakes and many of us deserve second chances. But when trying to sympathise with A-Rod, I still could not reconcile the issue of his *repeated* cheating. At some point, the responsibility to stay clean and avoid temptation was his. So, too, were the consequences.

For many years, Rodriguez lusted after what Ripken Jr. and Jeter had: respect, admiration and *appreciation*. If he played clean, perhaps those things would have happened naturally. His final game could have been a monumental event, on par with Derek's farewell. Instead, a sense of pity saturated his demise, and a tale of misplaced legacies took centre stage.

The unique selling point of baseball is its history, and those who cheat ruin a small part of that with every syringe to the buttocks and each lozenge on the tongue. Born in 1994, I lived through the entire Alex Rodriguez saga, and even as a passionate Yankees fan, in the end I was just relieved he could not do more damage to a game that gave him everything.

⚾⚾⚾

Chapman's presence on the Yankees was also drenched in scandal. Capable of throwing 106 mph, the bullpen ace was shopped by Cincinnati throughout the 2015-16 offseason. The Reds lost 98 games in 2015 and they were keen to rebuild. The framework of a Chapman trade was agreed with the Dodgers, only for allegations of domestic violence to surface and torpedo the deal.

Major League Baseball investigated Chapman under its personal conduct policy. He was accused of choking his girlfriend and firing gunshots at their Florida home. While no criminal charges were pursued against the Cuban, MLB suspended Chapman for 30 games as a result of the firearm usage and the impact of such behaviour on his partner. He was the first major league player ever suspended for domestic violence infractions.

Rather disturbingly, Cashman demonstrated his penchant for snapping up supressed assets, sending four minor leaguers to Cincinnati for Chapman in a December 2015 trade. Investigations were still ongoing at the time, and the Yankees appeared reckless in their zeal. I respected the Dodgers for passing on Chapman, just as I disagreed with the Yankees' decision to pursue him. It was impossible to comprehend.

Rooting for Rodriguez, a proven cheat, and Chapman, a domestically hostile tyrant, did not appeal to me. In fact, their actions tested my faith in the Yankees. I registered my displeasure and vowed never to root for those individual players, but a sour taste was still difficult to wash away.

Some troubled souls - mainly Red Sox fans - fail to understand that it was possible to root for the Yankees while disapproving of Alex Rodriguez and Aroldis Chapman. *The Yankees harbour cheaters and celebrate domestic abusers, so why would a moral*

person associate with them? How can you cheer for a team that
willingly employs steroid addicts and aggressive brutes?

Well firstly, Red Sox fans are in no position to lecture *anybody*
about cheating, so spare me the faux outrage. Secondly, the
scourge of PEDs was a baseball problem, not simply a *Yankees*
problem. Frequently, those caught using steroids were
egotistical lone wolves, acting out of inflated self-interest rather
than altruistic urges to win. They took it upon themselves to
inject illegal drugs. Nobody told them to do so.

Of course, teams were notoriously slow to break clubhouse
cliques that encouraged negative cultures to fester, but finding a
model franchise during such an unethical era was virtually
impossible. Every team has encountered problems with steroids,
from minor league scrubs to all-time greats. Moral point-scoring
should be confined to more nuanced subjects, because cheating
in baseball is so rife as to border banality.

Even Epstein, my original baseball hero, was mentioned in the
Mitchell Report regarding a shady acquisition of closer Éric
Gagné in 2007. Mitchell unearthed an email exchange between
Epstein and Marc DelPiano, a Red Sox scout, in which the duo
openly discussed Gagné's possible steroid use. Nevertheless, the
Red Sox still acquired Gagné, sending two prospects to the
Rangers for his services. Gagné later admitted using human
growth hormone to aid his recovery from injuries. This whole
situation is conveniently forgotten in Boston, even though Gagné
has a Red Sox World Series ring on his nightstand.

Meanwhile, Ortiz and Ramírez - twin terrors of the Boston
baseball revolution - failed drugs tests in 2003, according to the
New York Times. Ramírez was later banned on multiple
occasions for violating baseball's drug policy, casting doubt over
his monstrous productivity, while Ortiz' late-career power surge
was among the most improbable in baseball history.

That many New York Yankees used steroids is unavoidable.
Giambi, Sheffield, Pettitte, Clemens, Rodriguez, Cabrera, Canó -
the list is long and shameful. I will never defend anybody who
cheats to gain an advantage. However, the fire with which Red
Sox fans in particular disparage the Yankee *organisation* as a
result of individual misdemeanours is deeply hypocritical. It
serves an agenda rather than seeking retribution.

Sure, the players should be rebuked for their criminality, but Red Sox fans take these things personally. Such is their obsession with the Yankees, each transgression by a representative of that club is described as a fatal kryptonite for the Evil Empire. That the Red Sox' own success in recent decades may have been aided by steroids barely seems to matter.

Admittedly, explaining the Yankees' stance on domestic violence is a far more difficult task. This *is* an organisational problem, at least to the extent that Steinbrenner and Cashman apparently saw little wrong in employing a guy who fired gunshots to intimidate his girlfriend.

That Chapman throws harder than any pitcher in baseball history seemed to be the only concern for New York, setting a dangerous precedent of performance and results over behaviour and morals. A few years later, when promising Yankees pitcher Domingo Germán was also suspended for 81 games under the domestic violence policy, that paradigm was tested again. The Yankees went 0-for-2.

Delving further back, the infamous case of Luis Polonia was even more concerning. A Yankees outfielder in 1989, Polonia was arrested in August of that year for having sex with a 15-year-old girl. Polonia met the girl at Milwaukee County Stadium during a Yankees-Brewers game, and was wrongly informed that she was 19. Nevertheless, even after becoming aware of the girl's age, Polonia then had sex with her *again*, later being convicted of statutory rape.

Presiding over the case, judge Thomas Doherty said that, while the sex acts were consensual, Polonia still broke obvious laws. The Dominican was sentenced to 60 days in jail, suspended until after the baseball season, and fined $1,500. He also made a $10,000 contribution to a sexual assault treatment centre in Milwaukee. The Yankees made no formal comment and continued to put Polonia in left field. They even brought him back for two further stints, in 1995 and 2000, helping a paedophile win two World Series rings.

Horrifically, two of Polonia's Yankee teammates, Mel Hall and Chad Curtis, have also been convicted of sexual abuse and paedophilia. A third 1990s Yankee, John Wetteland, is currently awaiting trial after being indicted on three counts of aggravated sexual assault of a child. Meanwhile, Clemens is rumoured to have started a relationship with Mindy McCready, his long-time mistress, when she was 15. A deep inquiry into that era must be sanctioned.

The resurfacing of such uncomfortable truths brings me great distress. I weep at the depraved potential of sick human beings. Still, I manage to love my team in a global sense while challenging its behaviour at a granular level. It is possible to admire the Yankees for their history, heritage and overarching philosophical residue while dismaying at the decisions they make from day-to-day.

I will never condone domestic violence nor seek to explain it into acceptability. That scourge has affected some special women in my life, and the brute who destroys another human - mentally, physically or otherwise - deserves the harshest retribution. Likewise, sexual abuse is the most savage shade of barbaric human sins. It can never be excused.

Returning to events that transpired during my fandom, I believe the Yankees were wrong to trade for Aroldis Chapman. They were also insensitive when *re-signing* him to a five-year, $86 million free agent contract after his tour with the Cubs. Nevertheless, there is a clear distinction to be made between the enchanting veneer of sports teams and their often-gruesome underbelly. In this regard, the *idea* and *spirit* of New York Yankees baseball exists independent of the organisation itself.

"Loyalty to any one sports team is pretty hard to justify," comedian Jerry Seinfeld once said. "The players are always changing, the team can move to another city. You are actually rooting for the clothes, when you get right down to it. You are standing and cheering and yelling for your clothes to beat the clothes from another city. We are screaming about laundry."

All kidding aside, Seinfeld makes a pertinent point about sporting allegiance. There is an essence to fandom that overrides individual people and specific achievements. The day-to-day business of roster construction and personnel and marketing is separate to the overall *concept* of the New York Yankees, just as it is for all sports teams. As fans, we care more about the uniform than the people wearing it. Our loyalty is to the logo, not to the individuals who don it.

That beating heart, real but invisible, exists independent of what the team does at any one time or in any one game. It is buried deep in the soul of those who understand and those who believe. It is possible to love the New York Yankees *concept* while condemning the present-day machinations of the *organisation* itself. There is a subtle difference that must be acknowledged.

Not every Red Sox fan is racist because Tom Yawkey once owned the team. Not every Indians fan is xenophobic because Chief Wahoo is used as the team's logo. Not every Pirates fan loves cocaine because they once cheered for Dave Parker at Three Rivers Stadium.

Not every Dodgers fan is insensitive because city officials once bulldozed entire communities to build a ballpark in Chavez Ravine. Not every White Sox fan agrees with gambling because Eddie Cicotte took a bribe. And not every Giants fan injects stanozolol because they once had a poster of Barry Bonds on their bedroom wall.

Not every Cubs fan is a right-wing nut because the Ricketts family is a leading funder of Donald Trump's political career. Not every Reds fan is a Nazi because Marge Schott repeatedly praised Adolf Hitler. And not every Mets fans is a homophobe because Daniel Murphy once spoke of his disagreement with same-sex relationships.

Looking at the bigger picture, it is possible to stigmatise sports *as a whole* in such a negative mode of thought. If you sat at a computer for long enough, you could find a reason to hate every single sports franchise on earth, and that collective immorality debases criticism of any one specific team. The *industry* of sports is inherently rotten, so how can we criticise the teams that are but an outgrowth of that core? We still continue to love sports even though we know they are horrid. It is unwise to make judgments when we are all complicit in feeding the disgraceful system.

For example, since 1990, taxpayers have contributed more than $7 billion to build or refurbish baseball stadiums across America. In the wider scheme of society, that money would have been better used to fund hospitals and schools than to develop ballparks in Minnesota, Washington, San Diego or any other city.

Moreover, many people associated with baseball have also committed heinous crimes, but they still have great lives thanks to the sport and its financial reward system. Manny Ramírez was alleged to have slapped his wife at one point, but we still discuss his vintage home runs. Carl Everett has been charged with abusing various members of his family, once holding a gun to his wife's head, but we still joke about his quirky disbelief in dinosaurs.

Stephen Murphy was charged with 26 counts of aggravated felonious sexual assault, including rape, but he was still hired as a Red Sox clubhouse attendant when the team failed to complete adequate background checks. Donald J Fitzpatrick was a convicted sexual predator, but he was still the Red Sox' clubhouse manager for almost 30 years, committing many of his crimes in the bowels of Fenway Park.

Gazing at other sports, since 2000, there have been at least 110 reported arrests of active NFL players in relation to domestic violence incidents. Still, in the same timeframe, almost 345 million people have attended NFL games in person, clicking through stadium gates to support the teams that paid those players. How do you square that circle?

Lunging further, why do we watch the NFL *at all* when it glorifies such aggression, not only in the form of domestic violence but also in the guise of concussion-inducing combat? Why do we let the Washington Redskins exist when their name is pernicious? Quite frankly, why do we bother at all? There is no end to *reductio ad absurdum*, so we have to make our own choices of tolerance.

In a world where every decision we make will be considered wrong by *somebody*, the burden of ethical deduction must be removed from the public arena and placed in the lap of each individual. When the spectrum of politics, religion and culture is so fragmented, stretched and hyperactive, we cannot take a utilitarian approach to deciding what *is* and what *is not* allowed. Heck, when *life* is so disparate, a cookie cutter of self-righteous finger-pointing causes more harm than good. A more detailed exploration is required, far away from the breathless thrashing of showcase virtues.

The Roman Catholic Church offers a succinct corollary here. In recent decades, tens of thousands of lawsuits and complaints have been lodged against its priests around the world in relation to sexual abuse and paedophilia. The Church has spent hundreds of millions of dollars settling cases and dispensing compensation. Still, 1.2 billion people identify as Roman Catholics. That is 15% of the *entire global population*. However, not all churchgoers endorse sexual abuse, and it would be absurd to suggest so. There is nuance to each instance of individual worship that must be respected.

To truly appreciate contexts and to understand actions, we must separate the art from its artist. For instance, the music of Michael Jackson is still adored despite allegations of paedophilia surrounding him. The theories of Albert Einstein are still revered despite the fact he was a xenophobe and serial adulterer. The words of John Lennon are still worshipped even though he admitted to physically abusing women. Perhaps it is possible to love a product but loathe its producer. Perhaps grey exists between black and white.

We must also acknowledge the evolution of social norms before we tear up the history books in retrospective disgust. Regardless of who your hero is, they have probably done something terrible in their life. We all have. Besides, certain things that are deemed unacceptable now - smoking indoors, spanking children, making politically insensitive jokes - were once unremarkable aspects of daily life. Similarly, some things that are now socially *acceptable* – sleeve tattoos, same-sex marriage, swearing in music – were once frowned upon as taboo.

We change, folks. We mature. Therefore, a flexible approach is required when analysing misdemeanours. Revisionist debunking is a dangerous ideology because it lacks a standby button. There is no end to the demystification.

Sure, there will always be global truths that are non-negotiable. Osama bin Laden was bad. Domestic violence is evil. Stealing is wrong. But what each unique person deduces from those overarching maxims should be private, not informed by a subjective choir of vociferous opinion.

Let us consider an example. Today, Hugo Boss is a luxury clothing brand with annual revenues of $3.1 billion. Yet in 1931, Hugo Boss was a member of the Nazi party who just happened to manufacture uniforms for the SS, which killed millions of people in horrendous genocide.

Therefore, we all agree Hugo Boss was a pretty awful guy. Though he died in 1948, some of us may choose to boycott the fashion products hawked by his eponymous label in a show of solidarity. However, many of us may *not*, electing to wear a Hugo Boss t-shirt without reading *Mein Kampf* before bed. The brand's revenue would suggest a clear winner in that debate.

My point is that we must make clear distinctions between events and our reactions thereto. We all have our own internal taxonomies which should be respected in a non-judgmental manner. Foisting our own flawed contexts on external, changeable situations is fraught with danger because we ourselves are not infallible. Those who live in glass houses should not throw stones.

If, inside, I'm hurt by the Yankees' mishandling of domestic violence issues because I respect the universal unacceptability of such actions, but I complete an intensive private triage of the subject before reaching a nuanced conclusion, why is anybody else allowed to tell me that approach is wrong?

If, personally, I despise the actions of Chapman and Germán because my moral compass says domestic violence is wrong, but I devise a weighted protocol of checks that allows me to still root for the team that employs them, separating the two concepts, how can that be invalidated by somebody else?

Indeed, we need to appreciate the bigger picture before castigating *anyone*. For instance, since MLB introduced its new player conduct policy in 2015, a total of 12 players have been suspended for indiscretions related to domestic violence. Those players are drawn from 10 different teams, including the Red Sox, who recalled pitcher Steven Wright in 2018 after a 15-game domestic violence suspension. Boston even gave Wright a new one-year deal worth $1.3 million in the subsequent offseason, doing the same thing for which their fans earlier chastised the Yankees.

Here, we see how MLB *as a whole* must do more to educate its players and to protect its communities from harm. Yes, individual teams need to be more sensitive when acquiring and rewarding players who have been suspended for domestic violence, but the league needs to be assured in its interventions and consistent in its punishments.

Again, readers may question the validity of my thinking here. *What about your attitude towards the Dodgers, then? And why do you hate Liverpool FC so much if their daily actions are divorced from their overarching legacy? You disowned the Red Sox because their owners bought Liverpool, but you will not reject the Yankees for their misinformed approach to welfare?*

Well, in answering such questions, it is important to understand that I'm human, not a robot. These are hypocritical inconsistencies that I have spent hours trying to reconcile in my own mind, and finding a comfortable solution has often been impossible. I can offer no rational explanation, except to say that the heart does strange things to the brain, and that domestic violence is one area of Yankee fandom that can never be defended.

By the same token, I do not believe in a uniform brand of deductive reasoning. When I put Liverpool Football Club through my subconscious classification software, sirens whir and red lights flash. That is one individual computation, uninfluenced by any additional data. There is no connection to any other situation I have ever encountered. The disqualification is theirs alone.

Accordingly, to conclude that my continued Yankees fandom is causally contradicted by my earlier rejection of the Red Sox is like saying Mark Langer is a fascist because he is the current CEO of Huge Boss. Everything must be assessed on its own merits, in its own environment and by each person's unique moral infrastructure. The same broad lens does not capture every picture, and sometimes you have to zoom in to inspect different layers.

In the interest of full disclosure, and nothing else besides, it is also important to reiterate that Chapman was not criminally convicted in this case. Florida police did not arrest the pitcher, and prosecutors did not pursue charges, citing conflicting accounts and insufficient evidence in their rationale. Likewise, no charges were filed against Germán, who accepted his suspension and made a donation to Sanctuary for Families, a New York organisation that helps victims of domestic violence.

Thus, both Yankee players *were* punished by MLB, which levies its suspensions without pay. Chapman lost $1.8 million in salary while Germán lost around $260,000. Both also saw their reputations tarnished forever. They *were* disciplined within the context of baseball, and that should not be forgotten.

In fact, Chapman and Germán were suspended for far longer than the aforementioned Wright, even though the Red Sox knuckleballer *was* charged while the Yankee pitchers *were not*. Such discrepancies make you contemplate the validity of Rob Manfred playing sheriff. Such inconsistencies make you wonder why sports leagues can supersede police departments and courts of law in doling out punishments. Such disparities make you question the entire baseball institution.

Finally, neither Chapman nor Germán have committed further crimes since returning from their respective suspensions, so we must have *some* faith in civic rehabilitation. The Yankees also pushed both players through psychiatric evaluation and formulated bespoke counselling programs that became mandatory among their players.

Chapman showed little outward remorse, however, and that seemed at best tone-deaf and at worst incriminating. "I didn't do anything," Chapman told the *New York Times* upon his return. "I have not put my hands on anyone and didn't put anyone in danger."

The optics were terrible for the Yankees, who should have avoided Chapman in particular at all costs. Many Yankees fans were angry at the organisation for supporting these players, but they still remained Yankees fans, even while loathing the team's closer and its firebrand phenom. They adored the eternal ballclub while detesting its transient representatives. In my mind, that position is perfectly understandable.

When the Yankees later reupped Chapman to that long-term contract, Tanya Bondurant of *Pinstripe Alley* took a nuanced approach, donating $1 to the National Coalition Against Domestic Violence for every strikeout he recorded in the 2017 season. I vow to do the same for the rest of his Yankees tenure, and for that of Germán, offsetting my contempt for their presence on the team by helping charities that fight such unspeakable evil.

As Cashman dismantled his team, spaces became available on the Yankees' big league roster. Gary Sánchez, a truculent catcher, filled one of the spots, figuring to split time with McCann and learn under the veteran's wing. Instead, he totally outshone the burly backstop and bludgeoned his way to the front of New York's youth movement. A salve for sore eyes, all potential and shiny enthusiasm, Gary carried the Yankees' carcass to the precipice of respectability.

Sánchez reached 20 home runs quicker than anybody who has ever appeared on a major league diamond, breaking the plateau in just 50 games. At one point, the home runs were so plentiful as to spark murmurs of belief that the Yankees might even sneak back into the 2016 wildcard race. Those hopes faded, but Sánchez' travelling clinic did not. He just got better and better.

When Beltrán left town, Aaron Judge took over in right field, a 6-foot 7-inch colossus from the Jeter school of rectitude. Debuting at 24, Judge was groomed as the next Yankee icon. He launched a mammoth home run in his first major league plate appearance, a portent of greatness to come. I found a new baseball hero.

Elsewhere, the Yankees took a cautious yet productive approach with Severino, their ace-in-waiting. Just 22 in 2016, he epitomised the team's new philosophy: young, talented and focused on long-term attainment. Severino showed glimpses of greatness while adapting to the big league environment. Fans hungered to watch his exciting development.

Ultimately, then, the 2016 season was purgative for Cashman, who finally had total control over the Yankees' baseball operations department. In the absence of George Steinbrenner, and unburdened from controversial superstars on stifling contracts, Cashman came into his own. We finally caught a glimpse of his scuppered genius, and rival fans were shocked by the Yankees' resurgence.

Among the smartest executives in sports, Cashman saw the changing baseball landscape long before he was allowed to make the Yankees fit for it. Cashman championed the use of analytics and yearned to build a player development empire, highlighting the importance of sports science and psychosocial enrichment.

For all of his faults, Hal Steinbrenner listened more than his father, and although it was not necessarily glamorous, he gave Cashman the time, space, money and trust to realise a long-term vision for domination. It was a thrill to be part of that transformation from the start, and seeing it completed one day will be magnificent.

☙☙☙

In addition to my *Guardian* features, I continued to write for *Yawkey Way Report* in 2016, chronicling a Red Sox team that was swept by Cleveland in the ALCS. My work gained traction on social media, where I interacted with readers and editors alike. Opportunities came my way as a result, including the greatest honour of my career so far.

When the Cubs won the National League pennant in 2016, I received an email from Phil Gordos, assistant editor of the BBC Sport website. He was looking for an expert to cover the impending World Series, capturing one of the most cherished stories in baseball history. After years of unsolicited begging for opportunities, I stood out as a primary choice. We struck a deal with minimal fuss.

For a British kid who dreamed about being a professional baseball writer, covering the World Series for the BBC - our national broadcaster of global renown - was a mighty thrill. I could scarcely believe my luck. Unfortunately, I did not get to visit the ballparks, but reporting remotely on a phenomenal Fall Classic made me proud, nevertheless. My fantasy came true.

In sharp symmetry, the Cubs triumphed in seven games, winning their first World Series title in 108 years. Around 07:00 am on Thursday 3rd November 2016, without sleep in days, I filed one of the best stories of my career. It was published on the BBC website, teaching a worldwide audience about the billy goat curse and Epstein's magical cure. I kept the payment receipt, typed on BBC letterhead, for future inspiration. It would take something remarkable to surpass that achievement.

My feature on the Cubs' success earned rave reviews, and the BBC invited me on various radio stations across its network, where I answered basic questions posed by confused breakfast DJs. Spreading the gospel of baseball was hugely rewarding, and for the first time in my life I felt respected as an expert, regardless of my nationality. I had reached the mountain top, and the view was spectacular. For sentimental reasons, I'm glad the Cubs were somehow involved, even if their place in my heart had been permanently excavated.

Those who still knew me as a Cubs fan offered their congratulations on a famous world championship. Fellow rooters engaged in conversation about the topsy-turvy series, sharing their experiences. I did not have the heart to tell them about my changing allegiances. It all seemed so random and inexplicable. For once, I could not find the right words.

Further confusing matters, Chapman logged four saves for Chicago in the 2016 postseason, including Game 5 of the World Series. He also got the win in Game 7, the most sacred occasion in Cubs history. However, that did not invalidate the experience for generations of fans who waited decades to see a championship, just as Chapman's presence does not invalidate my rooting for the Yankees.

In such an emotionally charged context, harbouring a secret fandom for the Bronx Bombers became increasingly difficult. Even with the anonymous outlet of UK Yankee Fans, I lacked an authentic voice with which to declare my pinstriped affection. I cared too much about other people's opinions rather than living my true life. I kept my mouth shut, accepting platitudes that jarred with my soul. Looking back, it was a weird time in my life.

The self-doubt and endless panic about permutations frustrated me. I felt restrained and silenced, yearning for emancipation. However, the fear of being blacklisted kept me quiet, and so I fanned the flames of my own self-destruction.

To avoid the landmine of explaining myself to judgemental outsiders, I maintained a private love affair with the world's most lucrative baseball team. Yet without forewarning, my life changed immeasurably over the next 12 months, transforming my relationship with sports beyond recognition.

At 22, it was time for me to grow up and become a man. I outgrew my own shallow dreams, and I realised that life is more about surviving bullshit than it is about smelling roses. Every facet of my existence was tweaked and shifted, including the tragicomedy of my affiliation with Major League Baseball. I made essential sacrifices to facilitate my own maturation. Just like a decrepit old pitcher, the game told me that my time was finally up.

In the end, I had far more important things to worry about than men in pyjamas trying to hit a white ball on a massive field. Real problems replaced the fictional ones of my own creation, and finding a solution took years of soul-searching and change. That journey is still not entirely complete, and it altered my personality forever. I will always bear those scars, and I will never forget the transformation.

⚾⚾⚾

CHAPTER NINETEEN

Red Sox Relapse

In February 2017, I was approached by the owner of an environmental company in Wirral who was impressed by my work. We met in a Bromborough coffee shop and discussed opportunities. I was young, naïve and restless. The shark took advantage.

Tired of the fluctuating income and meandering security of freelance journalism, I accepted an offer to become the company's full-time Media Manager. For the first time, I had a proper job, and my starting salary was £18,000, a small fortune in my world.

I intended to keep writing and curating contacts, maintaining a passionate sideline in journalism. However, I had already scaled the mountain, and the realities of adult life soon became apparent. There was little time for such procrastination amid the 9-to-5 grind, and a lot of my momentum fizzled out.

Struggling to balance full-time employment with part-time happiness, I had to curtail certain paid writing arrangements. My Tranmere column for *Love Wirral* magazine was discontinued. My time at *Yawkey Way Report* came to an end. And the prospect of squeezing in features for the *Guardian* or BBC Sport faded rapidly.

By the time spring training finished, I was out of the baseball loop. Sure, I still subscribed to mlb.tv, but the concept of staying awake until 04:00 am every morning to watch Chase Headley strike out with the bases loaded lacked viability. I was up and out by 08:00 am now, a real man with a real job. There was little time for pondering the minutiae of baseball.

Sometimes, extra-inning games were still being played when I arrived at the office. I stepped on the treadmill of grim corporate adherence, and it was difficult to jump off as responsibilities mounted. Life comes at you fast, man. I often wonder how it all fell apart.

For the first time in my life, I was earning real money. At 22, the council estate kid had £1,200 in his bank account every month.

To most, that was not a lot, but to me, it was a stunning amount of money. I made a fraction of that as a writer.

I bought flashy clothes and expensive shoes. I ate at upscale restaurants and purchased the latest gadgets. I had the foresight to save a large chunk of my wage each month, but the guarantee of regular funds opened a different life before my eyes. Baseball did not really fit in.

I chased girls, obsessing over crusades of unrequited love. Suddenly, my time outside of work was consumed by Tinder, Snapchat, Instagram and Facebook. A late bloomer, I had my amorous teenage phase as a burgeoning adult. It was thrilling, but also deeply traumatic.

My innate shyness and chronic anxiety were exacerbated by a toxic workplace. Sitting at a desk for eight hours each day, often longer, engaging in small talk with invasive strangers, I quickly became exhausted. The relentless grind of full-time work was a huge shock to my system, and I typically crashed out on the couch each evening, dazed and confused.

Dangerously, I was also incredibly good at my job, which involved a mixture of bid writing, content marketing and public relations projects. When I delivered a new company website and launched its first social media channels to great success, the owner promoted me to Commercial Manager within six months. A pay rise and company car came soon thereafter.

Winning million-pound contracts, driving a new Mercedes-Benz and taking home £1,500 every four weeks, I was in a very good position. At least, that is how it looked to outsiders. In reality, though, I was drowning in stress, exhaustion and my own insecurity. There was too much pressure and not enough support. *Something* had to give. In the end, it was my mental health.

꩜꩜꩜

As the Yankees embarked on a premature quest for the American League pennant in 2017, I was preoccupied with romantic rejection and shiny Swiss watches. I occasionally watched day games, and I vaguely kept abreast of baseball news through Twitter, but my emotional investment was diluted.

In May 2017, one story did penetrate my identity crisis: the racial abuse of Orioles centre fielder Adam Jones by a minority of Red Sox fans during a game at Fenway. "It's unfortunate that people resort to those types of epithets to degrade another human being," said Jones, who also had projectiles thrown at him in the Boston outfield. I was shocked but not surprised, and the whole situation saddened me.

Aaron Judge broke the rookie home run record in 2017, mashing 52 bombs, while Sánchez, Gregorius and Aaron Hicks took huge steps forward in their development. Still under the stern command of Girardi, New York finished second to Boston in the AL East then managed to beat Minnesota in the wildcard game. When Cleveland took a 2-0 lead in the subsequent ALDS, I likely checked out, but the Yankees came roaring back to sweep the next three games and advance to the championship round.

Once again, Houston lay in waiting, and a rollercoaster ALCS went the distance. The Yankees also lost the first two games of that epic encounter before winning the next three. They were one victory away from reaching the World Series, only to capitulate and lose Games 6 and 7 at Minute Maid Park.

The Astros went on to defeat the Dodgers in the resultant World Series, but I can barely recall watching any of the games. I certainly could not stay awake to watch them live, although I may have streamed re-runs at more sociable hours. Who knows? Certainly not me.

Girardi was fired in the aftermath of a seemingly transformative season. After riding out the difficult years, answering questions about faltering veterans and injury-prone hopefuls, Girardi would not oversee the pinstriped renaissance. Cashman wanted a better communicator to spearhead his new culture, and Aaron Boone eventually got the job. A Red Sox demon came back to life.

Looking back, my growing indifference during that period is startling. For somebody who cares *so* much about baseball to effectively fall off the radar due to work and other commitments is astounding. I regret how life got in the way of me enjoying that span. I'm also remorseful at the loss of my own childlike innocence. I wish there was a way to get those months back. I feel cheated by my own confusion.

Like most things from 2018, the Major League Baseball season of that year is a vague mystery to me now. I was mired in a mental health crisis from spring onwards, worsening in the summer, and a full psychological breakdown rendered most things joyless.

At work, I was promoted again, becoming an executive Commercial Director, harbouring legal responsibility for organisational performance. There was a further pay rise, up to £26,000 per year, but I was rarely out of the office to spend it. More importantly, I was second-in-command of the entire firm, liable for its lawful performance, but a peek at the budget showed at least 15 people paid more than me, including those I hired and fired. I was the company MVP, yet my salary was that of a rookie. The whole thing was illogical.

Frequent were the 05:00 am starts and the 10:00 pm finishes. I travelled the country for monthly client meetings, spending time in London and even flying to Belfast, Northern Ireland, on a regular basis. I continued to win contracts with effective bid writing and business development skills. The revenue I generated for the company soared over £6 million, but I was still only 23 years old. It was all too much, too soon. I did not have the internal fortitude to shoulder such a burden. Why *would* I? Just 18 months earlier, I sat in my bedroom blogging about baseball all day. Those skills are not immediately transferrable.

Running from his own demons, my boss offered little support. In fact, he spent less time in the office as more work came in, burying his head and focusing on other businesses ventures. So good were my bid writing skills, he even began pimping me out to rival firms. I won contracts for them, too, receiving no commission or reward in the process. My one-man commercial department was understaffed and overworked. There was no way out.

The rigours of corporate success wreaked havoc with my personal life. Friends abandoned me with alarming speed, growing jealous of the fine accoutrements and becoming frustrated when competing deadlines and chronic exhaustion kept me from visiting the pub each weekend. I had to deal with vitriol and smear campaigns at every turn, losing key relationships every day.

In turn, my endless efforts to find romantic love were greatly impacted. I was insecure and anxious, tired and washed out. More pertinently, I was stuck with nowhere to go, spending hours at work even on weekends and lacking a social circle to meet girls in bars and clubs.

Racked by a negative body image and painful diffidence, my confidence was zapped. I felt abnormal, far adrift from mainstream coolness. My frames of reference were out of kilter, earning ridicule from the girls I tried to impress. Every day, there was a new perceived failure. I struck out with more potential lovers than can be accurately recalled. I was all over the place, awash in psychological turmoil. Professionally indispensable but socially superfluous, I did not know where to turn. I was paralysed by mental disarray, shrinking into a mute shell of angst.

When I came home from work each day, mustering the energy to live normally was often impossible. Each shift was an interminable war of fake smiles and contrived interest. I could barely talk about what transpired in any given day because nobody would understand. The demands of my job were *that* inhumane, and so I internalised my pain.

Capitalism relies on such anxiety because it is the fuel of consumerism and, thus, the elixir of profit. However, the effect it has on the agent of its progress is often overlooked. I typically crashed on my bed each night, wrung out from the trauma of it all, flicking endlessly through social media searching for something to distract me from the agony.

The harder I searched for ephemeral concepts – love, happiness, respect, appreciation – the more elusive they became. In turn, with each setback and each unfulfilled day, I tried even harder, sparking an endless cycle of mortifying agitation.

An ocean away, the Yankees were rolling to a 100-win season, promoting more young studs like Torres and Miguel Andújar, but I was lost in a sickly melancholy, adrift and indifferent. Cashman even traded for Giancarlo Stanton - the superhuman slugger who was paid more than any sportsman in history - to boost a vaunted lineup, but I followed along via occasional highlight reels and fragmented tweets. The thought of concentrating for three hours to watch a game was chastening.

Inspired by the poisonous work culture, my mental health deteriorated over the summer of 2018. The company for which I worked was relatively small, reliant on a few families and close friends to keep it running. Gossip, nepotism and sharp-tongued backstabbing were fuel for the corporate engine. My life was played out on the office floor, akin to a soap opera of personal chaos.

Every so often, my boss came up with another gift to compensate for the fact he was ripping me off every month on salary. I eventually grew wise to the tired act and began switching off. Rather than voicing displeasure, I typically shut down. That is exactly what I did at work, receding into a cynical ball of pecked tongues and cloudy headaches.

For months, I could not shift the ennui. Everything was cloaked in a thick blackness, devoid of meaning and purpose. I had everything and nothing, all at once. I had no way out, nor the energy to find an alternative mode of living.

My family was incredibly supportive, but my mind was a ticking time bomb. I did not know who I was anymore. I did not know what I was supposed to be doing, and the most innocuous tasks sent me over the edge.

I wanted to give up. I wanted to run away and hide. I wanted to cease existing and unburden the world from my annoying presence. There was a deep rage inside me, the rattling contradiction of a thousand failed plans, but I was otherwise powerless to release it. My life happened inside an angst-riddled bubble, of which I had no control.

Concerned at the degenerating pitch of my complaints, mum made an appointment with the doctor. I was initially fobbed off, told to relax and change my diet. When that did not work, I was diagnosed with depression and generalised anxiety disorder. The doctor gave me pills - antidepressants called sertraline - and they helped at first, only to quickly wear off. We experimented with a few other meds, finally settling on fluoxetine, or Prozac as it was once known in the US. That actually helped when we eventually found the optimum prescription.

I never missed a day of work, but fearing the toxic environment, I was reticent to disclose my psychological battles to anybody. I eventually told my boss, who feigned compassion before the office was transformed into a judgemental forum of prejudiced garbage.

Everybody had an opinion about my mental health, whether I asked for it or not. They used phrases like *wired* and *scatty*, saying I was *erratic* and *all over the place*. Lest anyone remember that I delivered a 2.2% increase in revenue year-on-year, even while dealing with the implosion of my own mind. Lest anyone remember that I revolutionised the company alone, making enormous sacrifices along the way. Lest anyone remember that I was closer to 17 than I was to 30. Those people were barbaric.

Managers questioned my medication dosage. Assistants whispered about my appearance and behaviour, freely discussing the weight and medical history of a *Commercial Director*. My boss even ordered me to stop taking the antidepressants, telling me to snap the pills in half each morning and gradually wean myself off. The guy could not even spell *doctor*, let alone maintain even a basic grasp of medical science. My life became a shitshow.

I began to struggle with stress-related panic attacks and their attendant consequences. For eight consecutive months, I either vomited, fainted or blacked out due to inner psychological strife. Twice, I passed out in the bathroom, laying on the floor in a bloody heap. Another time, I fell ill on a train and had to text my mum and brother to meet me at Bromborough station, such was my inability to operate. Doctors ordered blood tests and heart scans, tilt tests and pressure measurements. There was little certainty to any of the investigations, and I lost faith in the health system.

One doctor diagnosed syncope, which is marked by temporary losses of consciousness caused by falling blood pressure. On the contrary, DIY research later isolated cyclic vomiting syndrome as the real problem. Its trigger? Extreme stress, of course. I was a readymade exponent.

I paid £45 each week to visit a private therapist, who offered shelter from the demons but created new ones, too. She used phrases like *energy vampire* and *narcissist* and *mood hoover* and *gaslighter*, explaining the disastrous interpersonal relationships that ruined my life. Nevertheless, once those narratives were constructed, *absolutely everything* I mentioned was shoehorned in to fit the storyline. It became easy to demonise things, contributing to a pervasive negativity that demolished any progress I made through cognitive behavioural therapy. One step forward became two steps back. Old wounds were replaced by new bitterness.

A classic descriptor of depression is that the sufferer no longer derives pleasure from activities they once adored. Interests fade away and passions fizzle out. You stop attending that club or visiting that friend as hobbies are submerged in a sea of regret. I endured this timeless conundrum, losing all sense of sporting orientation and becoming anaesthetised to the daily rotation of news.

My beloved Tranmere won at Wembley, hoisting their first trophy in 27 years, but I experienced the moment through anxious caveats. Like everything else, football lost all meaning to me, and even my contempt for Liverpool FC was numbed comparatively.

When Liverpool fans sent death threats to Loris Karius, the club's own goalkeeper, after he made two costly mistakes in a UEFA Champions League final defeat to Real Madrid, I could not even muster the strength to get angry. Some fans wished cancer upon Karius' family, while several Liverpool nightclubs tweeted that the German was not welcome in their establishments. This is just who they are and that is just what they do. I wept for humanity that we allowed sports to mean so much.

A few months later, the Yankees and Red Sox faced off in a tense ALDS, their first postseason duel in 14 years, but I lost the ability to feel *anything* besides pain. Sitting through a five-hour baseball marathon became impossible. My attention span fizzled to zero, leaving me blank between the ears.

MLB even announced that, in 2019, the Yankees and Red Sox would travel to London for a two-game regular season series, but the thought of vying for tickets with day-tripping newcomers piqued my anxiety. I beat myself up for being such a lousy fan, lamenting the fact that other people had surpassed me in the ranks of British baseball media. A sneering resentment accompanied *everything* I tried to do. That shit was tiring, man.

As summer poured into fall, I was a mess. My mind was splintered, and the broken shards caused immense anguish. Everything was bathed in impenetrable gloom, and the slightest setback led to volcanic meltdowns that lasted days, sometimes even weeks. I lost the instruction manual for life, and putting myself back together again became a monumental challenge.

During one particularly dark episode, I remember uttering the word *suicide* for the first time, admitting my state of desperation to family gathered in the living room. I do not remember the date or month. I do not remember the chronology of events nor the definitive trigger. All I remember is hope seeping away, fear clouding the horizon and a dense weight of dark dejection crushing every fibre of my soul.

I remember the inability to think straight, the total absence of logic and the mute surrender to psychological entropy. I remember the silent tears of petrified trepidation and the fizzing ball of dread lodged in my throat. I remember seeing no way out. I remember wanting to run away, and keep running, and maybe cease existing altogether.

I remember slumping on the couch, paralysed by conflicting, inexorable emotions. I remember talk of medical help and professional guidance, of asylums and being sectioned. I remember my vision becoming distorted and my head throbbing with steamy confusion. I remember the pale pall of worry blanketing every family member accompanying me.

I remember my dad ringing HOPELINEUK, the telephone support service operated by PAPYRUS, a charity that works to prevent suicide among young people. I remember the phone call that saved my life.

Sitting upstairs, I spoke to a HOPELINEUK advisor, finally articulating the agonising thoughts, feelings and images that had popped in and out of my head during the darkest phase of a mental breakdown. The inclination to stay in bed for weeks. The idea to get in my car and keep driving for days, weeks, maybe forever. The vignette where I stood in the cold, dark night pondering the sinister river, so choppy and blustery, so capable of ending it all.

The advisor calmed me down, reintroduced logic to my tired mind, and gave me instructions to stay safe for that night. Give the car keys to someone you trust. Put on some pyjamas to lessen the likelihood of going outside. Stay away from water at all costs and listen to your favourite music. Stabilise today, recover tomorrow. There is so much left to live for. Just be yourself, because that is enough, no matter what anybody else says to the contrary.

Finally, those words penetrated the smog and settled in my soul. So many people had uttered similar instructions over the previous year, but this time it just clicked. There was something refreshing about a trained outsider providing guidance. I rediscovered hope, even if the process of growing that seed became a lifelong endeavour and a timeless fight against self-destruction. I learned to fight for another day of existence, even when the current one felt horrific. That lesson put me back on the rails, and I slowly rolled towards safety.

※※※

Boston outmanoeuvred New York in the aforementioned 2018 ALDS, clinching in four games. The third contest was a 16-1 rout at Yankee Stadium, the worst loss in franchise postseason history. Following the humiliation of 2004, so engrained in the Yankee psyche, this was too much to take for some fans. Cashman became a scapegoat while Hal Steinbrenner was castigated for perceived penny-pinching. Meanwhile, I was just trying everything to rediscover a baseline of *existence*. Baseball pain was a privilege I could not afford.

After working myself to the bone, unable to take holidays through fear of the company collapsing in my absence, I finally decided to bite the bullet and put myself first. I delved into my accumulated bank of annual leave, booking two weeks off to recuperate at home in October. The World Series was on at the same time, giving me something to focus on. That seemed vaguely pleasing, even if I did not particularly care.

Nevertheless, marooned in bed, attempting to rest, I stumbled upon the Fall Classic and became invested in the storyline.

Naturally, the Red Sox and Dodgers fought for the crown in a blast from my past. I still subscribed to mlb.tv, and I found myself awake after midnight again, watching as in days of yore.

Emotionally immature, thrust into a commercial rat race beyond my kin, I resented being an adult. Everything about it sucked, from the endless hours in front of a screen to the relentless passage of bullshit that coalesced into another day of survival. It became easy to see why people fall into drug and alcohol abuse, seeking a break from the stifling echo chambers of life. I associated with that same baseline sorrow, but my escapist narcotic just happened to be baseball.

I was lost, divorced from happiness. I was tired, detached from possibility. I was pessimistic, defeated by external worry. Watching the World Series made me nostalgic, perhaps even mawkish. There was something so soothing about the green hue of a baseball diamond, beamed through a television into the gloom of British night, into the heart of contemporary despair. I finally found relief from my mounting problems. For the first time in months, I could feel *happiness*, that most elusive state, and so I continued to watch, putting myself back together again in the process.

You see, that is the beautiful thing about baseball: it preserves the kid inside us all. We grow up with the game, discovering it at seven or eight, and a flame is lit inside us. A joyful flame. A *carefree* flame. No matter what happens in the world, those boys of summer will be there each night to provide escapism. *They* care, even if nobody else does, and that *means* something. That can be the difference between hope and despair.

Throughout life, we carry that flame with religious attention. We incubate it from destruction and we shield it from wind. We explain it to strangers and we defend it from attacks. Sure, life gets in the way sometimes, and the baseball flame will flicker, but in the soul of those who truly adore this pastime, the fire is never extinguished.

We watch baseball to honour that legacy. We watch baseball to keep alive the sensational freedom and enchantment of youth, when anything was possible and when everything was smiley. We watch baseball to construct meaning where otherwise none resides. We watch baseball to make ourselves happy.

Embroiled in the 2018 World Series, mentally ill but spiritually alert, I relapsed into a faint form of *association* with the Boston Red Sox. I would not call it *appreciation*, and it was certainly not outright *fandom*, but there was at least a twinge of *something* within me as they marched to a fourth World Series title in 15 years.

Confused and broken in my adult shell, I withdrew into that familiar introversion of childhood. I was comfortable there, away from sinister bosses and all-encompassing cash. I was protected there, unhindered from romantic affliction. There was time to think and dream and ponder inside that cocoon. Oh, and there always seemed to be a Red Sox cap nearby back then. Usually, it was on my head.

Pining for childhood, or at least the emotional cleanliness that came with its unadulterated innocence, I bought a new Red Sox hat and hoodie. Forgive me, Yankees fans. Bear with me, Tranmere acolytes. I know this is insane. I kinda *was* insane at that point. My mind was that of a sick man.

Alas, I sat awake watching the 2018 World Series wearing Boston garb. Not out of love for the baseball team or the city, you understand, but in a sentimental plea for salvation from the throes of adult entropy. For a moment, I was back in Bromborough library, sheltered from the march of irrepressible responsibility. For a moment, I was free.

Rejected by girls, abandoned by friends, abused by colleagues and hated by myself, I also found much-needed companionship in *Section 10*, a Red Sox podcast by Jared Carrabis and Steve Perault. Regardless of the team you root for, those guys are hilarious, and their podcast is arguably the greatest of its kind. Listening put a smile on my face, for whatever reason. There was a sense of community among followers, and no matter what team they spoke about, I felt the kid inside me come back alive episode by episode. *I* was still alive, and that felt pretty good.

When the Red Sox beat the Dodgers in five games, I was not especially bothered, in all honesty. The fleeting moment of reminiscence was over. My relapse lasted a couple weeks, tops, and I knew it was wrong. I felt dirty and hypocritical. There was no long-lasting renaissance, just short-term gratification devoid of meaning.

Sure, it was *nice*, in a dull, perverted, nonsensical sort of way, but the wider significance of a baseball championship melted away when I returned to work. There was no real connection between the Red Sox and me. Not now. Perhaps not *ever*. I was an adult, damn it, and there were more important things to worry about than Sandy León's OBP.

I liken my desperation during the 2018 World Series to that of a former heroin addict who is offered a fortnight of nostalgic indulgence without consequences. He has lost everything else and has sunken to the furthest nadir imaginable, so what the hell? May as well give in. Besides, who is going to be angry? The fair-weather 'friends' of yesteryear? Please – give me a break.

I was not so much moved by the Red Sox during this spell as I was transfixed by the eternal beauty of baseball. The *sport* offered calming companionship, and that familiar Boston team just happened to be immediately present. The 2018 Red Sox were like incense burning during meditation - they accentuated a pleasant experience via evanescent placebo.

In retrospect, I cannot escape the hypocrisy of my actions. Hands up. *Mea culpa.* I have been a jackass. There is no way to explain my momentary lapses of judgement, nor to articulate my phenomenally addled mind. I alone must bear that burden, and that is just what I will do.

Some will struggle with my story. I appreciate it is sanctimonious and contradictory. A lot of my experiences just do not add up, and my decisions have often been illogical. Hey, I'm human. We all fuck up occasionally. I can only apologise to anybody who has taken offence.

Many will argue that a history of routine defection invalidates my entire argument and debases this whole book. I respect that, and there is little hope of refuting those allegations. The reviews are likely to be a shitstorm. However, I'm keen to set the record straight and nail my colours to the mast.

I wrote this book to deal with my meandering trajectory, not to escape it. Sure, I could have conveniently overlooked the fall of 2018. Believe me, I would like to. But obfuscating the truth in that fashion would further tarnish my diminished credibility, and that is not something I want to do.

A wide swathe of claims and labels and accusations will be hurled at me, and I totally get that. I'm a guy who has changed his baseball rooting allegiance – no matter how temporarily – four or five times in the space of 16 years. In short, I have been a prick. There is little reason, beyond my own unproven word, to believe I will not change team again. There is little reason to invest in my future.

Yet, if readers could at least hear me out and attempt to comprehend the psychological challenges and logistical nightmares that underpin my life as baseball fan in Britain, they will see that I'm far from a gloryhunter or serial bandwagon jumper. Winning barely enters the equation. I might be a dickhead, but not through my own choice. My actions are always well-intentioned, and I have reached inner peace with my capricious past.

You see, a gloopy broth of emotional immaturity, chronic insecurity, debilitating shyness, manic depression, generalised anxiety and obsessive compulsion has seasoned my baseball fandom. Throw in the lack of a hereditary rooting interest and alienation thousands of miles away from the nearest major league team, and you begin to appreciate the scale of my problems. You begin to comprehend the utter chaos of my situation.

Of course, not every neurotic weirdo flitters between the Boston Red Sox and New York Yankees, sworn enemies of polar opposite constitution. Likewise, few anxious geeks oscillate between the Chicago Cubs and Los Angeles Dodgers for good measure, further complicating their situation.

I know this may read like an exercise in poor excuses and shamefully deranged self-justification, but I'm done apologising at this point. These things happened to me, for whatever reason, be they right or wrong, and I'm through explaining myself. I no longer wish to conceal the relatively unimportant decisions I have made about sports, which are fundamentally inconsequential in the wider sweep of our existence. If people are persistently angry about this stuff, I cannot help them. I'm just sorry it means so much, most of all in my own head.

CHAPTER TWENTY

Behind Enemy Lines

Two days before Game 1 of the 2018 World Series, I went on a date, using my enforced annual leave to good effect. The girl I met was from Poland, the ancestral home of Carl Yastrzemski, Bill Mazeroski, Ted Kluszewski, AJ Pierzynski and a select group of major league ballplayers. Her name was Patrycja Mitera, and I quickly fell in love.

We met in a dimly lit café on the Wirral waterfront at New Brighton. She was the most intelligent person I had ever encountered, academically and in her impressive grasp of common sense. Just sitting with her, waiting for hours to be served, was a spellbinding experience. A gust of fresh air blew into my life.

Following that first date, I rushed home with a smile on my face and told my parents how awesome Patrycja was. I spoke with a breathless tempo of excitement, explaining how she was once a star student at Tarnów University, not far from Kraków, a thriving urban hub. I hoped we would remain friends and likeminded scions of academia. After all, she was too beautiful to ever love me back.

However, that was the old me talking. The pessimistic me. The dejected me. The battered and bruised me, used and discarded by unworthy lightweights. Patrycja *was* interested, and she appreciated the real me, not some contrived persona I was forced to portray. We went on a few more dates and got to know each other well. Right from the start, our synergy was great.

Patrycja found it absurd that I took two weeks off work to watch *baseball*, a sport that barely registers on the radar in Poland, a snowy country obsessed with football, skiing and speedway motorbike racing. I told her about Pope John Paul II – *The Polish Pope* – delivering mass to 80,000 worshippers at Yankee Stadium in 1979. I sent her blurry photographs of the Polish chapter in Josh Chetwynd's guide to European baseball, attempting to explain my obsession. Patrycja did not care. Few people do.

When Boston won its ninth World Series title, I inexplicably posted a selfie on Instagram wearing my Red Sox cap and hoodie. Ever supportive, Patrycja was happy that I was enjoying myself, but that was the extent of her exposure to baseball. Even *she* did not know about my forbidden Yankee lust for the first six months of what became an exciting relationship. Such echoes of disloyalty do not tend to impress girls, and for once I managed to play it safe and avoid rejection.

Patrycja came to Merseyside in 2016, landing a work placement with a law firm in Birkenhead - of all places - using the Erasmus student exchange programme, funded by the European Union. She impressed so much during her two-month stint that the law firm reached out to her when a full-time vacancy became available a year later.

Bold and courageous, Patrycja packed her bags and journeyed to Liverpool, lodging with a Polish couple in Brunswick, near Toxteth. Early in our relationship, I drove through the tunnel for date-nights while Patrycja travelled across to Wirral via train. There was a sense of destiny to our relationship. We thought so, at least, even if nobody else did.

We were *Facebook official* by November and planning our long-term vision. Bound by common values and shared concepts of life, we brainstormed my exit from the corporate cesspit and spoke openly about children and marriage and houses. Many people scoffed at our enthusiasm, dismissing it as the giddy residue of lovebirds, but we believed in ourselves, and that is all that matters.

Throwing caution to the wind, we found a beautiful apartment on the Liverpool waterfront offering inspirational views across the river. We stumped up a deposit and made the leap, moving in together in February 2019.

Such was our romantic momentum, even the fact that I no longer had a job seemed only a trifling inconvenience. I flipped one day in the office, typed out my resignation letter and passed it to my boss. When we signed the tenancy agreement, I was two weeks into a one-month period of gardening leave, after which I would become unemployed. Sometimes you have to take a chance.

Given my native scepticism of Liverpool and my sworn hatred of its most famous football team, electing to live behind enemy lines in the city centre was a bizarre turn of events by anybody's gradation. Throw in my rapidly expiring employment, the return of a company car, and a monthly rent charge of £820 – well, suffice it to say that love does peculiar things to a man.

Slowly but surely, Patrycja and I pieced together our new life. On the whole, getting away from Wirral was a positive experience for me. It offered a clean break from the toxic relationships and incessant reminders of my own inadequacy.

I found another job before my gardening leave expired, remaining technically unemployed for just one day. The Wirral jobs market was predictably decimated, so I eventually took a role within the marketing department of a large international law firm in Liverpool. It paid the bills and allowed me to switch off at 5:00 pm each day. My work-life balance was greatly enriched, and I had time to contemplate my own emotions.

Patrycja and I bought a car with my first paycheck, getting back on the road literally and figuratively. Together, we gradually learned to be fully functioning adults, shopping for microwaves and gaining a newfound appreciation for the difficulty of laundering clothes.

For the first time in years, perhaps for the first time *ever*, I was happy. Sure, I still swallowed an antidepressant before my morning coffee, but there was purpose to my life. There was *hope*, that most important ingredient of all. Life was suddenly worth living, even if Liverpool's stadium *was* visible from my lounge window. I was alive, and that felt great.

⚾⚾⚾

Heading into the 2019 season, I vaguely identified as a Red Sox fan, although confusion ravaged my inner peace. Enjoying a fairer work-life balance, I became infatuated with baseball again. The prospect of watching games in my own living room for the first time was thrilling, and I welcomed Opening Day with treats from Dunkin' Donuts, a Massachusetts institution with a store in Liverpool.

With more free time, I became my own worst enemy, surrendering to the grasp of obsessive-compulsive disorder like never before. After transitioning from the autocratic dystopia of workplace hell, I thought things were better. I thought *I* was better. In actuality, though, I was living through a crippling overcorrection that drove me crazy in other ways. I rebelled against the machine, but the machine kicked back a lot harder.

I became vaguely obsessed with the idea of working from home in a desperate plea for independence. I discovered cyberspace clerics like Gary Vaynerchuk and Darren Rowse, energetic disciples of self-employed expressionism. *Turn your passion into your job*, they chanted repeatedly. *Make passive income using your phone.* It was heroin to an obsessive-compulsive like me, and I launched several ill-advised social media projects steeped in their flawed logic.

One such project was called *soxgent*, and I planned to develop it into a brand around life as an English Red Sox fan, musing loquaciously about games. I dabbled with a Twitter account and posted a few retro photographs on Instagram, but it was all so disingenuous and desperate. My heart was not in it anymore, while my head was about to explode amid relentless competing interests.

Still, I watched the games, gradually becoming numb with indifference. Assembled by Dave Dombrowski and managed by Alex Cora, the 2019 Red Sox yearned to defend their World Series title. In Mookie Betts, they had one of the most exciting players in baseball, while Xander Bogaerts, Andrew Benintendi and JD Martinez complemented him well. Nevertheless, that iteration of the Red Sox never really found its stride. Meanwhile, New York was just too good.

Without a division title since 2012, the Yankees meant business after consecutive years of playoff heartache. Losing to Boston in the 2018 ALDS was a bitter pill to swallow, but 2019 always figured to be the likely fruition point of Cashman's grand regeneration campaign. The window was open, and it was time for the Yankees to win again.

New York added DJ LeMahieu in free agency, and he was an instant success, anchoring their lineup with studious reliability. Injuries destabilised the Yankees out of the gate in 2019, but a monumental surge in May saw them develop a seven-and-a-half-game lead over Boston.

I swapped and changed allegiances almost by the day. I usually stumbled on a Red Sox game from Fenway and became hopelessly sentimental, only to wake up and question my own ethics. I would then fall into a period of Yankee appreciation - listening to John tell Suzyn how you cannot predict baseball - burning the candle at both ends.

Attempting to reconcile the quirks of my own mind was a daunting challenge steeped in hypocrisy. The low-level hum of dissatisfaction became a constant soundtrack, and correct answers were harder to find than anybody else who shared my problem.

I had never set foot in either Boston or New York, but I combed through the history of both cities, attempting to find a tangible link to my soul. I had never even visited *America*, let alone attended games at each respective stadium. Alas, my opinions of the Big Apple and Beantown were formed vicariously, pieced together from books, films, podcasts and Wikipedia entries. Picking a team to root for without spending time in its city was akin to building a castle on sand. It was not likely to end well, but I tried, nevertheless.

In one instance, I grappled with the fact that Liverpool FC has played matches at both Fenway Park and Yankee Stadium during its history, further confusing matters. The club played at Fenway in 2012 and 2014 while gracing Yankee Stadium in 1953 and 2014. A 2019 tour featured games at both venues, causing me untold pain and uncertainty. Every few days, a similarly cryptic missile derailed my progress.

In my eyes, Boston always seemed like a close-knit community of unflinching pragmatism. There was something endearing about the nasal accent, a real-world transparency that resonates with blue collar industry. Still, I could not help but wince at the city's conscious transformation in recent decades, ruing the loss of layman exasperation in New England.

Fuelled by disproportionate modern success, Boston sports fans have become unbearably entitled. Since 2001, the Patriots have won six Super Bowls, the Red Sox have won four World Series, the Bruins have lifted one Stanley Cup and the Celtics have won one NBA championship. Boston had 12 title parades in 18 years. A whole generation views such success as a birthright, and that jars with the region's wider traditional psyche.

For the longest time, Boston sports really *did* suck. The Red Sox never won a world championship for 86 years. The Patriots waited 41 years for their maiden title. Sure, the Celtics were always great, and the Bruins had a strong spell in the 1960s and 1970s, but Boston sports fans were known more for nervous breakdowns after losses than for self-aggrandising after wins. Old school rooters still have a hard time reconciling that juxtaposition.

Boston forged its place at the centre of American wit with incomparable self-deprecation. Nowadays, though, that seems to have been lost, or at least diluted, by the relentless procession of good news. The metamorphosis of actors like Ben Affleck, Matt Damon and Seth McFarlane from gritty, fraternal realism to sleek, mainstream glitz illustrates this troubling phenomenon, leaving a lot of unanswered questions. Boston appears to have lost its soul, in other words, shedding the plucky underdog spirit for samey cosmopolitan affluence. That does not exactly correlate with my worldview.

I'm not alone in this struggle, and battling its sporting consequences has preoccupied other Red Sox fans, as well. The aforementioned John Cena, once my brother's favourite wrestler, was born in West Newbury, Massachusetts, diehard Red Sox country. He was often seen at Fenway during the glory days, but has since changed allegiance to the Tampa Bay Rays due to a sense of alienation.

"Everybody in Boston wants me tried as a witch and burned at the stake," Cena once said on a *Sports Illustrated* podcast. "The Red Sox have become the team they used to hate. They have become the Yankees. They spend mega, mega money on talent and usually - nine times out of ten - they are in a bidding war with the Yankees.

"Fenway Park was a very different atmosphere when I used to go, and I have seen that place become a destination. I have seen it become a place where you go and buy a pink ball cap and a pink t-shirt and you do not know anybody on the team.

"I've always been me, but when someone changes that drastically, it is like, 'Ah, the franchise turned their back on me as a fan.' We used to be a bunch of rugged bums. Now we are a bunch of high-end guys. It's tough.

"The Rays just somehow make it happen. They are what the Red Sox used to be. Like, throw together a bunch of jumbled-up dudes and hope it happens. They are a team that loves baseball, and I dig watching them."

Conversely, New York seems to remain steadfast in its own uniqueness. What you see is what you get, especially in the Bronx and Manhattan, hardnosed boroughs of grime and steel. I have always been enamoured of the straight-talking, expletive-spewing, roof-raising *noise* of Gotham. Even from afar, the unapologetic arrogance is magnetic, and I struggle to resist the enchanting aura.

New York is the cradle of bold dreams and big ideas. It is the most linguistically and religiously diverse city in the world, with almost half its denizens fluent in more than one language and more than 7,000 churches, 1,000 synagogues and 250 mosques nestled within its sprawl.

Even as the spiritual home of global commerce, characterised by the financial speculation of Wall Street, New York remains proud of its heterogeneous makeup. Rich live next to poor. Whites mingle with blacks. Yankee fans heckle Mets rooters. There is a verisimilitude to it all that appears sacred, impenetrable and timeless. It pulls people in and adds them to the ballad. That is a magical concept.

Of course, as a Wirral lad, I know more about geographical prejudice than most people. I appreciated that, without visiting either city, my appreciation of Boston and New York is rife with preconceptions. I worked hard to invalidate or corroborate my hunches through rigorous study, but even words are no substitute for experience.

For example, I learned that, in 1976, the England national team played a soccer match at Yankee Stadium, facing Italy before a crowd of 40,650. "The goals came quickly and along with them came English flags decorating the railing of the upper deck of the refurbished Stadium," wrote Alex Yannis in the *New York Times*. This seemed promising, I thought. However, Liverpool defender Phil Thompson scored for England in the game, tinging even that fine vignette with melancholy caveats.

Digging deeper, I found that hundreds of big leaguers have played for both the Yankees *and* the Red Sox during their careers. Many of them are hated in Boston but loved in New York - Boggs, Clemens, Ruth, Wells. Some of them are loathed in New York but adored in Boston - Bellhorn, Youkilis, Tom Gordon, Nate Eovaldi. Some of them are disliked equally in both cities - Ellsbury, Canseco, Stephen Drew. But contrary to perception, more than a handful of players have been loved, or at least *tolerated*, in Boston *and* New York - Cone, Damon, Lowell, Lyle, Tiant, Pennock, Ruffing, Howard, Andrew Miller.

If *players* so frequently move back and forth between the mortal enemies, my situation did not look so bad as a pariah *fan*, even further removed from affecting the precious on-field outcome. If some of those guys enjoyed love on both sides of the divide, there was cause for optimism that I could one day be understood, too. Heck, even Clemens was inducted into the Red Sox Hall of Fame in 2014. There was hope for everybody.

To that end, much is made about the 2004 Red Sox personally hating the Yankees and using that as history-making motivation. Well, of the 25 players on Boston's World Series roster that fateful year, six went on to *play for the Yankees*. Almost a quarter of the Red Sox' rabblerousing idiots later wore pinstripes. That speaks to the alluring wonder of both teams.

Additionally, let it never be forgotten that, before he bought the Red Sox, John Henry purchased 1% of Yankees stock from George Steinbrenner. He *owned* a piece of both organisations *at the same time*, an altogether more egregious crime than my simultaneous rooting. The Yankees came before the Red Sox in his story. I guess nobody is perfect after all.

Time and time again, we see that, when it comes to this ancient rivalry, contradictions run both ways. For instance, when Henry stitched together his consortium to take control in Boston, The New York Times Company pitched in $75 million, good for a 17.5% stake in New England Sports Ventures, which was later rebranded as Fenway Sports Group. Accordingly, the *Times*, once a pro-Yankees paper, became a part-owner of their greatest rivals. You cannot make this shit up.

Naturally, while trawling the archives of both respective teams, I was also confronted by the Yankees' troubling history of racial intolerance, often overlooked by people who are quick to broach the Red Sox' systemic failures to integrate. Only three big league teams waited longer than the Yankees to promote a black player, while Hall of Fame general manager George Weiss left a litany of scandalous remarks between the 1930s and 1950s.

"The truth is that our box seat customers from Westchester County don't want to sit with a lot of coloured fans from Harlem," Weiss once told Roger Khan, rationalising his frequent decisions to stymie integration. Much like Yawkey's Red Sox, the Yankees also ignored exceptional Negro League stars like Willie Mays and Ernie Banks, scouting both players regularly but failing to extend contract offers.

Indeed, until Elston Howard broke the team's colour barrier in 1955, eight years after Jackie Robinson debuted with Brooklyn, there seemed to be an unwritten rule that precluded certain demographics from wearing the iconic Yankee pinstripes. That is a saddening concept that we must continue to challenge. Even today, we can all strive to be better in every facet of social mobility, baseball included.

In time, I came to understand the complex wiring that contributes to such anomalies every single day. Living with Patrycja, I matured and learned to prioritise my responsibilities while growing into adult life. Along the way, I guess the overall volume of my sporting intensity was turned down a notch, and working with authentic Liverpool fans introduced a human element to my relationship with the club. For a time, I was able to *tolerate* the Red Sox, even if *supporting* them left me remorseful. The Yankees, meanwhile, remained an ever-present fascination despite their conflicted past, tearing my heart in two.

Such a schizophrenic approach offered little comfort. In fact, it was living hell, as I judged my own stupidity. Deep inside, I knew something had to give, especially as both teams prepared to visit London. However, no matter how much I tried, reaching a consensus in my own mind was an arduous task that went unfinished. I was almost resigned to a life of baseball purgatory.

Making matters worse, my move to Liverpool coincided with a torturous period of success for the eponymous football team. Using the blueprint that brought success to the Red Sox, Henry and Werner revitalised a sleeping giant of world soccer. They did what I knew they would all those years earlier, back when the club first changed hands. They made Liverpool great again, and - suddenly able to *feel* once more - I could not bear to watch.

Anfield, their historic stadium, was refurbished and expanded, becoming a monolithic museum with a modern penchant for squeezing every penny out of visitors. Hello, Fenway Park.

Michael Edwards, a thirtysomething graduate of business management, was installed as Liverpool's head of analytics, taking control of player acquisitions and hunting for undervalued assets. Theo Epstein, eat your heart out.

Jürgen Klopp, an enigmatic visionary, was hired as head coach despite a mixed record elsewhere, spearheading a philosophical and cultural renaissance that resulted in relentless success. Terry Francona, huh?

Sponsorship deals flooded in. Star players were signed with the fruits of a juggernaut commercial operation. Liverpool made huge strides in sports science and empirical analysis. I had seen this movie before, and the ending was painfully predictable.

During the 2018-19 season, Liverpool embarked on a nightmarish run through the UEFA Champions League, European football's most prestigious club competition. After advancing to the knockout rounds, Klopp's team beat Bayern Munich and Porto to reach the semi-finals, where they met the mighty Barcelona over two matches.

Powered by Lionel Messi, arguably the greatest footballer who ever lived, Barça won the first leg 3-0 in Catalonia. I breathed a sigh of relief. There was surely no way back for Liverpool at

Anfield. I could chill out, safe in the knowledge that my nemesis would not be European champions in 2019.

Surprisingly, the Barcelona team stayed at the Hilton hotel in Liverpool's hectic city centre before the second match. Patrycja and I queued for hours to catch a glimpse of Messi in the flesh. To think that such an immortal slept just 15 minutes down the road was thrilling. I told everyone who would listen.

Woe betide, Liverpool produced one of the most sensational comebacks in football history to slay Barcelona and reach the Champions League final. Those damned Reds scored four unanswered goals, three in a 25-minute period, notching a dramatic winner in chaotic style.

Switch out *semi-final* for *ALCS*, and history repeated itself for Henry and Werner. On the brink of a championship game or series, down 3-0, their team somehow conjured a superhuman effort to win 4-3. Lionel, meet A-Rod. The trauma was otherworldly.

Holed up in my apartment, just four miles from the unfurling action, I felt the city quake beneath me. People screamed with disbelief. Objects crashed across apartments throughout the block. Car horns beeped with sickening delight. They actually fucking did it. Shit.

My exasperation grew with every Liverpool goal. When their unbelievable winner flew into the net, I erupted with rage. Fresh out of the shower, I lashed a towel onto the floor in disgust while my neighbours cheered in euphoria. My inner sporting monster reared its head for the first time in years. I was back in the real world, free from the pained nonchalance of depression's dulling grip.

Patrycja scolded me for being so hateful. No matter how many times I explained it, she simply could not understand my problem with Liverpool. "You should be happy that a local team won," she said. I went to bed disgruntled, covering my ears from the incessant celebrations.

Liverpool breezed past Tottenham Hotspur, another English team, in the subsequent final, winning the famous cup for a sixth time. Henry and Werner gloated on the field in Madrid, huddling for photographs. Henry even cradled the trophy on the plane home for dramatic effect. My nightmare vision came true. The end was nigh.

In the harshest plot twist yet, Liverpool City Council arranged an extravagant victory parade using taxpayer's money – yes, *my money*, thank you very much. Oh, and said parade culminated 100 yards from our apartment, down beneath the window I once adored.

A crowd of 750,000 fans encircled us, chanting and cheering. The colour red - now deeply offensive to my personal wellbeing - was everywhere. Red shirts and flags and scarves. Red flares and horns and banners. It was horrendous.

Though the event was dressed as a celebration of civic pride, I wondered how many of those people had actually witnessed their respective communities blighted by the very football club they worshipped. Since the mid-1990s, Liverpool FC has purchased dozens of houses around its Anfield ground with lowball offers, forcing residents out and leaving the properties unoccupied so they are easier to demolish amid lucrative stadium expansions. This has contributed to immense urban decay, widespread poverty and the loss of social cohesion in many local areas, all of which are conveniently blamed on other nondescript factors.

The club's famous anthem says fans will never walk alone, but whole neighbourhoods have been ransacked, abandoned, neglected, demolished and wiped off the map just so Liverpool FC can fit more people into its stadium. The sole motivator of that crusade is to squeeze every last penny out of each attendee, making billionaires out of millionaires at the expense of working class neighbours who do not seem to matter.

This elitist exploitation of poverty further contradicts Liverpool's curated image of leftist solidarity, and seeing so many duped everymen celebrating something that will only encourage their eventual destruction was actually rather sad. The more ordinary people venerate Liverpool FC for winning trophies bought with cash generated by working class subjugation, the more Fenway Sports Group will be empowered to expand that scandalous mode of wealth creation, destroying more communities in the process. It was like watching turkeys celebrate Christmas, and I could not comprehend the imbecility of it all.

Desperate for an escape hatch, I vowed to spend the weekend in Wirral, but likely traffic disruption stymied that plan. I tried to sit with the blinds pulled down, scrolling on my phone for distraction, but even after I muted dozens of Liverpool-related phrases on Twitter, the propaganda still seeped through. The Red Sox, of all stakeholders, sent a congratulatory message to Liverpool in their daily email newsletter. I unsubscribed faster than you can say *betrayal*.

The Liverpool parade bus passed by our apartment, to my eternal chagrin. Salt tumbled into open wounds and old scars resurfaced. I remembered why I fell out of love with the Red Sox, and any semblance of association with their values melted into a sea of discontent.

Freshly alive and mobilised from the darkened pit of depression, I became aware of my actions and obligations once again. Pride is a close sibling of hope, and rekindling the latter fortified the former. The Red Sox became an object of bruising frustration for me, and the quest to unpick that unquenchable enigma left me exasperated.

࿊࿊࿊

After Liverpool's coronation, attention turned to the MLB London Series, scheduled for late-June at the Olympic Stadium in Stratford. Despite being repeatedly disenfranchised, I was beyond excited. The prospect of finally attending real life ballgames – not just one, but two! – made me giddy, and the nostalgia was overwhelming.

After many failed attempts, we finally landed tickets for the occasion. I would travel to London with Patrycja and Nath. When the tickets arrived, it all became very real. I sat Patrycja down and told her the full story about my convoluted baseball fandom. She was shocked, but we laughed and joked about it all in the end. Patrycja teased me in good faith and eventually came to understand my plight. To her, it all seemed so trivial. I wish it did to me.

Mere weeks before the New York Yankees and Boston Red Sox came to my country to play a regular season series, I was back amid the wilderness, caught between conflicting emotions for both teams. Patrycja could see the whole thing eating me up, and together we devised a workable solution to the crisis.

We decided that, for all eternity, I would root for whichever team won in London. After years of struggling to manufacture spiritual bonds and traditional precedents with major league organisations, a lyrical opportunity presented itself, and I could not pass it up.

What better thread of motivational pride than seeing the team of my future beat its greatest rival *live*? That was the kind of magical yarn I could pass on through the generations, to my son one day and hopefully to his. It just made sense, in my absurd little mind. The idea released me from limbo.

Nath questioned the logistics of such a plan, querying the outcome of a split series. I decided that, in such a scenario, the team that scored more runs would win my eternal faith. If they scored the same amount of runs? Well, we would figure something out. There was always a way.

And so, what felt like a routine midsummer series for the Yankees and Red Sox was imbued with immense meaning and consequence for my future. The London Series meant the world to me in general, but the added prize – unbeknownst to the teams – made it the most important sporting event of my life. I could barely contain the exhilaration.

"I want to thank the good lord for making me a Yankee."
– Joe DiMaggio

PART FOUR

London Calling

CHAPTER TWENTY-ONE

A British History of Baseball

Major League Baseball is the most prolific sports league in history. Its unique schedule has necessitated more than 200,000 regular season games since 1903. Prior to the inaugural London Series, only 23 of those games had been played outside the United States and Canada. None had been played in Europe.

Nevertheless, baseball does have a strong footprint on the continent, especially in Britain, which has actually staked a claim to its very *ownership* in recent years. The British baseball community may be small, but its passion certainly is not, and neither is its history.

The earliest recorded game of baseball anywhere in the world was played indoors in London in November 1748. It involved the Prince of Wales and his family, quite remarkably, although cricket was deemed superior.

Similarly, the oldest surviving reference to baseball in global literature can be found in Surrey, England, where William Bray, a Guildford lawyer, wrote about playing baseball in his 1755 diary:

"Went to Stoke Ch. This morn. After dinner, went to Miss Jeale's to play at base ball with her, the 3 Miss Whiteheads, Miss Billinghurst, Miss Molly Flutter, Mr Chandler, Mr Ford & H Parsons & Jelly. Drank tea & stayed till 8."

Even the great Jane Austen, one of Britain's literary giants, referenced baseball in *Northanger Abbey*, written in 1797:

"It was not very wonderful that Catherine, who had by nature nothing heroic about her, should prefer cricket, base ball, riding on horseback and running about the country at the age of fourteen, to books."

The origins of baseball have been debated and dissected for eons. Scholars have generally agreed to disagree, explaining how the act of hitting a ball with a bat is so common and primeval as to defy a singular genesis. However, England has arguably the strongest of all creation hypotheses, and I will bang that drum forever.

Certainly, the notion that Abner Doubleday invented baseball in Cooperstown, New York in 1839 can be consigned to mythology. Brits had been swinging a bat, hitting a ball and running to stations correspondingly for almost 100 years by that point. The factual evidence holds firm: this game might be ours after all.

Obviously, any talk of dismantling the Hall of Fame and dumping it in Surrey is absurd. Baseball is synonymous with the United States of America. In every way, it epitomises all that is great about the stars and stripes. It is the *National Pastime*, god damn it. What more do you want?

However, even the very projects that consolidated baseball as America's defining sport - grand world tours organised by Sheffield-born pioneer Harry Wright and apparel magnate Albert Goodwill Spalding, respectively - had tangential links to Britain. Without those expeditions, the game's American fingerprint may never have been distinguished.

In 1874, Wright arranged for the Boston Red Stockings and Philadelphia Athletics to play games in London, Dublin, Liverpool and Manchester, exporting baseball as a US product. Then a young pitcher for Boston, Spalding competed on the tour against future Hall of Famer Cap Anson, who was a star outfielder for Philadelphia. The tour was not overly successful, however, as residual anti-American sentiment from the War of Independence percolated across Britain.

Still, Spalding enjoyed the experience, and in 1888-89 he organised another tour featuring the Chicago White Stockings against the best All-American team he could muster. Hoping to open new markets for his growing athletic retail empire, Spalding arguably did more than anybody to define baseball as a thoroughly American pursuit. That also had paradoxical benefits for baseball's international community, opening new avenues to exposure.

Engendering a sense of vicarious patriotic yearning was pivotal to Spalding's marketing strategy, which extended around the world. Spalding knew that, if he could package baseball as distinctly *American*, some kind of star-spangled elixir, people would hunger to associate with the inherent connotations of power and prestige. Games were duly organised in Hawaii, New Zealand, Australia, Egypt, Italy, Great Britain and Ireland as Spalding eyed fame, engagement and profit. His cavalier intentions were hard to define.

In the age of ship travel, such convoluted tours required immense planning. Spalding's assemblage sailed for six months, scattering seeds of capitalism and American imperialism on multiple continents. Baseball was always the dominant tool of transmission, but a hot-air balloon was also taken along to entertain crowds, in addition to the shameful presence of a black minstrel performer.

In the UK, Spalding's travelling circus stopped in London, Bristol, Leighton, Birmingham, Glasgow, Manchester, Liverpool - where the Americans were beaten by locals in a game of rounders - and Belfast. Dublin also staged a contest. On 12th March 1889, the future King Edward VII even watched one of Spalding's games at the Oval cricket ground in London, although he immediately declared his preference for cricket, too.

Amid confusing genealogy, that touring incarnation of the Chicago White Stockings is not the same White Sox team we know today. Eventually managed by Anson, those latter-day White Stockings adopted the Chicago *Cubs* moniker in 1903. Perhaps there was a certain historical symmetry to my fleeting Cubs fandom after all.

The *eventual* White Sox, famously owned by Charles Comiskey, *did* visit the UK as well, further obfuscating matters. In 1914, the Pale Hose beat John McGraw's New York Giants, 5-3, at Chelsea's Stamford Bridge during another global expedition. King George V was in attendance, but McGraw did little to ingratiate the touring party with their hosts, disparaging the comparative skill of British soldiers with insensitive remarks.

The Giants and White Sox also returned to Europe in 1924, playing in London, Liverpool and Birmingham before excursions to Dublin and Paris. However, crowds on that tour were so poor that planned jaunts to Brussels, Nice, Rome and Berlin were cancelled ominously. An uncertain future faced the continent's baseball diehards.

Citing the links to his beloved Chelsea, perhaps Jonny Gould should actually have rooted for the White Sox, not the Braves. Indeed, Stamford Bridge hosted a further baseball showcase in 1938, as 38,000 people watched the US Navy play the US Army. A tool of political engineering, the contest was again witnessed by King George V, along with prime minister David Lloyd George and future leader Winston Churchill. Nobody knows quite how genuine the whole thing was from a standpoint of growing baseball in the UK, but a neat footnote to the game's history was written, nevertheless.

It is similarly difficult to judge the overall success of Spalding's tour, partly because it had such esoteric objectives. However, the cumulative effect of such sporadic baseball exhibitions led to several leagues sprouting up across the UK. Seeking an option for summer recreation, many football teams became interested, with Aston Villa, Preston North End and Stoke City fielding successful baseball teams. A British form of the game was even spawned, with a flattened bat and underarm pitching, but the bloodline was decidedly American.

A key powerhouse of this early period was Derby County, which adopted baseball when famed industrialist Sir Francis Ley encountered the game on a trip to America. Ley was a doyen of local politics and commerce, and under his aegis, Derby became synonymous with baseball. The football team was later invited to share the home field of Lay's baseball squad, known fittingly as the Baseball Ground. Football was played there until 1997, although the baseball team folded in 1898.

Interestingly, my dad and his siblings – Harry, Helga and Renate – grew up in Derby after being born in Birkenhead. They lived at St Christopher's Railway Orphanage following the premature death of their mother, and my dad frequently attended football matches at the Baseball Ground, which became notorious for its awful pitch.

Such recurring problems with facilities added to the trouble of establishing professional baseball leagues in Britain. Issues within local politics, consistent advertising and general fan apathy also proved difficult to overcome. Nevertheless, the amateur game continued to thrive in the 1910s and 1920, and football clubs such as Arsenal, Tottenham Hotspur and

Nottingham Forest had fleeting baseball incarnations around that time.

On the continent, the model of football clubs adopting baseball was even more popular than in Britain. In Holland, for example, Ajax was particularly dedicated to extracurricular athletics, and legends like Johan Cruyff, Johan Neeskens and Marco van Basten all played for the club's baseball team. Accordingly, there is sweet poetry in my discovery of baseball being linked to Dutch football, as well. It often feels predetermined.

"Playing baseball, I learned many details that were useful in football," Cruyff wrote in his autobiography. "When you determine the flight of the pitch and judge it as a catcher without a perfect view. That sharpened one of my strengths as a footballer, having a wider field of vision. I learned to think ahead. It has many parallels with football: speed, acceleration, adaptation, balance, spatial awareness, anticipation and more."

Fuelled by this synergy with football, a second glory period for British baseball came in the 1930s and 1940s, when West Ham became a dominant force. A football institution, the Hammers routinely drew over 4,000 fans for baseball games, developing a loyal following and a strong tradition.

In Roland Gladu, West Ham harboured *The Babe Ruth of Canada*, and the third baseman's unmatched skill catapulted West Ham to glory. They even beat the US Olympic squad in a 1936 baseball contest before Gladu earned a big league cameo with the Boston Braves. Roland is the only player ever to hit home runs at the greyhound track in West Ham and at Ebbets Field in Brooklyn. He remains the ultimate folk hero of British baseball.

Decades later, the symbolism of West Ham's Olympic Stadium welcoming MLB to London was therefore pleasing for baseball romantics. Few British football clubs have made such lasting contributions to baseball, and the happy coincidence of history and logistics meant a lot to hardcore activists.

Even the legendary West Ham team struggled to generate national interest during their era of dominance, but baseball thrived at a regional level, nevertheless. Politician and philanthropist Sir John Moores was a major player in developing northern baseball, for instance, and he bankrolled several ill-fated pro leagues that stimulated participation.

Under Moores' guise, Merseyside was quite a hotbed for both American and British baseball, with the Liverpool Giants becoming a popular team. The aforementioned Tranmere and Everton great Dixie Dean played baseball for the Caledonians team, and legend states that he even met Ruth at one point.

Though historical records can be quixotic, many believe Ruth visited England on a handful of occasions, once to raise morale among troops during World War II. The Babe was apparently impressed by British finery, though, as he shipped tailormade shoes from Northampton for decades to come.

Amazingly, Tranmere even fielded a baseball team during this period. In 1944, the Merseyside National Baseball League formed as an eight-team circuit. Everton entered a team playing out of Goodison Park, while Rovers chairman Bob Trueman was keen to find opportunities to utilise Prenton Park in the summer. Baseball seemed trendy, and plans developed swiftly for Tranmere to field two teams, both using the hallowed turf on Borough Road as their base.

A new sound system was installed to allow announcements of each batter, while the pitch was altered to accommodate baseball. Tranmere also recruited well, as Colin Grove and Cecil Rutherford became notable additions from America. If only I had a time machine to enjoy their performances.

Sadly, interest in baseball waned as the new football season approached, and the Merseyside National Baseball League slowly petered out. Moores launched a North of England Baseball League in 1935, and that soaked up much of the residual interest at a regional level, but genuine traction has always been hard to stimulate.

Baseball is still played on Merseyside, however. In fact, the Liverpool Trojans are widely considered the oldest continuously existing baseball team in Britain. I briefly trained with the club after moving to Liverpool, but persistent injuries thwarted my career before it even really began. I was always more comfortable with a pen than with a baseball. You could say I'm more Roger Angell than Roger Clemens. The big league phone call never arrived. Well, not while I was awake, at least, even though the recurring dream never dies.

ಶುಶುಶು

Remarkably, a select few people *have* ventured from this emerald isle to major league stardom. Baseball-Reference.com lists 49 MLB hitters, 19 pitchers and 8 managers who were born in the United Kingdom. Two were born in Liverpool: Tom Brown, a 19th century outfielder, and Ned Crompton, who hit .154 in 18 career games. None were born in Wirral.

Measured by WAR, Glasgow-born Jim McCormick is the best Brit ever to play in the majors. McCormick won 45 games for the Cleveland Blues in 1880 amid a 10-year career of pitching excellence. However, the greatest 'British moment' in big league history was authored by another Glaswegian: Bobby Thomson, a clutch hero for the New York Giants.

Born in working class Scotland in 1923, Thomson moved with his family to New York City aged two. His father was a cabinet maker who carved out a niche career on Staten Island prior to Bobby's birth, and the Thomson family was subsequently reunited in a typical American setting.

After serving in the United States Army Air Forces, Thomson caught on with the Giants in 1946. A dependable third baseman and outfielder, he was a three-time All-Star who hit 264 home runs in a 15-year career. One long ball stands out from the rest, however, etching Thomson's name into baseball lore.

At the culmination of a gruelling 1951 season, the Giants and Brooklyn Dodgers were tied for first place in the National League with identical 96-win records. A three-game playoff was arranged to decide the National League pennant, and millions of eyes homed in on New York.

The Giants won Game 1 in cramped Ebbets Field, but the Dodgers fought back to even the series with a 10-0 blowout at the Polo Grounds 24 hours later. The decisive game was also held at the Giants' home ballpark as Manhattan bore witness to one of the greatest ballgames ever played.

In the decider, Brooklyn stitched together a 4-1 lead and hauled it into the bottom of the ninth. Al Dark and Don Mueller kickstarted the Giants' rally with two straight singles, only for Monte Irvin to pop out to first baseman Gil Hodges. Whitey Lockman followed with a double, scoring Dark and bringing Thomson to the plate as the potential winning run for New York.

Dodgers manager Chuck Dressen turned to Ralph Branca in relief of Don Newcombe. Branca threw just two pitches, the second of which was driven into the left field seats by Thomson for a one-out, three-run, pennant-clinching, walk-off homer. Bedlam engulfed the Polo Grounds.

"Now it is done," wrote famed sports journalist Red Smith in his game recap for the *New York Herald Tribune*. "Now the story ends. And there is no way to tell it. The art of fiction is dead. Reality has strangled invention. Only the utterly impossible, the inexpressibly fantastic, can ever be plausible again."

Indeed, a hardworking guy from Glasgow, Scotland hit arguably the most famous home run in baseball history, and if that does not rank as *utterly impossible* and *inexpressibly fantastic*, then nothing ever will.

Thomson's blast became known as the Shot Heard 'Round the World due to its dramatic impact and its stunning reverberation. That such an achievement was authored by a British chap is a source of tremendous pride, even though the dynastic Yankees flattened the Giants in the subsequent World Series.

Thomson returned to Scotland in 2003, celebrating his induction into the Scottish Baseball Hall of Fame. During the trip, Bobby visited the Edinburgh Diamond Devils, a local team, and provided some pointers on baseball.

"Team members presented Bobby with a traditional Scottish quaich, some single malt whiskey and a Devils cap," according to the *Baseball Scotland* website. "The day closed with Bobby kindly signing some autographs before having to leave for more media appointments."

Many Scottish baseball fans continue to root for the Giants because of this spiritual connection, and part of me regrets not learning enough about Thomson's life before falling in love with other teams. I could conceivably have been a Giants fan, seeing Barry Bonds break two home run records and celebrating three world championships in five years. Now *that* is gloryhunting, dear reader. Just imagine if I left my heart in San Francisco.

Despite such keynote contributions to the game's history, British baseball languished behind its continental counterparts after World War II. The Netherlands strengthened its prestige as a *honkbal* hub, while Italy also emerged as a European baseball force. By comparison, the UK was ravaged by splintered fiefdoms and connectivity issues, and our baseball leagues became fatally conflicted as a result.

Nevertheless, following in Thomson's footsteps, nine further British-born players reached the major leagues after his legendary home run. Les Rohr pitched six games for the Mets. Keith Lampard hit one home run for Houston. Danny Cox spent 11 years with the Cardinals, Phillies, Pirates and Blue Jays. However, on the whole, baseball interest waned throughout the country as exposure became almost non-existent. Even if people *wanted* to follow baseball, their options were so limited as to cause frustration.

In the late 1980s, though, a lifeline was extended when Major League Baseball began to look seriously at its global appeal. Based here in Britain, future sports presenter Mike Carlson was appointed vice president of European operations at MLB. Mike played a significant role in laying the foundations for eventual baseball success on the continent. His contributions should never be overlooked.

Under Carlson's command, MLB International made small advances towards its ultimate goal of growing the game across borders. In one grand experiment, Carlson helped arrange showcase home run derbies in London pitting baseball Hall of Famers Ernie Banks and Hank Aaron against cricket immortals Ian Botham and Graham Gooch. Generating mainstream attention was difficult, but executives persevered, conjuring further ideas.

In 1993, one of Carlson's blue-chip projects brought the Norfolk Tides and Pawtucket Red Sox to London for an exhibition series at The Oval cricket ground. Minor league affiliates of the Mets and Red Sox, the teams drew a smattering of attention. Future big league skipper Clint Hurdle managed the Tides, while future *Moneyball* star Scott Hatteberg played for Pawtucket. Bill Buckner was somehow lured along on a promotional tour, even facing questions about his infamous error from British journalists who knew nothing about the sport. Billy Buck must have rued his involvement from the start.

However, perhaps the greatest triumph of MLB International in those embryonic days was its relentless drive to find a broadcasting home for baseball in Britain. Carlson himself fronted a few early efforts, such as a brief baseball excursion by satellite station Screensport in 1991. Channel 4 and Sky Sports also tinkered with baseball coverage, only for Channel Five to create more genuine fans than at any point in the country's history.

MLB International played an important role in the early development of *Baseball on Five*, acting as a fulcrum of promotion and growth. For instance, Chetwynd, the man who did more to educate British baseball fans than anybody else, found his way onto our television screens via the governing body. Chetwynd was stationed in London as a communications executive for MLB, which encouraged him to try out for the lead analyst role with Five. The rest, as they say, is history. Sweet British baseball history.

Baseball on Five encapsulated a halcyon epoch for baseball on these shores. Never before had so many Brits associated with the sport, and never again could they access a greater pathway to understanding its nuances.

When I first discovered baseball, keeping abreast of events unfolding an ocean away required serious dedication. My mum recorded the Five shows using battered VHS tapes, setting her alarm for 01:00 am just to hit record while I pretended to sleep. It was a different age. A *simpler* age, and perhaps a *happier* age. I would go back in a heartbeat.

In the years following Five's decision to axe its baseball coverage, following America's national pastime from Britain became a sordid, solitary pursuit. The game existed only in the minds of devout believers, described by books, coloured by television, and preserved by boxscores.

Nevertheless, in modern times, British baseball has enjoyed a mini renaissance. Guided by head coach Liam Carroll, the Great Britain national team has achieved some remarkable results, threatening to advance in the World Baseball Classic on a few occasions. Former Padres great Trevor Hoffman was an honorary coach in 2017, while national team representatives such as Chris Reed and the aforementioned Antoan Richardson have spent time in the big leagues.

Off the field, the advent and refinement of mlb.tv has been a cherished gift for British baseball fans, allowing us to watch any game at any time on any device. Nevertheless, for the longest time, something was still missing from our national approach to baseball. I progressed way beyond my teenage years without hearing the crack of the bat or the chirp of Cracker Jack vendors in real life. That innocence of baseball-loving youth was still alive in this weary adult heart, waiting to be unleashed. At the age of 24, my chance to experience it all finally came around, though, and I was determined to enjoy every second.

As a kid, I dreamed of attending just one Major League Baseball game in my lifetime. Venturing to America from such meagre roots always seemed ever so slightly impossible, and I often doubted my ability to get there and to witness that ultimate game.

The struggles were multifarious – geographical, financial, familial and psychological – but the New York Yankees and Boston Red Sox eventually came to play competitive games in my homeland, and I was there to witness it all. For as long as I live, that will never stop being awesome. I will struggle to top that unbelievable high.

CHAPTER TWENTY-TWO

If You Build It, They Will Come

The concept of bringing baseball games to Britain has titillated pioneers for decades. From Henry Chadwick daydreaming in his study to Harry Wright, Albert Spalding, John McGraw and Charles Comiskey barnstorming the world, there has long been an implacable mystique attached to the export of baseball across borders.

Those bulwarks were united by an ardent lust for American capitalism. If something could make or save them a lot of money, they were interested. Comiskey was so obsessed with his balance sheet that, when the White Sox won the 1919 pennant, he gave his players a case of flat champagne instead of promised bonuses. Even back then, the dollar was king, and Comiskey's players illustrated that by throwing the resultant World Series against Cincinnati in return for illegal inducements.

To the archetypal businessmen of early baseball, then, there was always an urge to expand the game's purview. They knew there was a vast world out there, ripe for commercial exploitation, and they exchanged ideas about how best to unleash that potential. They never quite figured it out – at least not *totally* – but that trailblazing spirit imbued the game's soul for decades to come.

In 1953, for instance, the Boston Braves moved to Milwaukee, a comparatively rural outpost off the beaten track of Major League Baseball, seeking fame and fortune. The rise of Ted Williams consolidated Red Sock supremacy in Beantown, and Milwaukee lurked as an enticing hinterland of opportunity for avaricious owners like Lou Perini.

Embraced by baseball-starved Wisconsin, the Braves drew 1.8 million fans in their first season after relocation. No National League team had ever drawn more. Despite having the smallest catchment area of all major league teams, Milwaukee led the league in attendance for four straight years, piquing the interest of twitchy owners back east as local authorities became obstinate about funding new ballparks.

In Manhattan, Giants owner Horace Stoneham was particularly impressed by the Braves' resuscitation. As the Giants fell out of contention in the 1940s, attendances dwindled at the Polo Grounds, which became obtuse and dilapidated. The changing demographics of New York pushed denizens to the outer boroughs in search of housing, and the resultant changes in civic recreation strained the Giants' finances.

The team was New York incarnate, all big dreams and knowing power, but Stoneham was forced to look elsewhere for long-term baseball sustenance. Ever desperate for new accommodation, city officials wanted to raze the Polo Grounds and build houses on the plot. In turn, Stoneham flirted with cities in the Midwest, figuring Minneapolis was a strong synonym for Milwaukee.

While Stoneham became committed to the idea of moving his Giants, scheduling conflicts and the logistical challenges of doing so unilaterally stunted progress. To balance things out and ease the burden of cross-country travel, Stoneham needed to convince one of his fellow owners to move west, too. In Brooklyn, Dodgers supremo Walter O'Malley was initially hesitant, but he eventually led the project with concise vision.

Beloved by Brooklynites, the Dodgers were in decent financial shape when the spectre of westward expansion was first broached. World Series champions in 1955, O'Malley had a team of genuine stars like Jackie Robinson, Sandy Koufax, Roy Campanella, Pee Wee Reese, Duke Snider, Joe Black and Don Newcombe. The neighbourhood bums finally looked set to dominate, and the future looked rosy.

However, O'Malley wanted a new stadium to expedite the Dodgers' surge towards modernity. The innovative owner saw the coming importance of car travel, and he campaigned for a new ballpark in Flatbush with thousands of parking spaces and other cutting-edge amenities. New York planning czar Robert Moses did not agree, though, and a decade-long impasse frustrated both sides.

O'Malley was eventually wooed by Los Angeles, that booming city of the American future, forged by gold miners, railroad magnates and visionary schemers. Offered swathes of plush downtown land on which to build the stadium of his dreams, O'Malley fell in love with California. Cognisant of Stoneham's need for a moving partner, he duly convinced the Giants to embrace nearby San Francisco, transplanting the marquee rivalry 3,000 miles across the country. Accordingly, in 1958, MLB planted its flag on the west coast. For the first time, it was a national league in *essence*, not just in name, and that inspired further expansion projects across the country.

The Dodgers drew 1.8 million fans in their first Los Angeles season. That rose to 2 million a year later, when they won the World Series, then reached 2.2 million in 1960. Meanwhile, the Giants doubled their own gate in the space of 12 months before embarking on three straight years of attendance growth. San Francisco also won the pennant in 1962, taking a three-game tiebreaker from the Dodgers.

That two such fabled ballclubs could be cut from their traditional homes and stitched into fresh territory with enormous success whetted the appetite of major league decision-makers. Throughout the 1960s, new teams were added in, or expansion teams were gifted to, Anaheim, Washington, Minnesota, Houston, Oakland, Kansas City and San Diego. The Mets filled a void in New York, while the Braves moved again, settling in Atlanta as MLB's first southeastern team.

In the space of a decade, baseball sprawled across North America, with particular focus on the western seaboard. Seattle even got a franchise in 1969, while the Montreal Expos became the league's first Canadian ballclub. Texas got a team in the 1970s before Toronto expanded the league's footprint even further. New frontiers were conquered every single year.

Chasing the mighty dollar, ballclub owners welcomed ever more radical ideas to stimulate interest and - more importantly - revenue. When the domestic map was sprinkled with teams in every quarter, attention turned to international opportunities. Like the gunslinging trappers who chiselled America's modernity, baseball tycoons sought the next unconquered land and the freshest blend of potentiality. They found it overseas, just as their ancestors promised.

⚾⚾⚾

A sports-loving lawyer from San Francisco, Bruce Osterman likely enjoyed Giants games following their cross-country trek. A quirky guy with thinning hair and large glasses, Osterman became a test case for American involvement in contemporary

British sports, and his was a cautionary tale that debunked the invincibility felt by some US entrepreneurs seeking international expansion.

Osterman became fascinated by soccer, obsessing over matches of the San Francisco Scots, an upstart club in the North American Soccer League. After watching one training session in 1983, Osterman approached Ken Bracewell, the team's English coach, and asked to learn more about soccer on a participatory level. Bracewell was happy to befriend a passionate fan, and the pair became close, discussing soccer and its expansion around the globe.

When Bracewell told Osterman that England had the most professional soccer clubs of any country in the world, the lawyer was intrigued. He was fascinated by purchasing a club, more to satisfy his hobby than to make money, and Bracewell was soon tasked with finding a suitable option.

At the time, ravaged by hooliganism and the attendant defection of middle class interest, English football was in a dire financial position, so numerous clubs were up for sale. However, Bracewell did not get very far in negotiations on Osterman's behalf. An exclusive mentality guarded the English game, and foreign outsiders were unlikely to infiltrate its core. Nevertheless, in Wirral, his old stomping ground, Bracewell found a strong lead, and talks developed quickly.

In the mid-1970s and early-1980s, my beloved Tranmere Rovers lived a hand-to-mouth existence with financial problems lurking around every corner. Just to keep the club afloat, directors were forced to sell key players and scrape the barrel for other money-spinning initiatives. The cupboards were bare, and there was no rainy day fund to fall back on.

In 1981, the club only managed to survive in the Football League after being re-elected by a panel of members. A takeover bid by Birkenhead-born, US-based investor Billy McAteer failed, and chairman Gerry Gould announced that Rovers would close in three weeks' time without a new owner. "We are flogging a dead horse," he said rather grimly. The end was nigh for Tranmere Rovers.

Tony Kramer, a London businessman, became interested in buying the club, to the point where he promised lavish spending on famous players such as George Best should his bid be successful. Though the Tranmere board was desperate to find a buyer to stave off closure, it was unwilling to negotiate with Kramer, whose plans seemed deeply unrealistic. Kramer subsequently withdrew from the process, and Tranmere managed to survive only with last-ditch help from fans and a £200,000 loan from Wirral Council.

A reliable full-back during his playing days, Bracewell played for Tranmere between 1959 and 1961, so he knew the club well. Building on existing relationships, he brokered a deal for Osterman, who rocked up to Prenton Park in July 1984 and promptly bought the club. Tranmere Rovers duly became the first English sports club to have an American owner. I'm strangely proud of that fact.

With Bracewell overseeing day-to-day operations, Osterman vowed to "do a Watford" and take Rovers up through the divisions. While that seemed highly improbable, the initial reaction from fans was fairly positive. The San Franciscan spoke well, and his initial investment of £120,000 kept the club alive when otherwise it would have died.

"I did not come here to just stay in the fourth division," said Osterman in a documentary about his involvement at Tranmere. "Having said that, I have limited resources. I'm not a multi, multi-millionaire. This is an investment of the heart. I love this game."

Indeed, Osterman was a successful lawyer rather than a businessman of serious renown. Born in 1942, he graduated from the University of Washington Law School in 1966 before entering the world of insurance claims. While rich in a personal sense, his wealth simply did not correlate with the business plan required to make Tranmere competitive. Bruce Almighty he was not.

Osterman visited Birkenhead infrequently. Yet, when he *was* in town, the owner loved to train with his players. He was especially enamoured of the goalkeeper position, working hard to master techniques. That led to friction with team manager Bryan Hamilton, who left acrimoniously in 1985. Osterman then hired the flamboyant Frank Worthington as player-manager and tasked him with playing an entertaining brand of attacking football. If Kramer's plans were unrealistic, Osterman's actions were truly absurd.

A bubble of interest surrounded Rovers, with television cameras and journalists flocking to Prenton Park, if not necessarily fans. However, Osterman did not really understand all the fuss. "It is no madder than investing £1 million in a racing yacht," he said of his Tranmere involvement. "Everybody has their own horses and yachts and things like that, and they do strange things. But this is not strange. I put thirty people to work with my investment, and they earn their livelihood because of me. So, in that sense, I think it is a little more noble than racing the seas with some boat that sinks because its keel falls off."

Ah, the symbolism. Within a matter of months, Rovers began to sink under the weight of a poor business model. Osterman's initial investment was swallowed by excessive contracts given to new staff rather than contributing to the maintenance of Prenton Park or the signing of better players. Tranmere basically existed under a benefactor model, but that benefactor was neither exceedingly wealthy nor totally aware of English football's complex culture. As Osterman began chasing his money, things got nasty.

When training with the players proved an expensive hobby, and when the failing business struggled to yield a return, Osterman turned to selling assets as an exit strategy. Obviously, Prenton Park was the most viable option, and the owner conceived a plan to sell its land to a development company, which would in turn hand it over to the Tesco supermarket chain.

Osterman put all his eggs in this one basket, hoping that the £4 million sale would clear mounting debts, repay his initial investment and build a new stadium elsewhere. Aside from its financial improbability, that plan showed no understanding of how much Prenton Park meant to Rovers fans, who had called it home for more than 70 years. At best, it was an extremely risky proposition. At worst, it was wilful tampering with the future of Tranmere Rovers for personal gain.

Four directors resigned in protest at the plans, which were rejected at a council meeting. Osterman failed to earmark a site for a potential new stadium as his vision was exposed as self-serving and unmoored to any realistic foundation. Despite his threats to close the club down if the plans were stymied, Osterman was defeated by the council. In turn, the development company demanded its money back and Osterman attempted to bankrupt Tranmere while speaking to potential investors.

In 1987, to prevent the situation spiralling into an even worse mess, local director George Higham obtained an Administration Order under the new Insolvency Act, stripping Osterman and his directors of power before they could do any further damage. "I was betrayed like Jesus at the last supper," Osterman complained, but his own ineptitude fuelled such a demise.

On 20th March 1987, the debacle ended when Osterman's 260,000 shares were bought by Peter Johnson, a swashbuckling businessman of strong local stature. Under Johnson's leadership, Rovers managed to keep the relegation wolves at bay before flying through the leagues at a revamped Prenton Park. Tranmere never looked back, and there was still a club for me to support when I was born.

As for Osterman? Well, he became an avatar of failed American imperialism in relation to sport. While lower league soccer was a drop in the ocean compared to MLB, Osterman stood forth as a caveat whenever US magnates contemplated encroachment into foreign lands. The bespectacled barrister presented a compelling case *against* international indulgence, and it took decades for subsequent American investors to succeed where Osterman failed. Those pesky Tranmere Rovers, eh? Who knew they could be so influential?

ᴥᴥᴥ

Throughout the 1980s, the desire to expand Major League Baseball never ceased, but adroit operators were required to successfully navigate the operational, philosophical and financial morass of taking the game overseas. As Osterman showed, these things could quickly go wrong without a sharpened sense of awareness. Fortunately for MLB, it found a string of adequate trailblazers who nudged baseball towards a global audience.

Firstly, in Salem, Virginia, MLB discovered its oracle of logistics: Murray Cook, a trailblazing groundskeeper with uncanny skills in organisation and development. Few matched his eye for quirky solutions, and nobody surpassed his free-spirited belief in widespread exploration. When plans were conceived, Cook would make them work, and the depth of his expertise allowed baseball to fantasise.

A passionate fan, Cook yearned to invade the game's inner sanctum from an early age. As a first step, in the 1980s he helped out at Salem Municipal Field, home to a Pirates minor league affiliate. Cook ran errands and helped prepare the field for play, serving a valuable apprenticeship in groundskeeping. It soon became apparent that he knew more than his bosses about managing a field, however, and key recognition eventually trickled in.

When minor league officials hatched an elaborate plan to visit Eastern Bloc countries on a goodwill tour in 1989, Cook's reputation as a fearless improvisor stood out. Known as the USSR Diamond Diplomacy Tour, the excursion into communist crucibles was a tool of Cold War détente. A group of Double-A ballplayers played games in Ukraine, Estonia and Russia, and Cook was tasked with sourcing venues and constructing fields at each stop. He managed the tour with peerless class, raising eyebrows within the corridors of power.

Cook subsequently ran spring training facilities for the Braves and Expos before becoming a consultant for MLB. The God of Sod, Murray was ushered into the heart of league operations, offering powerful insight as a series of commissioners explored the viability of hosting games – and indeed *franchises* – outside North America.

In 1993, Cook worked with Mike Carlson of MLB International on the aforementioned minor league exhibition at London's Oval cricket ground. While often overlooked amid the deluge of baseball globalisation, that project offered a live breeding ground for Cook to further incubate and trial his revolutionary ideas. His bosses were impressed, and the London jaunt was something of a lightbulb moment in baseball's international awakening.

Around this time, MLB benefited from another visionary leader: the ever-productive Larry Lucchino, then in his transformative spell with San Diego. Projecting the future sprawl of baseball passion, Lucchino launched the first prolonged international outreach initiatives in big league history. "We are a baseball team with a foreign policy," he famously said while marketing the Padres to Mexico. Fernando Valenzuela was even signed to boost those efforts, while Lucchino made vital connections in Tijuana and Monterrey.

As with all major innovations, a little serendipity greased the wheels of international progress, too. When the Republican National Convention was scheduled for August 1996 at Jack Murphy Stadium in San Diego, the Padres were effectively booted out of their shared accommodation. Searching for contingency plans, Lucchino pivoted to Mexico, moving a three-game series with the Mets to Monterrey. They were the first regular season games ever played outside the USA or Canada, and Cook's flexible leadership made the project a success.

Looking to capitalise on these new, emerging markets, MLB hired former Nike public relations guru Jim Small as its vice president of international business. The momentum from Mexico was turbocharged by Small's globalist agenda, and his synergy with Cook delivered great success.

Cook proved his ability to recreate baseball facilities to major league standards in the most unlikely locales, and that meshed with Small's strategy for radical growth. Backed by brazen commissioner Bud Selig, the duo pushed the boundaries of possibility, staging more games in Mexico and looking further afield for new ventures.

One nation distinguished itself as an ideal long-term partner for baseball's worldwide development. Sadly, that nation was not Great Britain, but success in other continents increased the likelihood of games in Europe one day. Firstly, MLB ventured to the Land of the Rising Sun, where its product was devoured like few places on earth. Japan showed its unbreakable love for hardball, and that paved the way for other nations to see their aspirations come true.

⚾⚾⚾

Baseball was first introduced to Japan as a school sport in 1872 by Horace Wilson, an American professor of English at a forerunner to Tokyo Imperial University. A firm believer in physical exercise improving cognitive abilities, Wilson taught his young students how to play baseball, generating great interest on campus. The game caught on among different educational departments, and an embryonic tournament was soon arranged.

The local press was keen to understand this trendy phenomenon, and its coverage of baseball helped spread intrigue among budding athletes. Other schools and colleges began training and competing in games as the sport took on a certain mythical significance within the arena of collegiate competition. America's pastime found a new home on Japanese campuses, and rapid expansion came soon thereafter.

By 1915, a nationwide tournament of high school baseball teams was spawned at Koshien Stadium, which became sacred ground for baseball prodigies. Crowds occasionally swelled above 60,000 as a nation fell in love with baseball, or *yakyū*. An opportunity for commercial advancement presented itself, and early business pioneers took advantage.

Media mogul Matsutarō Shōriki assembled a Japanese all-star team in 1934 and arranged a 12-city barnstorming trip with legendary visitors from America. A mammoth crowd of 500,000 welcomed the travelling contingent - including Babe Ruth, Lou Gehrig, Jimmie Foxx and Charlie Gehringer - to Tokyo, from whence they travelled the country, playing 18 games.

When the tour concluded, Shōriki was eager to harness its momentum. After witnessing the adulation of Ruth in particular, Shōriki saw an opportunity to develop a professional product akin to Major League Baseball in Japan. Certain right-wing political factions protested the encroachment of a thoroughly American pastime into traditional Japanese life, but Shōriki pressed ahead and rebranded his all-star team as the Yomiuri Giants. Internationally, they became known as the *Tokyo* Giants, perhaps the most mystical baseball team of all.

In 1936, a professional baseball league was established in Japan. By 1950, that association morphed into the Nippon Professional Baseball League (NPB), which was generally considered the world's highest standard of domestic baseball outside North America. Efforts were made to solidify synergies between MLB and NPB, but the 1941 attack on Pearl Harbour complicated that important relationship. Likewise, the subsequent sprawl of

World War II illustrated the extent of US-Japanese polarisation, and that residual hostility took many decades to unstitch.

During combat, Japanese soldiers often presaged their frontline charges by disparaging famous baseball players, seeking to befuddle their American counterparts. "Fuck Babe Ruth!" was a popular cry, according to many retellings, and it was difficult to overcome such entrenched malice when attempting to rebuild civility.

For instance, when NPB pitcher Masanori Murakami joined the San Francisco Giants from the Hankai Hawks in 1964, becoming the first Japanese player to appear in a big league game, he was disowned as a pariah in Japanese society. The Hawks recalled Murakami in 1965, extending convoluted moral arguments and exerting control over his contract. The pitcher was routinely chastised in public upon his return, while NPB clubs did not allow their players to leave for America until the 1990s.

Those unwritten rules thwarted a hitting savant named Sadaharu Oh in his joust with the game's record book. A phenomenal hitter, Oh overcame racial prejudice and chronic misrepresentation to rival Ruth as the greatest ballplayer who ever lived. Gracing the Yomiuri Giants between 1959 and 1980, Oh hit 868 career home runs, a professional world record. He led the Giants to 11 Japan Series titles and transcended sports with stunning skill. Enormous crowds flocked to Giants games, hoping to see Oh hit a trademark missile. In his wake, Japan developed an unshakeable fervour for baseball and a distinct individuality that set it apart from all other national variations.

"No player outside of Babe Ruth himself has to date ever dominated for quite so long one of the game's top professional leagues," wrote Peter C Bjarkman of Oh for SABR. "And if the diamond sport is ultimately a game of numbers - as so many of its commentators contend - no single batter in any of the world's top circuits has left behind a more impressive and enduring numerical and statistical legacy."

Despite drawing inspiration from McGaw's *New York* Giants in terms of name and colour scheme, Oh's Yomiuri ballclub became known as the Yankees of Japan due to their unprecedented success. Indeed, at various times in the game's corporate progression, the two franchises joined forces in powerful partnership, sharing ideas on merchandise, retail and entertainment ventures. The Yankees knew a fertile market when they saw one, and Japan certainly matched their criteria.

Major League Baseball wanted a slice of the action, too. Launched in 1986, the MLB Japan All-Star Series was introduced as a coy marketing tool, an end-of-season tour every two years taking some of the game's greatest stars to Tokyo and beyond. In 1990, the Japanese all-stars beat a US team featuring Barry Bonds, Randy Johnson and Ken Griffey Jr. by four games to three with a further tie. The sun had fully risen.

Most of the Japan All-Star Series games were held at the Tokyo Dome, a 57,000-seat arena opened in 1988. Purposely designed for baseball, the dome was home to Yomiuri and the Nippon Ham Fighters of NPB royalty. However, it also gave yakyū powerbrokers a world class facility with which to further impress MLB with a view to greater competition and cooperation. Even Yankee Stadium was smaller than the Tokyo Dome, so mutual interest in corporate partnership simmered throughout the Pacific Rim.

That synergy was eventually enhanced by high-profile player transfers from NPB to MLB. Hideo Nomo joined the Dodgers in 1995, while George Steinbrenner captured Hideki Irabu for the Yankees in 1997. A posting system was formalised to construct a pipeline of talent between Japan and the major leagues, further codifying the intercontinental relationship.

Japan also showed its baseball force at the 1996 Olympics in Atlanta, beating Team USA on its own turf in a famous semi-final. An American lineup featuring future big leaguers like Troy Glaus, Jacque Jones, RA Dickey and our old friend Jeff Weaver was pummelled 11-2 by a Japanese team of superior focus and discipline. Japan was subsequently beaten by Cuba in the final, but guys like Kosuke Fukudome and Tadahito Iguchi went home with silver medals. The quality of their skill was clear to see.

Perhaps as a trade-off for agreement in the posting negotiations, MLB finally took a regular season series to Japan in 2000, satisfying generations of loyal fans across the country. A sellout crowd packed the Tokyo Dome to watch the Cubs and Mets play two games. Cook oversaw a successful operation, which burnished existing ties and developed new ones.

A fresh generation of Japanese fans felt involved with MLB, and those relationships encouraged long-term commitments on either side. When megastar Ichiro Suzuki signed with the Seattle Mariners in 2001, those bonds were strengthened, while the success of Yomiuri hero Hideki Matsui with the Yankees wrote a new chapter in the history books.

Matsui was serenaded when the Yankees played Tampa Bay at the Tokyo Dome to open the 2004 regular season. Hideki's titanic home run in the second game was a watershed moment for baseball in Japan. The crowd went berserk as an icon rounded the bases, and the sight of those pristine Yankee pinstripes gracing an Asian diamond was a huge boon for Cook and his mission.

However, when the International Olympic Committee dropped baseball from its program in 2005, removing the sport from future Games, some feared that Japanese baseball would be drained of its momentum. Without an elite competition in which to play against their contemporaries from around the world - particularly the US - Japanese players would find it harder to gain international exposure. However, a new tournament was introduced to assuage those concerns, and that competition *strengthened* the ties between Japan and MLB.

Modelled after the FIFA World Cup of soccer, the World Baseball Classic (WBC) was a bold project devised by the International Baseball Federation. Selig was quick to lend the support of MLB, offering use of big league stadiums and marketing cache. The first tournament was arranged for 2006, with PNC Park in San Diego hosting the showcase final.

Rising to another baseball challenge, Japan won the first *two* WBC tournaments, held three years apart. The legendary Oh was coaxed into managing the 2006 team, which featured stars such as Ichiro, Fukudome, Nori Aoki and Koji Uehara. Celebrated ace Daisuke Matsuzaka won tournament MVP honours on both occasions, ahead of innumerable stars, while his lucrative move to Boston between WBC championships created a hive of interest.

Dice-K started when the Red Sox opened their 2008 season against the Athletics in Tokyo, adding further symbolism to an established long-term arrangement. Once a novel idea frowned upon by traditionalists, regular season games at the Tokyo Dome became an accepted staple of the major league calendar by the time I discovered baseball. There was something timelessly evocative about it all, and I could not get enough.

Accordingly, Cook was busier than ever in the brave new millennium, flying between multiple countries on ballpark business. Just as in the USSR and in London, repeated success in Japan underscored his ability to plan and deliver baseball games not just in the Americas, but in entirely different continents, cultures, time zones and political contexts. No project seemed too daunting for Cook, who quietly delivered results in the shadows.

The road to major league games in Europe remained convoluted, but consistent success transplanting games elsewhere sparked hope, which seeped through to the continent's baseball underground. I fed on such nuggets of optimism, sharing fantasies with a hardy group of peers who refused to give up. In the end, we were all rewarded. *Our* turn eventually came around.

⚾⚾⚾

The most illustrious football club in England, Manchester United was itself no stranger to Japan. In 1999, United won the Intercontinental Cup before 53,372 at the National Stadium in Tokyo, a major coup in their plans to generate a loyal Asian fanbase. Meanwhile, the club's red shirts were exceedingly popular in Japan, connoting power, luck and respect at the confluence of traditional cultures. For the club's marketing department, Tokyo was a quick win.

Indeed, with such an evocative brand, United was beloved around the world, but the club traditionally struggled to make an impact in North America, which still had a complicated relationship with soccer as the new century dawned. United set out to change that, seeking a strategic partner to turbocharge their image across the Atlantic. World football's most famous club sought an American ally, and it headed straight to New York for support.

Experts told United that the Yankees were an obvious choice of stateside mentor. They were cut from the same cloth as United, and both were global powerhouses of remarkable success. The philosophical synergy was immediately apparent to Peter Kenyon, the United chief executive, and he subsequently met Yankee officials, including Harvey Schiller, an ally of George Steinbrenner who was tasked with building the YES Network.

Early in his project, Schiller encountered difficulty with Cablevision, which retained the rights to broadcast Yankee games for around $50 million per season. Attempts at ending that arrangement failed, and Schiller knew the importance of strengthening his negotiating position for future battles. The prospect of eventually carrying Manchester United games on the Yankees' pipedream network was instantly appealing, creating mutual ground for extensive discussions. Things came together quickly, with obvious gains brightening the horizon.

By joining forces, the Yankees and United strengthened their communal position with regard to broadcasting rights. In theory, international television networks would always be interested in showing their respective games, so it made sense to stoke bidding wars by marrying two different sports into one unique product.

While no money was exchanged, Kenyon and Schiller agreed to a marquee alliance of marketing, advertising and media expansion. Yankees merchandise would be sold in England, pushed through United's supply chain, while United garb would be available in New York, promoted by the Yanks.

Yankee Stadium and Old Trafford would feature logos and slogans of the other partner, respectively, while each club would promote their broadcasts together, pooling resources. United stars David Beckham and Fabien Barthez would be paraded to fans in the Bronx, while Bernie Williams and Orlando Hernández would visit Manchester. Crucially, the Yankees would coordinate a pre-season tour of America for United in the summer of 2003, using their expert knowledge of the market. It seemed like an ideal fit.

"The Yankees are not just about baseball, and Manchester United is not just about football," said Kenyon at a press conference announcing the formation of a superclub. "It is easy to just look at the US and the UK, but this goes beyond that."

Legendary United player Bobby Charlton attended the media briefing, and in a decidedly awkward encounter, he was asked to identify the Yankees' shortstop. Of course, Jeter was one of the most famous *men* in America, sports star or otherwise. Still, Charlton was stumped by the question, morphing into the bumbling personification of languid British arrogance with regard to North American sports.

"I'm not proud to say I don't know," stuttered Charlton. "We don't think Manchester United will produce baseball teams or the Yankees will produce soccer teams. We don't sell our soul to another sport. This is an alliance of an organisation that is as close to Manchester United as can be."

The London Stock Exchange reacted positively to the marketing pact, with United's share price improving by 13.1% at one point following the announcement. "I think this is colossal in terms of sports," said Barclays stockbroker Julian Buck in a news interview at the time. "It's the same as bringing together Coca-Cola and Pepsi in the drinks business - it is *that* big."

As desired, United *did* tour America in 2003, playing games in Los Angeles, Seattle, Philadelphia and New Jersey. It was the first time they had played in the States since 1960. However, beyond that trip, little tangible results were ever derived from the Yankees-United treaty. As the Premier League rights holder in the US, Fox refused to allow rebroadcasts of United games on YES once it was finally launched. Meanwhile, the respective teams seemed to underestimate their own traditionalism before entering such a progressive deal.

In essence, the Yankees and Manchester United were fuelled by hubris. They each believed their own claims to supremacy atop the global sporting ladder, and helping each other in that fight became fatally self-defeating.

When the partnership was announced, the Yankees had 25 World Series titles and annual revenues of $215 million. United had 13 Premier League titles, 2 UEFA Champions League wins and a yearly income of $230 million. In the end, some said they were just too similar. It was like arguing with the mirror.

With autocrats such as Sir Alex Ferguson and Steinbrenner guarding their fiefdoms, the Yankees-United relationship petered out within a couple of years, never really delivering benefits for either party. Kenyon switched jobs in 2003, taking up the reigns at Jonny Gould's Chelsea, while Schiller also moved on in a nomadic career. Any residual ties between the colossal cousins did not survive the change of personnel.

Nevertheless, I'm still reassured by the Yankees interacting with Liverpool's biggest rival, in keeping with the tribal miasma of this tale. Incidentally, Manchester United also helped save Tranmere when Rovers faced bankruptcy in Osterman's wake during the 1980s, playing a benefit game at Prenton Park to raise funds. You cannot buy such class, and you cannot question the Yankees' taste, even if their original soccer vision never quite materialised.

※※※

Rather like an NFL coaching tree, one spoke in the Yankees-United duality *did* proceed to affect real change in transatlantic interactions, however. Beckham left Manchester for Real Madrid in 2003 before joining the Los Angeles Galaxy of Major League soccer four years later. The Galaxy deal caused an earthquake in global sports, and Beckham's emigration had a strong subliminal impact on the growth of US-British collaboration.

"This is one of the biggest challenges I have ever taken on in my career," said Beckham of his headline-grabbing transfer. "Potentially, soccer in the States could be as big as it is everywhere else around the world, and I'm very proud to be a part of that."

Indeed, few people could remember such a positive jolt to Anglo-American relations as Beckham arriving in Hollywood. In a sporting context, certainly, there was no equivalent. Beckham joined an exclusive echelon of Brits beloved by America, sharing rarefied air with John Lennon, Stephen Hawking, David Bowie, JRR Tolkien and Tim Berners-Lee.

The Galaxy sold 11,000 additional season tickets after signing Beckham. They also landed a lucrative shirt sponsorship deal with Herbalife, while 250,000 jerseys were sold before he was even formally introduced at a Los Angeles press conference.

Still playing for the England national team, Beckham was truly beloved on these shores. Despite leaving the aforementioned United for Madrid in 2003, his personal brand became ubiquitous in Britain, with clothing lines and perfume collections earning mainstream popularity and many millions of pounds in yearly income.

David's wife, Victoria, was also extremely successful. A pop star who rose to fame with the *Spice Girls*, Victoria added style to the power couple, which transcended celebrity and enjoyed remarkable goodwill around the world. Posh and Becks became a de facto royal family in their own right. To many Brits, they symbolised the very best of our national potential. We wanted to be just like them, even if their outward image of serenity was often a work of fiction.

To that end, as a kid, I had Beckham's name printed on the back of my replica England shirt, just like everybody else. To many around the globe, even those without a morsel of football knowledge, Beckham was England incarnate, second only to Queen Elizabeth II in worldwide familiarity. He was our national team captain for six years, and only two people have ever represented England on more occasions. He was an idol to millions and he was an inspiration to Brits who dreamed big. He was *David Beckham*, for crying out loud, and that was always enough to at least spark a conversation.

While Beckham did not *directly* engineer pathways between major North American sports leagues and Britain, his move to Los Angeles greatly enriched the subtext of those debates. Instigated by President Bush and Prime Minister Tony Blair, the protracted war on terror in Iraq and Afghanistan following 9/11 placed strain on the so-called Special Relationship, and an undercurrent of suspicion permeated both sides. Subtly and smartly, Beckham personified the healing process, building bridges and flattening barriers. He gave us something to discuss besides weapons of mass destruction, and that was sorely needed at a turbulent time in our history.

Shortly after David's tickertape arrival, the Galaxy were special guests of the Toronto Blue Jays for an August 2007 game at Rogers Centre. Who just happened to be the visitors that day? Why, the Yankees, of course. Just as the gods drew it up.

As ever, Beckham was a focus of attention that day, chatting to Don Mattingly, then a Yankee bench coach, and posing for photos with Jeter, his baseball alter ego, in the clubhouse. The

Yankees were shocked by Beckham's casual approach, and they showed impressive respect for his global stature.

"He's a nice guy," said Jeter when asked about meeting Beckham. "You hear so much about him coming over here to this country. He's down to earth, and it was a pleasure meeting him."

Manager Joe Torre was keen to express his appreciation for Beckham taking time out of his busy schedule to interact with the Yankees. "He's a very engaging person," said Torre, never liberal with praise. "A very nice guy."

Of course, a soccer star cannot be credited with singlehandedly improving transatlantic commerce in this manner, but Beckham's successful transition to Los Angeles – plus the roaring economic glory of it all – made executives in every field reconsider their approach to globalisation.

In particular, Beckham's American Dream presaged an unprecedented rise in sporting interaction between the United Kingdom and the United States. His spiritual role in enabling top sports leagues to reassess Britain is often overlooked, but its transformative impact is inarguable.

Beckham was a great statesman given to unknowing ambassadorial excellence. With a flash of those pearly white teeth, and with a twinkle of those transfixing eyes, if not with an explicit speech beckoning international travel, Beckham made people think about England where else they may not have bothered.

Beckham got people talking about Britain and he made businesspeople contemplate its commercial potential as it pertained to sports. Without the trail forged by his wildcard transfer, other pioneers may never have found their calling. Beckham showed them what was possible, and the rest fell into place.

⚾⚾⚾

Just as the 1973 block parties of Kool Herc gave birth to hip-hop, and just as the 1994 launch of *Netscape* catalysed an internet big bang, the 2007 arrival of ice hockey and gridiron in London created a chain of future success for major North American sports in England. Without those inspired actions, we never would have seen the Yankees and Red Sox in our homeland. Without that insurgent *belief*, the dream never would have been realised.

Inspired by the success of MLB in Mexico and Japan, and spurred by Beckham's inadvertent diplomacy, both the National Hockey League (NHL) and National Football League (NFL) brought games to London in 2007. For ardent admirers, enthusiastic but isolated, dreams came true with remarkable rapidity. It was difficult to believe such a sudden change of fortune.

On 29th September 2007, the Los Angeles Kings and Anaheim Ducks faced off in the first of two NHL regular season games at London's O2 Arena. Just 29 days later, across town, the New York Giants and Miami Dolphins played the first NFL International Series game before 81,176 agog spectators at Wembley Stadium. In just over a month, more than 115,000 people watch competitive North American sports in our nation's capital. Things were never the same again.

With particular zeal, NFL commissioner Roger Goodell pressed ahead with visionary plans to develop a fervent fanbase in Britain, priming the territory for a potential expansion franchise down the road. NFL viewing figures in the UK were very strong, thanks to loyal broadcasters like Carlson, Coombs and Neil Reynolds, and Goodell conducted extensive research of such data points, circling London as the most receptive hub of his global development plan.

"The game in London was undoubtedly one of the highlights of the entire 2007 season," said Goodell in a statement after Super Bowl XLII. "The fan interest was tremendous. The passion they demonstrated for our sport that day continued throughout the season. We had an overwhelmingly positive response to the event from all involved, and we look forward to another spectacular event in 2008."

Indeed, the International Series became a yearly occurrence, with 31 of the 32 NFL franchises eventually playing regular season games at Wembley. Fan engagement campaigns were outrageously successful, and most games sold out within hours of tickets being released. The *lowest* crowd for an NFL game at Wembley was 76,981. More frequently, attendances soared over 84,000, while season tickets were sold for the annual slate of games. League officials fell in love with the British market.

Suitably impressed, Goodell brought two games to London in 2013. Three games came in 2014, 2015 and 2016, while four games occurred in 2017, split between various venues. The NFL caught lightning in a bottle, and its grand international experiment was an unmitigated success. A whole generation of British gridiron fans came to view London games as a birthright. We were living in different times, and a fantasy world replaced reality.

I had a passing interest in American football, but never to the extent of outright fandom. Sure, I watched the Super Bowl every year, and my earliest NFL memories involve Troy Polamalu and Ben Roethlisberger making the Pittsburgh Steelers a veritable powerhouse. However, I never really rooted for a specific NFL team. The Cowboys were impressive, and the Packers matched my values, but I could never make a decision. Sounds familiar, huh? I did not care enough about gridiron to be bothered.

Accordingly, the annual International Series games at Wembley, Twickenham and elsewhere held a bittersweet quality for me. I was happy that *any* North American sports league saw fit to visit my homeland, and the reward for ardent believers like Carlson and Coombs was well deserved. Nevertheless, football is not baseball, and every year I rued the missed opportunity that nobody else could see.

In the late-2000s, to believe that MLB would one day play regular season games in London was to sign up for rejection and ridicule. Josh Chetwynd released his *Baseball in Europe* book around that time, and he routinely fielded questions about the possibility of a baseball equivalent to Goodell's mission, but the outlook was rather bleak. Even JC sometimes struggled to muster optimism, and that is when you know a situation is dire.

The infrastructure of baseball in Britain lagged far behind that of American football. While the NFL established a permanent branch in London, complete with an office and - in Alistair Kirkwood - a fully-fledged director, MLB seemed reluctant to build a presence here. The level of interest did not support such a commercial decision, and Europe fell down the league's agenda.

When *Baseball on Five* was cancelled following the 2009 season, British baseball reached its lowest ebb in almost 20 years. If executives could not even negotiate a television rights deal, what hope did they have of finalising a framework to bring major league *games* to London? I winced at the injustice of it all.

In the ensuing period, baseball became even less visible to Brits, who became less inclined to develop rooting interests as a result. Hope of residual crossover from gridiron dwindled as disrespected agents of baseball progress were forced into isolated chambers of self-delusion. I was proud to be among that number.

While few listened, I continued to write about baseball, and I continued to campaign for MLB games in London. So many great people joined me in that crusade, making huge sacrifices for the good of British baseball. We must never forget those originals, those tireless boosters of our niche cause. People like Matt Smith and Joe Gray, Norman Wells and Liam Carroll. Their toil, often through grim adversity, kept the flame alive. More than that, it made the ultimate achievement possible, even if nobody believed it at the time.

⚾⚾⚾

Though it pains me to accept such concepts, the 2010 acquisition of Liverpool FC by Fenway Sports Group reawakened hope of major league games coming to London. The Red Sox sharing ownership with a real, live sporting institution - with real, live sporting facilities - here in England increased the logistical likelihood of a deal being discussed. Accordingly, I must acknowledge the role played by John Henry and Tom Werner in facilitating my dream, and that is more than a little strange.

Liverpool was previously owned by George Gillett and Tom Hicks, American owners who had links to baseball, but their Anfield tenure was marked by financial ruin and mounting controversy, stunting the potential for elaborate outreach initiatives. Hicks bought the Texas Rangers from George W Bush in 1998, and it was he who gave A-Rod that preposterous contract in 2000. Such fiscal ineptitude did not bode well for Hicks' time on Merseyside, and his demise was suitably predictable.

In truth, though, a lot changed between Bruce Osterman buying Tranmere in 1984 and the Red Sox owners purchasing Liverpool 26 years later. English football became generally more hospitable to foreign investment, and developments in America's knowledge of soccer - thanks again, Mr Beckham - eased cultural differences.

American tycoon Malcolm Glazer bought Manchester United for £790 million by gradually hoovering up shares between 2003 and 2005. A divisive figure, Glazer had the rare honour of outspending George Steinbrenner in the 1990s when the businessmen filed competing bids for the Tampa Bay Buccaneers. Glazer paid $192 million for the faltering NFL franchise before later adding United to his expanding portfolio. A resultant feud between Malcolm and George contributed to the aforementioned demise of Yankee-United relations.

Elsewhere, Cleveland Browns owner Randy Lerner bought Aston Villa in 2006, presiding over a similar decline in results, while real estate billionaire Stan Kroenke took over at Arsenal. The Premier League came to envy the franchise model of North American sports, while soccer's mass appeal intrigued entrepreneurs around the world. The synergies were irresistible, and transatlantic crossovers became far more frequent.

Opening an office in London, Fenway Sports Group revolutionised Liverpool and contributed to this linking of jurisdictions, which encouraged intercontinental ideation. Football became obsessed with pre-season tours of North America, while a host of British clubs participated in the annual MLS All-Star Game. There seemed no end to the stateside flirtation, and I began campaigning for true mutuality in the various relationships branching in and out of Britain.

When another Premier League club toured America on a money-making expedition, I asked when MLB teams would do the same, bringing their wares to Britain. When another marquee NFL franchise played at Wembley, I asked when similar events would be arranged for baseball. When MLB went to Japan, I asked when it would come to the UK. In short, I would not shut up, and that stubbornness was pivotal in fuelling our campaign.

After witnessing the NFL's mass appeal across Britain, the NBA brought regular season games to London in 2011. They returned for a seven-year run in 2013 as MLB became the only major North American sports league yet to host real games in Europe. I was motivated to make it happen.

Slowly but surely, the diehard baseball fans of Britain began to move the needle. Nuggets of news leaked out every once in a while, offering glimmers of hope. As a raw baseball journalist, I reported on developments for a range of publications, but few editors took my stories seriously. Baseball in London would never happen, some said, so why waste column inches on such a deluded concept? I carried on regardless, determined to find the truth.

In 2012, I developed a strong lead surrounding Ferran Soriano, a key executive at FC Barcelona who later became CEO of Manchester City. Soriano had pre-existing ties with Major League Soccer (MLS) commissioner Don Garber, who once sought Soriano's insight on possible expansion strategies. When Soriano got to Manchester, Garber rekindled those conversations, which were compatible with City's plan for a network of international partners.

At the confluence of Garber, Soriano and a soccer void in New York City, an agreement was hatched to create a hybrid MLS expansion team of benefit to all parties. Keen to develop a pipeline for US talent, Manchester City fronted the project, owning 80% of the eventual team. The extra 20% would ideally be sourced from an established force in the New York market, providing valuable support and guidance. That is when Ferran Soriano met Randy Levine. The rest is history.

Bombastic and forthright, the Yankees' president entered negotiations without a clear objective. For the Yankees, any benefits of partnering with Manchester City were not immediately obvious. Their unsatisfactory experience with Manchester *United* loomed large over negotiations, but Hal Steinbrenner wanted to enhance the organisation's social enrichment schemes. Bringing MLS soccer to New York City would add a new dynamic to those efforts while offering fractional income towards the Yankees' luxury tax bill. Hal told Randy to get it done.

In 2014, a deal was agreed, and the Yankees bought in at 20%. It was announced that New York City FC, the MLS expansion franchise born as a result, would play at Yankee Stadium until a purpose-built facility could be developed. Few listened to my giddy hypotheses, but another piece of the MLB London jigsaw slid into place.

"We are pleased to be associated with this move by Major League Soccer to enhance the opportunity for New York soccer fans to enjoy high-level play in their own city," said Steinbrenner. "We look forward to the opportunity to work with Manchester City to create something very special for the soccer fans of New York."

At that point, I wrote the article that changed my life, pleading for true mutuality in the partnership and reaching out to the Yankees for comment. That is when Cristina Campana sent the gift box that rocked my world. Putting things in perspective has been difficult ever since.

Behind the scenes, Levine and Steinbrenner were already engaged in exploratory talks about bringing Yankees games to England. In the dying embers of his premiership, Bud Selig wanted to go out with a bang, and taking MLB to Europe certainly fit the bill. The Yankees and Red Sox offered an easy inlet to that world, and discussions began in earnest.

"The idea has come up through Major League Baseball about us maybe coming over to play," Randy Levine told the *Telegraph* newspaper in London. "I don't think they have actually said it yet, but we'd love to come over to play at the Etihad Stadium [Manchester City's home ground].

"We think Manchester City are extraordinary partners for the Yankees. There are some great opportunities and we only team up with people who we think are first rate. They fit into our overall plan. Obviously, our brand is very well known. It is about winning championships and we are here to lend our support to make sure that happens."

Little by little, the picture became clearer. *Something* was happening, and I was right on the frontline, digging for the exclusive. I spent hours trying to connect the dots, and I did so in my mind before key announcements were made. There was tremendous excitement among British baseball campaigners that a deal could be reached, and I chronicled the story before it became a real *thing*.

I could see the momentum shifting before my very eyes, and I had to pinch myself that MLB games in Britain were back on a tangible agenda. There was still a long way to go, but for the first time in years my belief was justified. We had something real to fantasise about. We had genuine *hope*. There was no turning back now. We would fight until the end.

⚾⚾⚾

In time, the classic question of suitable facilities confronted those working on a possible MLB series in Britain. With 90,000 seats, Wembley seemed an unlikely fit but was not ruled out, while Murray Cook also undertook reconnaissance of London cricket grounds. Finsbury Park, our best baseball diamond, would barely be suitable for a spring training workout, and so Cook's expertise was required to find a workable solution.

In a pleasing quirk of fate, London held the Olympics in 2012, and a $480 million stadium was built purposely to host athletics events and showcase spectacles. When the Games ended, however, British lawmakers were eager to avoid the stadium becoming a white elephant. Talk of a true 'Olympic legacy' was ubiquitous, and local authorities were tasked with procuring new long-term tenants for the venue.

During a lengthy bidding war, MLB expressed an interest in the Olympic Stadium, as did the NFL, pushing its expansion blueprint. Cook scouted the stadium and reported favourably on its ability to accommodate baseball. Without such a visionary at its disposal, MLB may have abandoned the idea entirely.

Selig did not ratify a baseball bid for the Olympic Stadium tenancy, but he did concoct a more frugal plan entirely. The commissioner decided to approach the winning bidder and strike a deal. Cook's belief in the Olympic Stadium as a baseball facility was a real eye opener, and when West Ham was announced as the lead occupier, preparations for an MLB proposal were accelerated.

Further trips to Japan oiled the wheels of progress, while Selig settled on another unlikely destination for his international swansong. In 2014, the Dodgers and Diamondbacks played a two-game series in Sydney, Australia as MLB conquered another continent. I wanted England to be further up the queue, but the continued commitment to baseball travel was pleasing for veteran campaigners.

A loyal aide to Selig, Rob Manfred became commissioner in 2015, and he vowed to continue spreading baseball around the world. A March 2016 exhibition between Tampa Bay and the Cuban national team in Havana was attended by Barack Obama, the first sitting US President to visit Cuba in 88 years. Once again, Cook displayed his invaluable penchant for getting things right, and the Estadio Latinoamericano joined his peerless portfolio.

Some British baseball fans joked that MLB even went to an inhospitable communist outpost before it came to London, supposedly a hub of transatlantic relations. Nevertheless, Britain's chance was coming. It was just a matter of putting the pieces together.

※※※

In the autumn of 2016, the various cornerstones of a prospective MLB London Series were finally in the same zip code. Somebody just needed to figure it all out. That man was Sadiq Khan, one of the most misunderstood politicians in a *world* of misunderstood politicians.

Born in 1970 to a working class British-Pakistani family, Khan studied law at London Metropolitan University before joining the Labour party. He became a Member of Parliament for his home constituency of Tooting in 2005 and gradually climbed the slippery totem pole of British politics.

Khan was elected mayor of London in May 2016, replacing the enigmatic Boris Johnson. He inherited a complex situation as the UK negotiated its controversial exit from the European Union. Market uncertainty put Britain in a state of flux, and Khan had to tell the world that London, its dominant metropolis, was still open for business.

Accordingly, in September 2016, the mayor embarked on a five-day ambassadorial trip to New York, where he hoped to convince investors that London had a bright future. Manfred was one such investor, and he was willing to talk on behalf of the major league owners. While in Queens, Khan threw out the first pitch at a Mets game. Manfred helped arrange the engagement, a great opportunity to generate press and test the British appetite for baseball. Desire morphed into action, and momentum came naturally thereafter.

"I'm keen to make London the sporting capital of the world," Khan told the *London Evening Standard*. "I have been really encouraged by my discussions with MLB. I have told them there are huge baseball fans in London, all around the UK and in Europe."

Incidentally, Khan was a key ally of Ed Miliband, a former Labour leader who has a serious passion for baseball. Ed's father was a freelance teacher, and the family had two spells living in Boston, where Miliband fell in love with the Red Sox. Ed was later a visiting scholar at Harvard University and, upon returning to London, he was known to stay awake through the night to watch baseball games during his rise to prominence. It is fairly ironic, therefore, that Khan, not Miliband, played the role of baseball dealmaker. Behind the scenes, I'm sure Ed provided invaluable support.

Khan met Manfred on a few further occasions, while open dialogue sought to bring MLB games to London during the 2018 season. That date never quite materialised, as the Padres and Dodgers went to Mexico instead, but Khan was not perturbed. He pressed ahead with single-minded determination.

Working relentlessly hard, the mayor finally connected the dots between Liverpool and Manchester City, Fenway Sports Group and Yankee Global Enterprises, Major League Baseball and London's Olympic Stadium. Finally, on 8th May 2018, it was announced that, in 2019, as part of a two-year commitment, the Yankees and Red Sox would play two regular season games in London. Sleepy daydreams became confirmed reality, and veteran fans struggled to believe their fortune.

Khan and Manfred marshalled a press conference attended by dignitaries from both teams, including Henry and Steinbrenner.

Manfred spoke of his intention to make this a long-term arrangement, and ticket sales were encouraging. The Cubs and Cardinals were tabbed for a 2020 encore, and MLB launched community outreach ventures across the UK.

"We are excited to be bringing one of the most storied rivalries in sports to the passionate fans of London," said Manfred. "In our ongoing efforts to grow baseball, there is nothing as impactful as bringing live games and our talented players to fans. This is our most significant endeavour ever in Europe, and we look forward to showcasing Major League Baseball in one of the world's great cities."

I was adrift in the throes of anxiety and depression by that point, damaged from exposure to the capitalist coalface, but the news made me smile. I pumped my fist silently and managed a wry grin. British baseball's moment had finally arrived. I was right to believe in those unseen dreams.

⚾⚾⚾

Murray Cook faced a daunting schedule in 2019. That season, MLB planned to play eight regular season games outside the United States and Canada, an unprecedented number. There were two games in Tokyo as Ichiro said goodbye to his adoring public with the Mariners. There were four games in Mexico as Manfred harnessed momentum in Latin America. And, of course, there were two games in London as the warring factions of my heart travelled across the ocean.

When he was not on a field, shifting dirt and painting baselines, Cook was usually in an airport departure lounge or a small hotel room, crisscrossing continents with alarming regularity. It is a testament to the man that he did not go insane. Even more impressively, he delivered all of the games without a glitch, further enhancing his glowing reputation.

In London, transforming the Olympic Stadium into a venue fit for big league baseball took four weeks of exhaustive labour. Cook had 110 people working under his tutelage, and 16-hour shifts became the norm to meet tight deadlines.

Multiple layers of artificial turf were laid atop the football pitch, providing a smooth playing surface. Infield clay was imported from the US and fashioned into a beautiful diamond. Cook created a pitcher's mound with military precision, while bullpens were built and seating arrangements were finalised with impressive creativity. The bright yellow foul poles were crafted in Britain, a nice touch by MLB. Baseball's trademark mastery of detail was clear for all to see.

Allowing for an effective batter's eye in centre field and for adequate dugouts thronging the field, stadium capacity was reduced to 55,000 for the London Series. Still, that was bigger than Yankee Stadium and Fenway Park, making for an evocative setting. The rivalry had never known anything like it.

Designed for Olympic competition, the stadium featured wind-reduction technology to aid performance in disciplines such as javelin and discus. That created a stillness which, combined with roaring summer heat, saw the baseball fly. Early in the process, it became apparent that Cook was building a hitters' paradise. He did the best job possible with the resources he was given.

Irregular field dimensions underlined the batter-friendly environment. Straightaway centre field lay 385 feet from home plate, while the foul poles were just 330 feet down each line. At 382 feet, the left and right-centre field gaps became inviting power alleys. Runs would certainly be plentiful.

Seeking domestic broadcasting partners for the series, MLB teamed with BT Sport, which hired Chetwynd as a colour analyst for makeshift play-by-play man Darren Fletcher. It was nice to see the *Baseball on Five* bloodline come full circle. The BBC also carried coverage, and together the British baseball community sailed into uncharted territory.

Bringing the marquee rivalry to London was a huge display of intent by MLB, proving its seriousness about Europe. We were not getting the Rays and Twins in some dead-end series. We were getting the New York Yankees and the Boston Red Sox. There is no greater rivalry in sports.

The mortal enemies had played each other on 2,262 occasions between 1901 and the summer of 2019. Even more if you include spring training contests and exhibition games. Never had they met outside the United States, until London found a ballpark and beckoned those illustrious stars to Europe.

Accordingly, this was a series for all-time, a series that meant more. This was a showcase but also an awakening. This was British baseball's time to shine, and boy were the diehards ready.

This was for Gould and Chetwynd, Jansen and Lengel. This was for Macklin and Coombs, Carlson and Thomas. This was for Jupitus, the popular comedian with an uncommon love for the Red Sox, and this was for Colin Murray, Britain's only broadcaster with a portrait of Joe DiMaggio in his living room.

This was for Miliband, the only baseball fan ever to come within 94 parliamentary seats of occupying 10 Downing Street, and this was for Chadwick, the father of baseball born in Devon. This was for Spalding and Ley, Wright and Moores. This was for Bobby Thomson and his immortal home run.

This was for every jaded student who missed a morning lecture after staying up to watch Julio Lugo kill another Red Sox rally. And this was for every night-feeding mother who fell in love with Derek Jeter at four in the morning.

But most of all, this was for the 12-year-old me, the little kid with the baseball cap reading Dan Shaughnessy on the stairs. After all those years, I somehow landed tickets to watch the New York Yankees play the Boston Red Sox. It turns out childhood dreams can come true. Sometimes, you just have to wish a little harder.

⚾⚾⚾

CHAPTER TWENTY-THREE

The War for My Heart

"Accursed who brings to light of day the writings I have cast away," wrote Yeats, the great Irish poet. He could easily have been talking about baseball in London, because a similar sense of precious anxiety becalmed every diehard fan in this land as the two-game series approached.

Baseball is a game of such nuance and introspection that I was incredibly nervous about gifting it to mainstream Britain and sharing it with the modern orthodoxy. I'm very protective of this game, and I was somewhat scared of presenting it to a wider audience, undoubtedly raw and dangerously judgmental.

Baseball is alien here, and I hoped the majority would not embarrass the minority that actually cared. I just wanted London to do justice to Major League Baseball, because its mere presence on these shores was a remarkable gift that should never be eschewed.

I took annual leave from work to travel from Liverpool to London on 28th June 2019, a glorious Friday. Colleagues were accustomed to hearing about planned trips and tourist excursions to London, but my invoking baseball as rationale met blank faces and disbelieving frowns.

Baseball?

Why?

For an entire weekend, those resounding questions baffled a nation. The overwhelming majority did not know how to think, react or respond to the Yankees and Red Sox washing ashore. There was no frame of reference, but I did my best to educate anybody who showed an interest.

The Yankees flew to London atop the AL East, seven games ahead of Tampa Bay. Meanwhile, the Red Sox languished in third place, nine games adrift of their rivals. A Yankees sweep would spell disaster for Boston. It would also wipe them from my conscience.

Right from the outset, the teams approached their London expedition in very different ways. It was obvious who wanted to be there and who did not, and I have a nose for such subliminal messaging. It was clear what this meant to each respective franchise, and attitudes were surprisingly mixed.

The Red Sox chartered a luxury private jet for $500,000 to cross the Atlantic, and they did so with the grim-visage precision of trained killers. This was a business trip, first and foremost. The Red Sox seemed distant and unapproachable.

The Yankees, by contrast, made a huge effort to win friends and influence people. The New Yorkers positioned themselves as baseball missionaries, connecting fans and building relationships. That was greatly appreciated by baseball-starved Brits, who will never forget the Yankees' interest in us, not just our interest in them.

Sure, Red Sox players took advantage of pre-series downtime to sightsee atop red London buses, but Boston executives deigned to arrange any showpiece community events. Meanwhile, the Yankees organised a baseball clinic in conjunction with the London Mets, Britain's top baseball club. Perhaps Cristina Campana *did* feed along my ideas after all.

Staged at Finsbury Park, the event was attended by Hal Steinbrenner, Brian Cashman and a host of Yankees legends. Manfred even made an appearance, and no expense was spared in creating a great first impression.

With barbeque food sizzling on a distant grill, the Yankees taught baseball fundamentals to the London Mets' youth teams. Excited kids rotated from station to station, learning new skills from Yankees legends. They had the time of their lives, rubbing shoulders with baseball royalty. For many, such an event was beyond their wildest dreams.

Aaron Boone taught baserunning. Hideki Matsui roamed the outfield. Nick Swisher manned the infield. Mariano Rivera and Andy Pettitte demonstrated the finer art of pitching. Oh, and in the batting cages? Well, take your pick from Alex Rodriguez, Reggie Jackson or Carlos Beltrán. The menu was mouth-watering.

Never before had such a grand assemblage of baseball immortals gathered on a small patch of grass in north London. A total of 19 World Series rings were present, at least in a metaphorical sense. Cashman literally *wore* one of his rings, showing the local kids up close. That level of class is unprecedented, and I was very impressed.

The Yankees did not merely turn up to perform in a publicity stunt, take a few photographs and leave inside an hour. They spent all afternoon at Finsbury Park, eating charred hot dogs with locals, interacting with parents and signing hundreds of autographs. The depth of their gesture was even greater than its surface majesty.

As the earliest hints of twilight emerged, Steinbrenner gave a final speech to the assembled crowd, praising the London Mets' tireless ambassadorial work across England. Jokes were exchanged about how his father never would have praised the Mets – in London, Queens or anywhere else – before Hal pulled the chord on a surprise gift.

In a moving display of charity, the Yankees donated a huge truckload of equipment, apparel and merchandise to the London Mets, totalling $35,000 in value. Every kid got a Yankees cap, spreading the gospel. The team received catcher's masks and chest protectors, batting helmets and gloves, outfield mitts and more baseballs than many people had ever seen before. Rawlings seemed to be the main manufacturer of choice, in an ironic twist of fate. Somewhere, Spalding smiled, but the Yankees did it right, and even Albert himself would have approved of such thoughtful statesmanship.

"They landed as a first-place team and, in their initial group act, were first-class diplomats," wrote respected baseball insider Joel Sherman of the event. "The Yankees did well to make lifelong fans of the game and their team over a few hours on the only permanent baseball diamonds in London."

In showing such mastery of public relations, the Yankees distinguished themselves as classy and caring. Such gestures may appear tokenistic to some, but the minimalist manner of the Yankees' charitable engagement struck a chord with me. I was thankful for their interest in England and its baseball future. It reminded me of that special package I received all those years earlier, and the memories came flooding back.

In many years to come, I hope the Yankees find a way to return and witness their transformative impact on those young lives. London is home to some of the poorest urban neighbourhoods in England, and such goodwill gestures are genuine lifelines for some forgotten kids. I commend the Yankees' vision and I tip my cap to their power. Duly inspired, one of those kids may wear the hallowed pinstripes *for real* someday, representing our nation with class. I yearn to see that happen, and when it eventually does, I will weep with immeasurable pride.

The proliferation of British baseball fan groups, forums and websites was a positive by-product of the MLB London Series. So long confined to early morning silos, hardcore baseball enthusiasts across the country came together, creating a genuine community. Memories were exchanged and meetups were arranged. Our prosaic obsession ventured offline.

Ran by knowledgeable enthusiasts, *Bat Flips and Nerds* became a hub for news, views and analysis. Intriguing the world's press and gaining more than 40,000 social media followers, superfan Joey Mellows quit his job and travelled across America watching ballgames, morphing into *The Baseball Brit*. Every day, a new Facebook group sprang up for British baseball fans to share their stories. I sat back and watched proudly. This was barely even a dream when I discovered baseball. The progress was phenomenal.

Thanks to David Shaw, founder of the MLB UK Community group on Facebook, I managed to score tickets to Friday's pre-series workout session at the London Stadium, during which both teams took batting practice and spoke to the media. As a seasoned baseball writer, seeing so many iconic journalists and broadcasters up close was a sequestered treat. Spotting role models like Ken Rosenthal, Buster Olney and Sherman was surreal. So many Twitter avatars came alive before me.

Amid the scrum, I got to meet one such role model, Ken Davidoff of the *New York Post*. Ken became a professional sportswriter in 1994, the year I was born. He has subsequently covered the game as a Yankees beat writer and a national columnist for a string of publications, developing a strong reputation for quirky stories with a human thread. I have followed Ken's work for many years, relying on the information disseminated by him and many colleagues to form my appreciation and knowledge of baseball. It was a thrill to engage with such a consummate professional, and I never took the opportunity for granted.

I connected with Davidoff on LinkedIn a few weeks before the London Series, mainly seeking advice on how to develop my baseball writing aspirations. Ken enjoyed a blog I wrote previewing the London Series, and he suggested that we meet at the workout day. My piece was also featured by MLB.com, quite remarkably, and Davidoff sensed that I had an interesting story to tell.

Ken snaked through the stands to find me watching batting practice, smiling and agog. He rang my phone a few times, seeking my seat number. It was all very surreal. Davidoff asked questions about my love for baseball, pointing a Dictaphone under my nose. I later appeared in his *Post* article about Britain's most dedicated baseball fans. The thrill was unending.

"For Ferguson, who started watching MLB action in 2004, Saturday will mark his first game in-person," wrote Davidoff. "Ferguson estimated that he has '200 to 300' baseball books, and in line with his career ambitions, he said he'll enjoy the games without taking a side." Ah, if only the readers knew. I'm sorry, Ken. Now you know the real story, I guess.

I subsequently found myself just 20 feet from the aforementioned Jackson and Pettitte, two Yankee greats shooting the breeze. It was one of the coolest things I have ever experienced. I yearned to be in *their* world, chatting with baseball immortals. I wanted to *be* them, living the greatest life of eternal childhood. I needed to get closer, delving further into the game, but the protective netting offered a sad reminder of my mere mortality.

Judge and Sánchez put on a show in batting practice, and I enjoyed my first session of autograph-hunting by the Yankees' dugout. Coming within touching distance of players like Gregorius and LeMahieu was awesome. Previously, these people have only existed in my computer screen, pixelated figments of mlb.tv. Now they were here in London, ignoring *my* requests for a signed ball. What an honour. What a privilege. What a life.

Davidoff's article featured a photograph of Judge signing dozens of baseballs. In the top corner of the iconic shot, I stood in total shock and excitement, gazing at one of the planet's greatest ballplayers with bug-eyed exhilaration. I was totally starstruck, unlike any other time in my life. I had to pinch myself, unsure if this was all real.

Sure, you *hear* that Aaron Judge is 6 feet 7 inches tall and that *sounds* impressive. You watch on YouTube as he stands next to José Altuve, a hulking mismatch that speaks to the confounding beauty of baseball. But actually *seeing* this guy up close - seeing him cast a shadow over conventionally tall contemporaries - is awe-inspiring. I could not believe my eyes, and the *Post* photographer captured my astonishment. That picture will hang on my wall until I die, ranking among my most cherished possessions. It encapsulates a lifetime dream come true.

For the record, Aaron Hicks signed the most autographs, spending almost five minutes with a pen beside the dugout. I was impressed by his willingness to interact with the adoring public, and Aaron gained a new superfan in me.

While its vibe was distinctly British, the London Series also gave *European* fans a priceless opportunity to make a dreamy baseball pilgrimage. Around the dugout, I spotted fans from Italy and Spain, while a large Dutch contingent pined over Gregorius and Xander Bogaerts, both of whom represented the Netherlands in World Baseball Classic play.

While the Red Sox hit, I managed to meet up with Josh Chetwynd for the first time after years of internet correspondence. It was great to finally meet Josh and express my gratitude face-to-face. You will rarely encounter a more intelligent and passionate baseball man. Thanks, JC. You remain a tremendous inspiration.

The highlight of Boston's BP session was receiving a wave from manager Alex Cora and a ball from a nondescript reliever with a beard. Forgive me, whoever you were, but I forgot to bring my glasses. Thank you, regardless. That was another thrilling *first* in my baseball fandom, and it means a lot.

On the train back to central London after the workout day, I noticed a familiar face. Familiar to me, at least, if to nobody else. Only after instigating a conversation did I confirm the identity of Cliff Floyd, a solid outfielder who played for seven teams during my childhood, predominantly the Marlins, Expos and Cubs.

I shook Cliff's hand and expressed my respect for his solid career, during which he played more than 1,600 games and hit more than 200 home runs. Floyd won the World Series with Florida in 1997 and maintained a career batting average of .278. He appreciated my sentiment as an eager fan, if not the unprovoked attention on a busy train. I did not know how this was happening.

At the workout day, Red Sox fans far outnumbered their New York counterparts. It was quite surprising, therefore, to see so many Yankee shirts and caps on the tube heading to Saturday's opening game. These teams are a big deal, far bigger than even I appreciated. I felt fortunate to be part of this epic rivalry, and the big league intensity was very real.

Behind the marketing stunts and the advertising gimmicks, beneath the slogans and the montages, these fanbases really do not like each other. Even all these years later, in the post-Curse vacuum, there was a bubbling resentment among Red Sox fans towards New York and a feverish rebellion among Yankee fans towards Boston. They are diametrically opposed but somehow cut from a similar cloth. Such is the confounding nature of hostility.

Objectively, few people have had a more diverse experience of the Yankees-Red Sox rivalry than me. However, before the London Series, my participation in the feud was one-dimensional, cast behind a computer screen devoid of real intensity. I constructed much of the emotion myself, far removed from the frontline. Due to my isolation, *effort* was sometimes required to enflame emotions. It was all ever so slightly manufactured.

Up close and personal, however, I was presented with a stark dichotomy. Baseball is seen as a cuddly sport, but the discourse of this rivalry was hugely bitter. A broad church, the Red Sox fans I encountered were crude and uproarious. All weekend, my heart barked a message of pinstriped devotion, and I could not contain it. Perhaps there *was* a deep-rooted connection all along, and it finally got chance to mutate. Perhaps my journey was somehow *preordained*, and the attendant tribulations were just to add drama. Perhaps everything happens for a reason, and we should stop fighting fate.

Yankee class was everywhere, from Finsbury Park to exemplary on-field decorum. By contrast, an abrasive sense of entitlement emanated from Red Sox Nation, which appeared ever so slightly uncouth and unkempt.

All potbellies and scatty beards, the Red Sox fans I encountered were quick with derogatory slurs and slow with any modicum of grace. I admired the serious dignity of Yankee fans, which jarred with the giddy, arrogant homogeneity of Red Sox Nation.

Prior to Game 1, Judge embodied the chasm by interacting with fans and making dreams come true. He signed scores of autographs, posed for dozens of selfies, and even treated a handful of kids to some time on the field. Judge restored my faith in baseball stars. My soul had made its decision, even if my mind compelled it to await the outcome of the games.

Patrycja, Nath and I soon discovered that the tickets for our first ever baseball game were on the back row, deep in left field, way out in foul territory. I was the happiest person in the world.

That moment when I emerged into the seating bowl, amid a raucous crowd, will live with me forever. A lifetime of faith proved worthwhile, and vindication wore a star-spangled banner.

As the national anthems played, goosebumps trembled across my whole body. Tears formed in my eyes. I was struck by the sheer improbability of it all - of being there to finally watch a Major League Baseball game, but also of England being able to pull this off.

The logistics of bringing big league baseball to London were daunting. From the food and drink stalls right down to the bullpen mounds and the most innocuous pieces of equipment, there is a fine line between authentic and cheesy. London got it right, ever so blissfully right, and witnessing a crowd of 59,659 in my homeland, the largest for any major league game in 16 years, was one of the proudest feelings I can remember.

The fact that, across America, such events are staged *daily* from February through October renders me speechless. I can only applaud your peerless work ethic and commend your voracious appetite for sports. No other country could pull that off.

Despite Boston featuring as the home team in London, both franchises brokered a deal to wear their famous home uniforms throughout the weekend. The Yankees' hallowed pinstripes were sharp and elegant, while the Red Sox' red trim seemed lurid and somehow cheap to my discerning eye. I guess some would call that *confirmation bias*, and some would be correct. My Tetris-like quest for natural baseball fandom neared completion.

Before the game, we had a great view of Tanaka and Sánchez warming up in the Yankee bullpen. The Japanese hurler did not last very long in the game, however, as Boston and New York both scored six runs in the first inning. With rampant sunshine and grim humidity, the baseball flew through the air with slapstick rapidity. Our Olympic Stadium was akin to Coors Field on steroids. Batters had to stifle their laughter upon returning to the dugout.

The Yankees scored four runs on three consecutive doubles in their first turn at bat before Hicks, my new favourite underdog, hit the first ever major league home run on European soil, a two-run blast that energised the ballpark. The atmosphere was electric, and I was thrilled for the oft-maligned Hicks. Also, as baseball fans, we *got* it. There was nothing more to worry about.

Michael Chavis launched a mammoth three-run shot to punctuate the Red Sox' immediate comeback, knocking Tanaka from a freshly tied game. Brett Gardner nudged the Yankees ahead with a two-run bomb in the third, before another pinstriped explosion in the fourth was headlined by a line drive homer from Judge.

Eyeing the comic mismatch between Aaron's hulking physique and the shallow outfield dimensions, I called his shot. When the baseball soared out on a line to right field, clearing the wall and putting the Yankees ahead, 14-6, I stood up to applaud my newest baseball hero. Any semblance of impartiality was seeping away.

The Yankees and Red Sox combined for six Game 1 homers in total, decimating the ball with startling profundity. Chavis went yard a second time, while even the offensively challenged Jackie Bradley Jr. skied an opposite field dinger. In poetic symmetry, we saw the spiritual sequel to Carlson's home run derby, except this contest actually mattered in the big league standings.

As a nation, our first experience of Major League Baseball was therefore decidedly unrealistic, at least from an offensive standpoint. We saw an endless carousel of baserunners as Boston and New York combined for 37 hits, burned through 16 different pitchers and were eventually separated by just four runs in 30.

The Yankees outlasted the Red Sox, 17-13, in a game that fell within three minutes of being the longest ever for a nine-inning regular season contest. It was hard explaining balls and strikes to Patrycja, who lost the will to live amid stifling heat. I was mesmerised all day, however, bewildered in a state of utter bliss.

Around the ballpark, people taught one another the rules and history of baseball. Plenty of Americans made the journey, taking the chance to visit Europe. They joined in, too, using the famed British-American kinship to develop a mutual love for baseball. Everybody sang *Take Me Out to the Ballgame* together, a special moment of solidarity.

We stayed until the end, soaking up every second of the 4 hours and 42 minutes of rare baseball exposure. Participating in a mass rendition of *Sweet Caroline*, a staple of Fenway, was a cool experience, as was sneaking into the posh seats to watch the Yankees seal their victory. The stadium operators even played *New York, New York* by Sinatra after the final out, surely the first such serenading of a Yankees win at a Red Sox 'home' game that has ever been recorded.

We loitered around the Yankees' dugout well after the final chords floated into the dank London night. On three or four occasions, ushers asked us to leave, but I did not want the moment to end. I shouted onto the field, trying to draw the attention of A-Rod, who completed his work as a television pundit. I did not even know what to say to Rodriguez, if he ever responded to my calls, but potentially interacting with him seemed *meaningful* regardless of the content. Alas, he did not hear my pleas. Alex never did listen to others all that much.

We were eventually driven out of the stadium by security guards, perhaps an hour after the final pitch. Walking on water, bouncing on the sticky excess of happiness, we weaved through the streets of London, bona fide baseball fans at last. I could not stop smiling. I could barely believe my luck. MLB had conquered Britain, and my lifelong mission was complete.

ᔑᔑᔑ

Without the generosity of online friends, I would have missed Game 2 entirely. Tickets were quickly snapped up by touts in the first instance, while resale windows were hugely competitive. Some seats sold for more than £400. However, Mark Blakemore, a supporter of my baseball writing since the earliest days, gifted me a ticket. Without such enormous kindness, I would have been elsewhere while the Yankees and Red Sox played in my own country. Thanks, Mark. You saved my life.

A seasoned Yankees fan, Mark attended the game with his son and Kevin Rooney, better known as @CelticYankees on Twitter. It was great to meet these guys in the flesh after chatting baseball with them online for so many years. They have always encouraged my work, and I hope they enjoy this book.

I also briefly met Ed Miliband, the aforementioned politician, before Game 2, in another bizarre treat. Ed wore a Red Sox hat and disembarked the same tube train as me. I shook his hand, thanked him for his service, and wished him a pleasant day at the ballpark. I'm thrilled that the first general election candidate I ever voted for is a seamhead of serious renown, even if his choice of team is rather unfortunate.

Fortunately, my brother managed to find a last-minute ticket for the Sunday game, too, and we shared another fantastic afternoon at the ballpark. Nath has endured my garrulous baseball ramblings since he was a kid, so to see him engrossed in the game was magical. He also has a robust knowledge of baseball that will only grow with further exposure. One day, we may fret over big league strategy together as we do with Tranmere's chronic inability to play entertaining football.

Determined to soak up the occasion, we got into the stadium early. Unsure when I would next see the Yankees or Red Sox play live, I committed every detail to memory, capable of being recalled when needed most.

Nath and I walked around the entire ballpark, settling in the left field bleachers for batting practice. I brought my glove, and attempting to grab a BP home run made me feel like a kid again. In our world of restless irritation, such unfettered fun is an infinite good, and we must do everything to preserve such sacred traditions.

Just before first pitch, I managed to nab an autograph from Mark Teixeira, the former Yankees first baseman, as he exited the field following his pre-game duties for ESPN. Another World Series champion, Teixeira became just the fifth switch-hitter to reach 400 career home runs in 2016. This was a big deal for me. Everyone remembers their first signed ball, right? I will cherish it forever.

My view for the Sunday capper, down on the first base side, was spectacular. Like a veteran seat-hopper, Nath managed to shimmy down next to me, and we were ready to go. We were ready to soak up every last second of the action. We were ready to make a lifetime of memories.

Stephen Tarpley, a young southpaw, started for the Yankees before a crowd of 59,059. He received a rude awakening as the Red Sox erupted for four runs in the first inning. I winced as the Yankee hurler melted before our eyes. Bogaerts reached out and poked a two-run homer to right field, starting the carousel once more. JD Martínez went back-to-back with a soaring drive to right-centre before Christian Vázquez also dumped one over the tantalising outfield fence as the Red Sox fans in attendance fizzed with excitement.

I quickly realised that the series' aggregate score was 17-17 through the first inning of Game 2. Under the rules laid down prior to my London trip, this gave both teams less than one game in which to win my heart. Even all these years later, right from the Babe on down, they were still toe-to-toe, neck-to-neck and face-to-face. They were still inseparable, and that put a smile on this poet's face.

Yet, if truth be known, I was rooting for a Yankee comeback. Big time. The sense of expectation bubbled inside me, and I believed in their chances of staging a grand revival. One pitch at a time, I lived through pain with the New York Yankees as they chipped away in the pristine London sun. Facing Eduardo Rodriguez, the Yanks quickly loaded the bases with nobody out in in the second. Giovanny Urshela grounded out to bring home a run before Gardner smashed an RBI single to right. 4-2, Red Sox. 19-17, Yankees. Game on.

From a historically erratic start, the game – and indeed the series – calmed down from there. It was almost like both teams agreed to get the thing over with so they could head for the damn airport. Enough with the London bandbox already.

Entering the seventh inning, the score remained 4-2, Boston, as a tight duel captivated the monumental crowd. Then the Red Sox bullpen imploded, as it so frequently does. It was a beautiful sight to behold.

With a late Sunday train scheduled, Nath and I agreed to leave during the seventh inning stretch. Such a concept gnawed at my heart, but life waits for no man, unfortunately. I had to attend work early the next morning, and we still had more than 200 miles to travel home. I watched through watery eyes, unbelievably content but also sad at the unpredictability of when I would next see a live ballgame.

As if by destiny, the Yankees authored one of the most spellbinding half-innings of baseball in their recent history. As if for my pleasure alone, they confirmed my eternal fandom with a pulsating display of relentless hitting. As if by magic, New York pummelled Boston, and I cheered along with every pitch.

LeMahieu doubled leading off and Judge followed with a walk. Hicks thwacked a double to right, scoring DJ and moving Judge to third. Then Sánchez ripped a two-run, go-ahead single to left, putting the Yankees up, 5-4. I cheered like a mad man, wind-milling my arms to wave Hicks home.

The beat went on as a walk by Edwin Encarnación and a single from Torres were sandwiched between a Gregorius strikeout. Urshela then dumped a single to shallow centre field, scoring two more runs. Further hits from LeMahieu, Hicks and Sánchez left a trail of destruction. When eventually the Red Sox managed to record the third out, we skipped to the train station with an 11-4 lead. *We*, you will notice. Not *the New York Yankees*. *We*.

Didi homered in the eighth to stretch the lead before Boston threatened a late rally of its own, scoring four runs to make things interesting. Watching on my phone in London Euston station, I flinched a little as the score ticked to 12-8. Rafael Devers hit with two runners aboard, putting my glee in jeopardy, but Zack Britton induced a weak groundout to end the threat. Chapman then surrendered a leadoff double in the ninth but ultimately recovered to induce three swinging strikeouts, punctuating the Yankees' sweep of the inaugural London Series.

I smiled all the way home to Liverpool as this strange and conflicting country streamed past the murky train window. I wore that magical cap the Yankees sent me in 2014. A Jeter shirsey covered my heart. I typed away on my MacBook, writing the story of my life. Writing incredulous non-fiction that ultimately became this book.

I learned a lot in London, far beyond the boxscore. We saw 50 runs, 65 hits, 16 doubles, 4 errors and 10 homers, but it was about more than numbers. It was a celebration of unity and a tribute to fun. It was a feat of elite organisation and a showcase of immense skill. It was the greatest weekend of my life.

Everybody has heard of the New York Yankees. Ardent baseball fans are all too aware of their historical domination, while the ubiquity of Yankees merchandise in just about any western city speaks for itself. However, even I underestimated just how big the Yankees are, and belonging to that philosophical movement for the rest of my life is a truly uplifting concept.

This team means a lot to people. While the Red Sox are defined by distinct regionalism, the Yankees seem to embody some kind of national crusade. They are a grand expression of American pride, the most recognisable export of the States' most powerful city. Associating with that – hell, being a *part* of it – will lift me from the squalor of everyday banality. It will give me a pipeline to the finer things in life, and I'm ready to enjoy those trappings.

People complain about baseball games being too slow, too long and too stagnant, but that is kind of the point. Only a certain breed understands. A day at the ballpark is community in motion. It is learning and reminiscing, hoping and praying. It is taking time to stop and breathe in the otherwise chaotic whirlwind of contemporary life. It is relaxation, reconnecting with your younger self, and allowing the mind to wander. It is therapy, quite simply, without most people realising.

Baseball is the greatest sporting portal to introverted contemplation that exists in our lexicon. It is a kaleidoscope of hope that lets you discover yourself. Baseball is a wonderful thing that should never be broken, and I'm just glad I never changed the television channel all those years ago.

There is a unique rhythm to baseball, a lyrical tranquillity that calms the anxious and soothes the worried. In my battles with mental ill health, I discovered a new form of treatment: the gentle susurrus of a ballpark crowd, rising with each strike, undulating with every out and peaking in moments of mounting suspense, bowing to the majesty of pinstriped allure.

At the ballpark, you are free to just sit and think, sit and enjoy. You are free to just *be*, and be yourself, for there is no greater way to spend a summers' day than with the people you love obsessing over something of minimal mortal significance. That is why baseball is so special, because in a world where we are all just wasting time, you might as well do it with peanuts and Cracker Jack.

A million thoughts raced through my mind on that summer train ride home. I thought of Jonny Gould and those dusty VHS tapes of *Baseball on Five*. I thought of my own inner child, forever changed but somehow pleasantly refined. I thought of New York, hatching fantasy plans to finally make a pilgrimage.

A lifetime of distant baseball fandom flashed before my eyes. Sixteen years of nonsensical belief and blurry eyed squinting in the early morning hours – all suddenly worthwhile, all suddenly making sense.

After so much internal strife, harbouring secrets and living a baseball lie, swapping and changing teams like underpants, it was all over. I had reached inner peace. The war for my heart was over. The New York Yankees had won.

๑๑๑

RYAN FERGUSON

EPILOGUE

Pinstripe Galaxy

For years, I was stuck in the wrong body. Not in the classic sense of gender identity or sexuality, you understand, but in relation to my fandom of various Major League Baseball teams. Through fear of judgment, stigma and professional repercussions, I lived a lie, or more accurately *several lies*, losing myself as a result.

Writing this book has been a cathartic experience, and opening up about my struggles is exceptionally rewarding. I'm currently enjoying relief from the pent-up fear, anxiety and confusion. I'm finally living my truth, and that is a wonderful feeling.

In telling my story and admitting grave transgressions in the court of baseball opinion, I have derived great motivation and inspiration from the lesbian, gay, bisexual and transgender (LGBT) community. Equating mere baseball allegiance with any of those core concerns is myopic, but the spirit of discovery and emancipation fostered by that brave movement is certainly mutual to my journey.

In retrospect, caring too much has been a common factor in all my mental breakdowns. That baseline insecurity and frustrated narcissism lends itself to shyness, obsession, anger, depression, anxiety and social paralysis. For too long, I lived my life in the context of other people, attempting to fit in at great internal expense. My taboo baseball fandom was informed by that concept, and I modified my emotions for too long.

The first 24 years of my life were ruled by emotional immaturity. I had only a tenuous grasp of the real world, and my place within it seemed a harsh inconvenience. I developed fake personas just to fit in, neglecting my inner values for some vague, transient notion of communal respect.

After meeting Patrycja, I experienced a series of revelations. I did a lot of growing up – and fast. I discovered the uncomfortable truth that there is little overarching meaning to life except that which we create ourselves. Accordingly, we may as well create *positive* internal dialogue, because unceasing intramural chatter is all we can ever be sure of.

Through gritted teeth and innumerable meltdowns, I learned to stop giving a fuck about the opinions of other people. Nobody really gives a shit. And in the rare instance that they *do* give a shit, the modern attention span means they will scroll onwards after 30 seconds of indignation anyway, searching for the next nugget of instantly gratifying drama.

The sooner we understand that no single person holds more than a modicum of wider significance, the sooner we can get on with living happier lives. In the elaborate timespan of global history, what I say, do and achieve has infinitesimal importance. To a great extent, I do not matter. Therefore, your reactions to my story are also inconsequential.

When faced with this concept of futility, we tend to invest in things that help us escape its definitive tone. In *that* context, sports matter, and those people who view baseball as their chief alleviator of uselessness will find treason in my rooting for the New York Yankees after once adoring the Boston Red Sox.

However, in the broader scheme of life, and in our grander place among the tapestry of human existence, my interest in one baseball team over another has almost no consequence. Most people will raise an eyebrow, shrug insouciantly and sigh uncaringly before worrying about something else - some new thing that seems important but is actually rather meaningless as well.

Nobody cares. Everybody has their own problems that do not mean anything to anybody else. Such is the isolating complexity of chronic self-doubt and untamed arrogance. Such is the unsolvable dilemma of life.

Some people still know me as a Red Sox fan. Jonny Gould, for example. After all, I made huge statements of pride and passion back then, and those things leave an indelible impression on certain audiences.

A few people still remember me as a Dodgers fan. The good people at Amazon, for example, who recommend books about Clayton Kershaw because I once bought books about Orel Hershiser.

Other people still consider me a Cubs fan. Most of my British baseball friends on Twitter, for instance. I wrote a blog declaring my switch from Los Angeles to Chicago in 2013 and shared it across social media. It is hard to reverse such imbecility.

Nevertheless, to one and all, I hereby declare my eternal allegiance to the New York Yankees. A tryst that began with a letter in 2014 bloomed with Derek Jeter's heroics and culminated in London Series verification. Now the whole world will know, for better or worse. Now I can get on with just being a fan.

People may not believe me, and history certainly lends a suspicious eye to my trustworthiness, but whatever, man. I'm done with this. I'm done explaining myself. Deep within, I know this is true and lasting. I know this was meant to be. Now, I can simply let it all happen. I can simply watch baseball for fun.

Red Sox fans will hate me. Yankees fans will be wary of me. *Baseball* fans will disown me, calling me a bandwagon jumper despite my various teams winning just two division titles in 16 years while I was a fan. Fine. Okay. Go ahead. I do not care anymore, because I'm living for me, not for anybody else, and if I love the New York Yankees, then that is a personal choice immune to public consternation.

Living in Britain, following Major League Baseball is a lonely commitment. When you stay awake until sunrise to watch mundane regular season games in Baltimore, doing so with peer pressure rattling through your skull is not nice. When you get just 100 hours of sleep through the entire month of October, making huge sacrifices to enjoy playoff games live, only to be discounted as a bandwagon jumper, that sucks.

Recently, however, I have become aware that my baseball fandom is just that – *mine*. It exists in my mind, my heart and my soul, occasionally spilling onto my Twitter feed. Therefore, adjusting primal instincts to root for one team over another merely to appease some unseen baying mob of baseball vigilantes is a recipe for psychological meltdown. You can never please everybody, so you may as well please yourself.

Bidding for a healthier life, I merely tuned those people out and focused on what makes me happy. I realised that sporting allegiance is a pact between a team and an individual – nothing more, nothing less. I'm the one who is experiencing this, so why act to justify external opinions?

For more than six years, I never had the courage to 'come out' as a New York Yankees fan. It would ruin my career. It would shatter my identity. It would break bonds and undermine authority. It would be *uncool*. Well, here we are, ladies and gentlemen, and here we go. I'm a New York Yankees fan for life, and finally revealing that feels amazing. Please direct all feedback to John Henry, because I'm at peace with my decision regardless of what comes next.

⚾⚾⚾

Upon returning from the London Series, I hatched a strategy to resuscitate my old @UKYankeeFans persona. Dazed and frustrated, I curtailed the whole thing in 2016, but the Twitter account still had more than 500 followers. The thought of rekindling that hub of Yankees news, views, history and analysis excited me greatly, and so I logged back in.

With less than ideal subterfuge, I conceived a new name for the project, global in outlook rather than confined to Britain. Somehow, the @pinstripegalaxy username was still available on all social media platforms, and such an opportunity is too good to pass up.

I designed a new logo, evoking imagery of a Yankees-obsessed planet. I rebranded the Twitter page, concocting a grandiose bio. I trawled through the archives, deleting any social media posts that hinted at my identity as the driving force. It felt great to rekindle my passion.

All along, I intended to build a community of Yankees fans around the world and eventually reveal my involvement as the founder, in conjunction with the overarching tale of this book. Well, here goes, people. I'm the engine that powers Pinstripe Galaxy. I can only apologise for the uncertainty and anonymity hitherto. I hope you can understand.

As the 2019 season reached its climax, Pinstripe Galaxy gave me a new lease on life. Liaising with fellow Yankees fans - even behind an impersonal avatar - created an outlet for the steam created by my burdening secret. It was refreshing to have a voice again, and I shared my views openly.

When the Yankees lost to Houston in Game 6 of the 2019 ALCS, I was crushed. The ecstasy of LeMahieu's game-tying, two-run bomb in the ninth inning of that fateful contest was soon wiped out by the devastation of José Altuve's walk-off homer to beat Chapman.

In turn, *that* devastation was compounded by subsequent revelations that the Astros used elaborate schemes to steal signs from opposing teams, illegally gaining insights into what pitches they were about to face at bat.

Houston relied on outfield cameras to decode catcher signals, which were then communicated to hitters by the banging of a dugout trash can or perhaps via electronic buzzers. Former Astros pitcher Mike Fiers blew the whistle, and Ken Rosenthal and Evan Drellich of *The Athletic* reported the gory details.

Commissioner Manfred found the Astros guilty of cheating, suspending general manager Luhnow and field manager Hinch for the entire 2020 season. Both were subsequently fired as all credibility was flushed down a Houston toilet.

Elsewhere, Carlos Beltrán also landed in trouble. A prominent player on the Astros' world championship team of 2017, Beltrán coordinated the sign-stealing system among teammates. Hired to manage the Mets after the 2019 season, Beltrán stepped down before even stepping into a dugout, another feather in Manfred's cap. A more *Mets* thing has never happened in human history.

The MLB investigation found that Red Sox manager Alex Cora played a crucial role in establishing the scheme when he served as the Astros' bench coach in 2017. Cora and the Red Sox parted "mutually" amid the furore, as Boston's culpability was also probed by league officials.

After a protracted deep dive, Manfred found that, during their 2018 championship run under Cora, the Red Sox also decoded signs electronically, gaining an unfair advantage. While deemed less extensive than the Astros' system, Boston still benefited from in-game sign sequencing from video replay assistant JT Watkins, who was suspended for a year along with Cora for his misdemeanours.

"I find that, unlike the Houston Astros' 2017 conduct, in which players communicated to the batter from the dugout area in real time the precise type of pitch about to be thrown, Watkins' conduct, by its very nature, was far more limited in scope and impact," wrote Manfred in a statement. "The information was only relevant when the Red Sox had runners on second base (which was 19.7% of plate appearance leaguewide in 2018), and Watkins communicated sign sequences in a manner that indicated that he decoded them from the in-game feed in only a small percentage of those occurrences."

Ah, the old chestnut that cheating with runners in scoring position is fine. I mean, *seriously*? Whether it was 19.7% of the time or every damn pitch, the Red Sox cheated. In 2018, they had an .872 OPS with runners in scoring position, the best mark posted by *any* team in any of the previous 12 seasons. That they digitally untangled signs in those situations barely seemed to matter.

In addition, prior to that historic 2018 season, shortly after Cora was announced as their new manager, the Red Sox *just happened* to move their replay station from a remote upstairs location to a small room outside their dugout, making it more accessible for players and coaches during games. A total coincidence, I'm sure. Nothing to see here. Please move along.

In truth, the whole world knows that Watkins was thrown under the bus by MLB and the Red Sox. Such was the high-profile nature of Manfred's investigation, *somebody* had to take the fall for Boston's obvious transgressions. The humble video replay guy became an ideal protagonist, and Watkins did not have a leg to stand on.

The idea that a video staffer acted *alone* to illegally decipher signs and filter the decrypted information to Red Sox players during games is absurd. It is like blaming a McDonalds burger flipper for changing all of the restaurant's recipes around the world through deleterious means. These minnows do not have such authority, so blaming them unilaterally is illogical.

Once the Astros were punished, Red Sox personnel likely saw the torrential backlash from all quarters and battened down the hatches with regard to their own investigation. A storyline was likely crafted, featuring Watkins as a lone wolf, and that yarn was probably reiterated by every Boston employee interviewed by MLB investigators. The whole charade is laughable.

Of course, bending the rules to gain unfair advantages has a long tradition in New England sports. In 2007, the Patriots were disciplined for videotaping opposing coaches as they called plays. Seven years later, the same regime was found to have deliberately deflated footballs to aid the performance of quarterback Tom Brady.

Naturally, Boston fans and media personalities tend to defend their teams regardless of morality. Just as *Free Brady* t-shirts flooded the internet in 2014, the same Red Sox rooters who chastised Houston for cheating completed ethical gymnastics to defend the transgressions of Watkins and Cora. Their attempts smacked of hypocrisy. We had all seen enough.

Through the winter of 2019-20, then, a sense of grave injustice percolated among Yankees fans, me included. There is a very realistic prospect that the Yankees were beaten in three straight postseasons - and four of five - by teams that cheated. Our road to the World Series was repeatedly blocked by illegal means. That is difficult to swallow.

In 2015, 2017 and 2019, Houston prevailed with suspicious dominance, while in 2018, Boston won by historically unprecedented margins. Cora was a common presence in two of those defeats, and he was eventually outed as a prolific cheater. And to think the guy waved to me in London - jeez.

Amid the sign-stealing scandal, many uneducated baseball fans wrongly lumped the Yankees in with Houston and Boston. That bothered me, because any allegations against New York lacked validity.

In September 2017, the Red Sox were fined by MLB following a *New York Times* investigation into the illegal use of an Apple Watch to steal signs during games. A Red Sox trainer used the smart watch to convey signs to Boston hitters, gaining an illegal edge. Apparently, they never learned from their mistakes, huh?

The Yankees were also fined for *different* transgressions at the same time, rather confusingly. Indeed, by packaging New York and Boston together in one decision, Manfred did a huge disservice to the Yankees, who were never explicitly found guilty of stealing signs electronically.

Contrary to common perception, the Yankees were fined for misuse of a dugout phone in a season prior to 2017. They were not punished for stealing signs. Apparently, the internet is yet to hear that, because the amount of garbage spouted on social media is incredible.

Major league rules preclude the use of dugout phones for anything other than communication pertaining to pitching changes. A coach or manager is able to use the phone to instruct a reliever to warm up, for example, but any discussion of in-game minutiae is prohibited.

Yes, the Yankees misused their dugout phone. However, even the commissioner concluded that "the substance of the communications that took place on the dugout phone was not a violation of any rule or regulation in and of itself."

For all we know, Joe Girardi could have ordered takeaway pizza on the damn phone. Larry Rothschild could have requested a new pair of cleats for one of his relievers. The inane possibilities are endless. Hell, George Steinbrenner used to berate his managers on the dugout phone during games, criticising strategy. Mickey Mantle probably used the phone to pick up girls. Why are we splitting hairs here?

The Yankees' transgression was one of decorum, an eye-rolling failure to embrace MLB's ludicrous obsession with creating robotic role models. It was not a rule-bending tactic of gaining an illegal advantage. Never forget that, and never back down when presented with fake news.

Given the evidence that is currently available, any deduction that the Yankees illegally stole signs is, at best, wishful thinking on the part of those who dislike the organisation and, at worst, flagrant defamation from a biased mainstream media. I will defend the Yankees' cleanliness on this matter until proven otherwise. They did not cheat, whereas other teams did.

The sign-stealing scandal inspired fans to analyse where baseball currently is and where it is likely going. Personally, I believe the whole saga was a natural outgrowth of baseball's needless preoccupation with technology. There are some very clear ways of cleaning this up and ensuring it does not happen again. Scrap instant replay. Ban iPads in the dugout. Get rid of video rooms. Take back control of the sport and reintroduce its human instinct. We do not need this stuff. It is destroying the game.

Baseball men have always found ways to cheat. From Ty Cobb sharpening his spikes and Herman Franks operating a centre-field telescope to George Brett slathering pine tar on his bat and Manny Ramírez injecting female fertility drugs - these guys will always find a way to massage the odds in their favour. To a certain extent, we must encourage the baseline competitive urgings and incubate the fiery will to win, but we must also stop creating systems that, by their very nature, make it easier for people to cheat.

It is often said that *all* major league teams operate schemes similar to those exposed in Houston and Boston, but I do not necessarily agree with that notion. Cheaters like to believe that their actions are not unprecedented. There is safety in numbers, they think, and it is easier to justify a misdemeanour when *everybody* is guilty than when only a handful of guys bend the rules.

In truth, we will never truly know the extent of this sign-stealing boom, but do not let uncertainty tame your disgust at the Astros and Red Sox. Those teams were caught cheating, and those teams must be punished. Their championships are forever tainted in my mind, and I want to see genuine retribution.

⚾⚾⚾

As spring training began in 2020, rumours swirled that, once again, the Red Sox were about to trade away their biggest star for a generation. In early-February, Boston pulled the trigger on a woeful salary dump, sending Mookie Betts to the Dodgers along with David Price for three prospects. One of those prospects is called Jeter Downs, quite ironically, but the deal has been lambasted across baseball as lopsided and nonsensical.

It once seemed implausible that a guy named Mookie could succeed in Boston. After all, Mookie *Wilson* hit that ghoulish groundball to Buckner in 1986, banishing the name from households across Massachusetts. However, with a tireless competitive instinct and phenomenal skill, Betts became truly beloved around the league. As a Yankee fan, he was the one Red Sox player I hated to see at bat in close games. The outcome was typically devastating.

In six seasons with Boston, Betts hit .301 with 139 home runs, 470 RBI, 126 stolen bases and 229 doubles. He was a four-time All-Star, a four-time Gold Glover, a one-time MVP, and the leading light of that tainted 2018 championship drive. A small guy with searing speed and tremendous plate coverage, Betts became one of the best players in baseball. Just 26 through the 2019 campaign, he figured to break a slew of franchise records in the years ahead, except John Henry did not want to pay him.

For the sake of illustrative projection, let us assume that Betts has 10 seasons left in his career, retiring when he is 36. Extrapolating his typical yearly output to match that timeframe, adjusting for age-based regression, Betts has a legitimate shot at topping 3,000 hits, 400 home runs, 400 stolen bases and 100 WAR. No player has ever reached *all* of those plateaus, a sign of Betts' legitimate greatness.

The need to lock Betts to a long-term contract became apparent almost from the time he debuted in 2014. Ownership repeatedly undervalued Mookie in negotiations, however, reminding veteran observers of the Garciaparra fiasco in times of yore. Henry offered Betts a 10-year, $300 million extension before the 2019 season. When Betts countered with 12 years at $420 million, ownership balked and began exploring trades before Mookie became a free agent following the 2020 campaign.

One of the best players of all-time wanted to stay in a Red Sox uniform for a further 12 years, taking his total Boston tenure to 18 seasons. Let that sink in. Mookie Betts was *invested* in this thing. Yet despite earning more than $500 million per year in revenue, and despite a franchise price tag of $3.3 billion, and despite FSG being valued at $6.6 billion, and despite Henry's personal net worth resting at $2.6 billion, the team cut Betts because of money. The Red Sox axed Mookie over $120 million, to be precise. They earn that much *every three months*.

"No one this young and this good has ever been traded," wrote Ben Lindbergh of *The Ringer*. "Betts was already a top-10 position player in Red Sox franchise history, and he was just getting started."

Moreover, contrary to the revisionist narratives, the Red Sox were ensconced in win-now mode, replete with seasoned stars like Bogaerts, Benintendi, Martinez and Price. Boston missed the playoffs with an 84-78 record in 2019, and their luxury tax commitments were becoming a problem, but dismissing Mookie Betts was not the answer to that conundrum. The Red Sox screwed up. Again.

Indeed, it is worth revisiting the regularity with which Boston disowns its greatest and most iconic players. While the ballads of Clemens, Boggs, Nomar and Damon are detailed extensively in this book, the Red Sox have also severed ties with Vaughn, Pedro, Manny, Youkilis, Lester and Papelbon in my lifetime. These were huge fan favourites and major personalities. The way they were discarded leaves a bitter taste in the mouth.

Some will commend the Red Sox' lack of sentimentality with regard to player legacies and financial projections. However, such a data-driven approach strips the humanity from baseball and leaves it a poorer place. The same people who encouraged Boston to trade Betts likely canvassed New York to ditch Jeter when his defence began to wane. There are some things analytics cannot tell you, and they just happen to be things I adore about baseball.

In the past 40 years, only two beloved faces of the Red Sox franchise have finished their careers in Boston: Ortiz and Yastrzemski. Nobody else has come close. That speaks to systemic dysfunction within the club's front office, which sees players as computerised numbers on a spreadsheet rather than as fleshy heroes who are adored. There is no appreciation from Red Sox ownership towards the people who make them rich, famous and admired. There is no genuine respect.

Attempting to explain the absurd cost-cutting measures, Henry even had the gall to namecheck Nomar, comparing the deals and insinuating that a similar effect will be felt in competitiveness down the road. Meanwhile, Betts was cast as a deal-rejecting villain, adding to the biting subtext of Henry's remarks.

"I know many of you, particularly our youngest fans, are disbelieving or angry or sad about it," said the owner in a statement. "Some of you no doubt felt the same way in 2004 when we traded Nomar, who like Mookie was a hugely popular, homegrown player. All of us in this organisation hoped we could avoid ever having to go through something like that again, but most clubs face similar dilemmas from time to time."

Sure, the prospects obtained from Los Angeles - including Alex Verdugo, who has murky connections to a 2015 sexual assault investigation - may help the Red Sox win a championship in 2025, but Betts may have led them to *multiple* rings by that point, if embraced. Deferring those attempts at winning a World Series to save money makes no sense, and Mookie will now join Roger, Ruth and the rest in fulfilling his potential elsewhere.

Ultimately, I do not care anymore. It is not my money to waste, and the Red Sox are not my team to worry about. I feel lucky to have severed my ties with Boston before it did so with the best homegrown player it has developed since Clemens. Long may the austerity continue, and long may the Yankees reign. The curse may be over, but Boston's proclivity to derail its own progress is alive and well.

⚾⚾⚾

In a strange quirk of fate, the prospect of Betts entering free agency without ever playing a game for the Dodgers became increasingly realistic with each passing day. No, he did not sustain a horrific injury after swapping coasts. Rather, a global pandemic brought baseball to a halt in the spring of 2020, with no clear timetable for its return.

Emanating from Wuhan, China in late-2019, a novel coronavirus spread like wildfire across the world, causing unprecedented disruption to sports, business and everyday life. At the time of writing, over 6 million cases of COVID-19 - the potentially fatal illness caused by coronavirus infection - have been reported around the world in the space of seven months. Almost 400,000 people have died, including 24,000 in New York and 40,000 in the UK. Those numbers will have soared by the time you read this. My heart goes out to everybody affected.

The ease with which coronavirus can be transmitted necessitated aggressive social-distancing measures, and one third of the global population experienced some form of state-mandated lockdown. As I type this, Merseyside is in its fourth month of imposed quarantine, with people working from home and venturing outdoors only for essential grocery shopping, medical appointments and restricted exercise. We have never experienced anything like this, and the future has rarely felt so uncertain.

Naturally, the pandemic wreaked havoc with the world's sporting schedule. With gatherings of more than two people banned in many countries, stadiums were shuttered, leagues were suspended and games were cancelled. Tranmere played their last pre-lockdown game on 10th March, while MLB followed many elite leagues by pausing spring training two days later. We are still awaiting a plan for restarting our beloved sports.

In April, the 2020 London Series was cancelled with no immediate plan for bringing baseball back to the UK. I had tickets to watch both games between the Cubs and Cardinals, and it was disappointing to miss out on more live baseball. Nevertheless, public health is more important, and my memories of the Yankees' 2019 sweep became even more profound. Who knows if another MLB team will ever win a regular season game in England? I certainly hope so, but even hope is a transient privilege these days.

Incidentally, when the British government sought hospitals to receive expats returning from Wuhan, the first authority to raise its hand and offer support was Wirral Borough Council. Around 120 Brits flew home when the outbreak worsened, completing quarantine at Arrowe Park hospital in Birkenhead. I'm proud of the role my hometown played in spearheading our national fight against this deadly disease, and it stands in stark contrast to the standard shenanigans across the Mersey.

Indeed, while most people pulled together during the crisis, working their way through physical and economic devastation, John Henry botched his coronavirus response at every turn. At times, it was painful to watch his anachronistic ineptitude. Readers should discern patterns in his duplicitous behaviour by this point.

On 11th March, Liverpool hosted a Champions League knockout tie with Atlético Madrid at Anfield. Despite widespread knowledge of coronavirus thriving among large gatherings,

52,267 people crammed into the stadium, including around 3,000 from Madrid, a city already under partial lockdown at the time due to aggressive outbreaks of COVID-19.

Elsewhere in the Champions League and top continental competitions, matches had already been played behind closed doors at that point, with no spectators allowed inside stadiums. Nevertheless, Liverpool ignored scientific advice and allowed fans to gather in obscene numbers, accelerating coronavirus transmission in two different countries. Why? Capitalism, of course. The revenue from a large Champions League game was too good to turn down.

A subsequent study by the *Sunday Times* newspaper linked the match to 41 extra deaths in Merseyside hospitals up to five weeks after it was played. That number could well be larger, because the investigation did not account for people travelling from further afield and indeed overseas, including back to Madrid, to attend the game. All of those deaths were eminently avoidable.

Liverpool City Council has since launched an investigation into the public health effects of hosting the Atlético match without adequate safeguarding measures at Anfield. Do not expect any major findings to come from it, however, because the council is so far enmeshed with the football club as to render the whole thing a farce.

Appallingly, Liverpool refused to refund 290 Atlético fans who stayed home, obeying expert guidance, despite buying tickets for the match. Atlético stepped in itself to reimburse those supporters. At least Madrid won the match and ended Liverpool's defence of the trophy.

Amid fears of mass unemployment and financial hardship wrought by COVID-19, the British government created a coronavirus job retention scheme, whereby companies facing cashflow difficulties could furlough workers and let the state pay 80% of their wage for an agreed period. The scheme was roundly applauded from all quarters, but large firms began abusing the system before it even went live.

In early-April, Liverpool placed some of their non-playing staff on furlough leave, causing widespread consternation. The club agreed to top up the 80%, resulting in no loss of earnings for individual employees, but the manner in which a hugely profitable conglomerate sought to have the British taxpayer prop up its business model once again debunked the myth that Liverpool is a socialist football club.

Liverpool made a pre-tax profit of £42 million in the financial year to February 2020, with an increased turnover of £533 million. Yet even after saving so much money dumping Betts and Price across the pond, Henry showed no shame in using the furlough scheme, using working class Brits to protect his precious balance sheet.

Tranmere furloughed staff because they had no other choice. Such is Liverpool's strangulation of the local market, Rovers had enough resources to last a maximum of 12 months without income from fan-attended matches. Tranmere is a small business, the kind of company the furlough scheme tried to protect. By contrast, Liverpool is a multinational behemoth. Making the rudimentary taxpayer bankroll its immoral profiteering showed the real Liverpool to mainstream fans, and the outcry was vociferous.

Such was the weight of public disapproval, Henry was forced to reverse his decision within two days of it being announced. "We believe we came to the wrong conclusion last week and we are truly sorry for that," said club chief executive Peter Moore in a letter to fans. The vehement backlash sparked crisis negotiations with FSG and key stakeholders, and independent fan groups played the role of Henry's malfunctioning moral compass, suggesting the climbdown.

Meanwhile, back in Boston, the *Globe* drew criticism for refusing to drop its paywall on coronavirus coverage, in stark contrast to scores of media outlets around the world. Unbelievably, the *Globe* even placed targeted ads from health insurance provider Blue Cross Blue Shield on its coronavirus landing page. Nothing like a good old pandemic to spark an uptick in affiliate marketing dollars, huh? These people must be stopped.

With regard to the Red Sox, Henry instituted significant pay cuts across the organisation amid baseball's labour stoppage, with staffers said to be 'livid' at the decision. All Red Sox employees making more than $50,000 per year saw a reduction in pay, while those earning over $500,000 had their salaries slashed by 30%. The changes will stay in effect until 2021 at the earliest, while potential layoffs have not been dismissed, either.

As a whole, MLB mustered a terrible response to COVID-19 and its associated impacts. Even the Yankees cut 45 minor leaguers, to the annoyance of many fans, but Boston was particularly harsh in its cost-cutting campaign. The Red Sox released 22 players from their organisation, as well, adding to the absurdity. It was a terrible look for a billion-dollar industry that lost its way.

While we should refrain from scoring points during a universal health emergency, I believe the fallout of coronavirus has affirmed many of my instincts and substantiated much of my general argument. The Yankees were once lampooned for viewing everything through a financial prism, and Boston did much of the moaning. Now, FSG pinches pennies wherever it can, with little regard for the people who make its shareholders rich. I cannot wait to do battle again once competitive play resumes.

⚾⚾⚾

On Christmas Day 2019, I proposed to Patrycja and she said yes. We are now happily engaged, with a wedding to follow in Poland in the coming years. My priorities have changed from those early days of sporting obsession, and I'm past the point of caring about the fallout from this book.

I just ask that, when considering the machinations of my story, readers remain aware that people change. We grow and recede, expand and truncate. Our opinions evolve with the development of our values, conjured through experience, driven by maturity. Judging somebody without being privy to their journey is vacuous and unfair. Put yourself in my shoes before venting anger. Try to see this from my perspective.

Look, I have rooted for four different Major League Baseball teams in my life. That is strange, I know. That is abnormal. I will never attempt to argue otherwise. Before abandoning my carcass, however, you must also consider the fact that I was once a dickhead, whereas now I am not.

CONFLICT

I was 10 when Boston baseball first gripped my heart, a poor kid with no home internet connection and very few friends. If I knew about the Red Sox' history of racism and corporate inconsistency before watching that initial documentary, I never would have become a fan.

I was 16 when switching between the Red Sox and Dodgers, a spotty kid with unbalanced hormones. That decision was devoid of any thoughtful logic.

I was 18 when pledging allegiance to the Cubs, never a day spent employed and entirely devoid of even a remote understanding of the adult world. That decision was overly emotional and suitably immature.

I was 19 when the Yankees sent me a personalised letter and a gift hamper, all at sea and deeply impressionable. Falling in love with New York was not a decision at all, but rather a natural blend of destiny and happenstance.

I was 24 when Boston won the 2018 World Series, ravaged by mental illness and pining for the safety of youth. That was the darkest time in my life, totally hostile to positivity.

I was a fully-grown adult by the time everything made sense. Forgive me for growing up. I guess you expected me to have life figured out by the time I turned 10. I'm sorry to disappoint.

Looking back, I was immature, impudent, irrational, inauthentic, irascible, impressionable and insane. But that was then, and this is now. What matters is the present and the future, and I finally feel at ease in my own baseball skin.

A person can be wrong one thousand times, but if they eventually arrive at their own sense of truth, that is the most important thing. That is all that matters.

Sir James Dyson, the British inventor, worked through 5,127 failed prototypes of his eponymous vacuum cleaner, which eventually changed the market forever. Even I never loved *that* many baseball teams, so the voyage is not as important as the destination.

I'm a 25-year-old man. If everything goes according to plan, I will hopefully get to enjoy several more decades on this beguiling planet. All of them will be experienced as a New York Yankees fan, I guarantee, making those flings with Boston, Los Angeles and Chicago seem tiny by comparison.

In this world of pointless meaning and constructed purpose, the ultimate thrill for me is that I can one day raise a son or daughter and naturally pass down the most illustrious heirloom of all: traditional allegiance to the New York Yankees.

We will sit together and watch baseball games, something I never got to do with my dad. We will visit Yankee Stadium together and discuss the viability of trade rumours. We will laugh and cry, cheer and boo, believing in a common dream so hard in the making.

We will read about Babe Ruth and Joe DiMaggio at bedtimes. We will watch clips of Mariano Rivera on YouTube, reliving bygone glories in a bright and vibrant future. We will play catch and maybe start our own baseball team. Yeah, the Wirral Yankees sound great. How about that?

I cannot wait for those moments and those vignettes. I cannot wait for those memories and those feelings. I cannot wait for those gifts and those responsibilities. After all, that is what life seems to be about, even if it took me a while to figure out.

We are all in charge of our own happiness, no matter what anybody else may say. I'm ready to embrace that concept and to own that future, because nobody else will do it for me. I'm determined to enjoy the rest of my Yankee days, when all is said and done. I'm ready to root in public, not just in private. Even if Patrycja won't let me call our kid Derek.

Ryan Ferguson, June 2020, Baltic Triangle.

ACKNOWLEDGEMENTS

I would like to thank Patrycja, my fiancée, for pulling me through the meltdowns and for encouraging me to keep writing this book. I wanted to quit at various points, fearing my manuscript was too fragmented, but Patty is the best coach, and she told me to forget self-imposed deadlines and simply write with passion. I love you, Squishy.

Thank you to my mum, Cheryl, who took me to Bromborough library before we had internet at home just so I could check the baseball scores. We will donate a copy of this book to the library together.

Thanks also to my dad, Mike, who used to throw baseballs to me in the street as a kid, letting me jump into the hedges like a superstar outfielder. I hope you enjoy this book, dad.

Much love to my brother, Nath, who once randomly found a copy of *MLB 07: The Show* in a Rock Ferry game shop. Here's to many more years of attending the MLB London Series together. We might even see Ken Griffey Jr. on the train one day.

A special mention, too, for Kim, my sister, who used to order obscure baseball books for me using her Amazon account. Sorry for pestering you all those years ago, Kim. I have my own baseball book now.

Thanks to my brother, Carl, for his support. I promise to buy Snuggs a Yankees coat one day. Thank you, as well, to my uncle Harry for being a constant inspiration. Enjoy this book on your next trip to America, Harry.

Dziękuje Magdzie, Pauli, Wojtkowi, Wiktorowi i Kalince za Wasze wsparcie i kotlety.

Thanks to Dave Cooper, my best mate, and to Mark Henry, my professional mentor, for all of your support. It means a lot, lads.

I would like to thank everybody associated with *Baseball on Five*, without whom I never would have discovered this beautiful game. Jonny Gould and Josh Chetwynd, David Lengel and Todd Macklin, Erik Janssen and Mike Carlson, Mark Webster and Paul Romanuk – thank you.

Thank you to Nat Coombs, a true inspiration whose advice and guidance has been first class down the years.

Thanks also to Dan Louw and everybody at *Americarnage*. You guys kept talking about baseball in Britain when nobody seemed to care. This is a book fashioned in your spirit.

I'm grateful to Tom Lutz, Phil Gordos and every editor who has paid me to write about baseball. You helped my dream come true.

A few words, too, for the trailblazers who made this possible - for Henry Chadwick, the English father of America's national pastime; for Bobby Thomson and his Shout Heard 'Round the World; and for Antoan Richardson, the British guy who scored the winning run on Derek Jeter's immortal walk-off single.

Thanks to the captain himself, and to Babe Ruth, Joe DiMaggio, Mickey Mantle and Lou Gehrig. Thanks to Harry Frazee for his stunning contribution, and to Colonel Jacob Ruppert and George Steinbrenner for their ceaseless pursuit of glory.

I would like to place on record my eternal gratitude to everyone at South Wirral High School and Bromborough library. One taught me to write; the other taught me about baseball. This is the ultimate amalgamation of those passions.

Thanks to Mr Robinson, my only real English teacher. Without his advice and guidance during my teenage years, I never would have pursued my potential as a writer.

Thank you to Craig W Thomas, author of *Roads to Redemption*, the first great baseball book I ever read. I finally got my own baseball book published, Craig. I hope it rekindles your love for the game.

A quick thought, too, for every editor who rejected *The Olde Towne Team*, my childhood baseball manuscript. I got there in the end. Some of those scribblings are even embedded here, a respectful nod to my younger self.

Thank you to all the immortal baseball writers who inspired my style – from Ring Lardner and Grantland Rice to Roger Kahn and Roger Angell; from Dan Shaughnessy and Leigh Montville to Bob Ryan and Tony Massarotti; from Michael Lewis and Stewart O'Nan to Buster Olney and Jared Carrabis. There are too many to list, but rest assured that you all live on in my priceless baseball library.

A special mention for Baseball-Reference.com, FanGraphs, Baseball Almanac, SABR and Spotrac. Without those wonderful resources, researching for this book would have been incredibly difficult. Please support those independent websites if you have the ability to do so. Likewise, Wikipedia was a reliable friend throughout this process. The people there do great work.

Thanks to Rob Manfred, Sadiq Khan and Murray Cook for bringing Major League Baseball to London. Thanks to Aaron Hicks, Aaron Judge and the 2019 Yankees for making those games so memorable. And thanks to everybody who filled the Olympic Stadium, making memories that will last forever.

Thank you to Cristina Campana for her amazing generosity, and to everybody who follows Pinstripe Galaxy across social media.

My appreciation goes out to Mark Blakemore, Kevin Rooney and David Shaw for making the 2019 London Series so special. I owe you guys some tickets. A word, too, for Mike Head, the biggest Cubs fan in Bromley. Let's meet up again whenever the 2020 London Series is rearranged, mate.

Thanks to the New York Yankees and the Boston Red Sox, the Los Angeles Dodgers and the Chicago Cubs. You fought for my heart until the very end, and I would not change a thing.

I'm also thankful for the widespread availability of coffee, which fuelled the 06:00 am wakeup calls that allowed me to type in the early morning gloom.

Finally, I want to thank *you* for buying this book and for reading my stream of baseball consciousness. Getting it all out there and writing my story was incredibly cathartic. If anybody happens to enjoy the finished product, that is a happy coincidence.

Go Yanks!

ABOUT THE AUTHOR

Ryan Ferguson is a writer, author, blogger and journalist from Wirral, England. A passionate New York Yankees fan, he is the founder of Pinstripe Galaxy, a hub for global coverage of the team.

Ryan has been published by the *Guardian,* BBC Sport, *Liverpool Echo, Montreal Gazette* and *These Football Times,* among other outlets. Ryan's work has also been featured by MLB.com, while the *New York Post* profiled him as part of its London Series coverage in 2019.

In August 2019, Ryan published his first book, *Planet Prentonia,* a lyrical exploration of Tranmere Rovers history.

For more information, please visit ryanferguson.co.uk, and also follow Ryan on social media using the official accounts listed below:

- Twitter - @RyanFergusonHQ

- Facebook – Ryan Ferguson HQ

- LinkedIn – Ryan Ferguson

To support Ryan on his journey as a Yankees fan in the UK, please follow Pinstripe Galaxy:

- Twitter - @PinstripeGalaxy

- Facebook – PinstripeGalaxy

- Instagram – pinstripegalaxy

- YouTube – Pinstripe Galaxy

Printed in Poland
by Amazon Fulfillment
Poland Sp. z o.o., Wrocław